Curating Deviance

A CAMERA OBSCURA BOOK

Curating Deviance

Programming the Queer Film Canon

MARC FRANCIS

Duke University Press
Durham and London

2 0 2 6

© 2026 Duke University Press
All rights reserved
Project Editor: Bird Williams
Designed by A. Mattson Gallagher
Typeset in Arno Pro by Westchester Publishing Services

Library of Congress Cataloging-in-Publication Data
Names: Francis, Marc, [date] author.
Title: Curating deviance : programming the queer film canon / Marc Francis.
Description: Durham : Duke University Press, 2026. | Series: A camera obscura book | Includes bibliographical references and index.
Identifiers: LCCN 2025024295 (print)
LCCN 2025024296 (ebook)
ISBN 9781478033080 (paperback)
ISBN 9781478029632 (hardcover)
ISBN 9781478061847 (ebook)
Subjects: LCSH: Homosexuality in motion pictures. | Motion picture theaters—Curatorship. | Deviant behavior in motion pictures.
Classification: LCC PN1995.9.H55 F73 2026 (print) | LCC PN1995.9. H55 (ebook)
LC record available at https://lccn.loc.gov/2025024295
LC ebook record available at https://lccn.loc.gov/2025024296

Cover art: Ben Davis Collection, Bleecker Street Cinema calendar from June/July 1980 (detail). The Museum of Modern Art Department of Film Special Collections, New York.

To Nilo (and Melba)
Ruby
And my parents,
My rotating triple bill

Contents

Acknowledgments *ix*

Introduction *1*

1   **Promiscuous Programming** *23*
Filmic Eclecticism in Post-1968 Art House Cinema

2   **Deviant Repertories** *57*
The Queer Typologies and Taxonomies of Art House Curating

3   **Erotic Intertextuality** *97*
On the Programmatic Forms of Desire

4   **Repertory Time** *143*
Double Features and the Temporality of Queer Spectatorship

5   **For Shame!** *181*
On the History of Programming Queer "Bad Objects"

Afterword *207*
Curating Queer Cinema After 1989

Notes *215*
Bibliography *265*
Index *281*

Acknowledgments

Curating Deviance was written during a time of prolonged crisis taking place on personal, national, and global registers. I considered leaving this project behind multiple times due to the strained conditions of sparse research funding and precarious academic employment. Combine that with widespread environmental calamity, ongoing state violence, global currents of fascism, proliferating wars abroad, and a global pandemic. Through these rough waters, friends and loved ones helped champion this project's ongoing relevance. Conversations about cultural contradictions and sticking points in contemporary systems of gender and sexuality allowed me to see the ways this book is more than a historical study; it aims to push against today's righteous and individualistic politics coming from the right and the left, from religious conservatives to trans and queer communities. This book longs for profound and patient forms of coalition that seem inconceivable today.

    This yearning is a joint product of my personal experience and professional training, the latter of which places me forever in the debt of my mentor B. Ruby Rich. In 2013, Ruby took me under her tutelage, teaching me more than I have admitted to her—and perhaps myself, too. We have grown so close in part because we share many of the same values, worldviews, and viewing tastes. (*Many*, but not all!) I was granted the rare opportunity few mentees in the field get when my time with Ruby was extended at *Film Quarterly* for four years beyond my PhD program. I cherished her guidance at UC Santa Cruz and *Film Quarterly*, and our relationship continues to grow and deepen with the years. (And we now tend to be film festival buddies.) I have over the years referred to her as my lifelong *Doktormutter*, the German feminine for a doctoral adviser; I can find no more suitable term. Ruby's incomparable mentorship and spirit are reflected in the pages that follow.

There persist several myths about humanities scholars, that (a) they work in a vacuum of their own research and thinking and (b) even when they don't, they tend to only be influenced by and in dialogue with other scholars. This project is a testament to scholarship's expansiveness, from the collaborative settings of conferences and extended long-distance phone conversations, to its more casual contexts of post-screening conversations at the bar with queer elders and age peers, theorizing and historicizing together. This book, years in the making, is only possible through both these disciplined and spontaneous encounters and teachings.

The line between scholarship and friendship has become wonderfully blurred by the people I am honored to call both friends and colleagues: Linnéa Hussein (dare I say my *Doktorfrau*?), Annie Berke, Harris Kornstein ("Lil' Miss Hot Mess"), Damon Young, Ramzi Fawaz, Dolores McElroy, Francesca Romeo, Topiary Landberg, Neta Alexander, Kartik Nair, Ron Gregg, Alece Oxendine, Rachel Schaff, and Vika Paranyuk. I am especially indebted to film and media scholars who read drafts of chapters, or encouraged me to press on: Besides Dolores and Linnéa, Rebecca Prime, Peter Limbrick, Elena Gorfinkel, Rosalind Galt, Jack Halberstam, Jane Gaines, John Paul Stadler, Kiki Loveday, Janet Staiger, Amy Villarejo, Regina Longo, Yiman Wang, Jenny Horne, Carla Marcantonio, as well as the late Jonathan Kahana and Patricia Zimmerman. A special and effusive thank you to Patricia White, my editor at the *Camera Obscura* book series. Patty offered detailed feedback and line editing for a chapter that is significantly stronger because of her precise and generous insights. Thank you to the entire *Camera Obscura* Editorial Board for welcoming this book into their brilliant series. I stand among giants.

Teeming in these chapters is the collective energy and inspiration of queer friends with whom I watch movies and TV shows, discuss and analyze ad nauseum, and then repeat: Haroon Adalat, Federico Emiliano, Nick Austin, Erik Kenneth Staalberg, Gabriel Blanco, Michael Bednar, Robert Harter, BB Gunn, Sindri Galvan, JD Stuntebeck, Iggy Martinez, Zack

Oleson, Ernest Martin, and Jonathan Dalin. They remind me that camp is nothing without community. And to my other West Coast loves: Vanessa Peña, Lindsay Armstrong Vance, Lynora Valdez, Farron Feiner, Alexis Payne, Nikki Czech, Art and Gabby O'Leary, all anchors in precarious times. My Aunt Ruth and sister, Stacey Coleman, have supported my eccentric trajectory and work from early on. My best friend Mariam Kassem models great curiosity and reflection; rigorous conversation with her always makes my heart flutter with excitement. My brilliant colleagues at HBO, Warner Bros, and later, Paramount offered deep levels of encouragement over the years: Miriam Hobbs, Randall Luckow, Eric Lane, Max Sanchez, Natalie de Almeida, Graham Marshall, and Trisha Lendo, thank you for your generosity.

Programmers, past and present, who agreed to be interviewed by me provided a wealth of information coupled with idiosyncrasy. Fabiano Canosa, Edith Kramer, Richard Peña, Marcus Hu, Kim Jorgensen, Jane Giles, and Stephen Soba all took chunks of their time to teach me about their programming sensibilities. Mark Valen deserves distinct credit for all that he has offered me in interviews and conversations over the years. He has been more than a curatorial informant and mentor; he has been a giving and patient friend. At Pacific Film Archive's (PFA) Film Library and Study Center, Jason Sanders and Nancy Goldman provided me with stack upon stack of programs. Jim Nicola gave me access to the Nuart's archive and provided reproductions of calendars for the book. Ashley Swinnerton and the MoMA Film Study Center staff took time to organize program materials that had—to the best of their knowledge—never been requested or even cataloged; Collection Specialist Cara Shatzman helped with images. Vishnu Dass, who oversees the Steven Arnold Collection, illuminated a major part of neglected queer film history for me by showing me the Nocturnal Dream Show's posters and other materials.

At Yale, I am grateful for colleagues Diane Berrett Brown, Oksana Chefranova, Jennifer Newman, Brian Mecham, Marc Robinson, Moira Fradinger, Daisy Abreu, and Joe Fischel. I thank the committee at Yale who granted me the Fund for Lesbian and Gay Studies (FLAGS) Research Award to carry this book over the finish line. Haroon Adalat, a cherished cinephile friend and graphic designer extraordinaire, worked his Photoshop magic on a number of images in this book. At Duke, Senior Editor Elizabeth Ault and Assistant Editor Benjamin Kossak, the rest of the editorial staff, my two anonymous reviewers, and the Duke University Press Editorial Advisory Board all deserve esteemed recognition for helping shepherd this project to its current form.

This book is in part dedicated to my partner, Nilo Couret, for the laughs, the meals, and the intellectual rabbit holes. We challenge and influence each other every day; I couldn't imagine a better companion with whom to talk movies and TV, from the most obscure indie film to *RuPaul's Drag Race*. Our life together has been built on a love of travel and film, fitting given that it all started in Buenos Aires with a quote from *After Sunset*: "Baby, you're gonna miss that plane." And to our girl, Melba, who patiently waited to be walked while I wrote just another paragraph or two.

Last, this book is for my parents, Carol and Jerry Newman, who have supported me throughout this wild scholarly and professional journey. They might not have foreseen a future in which their names would appear in a book with "deviance" in the title, but I sense they will nevertheless recognize (and perhaps even identify with) aspects of the world described in these pages from the years they lived in NYC in their twenties. I am especially indebted to my mother, who watches and reads with delight, eagerness, and sensitivity; any attempt on my part to read reparatively and openly can likely be traced back to her.

Introduction

This book was conceived by way of a rather basic question: How were canonical queer films programmed and exhibited in the two decades following sexual liberation? While illuminating scholarship exists on the exhibition of New York underground films in the 1960s and on LGBT film festivals in the 1990s and beyond, I wondered about the intervening years, particularly 1968 to 1989, and those less exclusive screening spaces—that is, the art house and repertory cinemas common in cities throughout North America and Europe during the better part of the twentieth century. How peripheral were queer films in the larger filmgoing cultures of the time? What blends of queerness might everyday people have been encountering at their repertory and independent cinemas?

Curating Deviance attempts to recenter queer cinema in the history of art house exhibition by studying its programming and curation. Monthly calendars for urban art houses testify to the fact that queer films were far from marginal at this time; in fact, they were so prevalent that they wielded a gravitational pull that altered theaters' entire curatorial frameworks and their spatio-affective conventions. Programming, the practice of selecting and grouping films to be exhibited for a specific venue and expected audience, assembles disparate texts into a network of interrelations. I argue that post-1968 film programming marshaled together what have been deemed deviant subjectivities, animating insatiable publics who hungered for nonnormative perspectives on gender and sexuality. Additionally, the programmatic records of urban repertory and art cinemas, I contend, offer wormholes into queer and deviant imaginaries that traverse bizarre, disturbing, fantastical, and perverse sites of pleasure and embodiment. This book commits to unearthing these utopian remnants that break from the "respectable" gender and sexual paradigms of puritanical morality that still, in many ways, frustrate American culture and politics.

Curating Deviance uses post-1968 film programming to open a portal into an alternate sexual and gender politics of radical utopian inclusion, one that very much anticipates queer theory and politics but, crucially, also exceeds it in more perverse and deviant ways. A range of deviant practices that include but are not delimited by LGBT identities were regularly on the menu at urban repertory and art house cinemas: sex work, intergenerational desire, interracial desire, fetishism or paraphilia, swinging or nonmonogamy, bondage, domination, and sadomasochism (BDSM), and what Heather Love calls "other yet-to-be-specified experiences of stigma" filled the screens.

Films such as *Funeral Parade of Roses* (dir. Toshio Matsumoto, 1969), *Maîtresse* (dir. Barbet Schroeder, 1975), *The Night Porter* (dir. Liliana Cavani, 1974), *Cabaret* (dir. Bob Fosse, 1972), and *The Rocky Horror Picture Show* (dir. Jim Sharman, 1975), among many others in this book, covered a lot of ground in terms of gender and sexuality in a short time span—nearly the "whole repertory of human sexuality," as critic Parker Tyler observed in his landmark 1972 book *Screening the Sexes*.[1] His reference to *repertory* here seems far from coincidental; revival house programmers made use of the whole arsenal of film history, not just those films made in the 1970s and 1980s, to enact and visualize for viewers the wild range and variety of sexuality and gender.

Filmmakers John Waters, Bernardo Bertolucci, Liliana Cavani, Radley Metzger, Russ Meyer, Luchino Visconti, Pier Paolo Pasolini, Ulrike Ottinger, Andy Warhol, Paul Morrissey, Kenneth Anger, Rainer Werner Fassbinder, Oshima Nagisa, and a bevy of others brought to the big screen renderings of sexual and gender outsiders and perverts perceived as anomic within a bourgeois sensibility. These makers deployed divergent stylistic, narrative, and tonal strategies in their deviant politics, yet together they made up a panoply of voices calling attention to or attempting to extinguish the persistent forces of erotophobia. Through schedule configurations such as double or triple bills, thematic series, or proximate screenings days or weeks apart, curating clustered these outsiders into networks and revealed intersections in their stigma and oppression, as well as sources of *"outré"* pleasures.

What might studying the history of art house film programming do for queer film studies? What might it do for queer theory?[2] Queer theory has certainly confronted and opposed the exaltation of white hetero- and homonormative and binary gender logics. In addition to exposing larger structures of sexual and gender oppression and repression, queer theory has accented and celebrated the experiences, identities, communities, and imaginaries that break from those systems. Historically situated in cultural studies, it has also scrutinized highly ambivalent sites and modes of cultural production. That said, over the years, I have struggled to find in queer theory and queer film studies deep and sustained analytical engagement with the staggering range of gender and sexual subjectivities and imaginaries in the world. For instance, queer theory has taught its readers a multitude about fetishes, especially in relation to LGBT desire, but rarely are "straight" fetishes fully integrated into queer theory's web of kinships.[3] Queer film and media studies in particular tends to stay within the boundaries of LGBT readability/legibility, even if it manifests in coded or complex formal ways.[4]

As a response, this book joins other scholarly efforts in queer theory to recover the language and lessons of postwar deviance studies in sociology and its cognates in sexology. Following Gayle Rubin and Heather Love in particular, I seek to widen the criteria for queerness, including but not circumscribed by LGBT presence, to find a politics that might better account for expansive systems and structures of social alienation and stigma that are linked to sexuality and gender. Studies in queer visual culture might profit from this different set of criteria for studying the workings of gender and sexual alterity on film.[5] Thus this research, which benefits from many of the lessons of queer theory and queer film studies, has been driven by the following questions: Could art house film programming of the 1970s and 1980s be retrofitted to a new queer or, better yet, *deviant* thought? Might programming—an organizational tool that stimulates intertextual connection—rekindle or reorganize queer utopian imaginaries that feel lost or static?

This book endeavors to see what happens when "queer" reaches its analytical limits in the intertextual space of historical programming and begs for a new conceptual framework. Plunging into the film calendars from theaters in New York City, San Francisco, Los Angeles, and Chicago, *Curating Deviance* historicizes, by way of years of archival research, curation's power to signify and resignify texts, to create affective matrixes for cultural and political disruption, and to provide templates for deviant affinities and pleasures to take shape.

Take as an example the Canadian film *Outrageous!* (dir. Richard Benner, 1977), now virtually forgotten but programmed over and over in San Francisco Bay Area repertory cinemas between 1978 and 1980. This low-budget film stars real-life female impersonator Craig Russell (playing himself in many ways) as Robin, a drag queen whose best friend Liza is schizophrenic (fig. I.1). The film depicts the vicissitudinous affinity between these two social pariahs in scenes of mutual struggle and uplift. It was programmed in double features with popular films such as *Boys in the Band* (dir. William Friedkin, 1970) (at the Strand Theatre, the Castro, and the UC Theater), *Grey Gardens* (dir. Albert Maysles, David Maysles, Ellen Hovde, Muffie Meyer, 1975) (at the Roxie), and later *Harold and Maude* (dir. Hal Ashby, 1971) (also at the Castro). The clinical historical linkages between sexual and gender nonconformity and mental illness subtend all these films, both intratextually and intertextually; these themes then branch out into the difficulties and (offbeat) joys of other "degenerate" experiences: complicated gay male friendship, class descent into poverty and dispossession, and intergenerational romance, respectively. *Outrageous!* finds its queer kinships by way of its roaming signification, in individual double bills and in theaters around the Bay Area region, evincing deviant resonances over time in a sequential unfolding. This programming tells a diffuse story of the pains of ostracism and the ameliorative measures downtrodden subjects take to cultivate sources and sites of collective levity and support.

Curating Deviance engages with the programming of a wide range of canonical queer films frequently exhibited in the years between 1968 and 1989, including *Portrait of Jason* (dir. Shirley Clarke, 1967), *Satyricon* (dir. Federico Fellini, 1969), *Daughters of Darkness* (dir. Harry Kümel, 1971), *Les Biches* (dir. Claude Chabrol, 1968), *The Killing of Sister George* (dir. Robert Aldrich, 1968), and *Boys in the Band*, as well as curious examples of queer films such as *Multiple Maniacs* (dir. John Waters, 1970), *The Rocky Horror Picture Show*, and *Beyond the Valley of the Dolls* (dir. Russ Meyer, 1970), titles claimed more by straight cult fans at first and then later canonized as queer classics. This book also analyzes the intertextual implications of important "straight" films such as *Harold and Maude, In the Realm of the Senses* (dir. Oshima Nagisa, 1976), and *The Devils* (dir. Ken Russell, 1971), among others, that position taboo and abject forms of heterosexual desire queerly as representational scandal

I.1 Two outcast best friends in *Outrageous!* (dir. Richard Benner, 1977) with their guardian angel Marlene Dietrich in the middle.

(fig. I.2). These texts loiter awkwardly on the periphery of queer cinema, their deviant interventions about structures of repression and desire going undervalued, forgotten, or without a proper queer analytical framework. Here I recover them, placing them back in their viewing contexts within a nexus of films indicting sexual and gender persecution, or providing imaginative outlets for "abnormal" romance, desire, and gender identity to surface.

Situating Curation

Film programming or curation, as this book argues, is always working within textual constellations known as *intertextuality*.[6] Programming is intertextuality put into practice—in real time—forging authorial, formal, ideological, aesthetic, tonal, temporal, geographical, and cultural relations that emerge across the span of one sitting (such as at a festival, or a double or triple bill) or a longer period, such as an exhibition venue's monthly calendar. Although they have received scant mention in film studies, programmers have for the better part of film history mediated textual understandings through their assembled intertexts, steering how

1.2 A 1980 Bleecker Street Cinema calendar offers such perverse classics as *Death in Venice* (dir. Luchino Visconti, 1971), *Sebastiane* (dir. Derek Jarman and Paul Humfress, 1976), *The Damned* (dir. Luchino Visconti, 1969), *Tristana* (dir. Luis Buñuel, 1970), *Trash* (dir. Paul Morrissey, 1970), *In the Realm of the Senses* (dir. Oshima Nagisa, 1976), and many more. Ben Davis Collection, Bleecker Street Cinema calendar from June/July 1980. The Museum of Modern Art Department of Film Special Collections, New York.

audiences might read films' cultural and aesthetic relevance.[7] Programmers have played a pivotal role in the unique epistemic and affective work of the cinema, puzzling together films along syntagmatic lines to create coherent sign systems such as genres, as well as paradigmatic lines that alter the narrative and aesthetic meanings of texts based on their shifting arrangements.

Curatorial studies have underscored that *curate* comes from the Latin *cura*, meaning to care. Curators in this sense are caretakers or custodians of historical objects, taking responsibility not just for the material objects themselves but also for how they are presented to the public. David Balzer explains that in joining care and connoisseurship, curators lend "stylized independence to the act of caring for and assembling."[8] At the same time that curators, or in this case, film programmers, assert their unique visions of visual art, they are also in roles of subservience, as Balzer writes, "to institutions, objects, artists, audiences, markets."[9] In the process of balancing a distinguishing programmatic perspective with a subordinate position to the work and its makers, film programmers have used their unique tools of collecting, culling, and collating to both canonize certain films and filmmakers and resignify the work with each distinct screening and calendar arrangement.

Programming has played a central role in the histories of film reception, and it has done so in part through the process of classification. Programming can reinforce already existing cinematic taxonomies, which might coalesce around such themes or topics as nation, period, genre, wave, or movement (just to name the major ones), or it can initiate or establish a new classification. This might occur at a festival exhibiting new content, a film center identifying recent trends or patterns, or a repertory house reappraising and reclassifying older films. Whichever shape it takes, film curating is a robust classificatory tool that can further lodge established knowledge into place or bring about new knowledge to the film discourses shared by critics, cinephiles, and scholars. Programmers of the late 1960s to late 1980s did not fully jettison existing filmic categories, but many were also experimenters—laboratory scientists of sorts—mixing intertextual compounds that could reveal taxonomic congruencies and homologies among deviant depictions and their formal illustrations. Constellating texts into intertexts, programmers drew up provisional and idiosyncratic categories or schema befitting of outcasts such as fetishists or sex workers, types often left on the fringes of decency, political visibility, and thus political class membership.

Film curators from 1968 to 1989 may not have been held to the deity-like status of auteur that their cinephile patrons worshipped (with the exception, perhaps, of preservationist-curator Henri Langlois of the Cinémathèque Française), but they were known by cineastes and critics for making their stamp on a particular screening venue's personality, politics, and vision. Think here of Jewish-Austrian emigré Amos Vogel of Cinema 16, gay and black programmer Albert Johnson of the San Francisco International Film Festival, Richard Peña of first the Chicago Art Institute and then the Film Society of Lincoln Center, and Dan Talbot and Toby Talbot of the New York Theater, all programming cinemas frequented by contemporaneously or soon-to-be influential critics, artists, filmmakers, intellectuals, and cultural producers in their debt.[10] Even if they identified as heterosexual, some of these esteemed programmers were outsiders in other ways, their selections suggesting they latched onto representations of other social pariahs.

Scholarship and histories of film programming provide many useful analogies for the figure of the curator or programmer, which appear across the following chapters: the programmer is at once a cultural gatekeeper, presenter, tastemaker, intermediary, educator, showman, ambassador, culler, herder, and bricoleur. *Curating Deviance* treats the film programmer or curator above all else as a discursive formation, a role that directs politics, aesthetics, sensibilities, and tastes. For this reason, rather than track biographical, anecdotal, or institutional histories of important programmers, or provide historical insights into the ins and outs of exhibition (e.g., print availability, budgets, etc.), I remain attentive to the queer political stakes and possibilities that are located in the post-1968 film program.[11] To this end, I am less interested in the programmer as a person, even as part of a decision-making team, than as a *force*, more a cultural sculptor or bricoleur, that offers the public new ways to see, hear, know, and feel.

When particularly illuminating, some curators make repeated appearances, such as Richard Schwarz, the gay programmer and owner of the Thalia Theater in Manhattan; the aforementioned Amos Vogel, whose insights extend into the 1970s with his book on "subversive" cinema; Brazilian gay programmer Fabiano Canosa of the First Avenue Screening Room and Papp Theater; as do certain exemplary cinemas such as the Nuart Theatre in West Los Angeles, which began Gary Meyer, Steve Gilula, and Kim Jorgensen's Landmark Theatres chain venture; Sid Geffen and Jackie Raynal's Carnegie Hall and Bleecker Street Cinemas in Manhattan; and the Roxie in San Francisco. *Curating Deviance* pays critical attention to their historical, geographical, demographical, and architectural particularities.[12]

Longtime Pacific Film Archive (PFA) curator Edith Kramer describes a film series as a "journey" with peaks, valleys, and tangents that guide the audience toward interpreting how the films "relate to each other."[13] Similarly, Peter Bosma writes, "A film curator is a storyteller, telling a story about the value of films," asking critical questions like, "'Why is this particular film important,' or 'Why is this specific combination of films interesting?'"[14] *Curating Deviance* dwells on this second question because it pinpoints why programming merits distinct intertextual study. I insist programming is more than a practice of selecting, booking, and arranging a group of films. And in the context of queer film history post-1968, it did more than expose publics—LGBT and "straight"—to evidence of queer existence. Programming *built* deviant worlds and generated out of its dialogic structure new ethical strategies of pleasure and care for those belonging to the lower castes of the sexual and gender hierarchy.

Deviance Terms, Deviant Times

Curating Deviance begins in 1968, a year that approximates the inauguration of monumental change in the United States' public sphere.[15] The legalization of the birth control pill and then abortion, along with women's liberation, gay liberation, race empowerment, and anti-colonial movements set the scene for what became known as the era of sexual liberation or revolution. Cinema reflected and inspired these sea changes, marked by the end of the then-declining Hays Code, to be replaced with the Motion Picture Association of America (MPAA) ratings system in 1968. Art and graphic sex had merged several years before in the New York Underground and Warhol Factory in what Ara Osterweil calls the "corporeal turn" of art cinema, a "participatory realm of assault and seduction"; by the early 1970s this corporeality had become an integral part of art cinema.[16] Various sex acts—homo-, hetero-, and bisexual—were now regularly viewable in art and porn theaters that even middleclass couples would visit together, enticed perhaps by the "X" rating given by the newly minted MPAA.

Film scholars Linda Williams, Elena Gorfinkel, Eric Schaefer, and Damon Young have discussed this flood of sexually explicit content in grindhouses, exploitation houses, art houses, and even mainstream cinemas as an expression of excitement as well as anxiety around sexuality's new auditory and visual accessibility. Far from being simple celebrations of bodies and desires, these new films delivered irresolvable and befuddling ideological antinomies, articulating the contradictions of "making sex public," as Young phrases it.[17]

Fraught or messy as they were in their depictions, the sheer range of blatant acts, desires, identities, and practices displayed "on/scene," as Williams puts it (in contrast to what had been deemed "obscene"), was unprecedented. No longer relegated to subtext, themes of hustling or sex work could be found in a mainstream sensation such as *Midnight Cowboy* (dir. John Schlesinger, 1969), or in art house successes *Belle de Jour* (dir. Luis Buñuel, 1967) and Paul Morrissey's trilogy of films starring underground Warhol Factory hunk Joe Dallesandro. Ken Russell's hit art films *The Devils* (1971) and *The Music Lovers* (1970) allegorized the effects of sexual repression by featuring characters driven mad and tortured by their buried lust.

I.3 Poster underscoring sexual depravity in Ken Russell's *The Music Lovers* (1970).

Russell's films strangely delighted in a maddening repression that only intensified abject perversions, turning "the straight into the kinky," as critic Parker Tyler rightfully noted.[18] Although it often employed sensationalizing qualifiers (such as "bizarre," "strange," and "outrageous") in marketing materials, post-1968 programming assembled these "degenerate" characterizations into comparative schemata, inciting opportunities to witness and feel the alienation and pleasure of ostensibly disparate experiences of sexual and gender outcasts (fig. I.3).

Deviance is the most apposite social concept for capturing these objects. My usage of *deviance* carries with it broad queer epistemologies, but I simultaneously attempt to leave behind the centralizing of LGBT in the demarcation of sexual otherness, stressing instead the interdependence of social categories by which we might adopt an inclusive ethical framework.[19] Defined by the negative, that is, what is *not* normal, *deviance* risks covering too much ground, perhaps even more so than the intentionally amorphous *queer*. The capaciousness and elasticity of *deviance* is both an asset and risk. *Deviance* unifies as it limits; it brings together the array of perverse and unthinkable depictions of sexuality and gender in art films of this era while underscoring the difficulty of advancing a unified political front of sexual liberation that can (or sometimes even should) accommodate such varied difference. *Deviance*, then, can be seen as an amalgamation of social alterity that helps train the political and ethical imagination for radical inclusion.

The image of the deviant invokes flashes of a history replete with demonized and feared archetypes: sideshow freaks like the bearded lady, dwarf, or limbless man; in the United States, the Cold War–era pervert (e.g., the homosexual-pedophile); the "welfare queen"; the sociopathic convict; the communist; the oversexed, nymphomaniac-fetishist; and the "cripple" subject to endless stares. (Note how many of these bogeymen persist to this day.) Photographic and cinematic technologies have from their beginnings played a vital role in assigning and codifying physical difference as deviance. Allan Sekula explains that "photography came to establish and delimit the terrain of the *other*, to define both the generalized look—the *typology*—and the *contingent instance* of deviance and social pathology."[20] Studies in disability (especially crip theory), sexuality, and race have documented these intersectional histories, attesting to how distinct forms of deviance have an interlocking character because their classificatory origins are grounded in moral panic about visual markers of social difference.[21]

This troubling (if not violent) history leads Dana Seitler to a potent articulation of *sexual deviance*, one that I want to underscore and adopt in defining deviance within the context of film programming. She writes, "Sexual deviance ... specifies an affiliation—an intricate, nonfamilial kinship web of human aberration in which an assortment of anomalous characteristics exist within a larger schema of human variation."[22] Seitler here observes that the dispositif of sexual deviance produces bound subjectivities, a skein of difference that ties one deviant type or form to another as a modern condition that is a priori baked into conceptions of "aberrant" subjectivities.

Moreover, Seitler notes (as she reads sexologist Havelock Ellis's 1900 study of homosexuality as gender inversion) that sexual deviance "could only be cognized relationally, or more to the point, *serially*."[23] This early twentieth century (re)cognizing of deviance might indeed live on in the structuring of the deviant film *series*, a word that shares its etymological root with "serial." If, as Edith Kramer and Peter Bosma suggest, curation tells a kind of story, programming is serial in structure—even with loose, nonlinear, or tangential tendencies. We might say then that post-1968 film curating made legible and even fortified deviance's relational basis through the time-based method of sequentiality. In this sense, deviance operates as its own sign system, relying on accumulating and interconnected representational codes and formal motifs of nonnormative erotic jouissance as well as distressing moments of persecution. Over time, programming can reveal narrative, typological, and aesthetic connections across a sign-system omnibus of taboos.

For some, *deviance* is an irredeemably charged term that cannot be isolated from its violent clinical, medical, academic, and legal historiographies. Although it is thorny work, I recuperate and repurpose the beneficial aspects of some social scientific deployments of the term, specifically in the invaluable work of anthropologist Gayle Rubin and sociologist Erving Goffman, as well as controversial sexologist John Money's crucial (if not ambivalent) thinking on paraphilia. My use of *deviant*, which draws on but is distinct from *queer*, maintains an uncomfortable yet productive distance from the social sciences; in keeping with Heather Love's recent work on queer theory's disavowed entwinement with 1960s deviance studies, *deviance* seeks to remind us of the ways that scientific inquiry has kept nonconforming identities, bodies, practices, and experiences enmeshed with one another, even as queer theory assures its readers to have "moved on" and distanced itself from those outmoded prejudicial groupings and analyses. The positivistic shaping of those social associations, I will go on to argue especially in chapter 2, is not an entirely bad thing.

Some of these sociological and sexological concepts rippled out into the wider public sphere beyond academia, influencing critics, filmmakers, cinephiles, and film programmers in their encounters with deviant film texts. Historical correlations exist between this era's art house film programming and the public's interest in the sociology of deviance (a.k.a. deviance studies), both in its pseudo-scientific forms in exploitation films and "shockumentaries" (such as *Mondo Freudo* [dir. Lee Frost, 1966]), and by "legitimate" institutional means such as Erving Goffman's research, and that of popular postwar sexologists Alfred Kinsey, Wilhelm Reich, and John Money.[24] In many ways this complicated research better suits the historical articulation of outliers who are not easily slotted into queer theory's imagined vanguard. We might then see deviance here as a useful *analytic category*, in Joan W. Scott's usage of the term, with potential for ethical reconfiguration along manifold axes of age, labor, gender variation, and communal practice, employing an array of archetypes, from the chronophile to trans person to sex worker to sadist and masochist (or some mixture thereof!), to populate its representative motley.[25]

This book takes the position that sexual and gender deviance binds subjects to one another through their failure to meet ideologically entrenched standards of propriety, and that art house programming from 1968 to 1989 guided curious audiences through profound meditations on these interrelated histories of both queer (i.e., primarily LGBT) and other "deviant" subjectivities. Intertextual analyses in the pages that follow intend to drastically revise orthodoxies in the study of queer visual culture, to incorporate widely unthinkable outlier pleasures that lurk in the margins of queer discourse. This is precisely why I read for deviant typologies overlooked in queer theory (chapter 2) or for erotic forms that confound tidy demarcations between straight and queer desires (chapter 3). *Curating Deviance* ventures to traverse other critical modalities for the study of sexual and gender alterity and the moving image in the hopes of bringing hitherto neglected deviant exiles into the queer fold.

From Text to Intertext

My reading practice for film exhibition in this book deviates from the usual protocols of intertextual analysis. Literary and film scholars tend to focus on instances of intertextuality that take the shape of quotation, reference, allusion, parody, adaptation, revision, remaking, plagiarism, metafiction, and parallelism in the ramified genealogies of artistic work. These studies attend to how a text becomes present and known within the body of another text, whether by the author's intent or uncovered by the reader. In *Curating Deviance*, however, intertextuality figures the embodied real time of film viewing within the concentrated comparative textual conditions of the cinema.

Studying the film calendars I found in archives at the Museum of Modern Art (MoMA), the Berkeley Art Museum and Pacific Film Archive (BAMPFA), and even the theaters themselves, with deteriorating calendars stacked in cardboard boxes, I read for homologous as well as clashing textual forms, narrative schemata (including standout indicators such as sex scenes, fantasy sequences, and endings), tones or sensibilities, and star and director filmographies that might connect films with otherwise vague shared intertextual properties. At times, I find it more useful and specific to refer to the *interdiegetic* rather than the *intertextual* because of the ways programming forges, if not fuses, together the narrative, stylistic, and tonal qualities of distinct film worlds.[26] The *interdiegetic* gets us inside the shared and overlapping textual (il)logics and sensibilities that make films programmed together sudden siblings when they would in other viewing contexts be perceived as distant cousins or perhaps even completely unrelated.

My version of intertextual analysis rejects wholesale monotextual assumptions about spectatorship; the intertextual praxis of film curating means that no text or object within its viewing context can rest on its own production of meaning. Programs are contact zones of signification that amplify the kinds of textual multivalence and elasticity that literary theorists such as Laurent Jenny, Roland Barthes, Julia Kristeva, Jacques Derrida, and Umberto Eco, among others, have advanced. Following their theories of intertextuality, I contend that curating enacts textual *contingence* that magnifies hermeneutic *contingency*, in which textual meaning depends on webs of relationality.

Repertory or revival house programs are paragons of concepts in semiotics such as Eco's unlimited semiosis or Derrida's *différance*, both describing the proliferating flows of meaning and shifting hermeneutic relays or chains that stretch onward in time. Commercial repertory cinemas, along with museums such as MoMA, programmed films from the past in altering configurations that maximized potential for their resignification. Performance scholar Diana Taylor nicely illustrates how notions of revision and regeneration are embedded in the word *repertoire* itself. *Repertoire* etymologically means "'a treasury, an inventory,' . . . referring also to 'the finder, discoverer,' and meaning 'to find out.'"[27] Counterposed to the *archive*, the *repertoire* lends itself to impermanence and ephemerality, living in a community or culture's "embodied memory" in ways that can create meaningful resonances that are dynamic and historically contingent. Repertory and revival cinemas thus frustrate notions of crystalized knowledge, wielding *repetition* with variation, recycling films while recasting signification through protean thematic framings, as well as by geographic and temporal viewing contexts. These heterotopic sites hold the utopian promise not only of rediscovery in a nostalgic or historical sense but also of reframing texts within the shifting temporalities of past, present, and future that recalibrate how audiences think and feel.

As I suggested earlier, programming provides a wormhole into historical spectatorship as well as a different political imaginary for needed sexual and gender inclusion. I base these theories in the viewing practices of spectators at the time, grounding my readings in the intertexts on offer at local cinemas. Speaking with baby boomers who frequented art and repertory houses in the 1970s and 1980s, I learned that it was common for urbanites to go to the cinema weekly, sometimes daily, and stay for entire double features, even if they had seen one or both films before.[28]

That devout communities of cinephiles attended many of these urban cinemas on a regular basis fortifies my intertextual analyses, yet this fact does not fully undergird my readings. As BAMPFA's programmer Kathy Geritz has noted, "Nobody comes to every [screening] ... so [the programmer is] making connections for history, for when people go back and look at the programs."[29] Geritz, echoing her mentor Edith Kramer's equation of programs to journeys, suggests that even without total consistent attendance, the film program maps the conscious and unconscious life of a given historical moment; the film calendar is a compendium of assorted desires, fantasies, hopes, questions, curiosities, grievances, propositions, and provocations that structure and chronicle the public's complex emotional and political life. More than a mere reflection, programs and calendars provide the building blocks for unmaking and remaking the world through the public fantasy that is cinema.

Case in point: consider, in another Bay Area example, the manner in which these two double bills were arranged: Federico Fellini's *Satyricon* (1969) and Pier Paolo Pasolini's *The Decameron* (1971) were paired together in San Francisco Bay Area theaters over six times from 1975 to 1978, half of them at the Roxie Theater (figs. I.4 and I.5).[30] Clearly successful with audiences, this duo of popular Italian art films about unbridled premodern sexuality channeled the spirit of an emergent transnational sexual liberation by entertaining Dionysian fantasies about a sexually permissive and fluid era centuries in the past. Another popular pairing of Italian films screened twice at NYC's Carnegie Hall Cinema, first in 1974 and then in 1978, was far less euphoric: Luchino Visconti's *The Damned* (1969) was exhibited with his *Death of Venice* (1971), meditating on the quite literal lethal effects of sexual repression. *The Damned* ends with a depiction of the Night of the Long Knives and *Death in Venice* with the protagonist in an agonizing state of pederastic longing before a heart attack claims his life.[31] These antonymous programs, both representing queer Italian history, one on the side of romanticized sexual liberation and the other a brutal indictment of pathology, power, and repression, testify to the fact that art house depictions of deviant sexuality and gender were not always "freeing" or uplifting; they also carried critiques or expressed ambivalence or even confusion about how nonnormative practices and social types related to the domains of culture, politics, and history.

In this vein, I read historical programming documents such as calendars, schedules, press releases, and program notes—both in their text

1.4 Showcasing sexual decadence in publicity for Fellini's *Satyricon* (1969).

I.5 Lustful nuns take turns having sex with the new gardener in Pasolini's *The Decameron* (1971).

and design—as intertextual guides for a world envisioned otherwise. In its commitment to reenvisioning political imaginaries that have grown stale, this book takes an avowedly reparative approach to queer intertextuality, reading for critical openings that help imagine obscured forms of kinship, sex, and love. My critical reading practice can best be described by what José Esteban Muñoz calls "utopian hermeneutics," a "backwards glance that enacts a future vision."[32] In attempting to circumvent the "present's stultifying hold," Muñoz reads past cultural objects for their ecstatic longings for idealized states of queer passion and pleasure. Similarly, I suggest these utopian horizons of potentiality appear through programmed intertexts, providing inspiration for coalitional opportunities in the types and practices clustered in the program, or formally by giving shape to paraphilia or fetishes that otherwise appear as outliers or anomalies in film and cultural history.

Art houses of the time were in good company; utopian sexual and gender topographies surfaced in many 1970s LGBT and nonwhite counterpublics, reflected best in the Third World Gay Revolution, which advocated for anti-racist, anti-sexist, and anti-capitalist transformation along with one of queer inclusion, in addition to lesbian and feminist separatist movements.[33] Independent and experimental films of the era such as Lizzie Borden's *Born in Flames* (1983) and Barbara Hammer's experimental shorts wedged open a feminist filmic space for imagining love, sex, and activism within egalitarian, liberated communal bounds.

With far less racial or geographical diversity than the Third World Gay Revolution or *Born in Flames*, post-1968 film curating still marshaled its own coalitions through comparative models of stigma or paraphilic desires, converging identities, types, and practices relegated to the depths of the social strata. Exemplary is John Waters's films, such as *Female Trouble* (1974), *Multiple Maniacs*, and *Pink Flamingos* (1972), with "maladjusted" subjects such as fetishists, genderqueer or trans characters, and antisocial queer convicts commonly mingling in the space of programs with films that have similar character typologies, namely the work of Rainer Werner Fassbinder and Pier Paolo Pasolini. (See chapter 2 on the Nuart's "Outlaw Cinema" series.) Whether these films' interventions took the form of critique or pleasure, or some mixture thereof, the film series gave these deviant forms and practices a meeting ground unavailable in the repressive status quo.

Reading for utopian aspirations in the intertext—whether it takes the form of sharing in one another's vexed status or releasing and celebrating a taboo desire—does not imply a romanticizing of the intertext or era of its programming. There is plenty of cause for casting suspicion on this tunnel-vision gleaning of the past. After all, creative treatments of social deviance were often used as metaphors or vehicles for abstracted "anti-establishment" positions, in effect diminishing their applicability in the embodied, material realms of political life. These *gestural* anti-normative politics also came at the price of personal injury, proof that sometimes behind the optics of liberation hides exploitation. Case in point: actors Maria Schneider (in *Last Tango in Paris* [dir. Bernardo Bertolucci, 1972]) and Björn Andrésen (in *Death in Venice*) were taken advantage of and assaulted by their directors, becoming casualties of a widening representational field for nonnormative desire.[34] The depiction of BDSM in *Last Tango in Paris* and chronophilia or intergenerational desire in *Death in Venice* thus came at the expense of the films' vulnerable actors. Production backstories like these forestall a comprehensive recovery of film programming history.[35] Distinct from wish fulfillment or "cherry picking" history, *Curating Deviance* invests in the reparative or utopian work of retrieving history's abandoned promises, its lost openings for "future-dawning, anticipatory illuminations of the not-yet-conscious," as Muñoz explains it, for a political moment to come.[36]

Chapters

Curating Deviance is organized roughly into two parts with interrelated topics: the first half (chapters 1 and 2) tends to focus on the ideological role of the programmer as an intertextual designer of the cinematic experience; the second half (chapters 4 and 5) speculates more on the role of the historical spectator in their cognitive-affective encounter with programming; and as a kind of interlude or midpoint break, chapter 3 attends closely to questions of intertextual form. Each chapter presents its own theoretical framework for thinking about film, sexuality, and gender in novel intertextual terms, and does so by either proposing new terms (e.g., *promiscuous programming* and *repertory time*) or adapting established ones (e.g., *deviance* and *reparativity*) to elucidate the schemata and stakes of film programming's deviant ethics.

Chapter 1, "Promiscuous Programming," delineates a shift in late 1960s programming practices in which exhibitors moved away from a model confined to "sophisticated" auteurist traditions. Instead, most urban repertory and art houses in the years between 1968 and 1989 unabashedly assembled for public consumption an eclectic blend of films that ranged greatly from Classical Hollywood to exploitation films to foreign or art films to experimental shorts to blockbusters. I call this heterogeneous approach *promiscuous programming*, doubling in meaning to express the eclectic reshuffling of taste strata as well as the racy and salacious content that permeated this period's film programs. A large portion of the chapter sketches a genealogy that links the programmatic sensibilities of Iris Barry (of MoMA in the 1930s), Amos Vogel (of Cinema 16, 1947–63), Pauline Kael (of Cinema Guild, 1955–60), and other programmers and exhibitors who revised conventional taste codes and laid the groundwork for a veritably multifarious curatorial attunement. The historical concept of *promiscuous programming* also identifies a spatial relation in which film viewing and nightlife leisure practices (such as dancing, performance, and drug use) spilled into one another, infecting each other in their use and enjoyment.

Chapter 2, "Deviant Repertories," the title chapter and theoretical heart of the book, lays out *deviance* as a critical category for film history. It positions the post-1968 programmer as a kind of lay sexologist-cum-sociologist who mediated persistent structures of erotophobia. These queer and straight (mostly male) programmers classified and reclassified films via malleable deviant categories inspired by and in defiance of the ordered knowledges of sexology and sociology. These two social sciences,

I argue, are valuable because they describe phenomena that fall outside of reproductive heterosexuality and thus provide robust queer rubrics for programming's coalitional aspirations. Here I focus on a number of 1980s programs, such as a Marlene Dietrich and Josef von Sternberg retrospective at San Francisco's Roxie in 1988, a series called "Sexuality in Cinema" at Film Center at the School of the Art Institute of Chicago in 1984, and a weekly series called "Outlaw Cinema" at the Nuart Theatre in 1981, to analyze programmers' deviant strategies for stitching together seemingly incompatible types, practices, and identities.

Chapter 3, "Erotic Intertextuality," breaks from the dyad of programmer and spectator to traverse the perverse formal terrain of what I consider to be erotic intertexts. Programming, I argue, pushes eros askew, congealing homomorphic patterns of editing, production design, performance style, and frame composition to make form itself the object of mimetic desire. As my central case study, I select the Nuart's 1978–79 winter calendar, which included deviant cult classics *Salon Kitty* (dir. Tinto Brass, 1976), *The Night Porter*, *Salò, or the 120 Days of Sodom* (dir. Pier Paolo Pasolini, 1975), *Beyond the Valley of the Dolls*, *Women in Love* (dir. Ken Russell, 1969), *Maîtresse*, *Sebastiane* (dir. Derek Jarman and Paul Humfress, 1976), as well as a Marlon Brando retrospective, to do a close intertextual analysis of the calendar's erotic scales, textures, and durations.

Chapter 4, "Repertory Time," examines the phenomenon of double bills or double features once ubiquitous among repertory houses. While it is almost entirely neglected by film studies, this paradigm offers, by virtue of its dyadic nature, a constantly refreshed platform for intertextual re-readings. I suggest that double bills function as highly concentrated microcosms for the larger schemas of entire weekly schedules or monthly calendars. This chapter lays out the terms and implications of what I call *repertory time*, an elongated viewing modality in which spectators were immersed in queer worlds that rejected routine heteronormativity and endorsed carnivalesque, heterotopic transgression. As exercises in intertextual cross-pollination and juxtaposition, double features indicate how programming made critiques and pleasures affectively immediate for repertory filmgoers.

Chapter 5, "For Shame!," engages with the reclaimed "bad objects" or "guilty pleasures" of the queer canon that, once reviled by lesbian and gay liberationists, have acquired cult fandom and signal ways to liberate "contaminated" forms of enjoyment. The Frameline Film Festival's series on women-in-prison films (1990) and lesbian vampire films (1987), as well as MoMA's program on Russ Meyer's sexploitation films, provide fascinating examples of lesbian feminists' concerns with women's representations in queer films that shift by the late 1980s. To this end, I connect the critical efforts of queer feminist thinkers such as B. Ruby Rich, Judith Mayne, and Andrea Weiss with reparative thinking in queer-of-color critique. Ultimately, I connect this criticism to diachronic programming techniques, which loosened the traumatic grips of individual texts and thereby transmuted forced viewer identification with clichés into spectators' risible recognition of the tropes.

In the chapters that follow, post-1968 programming histories hold the capacity to help redirect queer energies and to draw attention to deep structural hierarchies and systems of stigma, moralization, and infighting that sustain sex moralism and judgment on the right and left, and which beleaguer contemporary attempts at collective protection and advocacy of some of the most vulnerable to attacks of a sexual and gender nature. Post-1968 programming is uniquely positioned to revise the criteria for queer affinities yet also to discover existing tenuous ones. *Curating Deviance* reminds us that the cinema is a site of pleasure that can prompt spectators to share in each other's perverse differences, discovering the variegated oddity and waywardness of bodies and desires not their own, though somehow strangely familiar. In this vein, historical programs act as the abandoned itineraries of an unfinished sexual revolution, an undertaking burrowed in the cobwebbed recesses of the forgotten repertory and art houses, not lost forever, but certainly in need of loving repair.

Promiscuous Programming *1*

FILMIC ECLECTICISM IN
POST-1968 ART HOUSE CINEMA

Throughout the twentieth century, art house cinema reinvented itself over and over again—from the Parisian 1920s "cine clubs" to the repertory houses of 1950s New York City, from its strictly experimental origins to its later auteurist embrace of Hollywood classics. By the mid-1960s, art cinema in North America and much of Western Europe had subsumed under its pliable name a host of films from various parts of the globe, as well as a blend of traditions, production values, and ideological positions. The mid-1960s movie listings page in a newspaper like *The Village Voice* is especially representative: lined with postwar favorites from Europe and Japan (especially by directors such as Godard, Fellini, Bergman, Kurosawa, Mizoguchi, and Ozu), Hollywood features from the golden age, redeemed with the help of Andrew Sarris's "auteur theory" that he imported from *Cahiers du Cinéma*, and peppered with US independent fare (avant-garde and new wave directors from Brakhage to Cassavetes).[1]

By 1969, however, the programming listed in the same section of *The Village Voice* appears as if beamed from another planet. For example, in May 1969, the Regency, a repertory house in Manhattan, publicized Russ Meyer's landmark sexploitation classic *Vixen* (1968) with an advertisement that took up a third of the page. On the adjacent page, the Elgin in Chelsea showcased Marlene Dietrich and Marilyn Monroe double bills for a week in May.² The lusty subtext that had been part of art cinema for decades was now unabashedly on display, couched in a far-reaching variety of films from around the world and ranging in taste, from "foreign" highbrow to middle- and lowbrow mainstream or "commercial."³

In a survey of local theaters in 1977, the *Los Angeles Times* observed—rather belatedly—that Los Angeles theaters were "specializing in a new sort of presentation," wild in its eclecticism. These programs, the article reads, showed "cult films (*Harold and Maude*), classics (*The Maltese Falcon*), movies of redeeming value that missed commercially (*Medium Cool*), older foreign entries (*La Dolce Vita*), all-time favorites (*Singin' in the Rain*), and a general grab bag assortment, from Woody Allen (*Sleeper*) to Lina Wertmuller (*The Seduction of Mimi*), from Chaplin (*The Gold Rush*) to Fields (*The Bank Dick*)." Patrons, the piece points out, were by then calling this eclectic programming interchangeably *revival* and *alternative*.⁴ In merging *revival*, once considered the stuff of historical value and appreciation, and *alternative*, a euphemism for that which existed on the fringes of aesthetic and social decency, programmers and their audiences were upsetting the terms of art house as they had once been understood.

By 1968, a year that programming historian Ben Davis asserts inaugurates "the second wave of the repertory theater movement" in New York, films of disparate traditions, genres, and taste strata were beginning to regularly intermingle in art house programs in major US and European cities.⁵ With a focus on the US context, this chapter unpacks this major shift in film programming that materialized in the late 1960s and lasted through the 1980s. During this period, I argue, repertory and art house programmers exercised an eclecticism not seen before, mixing filmic traditions, genres, and low-, medium-, and highbrow tastes; effectively ditching thematic or tonal coherence; and concomitantly embracing carnal depiction. Programmers borrowed from anti-hierarchical sentiments based in liberation struggles of the time, and audiences likewise craved experimentation in presentational modes of entertainment and leisure that could further disrupt taste economies that had separated "art" from "trash."

Urban art house exhibition practices between 1968 and 1989 can best be described by what I refer to as *promiscuous programming*. The word *promiscuous* serves multiple functions here. Following its original Latin usage, it denotes the adulterous and indiscriminate mixing of different elements belonging to different classes. In the context of art houses and repertories, incompatible kinds of fare found themselves sharing the same monthly calendars to a degree never seen before. Following its later and more common contemporary usages, *promiscuous* also describes many of the films' own depictions, especially sexploitation, cult, and European films, which feature nude bodies performing simulated and unsimulated sex acts or enacting various kinds of kink and fetish play on-screen with any number of bodies. Last, *promiscuous* too carries a spatial quality, identifying film viewing spaces that spilled into other sites of artistic production and vice versa, including nightclubs, performance art and live theater spaces, and concert venues. These varying and enmeshed usages of *promiscuity* describe an overall mood and atmosphere of bodily and medial interplays that characterize art house and repertory programming and spectatorship of this era.

Promiscuous programming is not limited to this period; it is a style and a philosophy—a utopian aspiration of classlessness—that exists in traces throughout the past of film exhibition and into today's film cultures. Its antecedents are found in the innovative practices of a number of programmers whose tenures predate the period under focus in this book. This chapter produces a genealogy of renegade programming pre-1968, pointing to models that diverged from the typical itineraries more conventional programmers of that time plotted. Programmers such as Iris Barry, Amos Vogel, and Pauline Kael intentionally polluted the taste ecologies of the elite spaces they curated. They set the foundation for and influenced repertory and art house programmers of the 1970s and 1980s, when promiscuous programming became the norm in urban repertory houses especially. In charting promiscuous programming of film programmers stretching back to the 1930s, I am also providing a roadmap of filmic taste and its historical ruptures. This roadmap leads to 1968 as an approximate turning point, when content once considered sleazy or trashy, with no place at the art or repertory house, becomes a staple of its programming. Promiscuous programming, once marginal, becomes dominant and standard among art and repertory houses by the early 1970s.

These key players embody shifts in tastes and sensibilities that help to redefine not only what "art" is in a cinematic context but also the affects that might accompany such a category. In telling this programmatic history, I provide useful—albeit imperfect—homologies that the programmer shares with other figures who already occupy a place in cultural theory, namely the art dealer and the bricoleur. In a perhaps rather cynical light, Pierre Bourdieu's description of the art dealer encapsulates the programmer's influence over the public's taste and his role in reception economies. In a more romantic light, critical theory's reflections on bricolage and the role of the bricoleur bring into focus the imaginative, diversified practices of the

1970s and 1980s repertory house film curator. Promiscuous programming melds these two figures together—on the one hand translating "art" into capital (art dealer), and on the other, testing the correlation between cultural capital and its objects via the act of heterogeneous mixture (bricoleur).

Finally, I look at the geographical and spatial dimensions of city life that contributed to the explosion of promiscuous programming. This involved the geographic proximities of cinemas to one another, the bodily proximities of divergent audience demographics sharing viewing spaces, as well as the dissimilar yet complementary adjacencies of cinema spaces to other leisure and art forms such as music, dance, and performance. Such confluent processes were inextricably shaping and being shaped by the kinds of unruly and layered intertextuality seen in film programming of the time. These spatial conditions helped form new knowledges of the body and its relation to other bodies in space, thereby bringing about queer forms of knowing and questioning for the attending public. The relationship of viewing spaces, film texts, and exhibition styles or formats to one another, I demonstrate, was fluid and symbiotic rather than linear in cause and effect; these forces continue to tug on and propel one another starting in the late 1960s and continuing into the late 1980s.

Proto-Promiscuous Programming, 1935–63

Programmers, like all curators, are gatekeepers. They steer tastes by way of selecting certain films and omitting others from exhibition. On a deeper level, they arrange the viewing objects in such a way as to communicate meanings to their audiences, asking questions, provoking their senses, and expanding aesthetics and worldviews. If such cognitive and bodily processes are meant to elicit pleasure on the part of the paying public, wedging open their appreciative capacities for and attunements to creative objects, programmers, like fine art curators and dealers, set the terms of taste, in a deeply hierarchical, classed sense.

Within cinema, a populist entertainment medium and commodified form from its start, the "artfulness" of "art cinema" holds distinct and unique, if not complicated, prestige; it must distinguish itself from a larger money-driven and standardized industry (e.g., Hollywood). One of the most prevalent understandings of art cinema, which remains pervasive today, is that it follows high art and literary traditions, adapting for the moving image the aesthetic aptitude and philosophical interests of the intelligentsia, and thus sustaining investment in modes of elite cultural appraisal.[6] Barbara Wilinsky argues, in one of the most insightful studies of postwar art-cinema-going culture, that the description of art cinema as distinct and, oftentimes, against the mainstream, anti-Hollywood, outside commercialism, and reserved for educated and high-class populations reflects more the image that art cinema produced for itself than what the actual history of its content and reception suggests.[7] One historical explanation for this is that the middle class—from the postwar era to the present—have used art films for cultural capital, giving them access to highbrow culture historically reserved for the upper crust of society.

The launch of MoMA's film initiative beginning in the 1930s, helmed by archivist and curator Iris Barry, perfectly embodies this paradoxical effort to preserve and distinguish art cinema, as well as make it available to the masses. Haidee Wasson has skillfully tracked the dialectical development of MoMA's aims to make art accessible to the general public in the Depression-era United States while maintaining the sense of distinction that museum spaces need to sustain their position as custodians of history and culture. During this period, museums were drifting away from being sacred spaces for upper-crust patrons and moving toward a model of inclusion and education for the masses. Barry's curatorial position on that exact fault line—between populist appeal and cachet—is precisely what fueled her to expand the borders of artful taste in the context of cinema.

When Barry began programming films at MoMA in 1935, critics and intellectual circles in the US and Europe reserved artistic merit for the mostly experimental films made by the surrealists, Dadaists, and expressionists coming out of Europe and the United States, as well as Soviet filmmakers.[8] Barry's controversial approach, however, was not to expose audiences only to the "great work" of those mostly European directors already initiated into the modernist art canon (e.g., Luis Buñuel, Fritz Lang, F. W. Murnau, Fernand Léger, and Jean Epstein), but to also persuade the public that commercial films from the United States contained their own brand of formal and technical artistry.[9] For example, when it was unpopular to do so in a presumptively high art setting, Barry showed such early films as *The Great Train Robbery* (dir. Edwin S. Porter, 1903), *A Trip to the Moon* (dir. Georges Méliès, 1902), and *Intolerance* (dir. D. W. Griffith, 1916).[10]

Those then-outdated early films did not necessarily go over well with audiences. Wasson notes, "They talked loudly during screenings ... They laughed at tragic heroes and weeping women, cackling with abandon at the sight of violent deaths."[11] Strikingly, Barry continued to screen these early films despite their unintended response. For her, a history lesson did not always have to be serious—in fact, on occasion she described this laughter as a sign of affection for older films.[12] Embracing the audience's affective range in their encounters with the by-then crusty objects, Barry seemed to previse early cinema's later appreciation. Just wait, she seemed to suggest, these films will be seen as art in time. In this sense, Barry, like other maverick programmers, was anticipating a future to come.

Barry continued to blur the boundaries of genre and taste throughout her tenure at MoMA. One telling series from 1939 integrated documentaries and genre films (such as the western and the gangster film) into its aggregate of art and popular offerings, which would have been virtually unseen at this time, from the early revival house to an exclusive cinema society such as Frank Stauffacher's slightly later Art in Cinema film society.[13] In straddling the line between populist and intellectual appeal, Barry's programming was a mixture characteristic of MoMA's institutional politics and financial exigencies at the time, doubly elevating mass-distributed films to the status of art while rendering art itself as a category that could be accessed and experienced by the common person. Barry's proto-promiscuous programming, therefore, was an attempt to reorient the ways in which art was conceived, determined in large part by who should be included in its address and how it should be received, intellectually and affectively.

The democratic ideals of Barry's highly eclectic programming style would be followed later by Amos Vogel, an Austrian émigré-turned-film exhibitor. Vogel, along with his wife, Marcia Vogel, founded the membership-based film society Cinema 16, which ran from 1947 to 1963 (fig. 1.1). Renting out different affordable event halls, theaters, and other venues throughout Manhattan, the programming team at Cinema 16 (which, besides the Vogels, included assistant Jack Goelman) exhibited work assumed to be of "marginal interest." Vogel and his indispensable team strove to serve a "double purpose": to promote appreciation of "superior and avant-garde films" as art forms and to "provide its audience with a more mature realization of the nature of this world and of its manifold problems" through scientific and educational films, or documentaries, according to its mission.[14] One 1950 program is indicative of this goal: Vogel showed Luis Buñuel and Salvador Dali's surreal classic *Un Chien Andalou* (1929) alongside Pare Lorentz's Marxist-inflected *The Plow That Broke the Plains* (1936).[15] In a somewhat counterintuitive gesture, Vogel paired films that might conflict stylistically but dialogically worked together to revise the aesthetic and political perception of the spectator—to allow them to see the world anew. Many of

1.1 Young Amos Vogel looking at small-format film, with Joan Crawford looking over his shoulder.

Cinema 16's programs had clear politics to them, often showcasing work with leftist leanings in content and form.

Barry's heterogeneous approach was a clear precedent for Vogel's alchemical style, yet Cinema 16 was only populist in its programming, not in audience inclusion. Vogel relied on a devoted membership base; therefore his model was one of social exclusion. However, Cinema 16's cliquishness was done out of institutional protection, not intellectual arrogance. They used the membership model as a way to maintain a steady flow of money that could be used for space and print rentals.[16] The exclusive premise of the film society also allowed them to exhibit provocative and even illicit films that would experience intense censorship and many times print seizure, especially within the anxious sociopolitical climate of Cold War America.

By policing its boundaries, Vogel was able to show the audacious work of avant-garde makers such as Maya Deren, Shirley Clarke, Kenneth Anger, and Gregory Markopoulos, all of whom integrated perspectives on gender and sexuality that existed on the fringes of public discourse at the time. Including such work thus further inscribed within art house cinema queer affinities that would become unmistakably prominent by the late 1960s, which I will discuss later.

Based on his programming alone, Vogel might read today as a curatorial egalitarian, fighting for the place of marginal voices (e.g., women and queer makers) within the grand scheme of "art." Questions and definitions of art and taste better explain these programmatic maneuvers than do a politics of social inclusion. Not unlike Barry, Vogel at times seemed poised to lower the esteemed classification of "art" through the expansion of its borders, whereas at others he appeared to argue, in the spirit of *Cahiers du Cinéma*, that film fit within tight formal definitions of "art" as it had been classically delineated. Within his oscillating definition of "art," then, something like Kenneth Anger's short films, for example, which are full of popular cultural references, subcultural queer practices (e.g., BDSM and the occult), and formal experimentation, were compatible with Cinema 16's mission as well as with Vogel's variable classification of subversive filmmaking, which he would later describe in his 1974 book *Film as a Subversive Art* (which I discuss in chapter 2). They were representative of his mixed intentions—at some times to subvert the notion of art writ large and at other times to question and thereby redefine the definition of "highbrow taste."

Vogel's interest in Kenneth Anger's work demonstrates a larger change in the formal and aesthetic politics of the time. The emergent modernisms of the 1960s, of which Warhol and the Factory were emblematic, provide well-documented evidence of changing definitions of art. Pop art signaled the undeniable blurring of popular and underground systems of signification that had existed only in traces dating back to previous modernist movements. As cited by Noel Carroll, Parker Tyler, Douglas Crimp, Reva Wolf, and many others, these modernisms were saturated with intertextual forms of generic allusion that emanated from cultural objects belonging to various tiers of the taste strata.[17] Beyond Warhol, the French and Japanese New Waves incorporated aesthetic influences from Hollywood as well as avant-garde traditions, despite their place in what Peter Wollen once called "counter-cinema," an independent antidote to the Hollywood capitalist machine.[18] In truth, as early as the 1940s, Vogel was piloting a nascent aesthetic vocabulary that would, by the 1960s, come to blend formal visual signifiers from different tiers of the taste hierarchy.

If Barry's and Vogel's film curating dating back to the 1930s and 1940s, respectively, was marked by its penchant for eclecticism, mixing the popular with the avant-garde, the supposed highly unartistic (e.g., nontheatrical/ institutional documentary) with the highly artistic (e.g., surrealist cinema) and the middlebrow with the highbrow, then influential programming of the time both heralded the global new waves and pop art movement to come, and played a crucial and formative role in molding those artists, directors, and critics, who reflected the array of visual and aural textures they received in these art cinema spaces. Just as the Cinémathèque Française sculpted the sensibilities of an entire generation of French filmmakers and spectators with its range of films on tap, so too were the New York audiences attending Cinema 16's and MoMA's series made in the image of the low-, middle-, and highbrow work they experienced.

Matters of Taste

In no way did this proto-promiscuous programming, nor even its later fully formed version, eradicate taste boundaries and hierarchies. As the above art movements show, taste has a highly durable character even as it can transform the category of "artfulness," a quality that is still dictated by a certain privileged caste of individuals. As Pierre Bourdieu writes in the introduction to his study of taste, "To the socially recognized hierarchy of the arts, and within each of them, of genres, schools or periods, corresponds a social hierarchy of the consumers. This predisposes tastes to function as markers of 'class.'"[19] Wilinsky reminds us that art cinema is a marker of class—of cultural capital—even if its correspondence to that (high) class is, in reality, dubious.[20]

Whether Barry's and Vogel's programming was in its time seen as adhering to the codes of artfulness or can only be seen as such from a historical vantage point, it is still endowed with sophisticated and specialized taste. Even as taste remains a dynamic feature of society—one that is institutionally unfixed and culturally situated, and that continually shifts over time with changing mores, class or educational structures, and demographics—the programmer, like other art curators, still wields the ability to police or expand art's borders. As arbiters of taste, they both take the pulse of art and popular culture, and often aim to steer culture in opposing directions.

Elaborating on his thoughts in *Distinction*, Bourdieu later explains that "the work of art is an object which exists as such only by virtue of the (collective) belief which knows and acknowledges it as a work of art."[21] In order for an object to be considered "art," it must be labeled as such by an expert or set of experts, such as publishers or art traders/dealers, as having value, both monetarily and intellectually.[22] Bourdieu emphasizes that the dealer has a financial stake in the product to whose endorsement he must fully commit. Note Bourdieu's description of this production-distribution process, which bears some resemblance to film exhibition as well:

> The ideology of creation, which makes the author the first and last source of the value or his work, conceals the fact that the cultural businessman (art dealer, publisher, etc.) is at one and the same time the person who exploits the labour of the "creator" by trading in the "sacred" and the person who, by putting it on the market, by exhibiting, publishing or staging it consecrates a product which he has "discovered" and which would otherwise remain a mere natural resource; and the more consecrated he personally is, the more strongly he consecrates the work.[23]

Here challenging the naturalized role of the artist-as-author, Bourdieu reminds us to take into account the "cultural businessman" who effectively classifies a work as "art" and helps to produce those knowledges of value. The film programmer is such a "cultural businessman," working in concert, of course, with distributors and marketers, to determine whether audiences could even see certain films, as endorsed and therefore exhibited by the programmer. This is what I mean when I say the programmer is a gatekeeper as well as a tastemaker whose role should not be downplayed within film culture and consumption.[24]

Bourdieu classifies the role of the curator as similar to the critic, protector of a field's respective canon of "consecrated" work. One could say programmers and curators, as part of their practice, filter out the many options for screening based on their discriminatory tastes, while critics, in written, rhetorical form, guide spectators toward certain directors, genres, and trends by many of the same guidelines as programmers. Critics and programmers together direct audiences to certain objects over others that may (or may not) be available in the cultural field.

The economics of programming are unavoidable, as they play a crucial role in the curator's practice. Programmers must sell tickets to keep theaters or institutions running, if not financially thriving. In the shift toward promiscuous programming, financial realities remain pivotal. At the same time, and perhaps less cynically, the post-1968 programmer's love of unruly mixtures of traditions, genres, and tastes produced audience affects that cannot be reduced to mere financials. As I will describe, the idea of the programmer as a kind of bricoleur might add flesh to not only the goals of promiscuous programming but also its effects and affects.

In the spirit of the leftist youth countercultures that were engulfing artistic production and even popular media, programmers post-1968 applied Marxist, revisionist, and liberation ethos to their craft. This did not mean that aesthetics and taste merely dissolved. Rather, the terms of "taste" became highly elastic; one could cite a work's political value *as long as* it fit within the loose parameters of "taste." Still, many programmers of the time treated eclectic programming as a political act, as random and frivolous as it may seem on the page at times. The implication spoke volumes: their programming suggested that no longer could culture and subculture be neatly divided. No longer did films correspond essentially with any class category. The floodgates had opened, calling all kinds of freaks and weirdos to its doors.

Arty Trash/Trashy Art

Promiscuous programming would not exist if it weren't for the shifting relationships audiences had to art cinema, moving it from an oft-required state of reverence to one of critical disobedience and even sometimes mockery. Film criticism in the 1960s was vital to this transformation, exemplified by the work of Parker Tyler and Pauline Kael, the latter of whom spent years as a programmer before rising to fame as a brazen critic dispensing what today would be called "hot takes."

Kael became wildly popular in the 1960s and into the 1970s, making a name for herself not as a serious cineaste but as a playful critic and lover of trash—a shrewd polemicist skewering pretentious and elite cinephile attachments. Before her rise to critical stardom among cinephiles, she programmed at the Cinema Guild in Berkeley, California, from 1955 to 1960. Kael's bookings were by no means that different from contemporaneous trends. By then, a mixture of world art house, Hollywood genre films, and classics was boilerplate, and Kael didn't stray far from this template. What stands out, however, was how her program synopses and descriptions were nascent blueprints for the kinds of witty and oftentimes cheeky reviews she would become known for as a critic.[25] Described by Kael's biographer, Brian Kellow, as "hilariously personal and direct," her programs "were anything but public relations fluff. Pauline didn't hesitate to poke fun at some of the films being shown at the Guild, but even when she was taking swipes at them, her energetic critical tone seemed only to make people all the more determined to turn up to see them."[26]

Distinct in form and tone from a film review, the program note is meant to be a sober yet complimentary description and contextualization of a film; it persuades an audience of a film's aesthetic and cultural value. Kellow suggests that Kael editorialized in her program notes beyond the categories of "good" or "bad," setting a different standard that made a film worth watching regardless of its supposed esteem or rottenness.[27] Her program notes laid the basis for a pro-trash sensibility that would unabashedly materialize in her groundbreaking piece, "Trash, Art, and the Movies," first appearing in *Harper's* magazine in February 1969.

Kael's 1969 treatise was a call to claim a cinephilia that dare not speak its name. Characterizing cinema as a "sullen art of displaced persons . . . and masochists," Kael reaches out from the page to a reader whose company affirms anti-art sentiments. In a you-know-who-you-are moment, she writes, "You talk less about good movies than about what you love in bad movies."[28] Unapologetically anti-academic and anti-intellectual, Kael imagined a cinephilia that departed from the quiet reverence for supposed great films. Rather, the cinema, even when it could be designated as "art," was better used as a conduit for arriving at delicious descriptions and unpredictable thought experiments.[29] Moving effortlessly through the taste strata, Kael knew all the same that the best films—not the most dignified or sophisticated ones—afforded audiences insights, gave them pause, and made them feel deeply, from states of sorrow to glee. Kael's displacement of the binding principle that only texts deemed "deep," "philosophical," or "artful" yielded profound exercises in thought and feeling was radical in mainstream film reception.

American International Pictures, a leading exploitation movie house that got its start in the 1950s, gets several mentions in her essay, reminding readers that the "great appeal of movies is that we don't have to take them too seriously."[30] To say that Kael *only* liked low fare, however, would be to mischaracterize her taste. Pleasure was central to Kael, regardless of the object's status in the larger taste economy.[31] Throughout "Trash, Art, and the Movies," Kael professes her delight for Zeffirelli's *The Taming of the Shrew* (1967), *Bonnie and Clyde* (dir. Arthur Penn, 1967), *The Manchurian*

Candidate (dir. John Frankenheimer, 1962), and even—with qualification—Godard's *Les Carabiniers* (1963), work that spans middle- to highbrow ranges by standards then and today.[32] Given the sheer range of celebrated objects in her writing, Kael's criticism and program notes can be seen as a kind of declaration for promiscuous programming and the array of affects it invites. Promiscuous programming, characterized by intermingling disparate traditions, genres, and tones, reflects Kael's programmatic and critical investments in cinema, which claims it as a medium that always has been and probably always will be a crude popular art form, and any attempt to rescue it from the depths would do a disservice to it.

Kael established a new tone and set of expectations within intellectual audiences who were encouraged to greet films with incredulity, sardonicism, and wonder more so than the earnest generation of cinephiles that came before them. She could easily be placed within a genealogy of queer wit, though by all accounts she was heterosexual. Along with distinctly queer-voiced essayists Parker Tyler, Dorothy Parker, and Oscar Wilde, Kael's snarky commentary was intent on delighting in the bad and transforming the boring into fodder for ridicule, and thus remaking attachments in the image of camp pleasure. Further deepening her queer resonances, Kael despised the pretension of respectability, both in the activity of moviegoing and in what she saw as the pompous and ostentatious aesthetics most conspicuous in art cinema. Such an attitude, one could easily argue, was compatible with a fair amount of queer work that itself questioned, if not rejected, the respectability of (re)productive life within sanitized social, sexual, and gender systems.

Kael's reading practices were far and wide, garnering her a devoted following with fans and protégés known as "Paulettes."[33] One such Paulette was Fabiano Canosa, a gay Brazilian émigré and programmer of the esteemed First Avenue Screening Room, starting in 1973, and later, the Joseph Papp Public Theater, beginning in 1979. Canosa's penchant for unpretentious textual intermingling and his eclectic queer approach to programming reflected Kael's own attitudes toward cinematic pleasure.[34] Even if Canosa, a self-identified gay man, rarely, if ever, programmed series that directly named sexual politics, he frequently incorporated queer tastes and sensibilities into his programming, and kept a political and cultural awareness of films that appealed to many kinds of marginalized perspectives.

One such example of Canosa's programming was Toshio Matsumoto's 1969 film *Funeral Parade of Roses*, a topsy-turvy retelling of Oedipus Rex set in the underground art scene of Tokyo's queer Shinjuku district, featuring a

1.2 Transgression in the men's bathroom in *Funeral Parade of Roses* (dir. Toshio Matsumoto, 1969).

young trans woman in the role historically designated to a male protagonist (fig. 1.2). The film is part fictionalized panorama of Shinjuku's nightclub and sex work scenes, part flashback to the lead character's traumatic upbringing, and part *verité* documentary, interviewing trans and queer denizens of Shinjuku about their communities, identities, and aspirations. It is both a fiction and nonfiction testament to and treatment of flourishing queer life in late 1960s Tokyo.[35] According to J. Hoberman, the Canosa-programmed First Avenue Screening Room was the first New York theater to exhibit the film when it did so in 1973.[36]

This was not the first time it had been exhibited in the US, though. In 1970, Albert Johnson, a gay Black man who was director of programming for the San Francisco International Film Festival, screened it in what appears to be its actual public debut on the continent. Despite the fact that neither Johnson nor Canosa could be said to have curated with a "queer" or "gay" sensibility distinct from their "straight" contemporaries, I would also not want to reduce to mere coincidence their decisions to book this film. That two gay men were among the first to show the film suggests that a film's queer appeals (in the realms of aesthetics and deviant politics) likely had something to do with the film's inclusion, even if it was not its predominant justification.[37]

Canosa's former assistant of many years, Stephen Soba, identified their style of programming at the Papp as "spontaneous" and "ad hoc."[38] Soba recalled many moments in which Canosa would work himself into an ecstatic frenzy with temporary fixations on auteurs, stars, or national cinemas. Soba named several auteur-oriented series that memorialized the work of Luis Buñuel, Sam Fuller, Nicholas Ray, Bernardo Bertolucci, Chantal Akerman, and Douglas Sirk, among many others. They also developed retrospectives that centered on stars with queer followings such as Judy Holliday and Elizabeth Taylor. These retrospectives incorporated queer content across sensibilities and eras that did not stay strictly within the bounds of Hollywood cinema with mass appeal, nor did they care to include the avant-garde work of filmmakers whose films announced their queerness, usually by way of on-screen displays of sexuality.

Soba gave the example of "films of the civil rights movement" as a program more socially and thematically based than others. They also created programs that honored marginalized national cinemas (such as that of Hungary or Canosa's native Brazil). Canosa thus used his programming to underscore what we might call a *politics of marginality*, putting to social use what Soba referred to as "Salonified" and "eclectic" approaches to arrive at comparative, perchance even coalitional, forms of thinking. In 1975, a year before the First Avenue Screening Room would go out of business and become a gay porn theater, Amos Vogel wrote lovingly of "sleuth-cineaste-programmer" Canosa; mentioning Arzner's *Dance, Girl Dance* (1940), Oshima's *Death by Hanging* (1968), Fassbinder's *Ali: Fear Eats the Soul* (1974), and Guerra's *The Guns* (1964), Vogel writes, "The emphasis here is clearly not on shorts or the American underground, but on features (at times close to the commercial area in its creative aspects), Third World films, neglected countries, social and aesthetic concerns."[39] As Vogel highlights, Canosa's curating beckoned a spectator who perhaps felt excluded from the fare available at mainstream commercial cinemas, longing to understand and come in contact with all the difference Canosa's programming had to offer.[40] Canosa's programming also offered relief from the superciliousness of exclusive and cliquey underground circles, which would have ignored Third Cinema and non-experimental international cinemas, and which any true Paulette would have shunned for their "pretentiousness."

Canosa's work at the First Avenue Screening Room and the Public Theater was not without precedent or contemporaneous parallel. His goal to put certain filmmakers who had otherwise been overlooked or seen as inferior (in the case of B-movie directors Nicholas Ray and Samuel Fuller) on the map typified the art house programmer's quest in this era to expose audiences to work they had not encountered before. Canosa's taste, as representative of other promiscuous programmers at the time, was "all over the map," without allegiance or devotion to one school or approach to filmmaking, and redrawing parameters for what subjectivities mattered and were worthy of thoughtful attention.[41]

The promiscuity and variety that defined the repertory programming of many New York repertory houses, as well as a host of others across North America and Europe, translated to a politics of taste in which audiences were reoriented away from the auteurism that reigned in the 1960s and toward a varied mixture of Hollywood genre films, blockbusters, foreign and domestic independent films, and experimental work. With or without the programmer's intention, this seemingly random intertextual play that permeated 1970s and 1980s art house and repertory cinema went hand-in-hand with the taste cultures Pauline Kael beckoned. Programmers such as Fabiano Canosa and Richard Schwarz (whom I will discuss shortly), among an array of others who will get mention throughout this book, emblemized the "salonified" approach, as Soba put it, to film curating in a social and political climate highly amenable to such persuasion.

Textual Promiscuity's Queerness

By the early 1970s, the incorporation of cult, exploitation, and B-movies into art house curating programmatically realized the already-present linkages between art films and tawdriness. Art house cinema's reputation between the postwar era and the late 1960s had been paradoxical in this regard: on the one hand, elite, dry, and cerebral, and on the other, synonymous with nudity, adult themes, and the showcasing of sexual taboos. Films by Ingmar Bergman, Louis Malle, Roger Vadim, and Roberto Rossellini were among those heavily scrutinized or censored for their references to or depictions of fornication, homosexuality, and other unmentionable subjects. By the 1970s, however, art house cinemas no longer cared to submerge, disavow, or eclipse their prurient connections. Within the backdrop of shifting sexual norms, they could now flaunt and further profit off their ill repute, which would lead them to welcome the "trashy" content to which they had, at worst, repudiated or, at best, avoided in the previous era.

Landmark legislation to decriminalize the sale, distribution, and purchase of pornographic material made it all the more possible for art house programmers to invite softcore and "art porn" into their spaces.[42] The baby boomer demographic, who no doubt comprised an overwhelming share of these audiences, especially for evening or late-night screenings when older patrons were presumed to be at home in bed, hungered for such depictions. Alongside their patronage at the revival and art houses, baby boomers were central to what became known as the "sex industry" of erotic commodities, from manuals/guides such as *The Joy of Sex* to magazines like *Penthouse* to 8mm and 16mm porn films to toys such as vibrators playfully rebranded for the liberated consumer. John D'Emilio and Estelle B. Freedman describe this as a time when "Americans came to accept pleasure as a legitimate, necessary component of their lives, unbound by older ideals of marital fidelity and permanence."[43] With the notion of "marriage as the privileged site for sexual expression" burst asunder, singles and unmarried couples found themselves going to the cinema to seek out representations of sexual and romantic interaction that had before their generation been largely unthinkable. Art house cinema satisfied this liberatory drive to explore, probe, question, and ultimately discover new pleasures, serving as "sex aids" in many cases, as Linda Williams calls them.[44]

The definition of art house cinema as, like the museum, a space of education, reflection, and intellectual exercise and exchange began to further erode by the early 1970s, when films such as *I Am Curious Yellow* (dir. Vilgot Sjöman, 1967), *Belle de Jour*, and *Last Tango in Paris* became "must-sees" for many regular urban moviegoers, not only the sophisticated cineaste. As a consequence, art house cinema's association with graphic or explicit sexual content further deepened. Nevertheless, as Linda Williams has noted, art house audiences could claim the alibi of narrative sophistication so often connoted by the "tasteful foreign film" in order to distinguish *their* actual scopophilic tendencies from those elicited by hardcore pornography. *In the Realm of the Senses*, a sensation at the time on multiple fronts, embodies this paradigm whereby perverse content is housed within the arty style, in this case, characteristic of Oshima Nagisa's work. The sex, however, rather than being tempered by the sublime artiness of the film's aesthetic, was all the more shocking and, at the end, horrific because of it.[45] *In the Realm of the Senses* (which I will return to several times throughout this book, given its significance) does not stand alone in its visceral depiction of perverse erotic life. The films of Ken Russell, Pier Paolo Pasolini, and Bernardo Bertolucci, to name a few, wrested audiences out of their conventional knowledge about sex while retaining the prestige of "art," within and without its shifting guises.

At this time, Paul Morrissey's films became among the most programmed in repertory calendars, as he emerged as an auteur of a growing subgroup of amateurish low-budget art-trash films. His low aesthetics, which became so central to promiscuous programming, diverge from assimilationist lesbian and gay politics and representations of the time, following in the stylistic footsteps of Andy Warhol (who produced most of Morrissey's films, including his name in many of the titles). Morrissey's trilogy, *Flesh* (1968), *Trash* (1970), and *Heat* (1972), which features regulars (many of whom were gender nonconforming) from Warhol's Factory such as Holly Woodlawn, Jackie Curtis, and Candy Darling, further enlarged the Warhol brand in broader art house outlets. As early as 1969 (the same year of the Stonewall Riots), Morrissey showed *Flesh* in MoMA's Cineprobe series, a program devoted to socially and stylistically provocative work. Handheld camera work, long takes, improvised dialogue, oddball characters who spanned the gender and sexual spectrum, and transgressive themes of sex work and drug use ran through Morrissey's films. His intent, as he made it known, was to comment on the moral dissolution and degeneration of the American family, but many critics notice that the films appear more to be humorous experiments in taste, art, and form.

Janet Staiger has shown that the underground work of Warhol, along with that of Kenneth Anger and Jack Smith, must be placed in a pre-Stonewall nexus of queer underground production that laid the groundwork for later gay liberation efforts. Staiger suggests that it was not the outright politics of those films that were funneled into gay liberation politics post-Stonewall, but rather their ability to break with the "accommodationist" appeals of the prior "homophile" movements, which had been caught between the poles of pathologization and respectability. Staiger describes a scene where male heterosexual programmers such as Jonas Mekas (founder of the Film-Makers' Cooperative in New York City) and Amos Vogel played key roles in leading queers to "de-shame" their identities, histories, and sexual practices. Staiger animatedly writes that, "for one thing, these films were not embarrassed by their sexual deviance. They flaunted it and played with it. For another, the sexual deviance was, within its contemporary gay hierarchies, the most underprivileged—it was directed toward fairies and drag queens, not respectable middle-class gay men."⁴⁶ An inchoate form of supposed trash was already welcome in some art house circles in the mid-1960s; as Staiger notes, the "flaunting" of sexual otherness was central to the artistic production of this work and, by the 1970s, the presence of these unabashed depictions of perversion was prevalent in art house programming.

Lusty Adjacencies

Programmers and spectators alike have been heavily informed by their urban contexts.⁴⁷ New York City, San Francisco, Los Angeles, Chicago, and other major US cities were contact zones of converging political discourses, in which people of different identities, experiences, backgrounds, and proclivities met in the streets, in bars, and in the theaters. In New York City, each art house theater of the 1970s and 1980s channeled the distinct flavors of its encompassing neighborhood. The Village, where the Bleecker Street Cinema, Film Forum, and the Quad were located, was a contact zone for all kinds of social deviants: the gays and lesbians of the West Village, the gangs and punks of the East Village, the homeless population on the Bowery, and bohemians of all stripes. Across the neighborhoods, they carried on the iconoclasm that had come before them in the moody energy of the beatnik generation of the 1950s and the idealistic humanism of the hippies in the 1960s.⁴⁸

New York City is a particularly striking spatial example because of its multiple conflicting cultural and historical associations with, on the one hand, elite intellectualism and, on the other, vice such as prostitution and pornography. Art house cinemas merged these associations, in part because they programmed European films, attacked in the United States for their morally lax depictions of sex and sexuality. No doubt there is a history there. In the postwar years, Wilinsky argues, the censors and Hollywood constantly condemned art house films for using obscene and overly sexual content to sell tickets (which was sometimes true but often inflated by moralists). In 1949, *Variety* commented on one film society's advertisements: the Foreign Films Movie Club's "promotional literature," they said, "is frequently angled like an exploitation house's marquee."⁴⁹ Wilinsky says the same worked in reverse: "Because of the connection between foreign films and risqué entertainment, 'grind houses' specializing in exploitation films, such as Chicago's LaSalle and Studio Theatres, also showed foreign films."⁵⁰ Repertory and porn theaters in Times Square, an area known for vice, could also be found mixing their content because of these associations or, in the very least, absorbing the logics of nearby theaters if not their actual content.[51]

In light of this mixing, disparate audiences found themselves convening in previously uncharacteristic spaces, some devoted to the "skin flick" and others more to art cinema. Elena Gorfinkel summarizes several accounts from the mid-1960s of the veteran "hard-breathers" sharing the house with "Vassar girls in pony tails and young men with beards" curious to see what had been forbidden.[52] Gorfinkel notes that Russ Meyer and Radley Metzger were especially central to this pivot. Metzger aimed his films such as *Camille 2000* (1969) and *Therese and Isabelle* (1968), both of which depict homosexuality, to appeal to, as a critic at the time wrote, "'sophisticated married couples in the mid-30s' rather than aging insurance salesmen with their finger poised behind their suitcases."[53] Metzger's films retained a liminal status, balancing art house with soft-core pornography, and thus attracting audience members from both sides of the aisle.

Likewise, Meyer positioned himself as an auteur of the erotic, wielding the ability to cross over from the soft-core circuits of adult movie theaters into the repertory and art house spaces, and finally, the mainstream with the Twentieth Century Fox release of the Roger Ebert–scripted *Beyond the Valley of the Dolls*. Surprisingly, both Metzger and Meyer were invited (separately) to MoMA in 1971.[54] One of Meyer's visits that year was framed within an effort to discuss censorship. Despite an attempt to elevate the film from a lower taste status, it elicited what Gorfinkel describes as a "collision between differing cinematic taste publics."[55]

According to accounts, working-class spectators came out to the museum and did not hesitate to audibly react to the film throughout. Their boisterous and supposedly bodily affect met in a contact zone with the average MoMA patron, who had been lured by the purportedly intellectual considerations of Meyer's experimental style and creative freedom. These accounts of differing demographics grappling with their copresence in the theater demonstrate the deepening blurring and troubling of taste boundaries, which prompted the blurring of spectatorial boundaries as well. Where once a person could count on MoMA's screenings to be reserved for populations proficient in highbrow intellectual traditions, there now existed the possibility of uncertain encounters with surrounding bodies as well as the films themselves.

Despite the observed tension at MoMA, it could easily be argued that such conflicting affective forces encouraged those present to rethink the object at hand (even at a non-conscious level). Accordingly, we might say the space itself is *promiscuous* in an archaic use of the term, which up to the end of the nineteenth century denoted a mixture of people of various socioeconomic classes, educational backgrounds, and other markers of difference congregating in a public space.[56] As such, Meyer's films lack a stable taste assignment; this occasion might engender the intellectuals to infuse sensation, desire, and camp into their readings, just as those who enjoyed Meyer's work as shallow entertainment might find an opportunity to reframe their knowledge within the elevated museological context. This moment returns MoMA to the spirit of Iris Barry's curation of early silent films decades earlier in an attempt to resignify them as art objects. If bringing Russ Meyer's sexploitation films into MoMA also had a populist bent to it, this time questions of taste and form were tightly bound to ones of (in)decency and (im)propriety, the issue of censorship preceding that of virtuosic style.

As Gorfinkel notes, the sexploitation genre, once one of the few ways to get a peek at nude bodies alluding to or simulating sexual acts in filmic motion, became, by the 1970s, a source of campy humor for sophisticated urban audiences. Films self-conscious about their obscenity now reeked of datedness if not cultural irrelevance. But crucially, their programming continued, not in the porn theaters where hardcore was now the main entrée, but in revivals and art houses. The shifting attitudes toward sex are pivotal to this transformation, but sexploitation's staying power also suggests an accrual of affective possibilities that had either not been present before the 1970s or only existed in sensed form; a collage of affects, if you will, is produced out of their multivalence. Based on their selections, programmers considered the many audiences for these films as well as their attendant pleasures: for some, sexploitation films had historical meaning, while for others, comedic value, and still for others, perhaps even titillation, be it residual or a fetishizing of the past, or a mixture of both. Programmers, in their promiscuous sensibilities, tried to predict and stay attuned to this motley of affects, and to distribute resonances across potential audience types and their assumed attachments.

As taste borders were trespassed, so too were those between sexual identities. In the 1970s, young heterosexual urban dwellers had started to take note of the gay male practices of cruising, group sex, and nonmonogamy that had been in place for some time, but were now gaining new cinematic visibility. Historians of sexuality have intimated that heterosexual couples and singles alike wanted "in" on the fun, too.[57] Although it is often overlooked, the cinema played a major part in this cross-pollination. One primary example is the exhibition of *Boys in the Sand* (dir. Wakefield Poole, 1971).[58] Wakefield Poole's Fire Island–shot gay hypnotic pornographic fantasy, it has been documented, was seen by straight as well as gay audiences upon its release in 1971, as well as in cities across North America and Europe, where it was programmed repeatedly throughout the decade.[59] More documented and analyzed among historians at length is *Deep Throat* (dir. Gerard Damiano, 1972), by and large the first pornographic film that made it acceptable for couples to watch explicit content in (semi-)public spaces together. One could argue that *Boys in the Sand* stands as a precursor to this moment. Heterosexual couples and singles may not have gone to see *Boys in the Sand* because they necessarily desired to see gay sex (though, of course, they could have), nor only to experience Poole's sophisticated mise-en-scène and editing, but to learn what it meant to be sexually uninhibited, to be empowered to deepen one's own erotic imagination, and to be infected by its picturesque and exuberant depiction of sexual freeness as an aspirational spirit.[60] HBO's TV series *The Deuce* (2017–2019) fictionalizes this encounter in its first season when a sex worker takes her gangster boyfriend to see the film. Even as the boyfriend, played by James Franco, tries to avert his eyes, he remains intrigued by the sexual technique on-screen.

With the rise of hardcore pornography and censorship cases' victories in the courts came a proliferation of porn theaters in several US cities, none more concentrated than New York City. Samuel Delany, in *Times Square Red, Times Square Blue*, explains that by the early-to-middle seventies, large movie houses underwent a mitotic conversion into smaller theaters that would serve a sexually awakened, largely male, public.[61] Delany lyrically recounts his days frequenting these theaters and the sexual encounters that would take place there. Delany writes that the absence of male homosexuality "from the narrative space on the screen proper is what allowed it to go on rampantly among the observing audience."[62] The theater here becomes a meeting ground for straight, gay, bisexual, pansexual, and curious men seeking the shared atmosphere of arousal that such a semi-public space could offer. Perhaps it makes sense that in this era of intense gay and lesbian identity politics, from the days of gay liberation in the 1970s to the ACT UP and AIDS activism of the 1980s, the darkness of the theater provided opportunity for unclear or uncertain subject positions, a space of contingency within which inchoate pleasures could emerge.

In discussing the "seedy ambiance" of rundown repertory and second-run houses, Ben Davis adds, "The funky life of these theaters was also well-known for their balconies and bathrooms, which were often choice places for anonymous, generally gay, sex, although heterosexual groping also occurred."[63] The back-to-back continuous performances of films in long periods of darkness (which I describe in chapter 4 as "repertory time") likely established the repertory house as a setting for indecent acts to take place without the threat of a watchful eye. One might then be tempted to call the repertory house itself a deviant space.[64] Certainly "necking and petting" at the movies had long been hallmarks of dating cultures, with the drive-in as the most salient example, but Davis here addresses a phenomenon specific to the shabby architecture of repertory houses. Davis cites one description of the Bleecker Street Cinema, for instance, as a "classy dump."[65] The Elgin, situated in a pre-gentrified and racially diverse Chelsea, had a "tacky" and "rundown" facade, with a "marquee that lacked apostrophes."[66] Add to it the dingy and uncomfortable seats coming apart at the hinges and the scent of transient populations mixed with stale popcorn, and the repertory house in a state of disrepair and neglect may very well have symbolized the sense of rejection, marginalization, and disrepute that queers had long been subject to and felt.[67]

The programming too boosted this association. Repertory fare, against a mainstream market that prizes freshness and originality over longevity, is waste product—irrelevant and tired—and misaligned with the contemporary moment. The work of Elizabeth Freeman and Heather Love illustrates the ways in which queer cultural production indexes feeling *out of sync* with the normative time (Freeman calls it "chrononormativity"; for Love, "feeling backwards") of supposed social progression, of longing to linger in feeling adrift, discarded, and "off."[68] Perhaps this kind of queer temporal deviation is one explanation for queer love of "the classic"—the abandoned object—that might run counter to the backward figure or stereotype of the "old queen" who romanticizes a pure moment that never was. Repertory fare might be regarded as the queer unwanted stepchild in the larger exhibition family.[69]

During this era, entertainment spaces such as live concert venues and nightclubs were increasingly adjacent to theaters.[70] The Fox Venice in Los Angeles, as the *Los Angeles Times* commented, "prides itself as a community center with segues into live, ethnic shows, political benefits and concerts"[71] The theater's owner told a reporter at the time that "the whole idea is that the local movie theater doesn't have to be a crass supermarket, a cold image with people sitting in a cold box watching film on a cold screen."[72] In *Midnight Movies*, J. Hoberman discusses the venue "Club 57 on St. Marks Place—a Polish social club that the punks and new-wave types used to rent on weekends. That had strange programs—dated exploitation films by people like Roger Corman and Hershell Gordon Lewis, old TV shows, Zsa Zsa Gabor flicks."[73] While cinema had been intertwined with civic activity in multipurpose spaces since the early twentieth century, the latter half of the century returned it to its almost vaudevillian roots, in which films and other communal and entertainment events were conjoined, only this time differently invested in new music genres (e.g., punk, disco, techno), art movements (e.g., performance art, guerrilla theater, "happenings," pop, feminist), drug use (e.g., weed, LSD, cocaine), and leftist political causes (e.g., civil rights, national and indigenous liberation, feminism, gay liberation, Marxism).[74]

Perhaps no better illustration of the spilling of nightlife, performance, and film exhibition into one another exists in the US context than the Nocturnal Dream Show at the Pagoda Palace Theater in North Beach, San Francisco. In March 1969, queer filmmaker and visual artist Steven Arnold began midnight screenings at the Chinese American–owned theater, with a "vintage '30s interior . . . lavish, with overlapping wall motifs from the original Italian art nouveau designs . . . [and] art deco chandeliers . . . [with] Chinese opera trappings."[75] Arnold programmed a ragtag set of films, clustering queer or sexually suggestive live-action and animated shorts such as *Betty Boop* and the *Flash Gordon* serials (fig. 1.3).[76] These might be shown with treasured early cinema and early Hollywood classics, including Méliès's magic-trick shorts, Busby Berkeley films, and Tod Browning's *Freaks*. Arnold also favored avant-garde films with queer and surreal motifs, notably Kenneth Anger's *Kustom Kar Kummandos* (1965), Maya Deren's *Meshes of the Afternoon* (1943), and Yukio Mishima's *Patriotism or the Rise of Love and Death* (1966). A short or two would also accompany campy features such as *Duel in the Sun* (dir. King Vidor, 1946) or *Flamingo Road* (dir. Michael Curtiz, 1949), the latter starring queer icon Joan Crawford. Arnold, like the glittered-coated drag performance trope the Cockettes, who would get their start performing at those midnight shows, was inspired by the style and decadence of early Hollywood and bohemianism of those earlier avant-garde movements.

The Cockettes were born out of the midnight screenings at the Nocturnal Dream Show, where Arnold supposedly took note of Hibiscus, Rumi Missabu, and the other faeries draped in overlong necklaces and hippie fabrics, and asked if they would try their hand at performing.[77] Rumi Missabu describes the Nocturnal Dream Show as a kind of Dionysian affair, where it was typical to "smoke dope in the balcony . . . and

1.3 Psychedelics meet bohemia in the design of the Noctural Dream Show's September 1969 poster. Courtesy of The Steven Arnold Museum and Archives.

have sex anywhere we wanted."⁷⁸ Original Cockette member Pam Tent describes the environment in carnivalesque terms, with talent shows, costume contests, poetry, dancers, and other entertainment before, during, or after screenings. The Palace was an intermedial environment to say the least, in which the programmed cinematic fare inspired live performance and stimulated spectatorial behavior that reflected the debauchery and perversion projected on-screen.

To that end, then, it is no surprise that the psychedelic drag troupe was extended an unofficial residency at the Nocturnal Dream Show, which then led to their show entitled *Hollywood Babylon* (explicitly named after Kenneth Anger's salacious history of Tinseltown). Hollywood history wasn't just superficial allusion; the performance included a bizarre mixture of shorts, from a 1935 Gene Autry Western serial to Buster Keaton's *The Paleface* (1922). As Pam Tent explains, "The Babylon scene from D. W. Griffith's silent classic *Intolerance* provided the backdrop for our opening scene, where we belly-danced onstage as a 3-D extension of the orgy on film."⁷⁹ Here the film's projection literally spills out into the audience in the live performance that mimics the action on the screen. (Without overdetermining a direct link, this seems to set the groundwork for the later live reenactments at *The Rocky Horror Picture Show* midnight screenings, exemplary of how the undisciplined audience becomes a prevalent feature of the repertory house.) The Nocturnal Dream Show infused its programming and viewing atmosphere with a promiscuity in every sense of the word, encouraging a sensuous boisterousness and sexiness that violated normative boundaries between spectators, as well as those of audience to screen, of one artistic medium to another, and of one kind of film to another.⁸⁰

The importance of these phenomena vis-à-vis the shift toward promiscuity in repertory programming is that the cinema's bodily and sensorial connotations shift with this rise of porn theaters and nightclubs, themselves proximate to and sometimes cross-fertilizing with art cinemas. Delany's treatment of sex as a hobby, as well as the Cockettes, and Nocturnal Dream Show's carnivalesque environment, repurposed the space of the cinema and its dominant ontology, which requires of its spectators that their attention be directed forward and at the screen. By the 1970s and 1980s, the cinema as a quiet, disciplined site primarily designated for affectively restrained viewing is undermined by the many co-constitutive adjacencies and permeations of the art house, and thereby conjoining it to the spheres of nightlife, pornography, music, and live performance. These lusty adjacencies find themselves encoded in the filmic texts themselves too, which respond and are tailored to the increasingly lively programmatic environment of the art house and repertory cinema.

Promiscuous Programming

Promiscuity is a term that captures more than just the intertextual relations within a film calendar and boisterous depictions of uninhibited, wanton sex within many of the era's art films. Spatial spillages suggest a promiscuous interaction among a range of media and art practices or creative expressions during this era.[81] Channeling these energies, the programmer acts as more than a gatekeeper and tastemaker who mirrors the practices of an art dealer or critic; the programmer here is akin to a bricoleur, cobbling together disparate parts of traditions and styles within the sphere of exhibition.[82] As Hal Foster defines it, "*bricolage* is a process of textual play, of loss and gain ... *bricolage* cuts up, makes concrete, delights in the artificial—it knows no identity, stands for no pretense of presence or universal guise for relative truths."[83] Foster's description expresses the playful sensibilities of promiscuous programming to strive for heterogeneity over unity, proposition over thesis. Promiscuity borrows from bricolage values of anti-institutionality and anti-allegiance, deploying improvisational strategies and sensibilities associated with punk, anarchist, and DIY cultural production.[84] In short, promiscuous intertextuality and bricolage are at their root about making up the rules as one goes along.

There is no denying that programming of the post-1968 era still very much recycled old modes of organizing film history, though. For instance, genre- or auteur-focused retrospectives and series were still popular, as they remain so to this day. Further, US art cinema curating at this time was limited geographically, due, on the one hand, to the logistic and financial difficulty of obtaining prints from faraway countries and, on the other, a pervading Eurocentrism in taste.[85] (A more expansive global art cinema that includes films from the Global South would emerge decades later, as Rosalind Galt and Karl Schoonover have underscored in their research.[86]) At the same time, there also existed a concurrent phenomenon in which exhibition sites sought to undo rather formulaic approaches to film curation. It did so simply by producing rather unusual arrangements, revising associations, even previously wholesome ones, of a film or set of films, to have them instead brush up against their diametric opposites.

Gay programmer Richard Schwarz could be said to be a bricoleur of sorts in a quite material sense of the word. Schwarz earned a name for

1.4 Street and facade view of the Thalia, date unknown.

himself after reopening the Thalia, a treasured New York revival movie house from the 1940s to 1960s, in 1977 (fig. 1.4). Ben Davis provides several accounts of patrons who considered Schwarz's programming to be unique among the assortment of repertory houses. "While Schwarz programmed the typical fare of a serious cinematheque . . . he mixed these with the quirky, rare films that he unearthed," from forgotten cartoon shorts to the "first retrospective of silent screen legend Louise Brooks, including a rare showing of her bizarre B-Western swan song, *Overland Stage Raiders* (1938), opposite John Wayne."[87]

The Thalia's programs were historical exercises in facetious recovery and respectful infidelity. In May 1979, Schwarz and his team curated a series called "Four-handkerchief Classics: 35 Years of Tearjerkers" with melodramas that, according to the calendar's description, provide a "celluloid link between Victorian repression and sexual freedom."[88] Acknowledging room for these films to be received as "nostalgia, camp, or the moral fables they were initially intended to be," the Thalia subdivided these melodramas into double bills with headings that invite a number of deviant attachments. For example, the decadent double bill, "WAGES OF SIN," featured *Blonde Venus* (dir. Josef von Sternberg, 1932) (echoed in a von Sternberg–Dietrich pairing in a 1988 series called "Fascinating Fetishism" at the Roxie in San Francisco, which I will analyze in the next chapter) and *The Old Maid* (dir. Edmund Goulding, 1939) (with Bette Davis); "UNWED MOTHERS" paired *To Each His Own* (Mitchell Leisen, 1946) and *Johnny Belinda* (dir. Jean Negulesco, 1948), both films about "fallen" women; and "Unhappily Ever After" told the tale of heteronormativity's failings through *Make Way for Tomorrow* (dir. Leo McCarey, 1937) and *Come Back Little Sheba* (dir. Daniel Mann, 1952).

There are a myriad of intriguing implications and conclusions to draw from these subcategories, produced during the late 1970s when sexual and gender normativity was put under the immense pressure of sexual and women's liberation, but here I want to highlight, first, that the Thalia did not dispose of the general category of melodrama (or its cognates such as "weepie," "women's film," or even more colloquially, "four-handkerchief classic").[89] Rather, the Thalia accented the genre's varying messages, morals, pathos, and pleasures by breaking them down into their thematic factions, thereby troubling the genre's routine hermeneutics.

These invented melodramatic subclasses together offered a renewed vision of an old genre.[90] The subclasses suggested that melodrama's appeal cannot be reduced to or explained by gay male idolization of diva actresses (such as Bette Davis, Joan Crawford, and Lana Turner) or identification with their suffering, or as corrective of sexism and patriarchy; melodrama here, by way of its balkanized variants, invites other queer attachments, acknowledgments, and provocations to form, be it couched in transgressive desire ("wages of sin"), disreputable type ("unwed mothers"), or the experience of social failure ("unhappily ever after").[91] The typical gay and feminist appeals of melodramatic fandom might thus be repositioned along more deviant axes of pleasure and identification, emitting vectors in search of alternate worldviews that unite perverts and failures in their social abjection.

Schwarz and his teams' subdivisional approach could be explained by the fact that repertory curators had to find ways to repackage, rebrand, and resell material that was repeatedly in circulation. Along these lines, promiscuity and deviance might be seen as a commodity in art and film cultures of the time (perhaps especially necessary during the 1970s economic recession). But such commercial strategy also led to epistemic ingenuity; by teasing out the *many* queer resonances in name (as subcategories), this curatorial approach could dislodge the logic of sex moralism and gender oppression that by then ran counter to the consciousness of the emergent sexual and gender political movements coming to a head in the late

1960s, augmenting them by criteria yet to be identified. As a result, Richard Schwarz found a way to make melodrama even queerer, subdividing the genre in order to enlarge its coverage beyond gays and women, welcoming social outcasts and failures whose experiences and lives might also disqualify them from the dull and impossible prize of normative life (to borrow from the sentiments expressed by Aunt Ida in John Waters's classic *Female Trouble*). It offers fantasies of unbridled desire as well as somber tales of social alienation, making room for spontaneous forms of affinity for and with othered others.

Schwarz also became known for editing together compilations of Hollywood outtakes whose copyrights had been left in the public domain, screening them at the Thalia, and then offering them for distribution. In a practice that lends itself to bricolage as much as to facetious recovery, these outtakes included stars such as Humphrey Bogart, Bette Davis, and Errol Flynn in vulnerable and comedic moments that might run counter to their image as poised, disciplined actors. Editing together these compilations, Schwarz exemplifies the bricoleur described by Foster, assembling the neglected or discarded shards of film history for (perhaps perverse) public consumption. The programmer here gleans the shards of cinematic history, picking up the pieces no one is supposed to want. When repurposed, the parts might produce new pleasures and insights. In a manner that articulates in material form the curatorial practices of post-1968 programmers, Schwarz elected to mold out of the debris of filmic past an assemblage that scavenges the literal trashcan of film history.[92] Schwarz's practice is marked by a queer irreverence for otherwise idolized cultural objects (especially movie stars), turning paratextual waste into his play things, augmented by a queer desire to "re-cut" Hollywood film history out of one's own castoff image.

Textual promiscuity, a highly eclectic and concentrated form of intertextuality, embraces the clashes and concedes that one's subjectivization is a product of scenes of stylistic, tonal, and taste collisions. Such an admission casts doubt on attempts to isolate spheres of influence from one another. Vogel showcased this when he programmed educational and scientific documentaries alongside avant-garde films. Vogel's motive was to lay bare the social and aesthetic educational value of both modes, however starkly different in production and intent, but it also revealed the ways that scientific films wielded a lyrical treatment of the physical world surprisingly akin in aesthetic criteria to experimental cinema.[93] Scott MacDonald frames Cinema 16's collisional form of programming as "dialectical." He observes, "One form of film collided with another in such a way as to create maximum thought—and perhaps action—on the part of the audience, not simply about individual films but about film itself and about the social and political implications of its conventional (or unconventional) uses. The similarity to Eisensteinian dialectic is more than accidental; Vogel and [his assistant] Goelman were great admirers of the Russian filmmaker."[94]

MacDonald's deployment of "dialectic" casts Vogel's programming as having a montage-like quality that physiologically and cognitively reformed spectators' understandings of the world. Certainly some of Cinema 16's programming was dialectical, but much of it was not so deliberately political in the Marxian sense (even if the "dialectic" here means to engage other forms of classed difference). Vogel's programming also contained various kinds of oddities that placed emphasis on the affective experience over the strictly formal or political one. In this sense, Vogel's approach had more so a promiscuity to it, his bookings being exercises in programmatic form that keeps the different receptions for that form open-ended.

Later repertory and art houses took cues from earlier film programmers, such as Amos Vogel, and, influenced by the changing cultural and subcultural currents, amplified a promiscuity that had to a lesser extent already existed in art cinema exhibition. Even more than programming between World War II and 1968, when Hollywood classics commingled with mostly European and Japanese art house films, post-1968 programming returns a notion of promiscuity to its Latin usage, from *conubium*, which means mixing indiscriminately, "done or applied without respect for kind, order, number, etc.; confusedly mingled, indiscriminate," before the nineteenth century when it came to primarily describe a person who is sexually prolific.[95] The word's usage from antiquity up through the eighteenth century did not have an inherently negative valence, often neutrally meaning a public congregation of different types of people, but in ancient Rome it had a classed and racialized usage too, sometimes denoting cases in which Plebians (commoners) and Patricians (noblepersons) would marry (*conubium*).[96] The word also has a trans or androgynous etymology, "used occasionally to signify a person belonging to one sex but having the characteristics of the other, or of neither."[97] The word's own semantic promiscuity lends itself to a deviant genealogy of boundary-crossing and defying the laws of distinction and separation. Even its neutral valences suggest contact among disparate people and objects, leaving room for all kinds of implications that might emerge from those experiences.

Promiscuous programming does not eradicate those crucial differences among objects, as a postmodernist reading might argue, but it does make films belonging to varying taste strata, historical and geographical contexts, and genres elastic and subject to wild reinterpretation.[98] Promiscuous programming, by virtue of its range of objects, abandons the course of prescribing, even determining, how spectators should think and feel in the cinematic encounter; meeting such a motley assemblage offers only entry points of connection that can careen into a number of directions, reshuffling the spectatorial sensorium as it encounters the world within and beyond the cinema.

Promiscuous programming may not be intrinsically queer, but if such a curatorial style tends toward disorder and even at times incoherence, it magnetizes queer texts that themselves throw off kilter a normative schema of desire that gets treated as rational and tidy. Further, most urban art house and repertory calendars at this time contained queer films that were by then canonical or were canonized later, infecting and infusing the entirety of the organism that is the series or calendar with forms of queer defamiliarization. Even the "straightest" of films, then, might be read queerly because of its dynamic proximity to queer or deviant texts, whether they are experimental shorts by Kenneth Anger or Jack Smith, Hollywood classics with Greta Garbo or Bette Davis, or international art films such as those by Pedro Almodóvar. Queer reading practices were not only encouraged by programmers who selected the assortments spectators might encounter; they were stitched into the very fibers of film series and programs, making deviance immediate for straight and queer viewing publics alike.[99]

Coda

By the early 1990s, repertory houses had shuttered in droves and with them the idea of promiscuous programming. *Village Voice* listings, like the ones that began this chapter, show a thriving scene of US independent film exhibition (the peak of the Sundance moment) and a nearly absent repertory scene by the mid-1990s. The remaining art cinemas operated on new releases, the idea of double bills also a thing of the past. It is difficult to point to the exact cause: home videocassettes (VHS), cable TV, the increase in urban rent costs, the rise of the indie film movement? All likely played a part, making it more difficult to sustain the business of recycling titles for audiences who did not have many viewing options but to go to the repertory cinema to watch them.

The idea of promiscuous programming thrives on a ragtag approach to assembling texts. Promiscuity should not be mistaken for randomness, given that much repertory programming pre-1968 was not ordered into series or other framing devices; however, promiscuity does seem to flourish when a calendar's scheduling is not organized solely by way of series. Ben Davis discusses that the debate around whether to continue with a kind of eclectic, "scattershot" programmatic gained traction by the mid-1980s, just as many revival houses in New York were closing or converting to first-runs.[100] The programmers at the Regency Theater in New York City professed their love of series or "theme bills" instead of what Davis deems "random programming."[101] One programmer even suggested that the future of repertory cinema exhibition *depended* upon theme bills. "The *Harold and Maude, Casablanca, King of Hearts* thing is just passé," he told *Newsweek* in 1987. "But if you bring back *Harold and Maude* as part of an intergenerational sex film festival, you have a hit."[102] The other side of the debate saw limitations in this model, which might wholesale turn off moviegoers who weren't fans of a specific genre, star, or movement.[103]

There is a little doubt as to who won this debate. The series became repertory programming's modus operandi by the 1990s and has persisted to this day. Fast forwarding to the present, unlike in the 1970s and 1980s, media consumers can take for granted the digital availability of classic, older, foreign, and independent films, so they need justification for why to show up in person to the cinema. Several factors can draw a contemporary audience to repertory screenings: recent restorations (usually presented as a Digital Cinema Package [DCP]), the availability of 35mm print versions, live Q&As with talent (e.g., filmmakers, actors, etc.), and anniversaries all appeal to contemporary repertory audiences. In terms of scheduling arrangements, repertory programming relies heavily on the thematic or focused series as a way to frame a film's exhibition. A highly useful promotional tool that has been around since the near beginning of formal film curation, thematic and focused series—even when they contain varying types of films—seek prescriptive logic, coherence, and perhaps even an epistemic enclosure.

Sexual and gender nonconformity—especially as it moves outside the also routine categories of LGBT—now has become more difficult to encounter if it is not within one's generic taste parameters. Perhaps this is one the reasons that several once-canonical queer films by such filmmakers as Ken Russell and Russ Meyer have dropped out of the canon and many programming circuits (as of the time of this writing). Without a secured fan base or a clear location within the queer spectatorial imaginary, programmers are unlikely to take the financial risk to show films that do not fit neatly into a taste, genre, style, tonal, or even identitarian classification.

Given this loss, I engage more closely with these forgotten films, such as those dizzying and perverse explorations of Ken Russell, or a film such as *Myra Breckinridge* (dir. Michael Sarne, 1970), in the chapters to come. Correspondingly, promiscuous styles of programming may remain in the backdrop of the rest of the chapters in this book, but it is pivotal to theoretical interventions I will be laying out. Its implications percolate outward into intertextual questions of deviant typology, erotic form, and queer world imagining and building. Promiscuity is thus a practice of expansion and openings—textually, perceptually, consciously, sensorially, and libidinally—in the face of normative dictates of consistency, coherence, legibility, congruity, and polish that still inform both exhibition styles and sexual politics alike.

Deviant Repertories

THE QUEER TYPOLOGIES AND TAXONOMIES OF ART HOUSE CURATING

Parker Tyler's landmark 1972 book *Screening the Sexes: Homosexuality in the Movies* is unanimously regarded as the first book devoted to LGBT representation in cinema. Deceptively subtitled *Homosexuality in the Movies*, the book instead presents an expanse of sexual alterity that extends well beyond homosexuality. A dizzying encyclopedia of queer—or, better yet, deviant—Hollywood, art house, and experimental films, *Screening the Sexes* parses a panoply of "degenerate" types and fantasies the cinema had amassed in its seventy-odd years. A better subtitle might have been *Sexology at the Movies*, given Tyler's interest in sexual practices that were, especially at that time, in the "outer limits" of the American public's sexual imaginary. As fascinated as he is tickled by these oddities, Tyler moves amorphously among figures of aging queers (inventively listed in a confounding table of contents as "green carnationists, kittenish werewolves, [and] tired but true blue poets)" to what he calls "ambisexuals" (proximate today to "nonbinary pansexuals") to military and school uniform fetishists.

In many cases, Tyler anticipated a gay and lesbian film studies to come, such as with his in-depth look at films centered on heterosexual male friendships with homoerotic undertones, or "buddy films," which would be later dubbed "bromances," or his interest in literal and figurative blood-sucking lesbians, taken up by lesbian film scholars from the 1980s onward (see chapter 5). The book also exceeds a future queer film studies to come, committing to the study of taboo heterosexual practices and behaviors as well as LGBT typologies and practices. In this vein, Tyler is a film-sexologist as much as he is a film critic and historian, attempting to endlessly exhaust what he calls the "whole repertory of human sexuality" by mischievously chiseling out new lexicons and classifications.

I begin with Tyler because, though he was not a programmer by profession, his canonical yet paradoxically undervalued book on sexuality and cinema, more than any other critical or scholarly record of the time, renders a vivid image of the queer spirit of 1970s and 1980s film programming, which runs counter to gay liberationist politics of the time. Tyler's writing brings into focus the era's curatorial penchant for a cheeky and somewhat improvisational style of taxonomizing queer film history, importing while caricaturing the logic of a social scientific approach to gender and sexual otherness. Although art house curating used as its tools schedules rather than prose or test subjects, double bills rather than comparative data sets, like Tyler, it was constantly reshuffling texts into idiosyncratic classes, thereby throwing into crisis the orderly identity politics emergent in this era; these programmatic schemata or themes coalesced less around the dull dyads of "gay" and "straight," male and female, and more broadly around those profuse taboos and stigmas that bind people and experiences across the gender and sexual continuum. In this sense, programming, like Tyler's taxonomy (no doubt inspired by the film programming in Manhattan where he lived), expresses a critical modality adopted from the social sciences to indefatigably produce classes and knowledges about those whose lives and practices were (and still often are) unthinkable and ostensibly on the fringes of society.

This chapter suggests that programmers of the 1970s and 1980s acted as lay sexologists-cum-sociologists for the filmgoing public. They did so by going beyond the mere public exhibition of deviant texts; by generating series and double features predicated on deviance, they invented new social classifications and redressed old ones for a generation of film viewers whose attitudes were dispensing with postwar mores that by then smacked of old-world repression. Repertory and art house programmers—those showmen-codifiers of perversion—provided for the hungry viewing public a deviant menu of lusting nuns, "ambisexual" hustlers, and cross-generational star-crossed lovers. It is no understatement to say that patrons were, by the early 1970s, inundated with an omnibus of perversity outdone only by the *Diagnostic and Statistical Manual of Mental Disorders* (DSM) or Freud's early writings that emerged from Victorian sexology.

Certainly, cinematic deviance exists in a single text's representation alone. Popular films of the post-1968 era directed by John Waters, Pier Paolo Pasolini, and Russ Meyer testify to this. However, programming bolsters the deviance of such content by drawing networks of films bound by their sexual and gender outsiderness. The programmer has long served as a classifier of films, working alongside a multitude of factors that include industry, period, style, and technology to create and sustain genres, temporally and geographically particular and expansive.[1] By the late 1960s, programmers were constructing a "deviance genre" of sorts, aggregating disparate representations of social outsiders that had been dissected and analyzed in the fields of sociology by the likes of Erving Goffman, Philip Toynbee, William Simon, Evelyn Hooker, and John H. Gagnon, and then later and polemically, Gayle Rubin, and in sexology by almost a century's worth of study, from Magnus Hirschfeld to Alfred Kinsey to John Money.[2] Together, art house cinema and these academic disciplines—what I consider discourses of deviance—were sites of knowledge accumulation that shaped the public's perception of sexual and gender difference in its multitudinously expanding typologies.

What specific politics of sexual and gender deviance, then, were programmers generating by way of their practices of selection and arrangement? With a wealth of nonnormative representations at their fingertips, urban art house and repertory curators of the late 1960s to late 1980s served as taxonomists both channeling and challenging social scientific traditions fixated on forms of sexual and gender alterity. Not experts in the fields of sociology and sexology themselves, curators were instead nonexpert codifiers, reflecting how the social sciences had seeped into the public domain through a range of media and discourses, even sometimes via films and through the visions of erudite, omnivore makers such as John Waters. Reflecting sexology's long-standing fascination with paraphilia and sociology's obsession with the social category of deviance, programming pushed historically maligned and marginalized sexual and gender subjectivities into conversation, forging coalitional alliances where viewing publics might not have seen them. Ejected from normative spaces and circles, deviances of all sorts found their homes in the urban art house cinemas of the 1970s and 1980s, where they were flaunted, monetized, exploited, relished, sensationalized, memorialized, and worshipped.

Spanning depictions of interracial desire, sex work, or a taboo fetish, art cinemas at the time made overlaps and connections in these experiences visible and felt. Urban film programming of the 1970s and 1980s, I argue, time and time again grouped the social lepers together. Because of this, programming brought the scientific mediation of social difference into sharper focus, stressing the experiences of those deemed outsiders or pariah for their nonnormative desires and modes of identification. One might say that, *figuratively*, programmers used films as their test subjects, venturing to see how textual arrangement might alter or influence public sexual and gender knowledge formations.[3] Art film exhibition presents its litany of typologies and sociological examples couched in film style and narrative and, in response, spectators bring any number of hermeneutic techniques to their viewing experiences. Whether tragedies about deviants, sometimes received as camp, or portrayals deemed affirming or sympathetic, art cinema, by virtue of curating, invited spectators into not only narratives of outsiders, and the means by which they are represented, but also programmatic occasion to *compare* those narratives and representations.

In this chapter, questions about politics of representation and film style will work in service to those of typology and taxon. Typology allows us to look beyond the LGBT of queerness, to survey the motley of sexual and gender deviant acts, practices, and identities that post-1968 programming assembled and brought into intertextual contact. For example, one series I will analyze here is a 1988 retrospective of Marlene Dietrich–Josef von Sternberg collaborations titled "Fascinating Fetishism" at the Roxie in San Francisco. The mise-en-scène fetishism in Dietrich's performance style, as well as the use of costumes and props, ravishing the screen with fulsome erotic textures and symbolism, creates multiple overlapping deviant typologies. The series invites a lesbian and queer typology, given diegetic and extradiegetic evidence of Dietrich's same-sex desire and relationships; it simultaneously invites a spectator drawn to fetishistic materials and practices. Series such as this one and others I discuss in this chapter reveal not only cinema's expanse of deviant typologies but also the theoretical implications of their curated intertextuality. These programs functioned as meeting grounds—or contact zones—on which difference could be compared and then metabolized into ethical arrangements of shared (and simultaneously distinct) oppression and, alternately, modes of pleasure.

Programming, scholars have implied, is a kind of classification apparatus, and by the late 1960s it extended its classificatory capacities to make pliable or elastic social scientific methods of organizing sexuality and gender.[4] Programmers transformed the taxonomic act into a queer practice, a game that creates, paradoxically, order and disorder simultaneously (akin to Parker Tyler's approach in *Screening the Sexes*, with which I began). In some cases, programmers were, whether intentionally or inadvertently, integrating the redeeming and generative aspects of scientific rationality and rejecting its vacuous or harmful—even dangerous—aspects. In short, film programming subverted the dominant discourses of deviance found specifically in sociology and sexology's persistent classificatory traditions, while also taking cues from their disciplinary logics. Programmers thus took seriously the potential political implications of assembling sexual and gender pariahs together, while also exaggerating and lampooning the bizarre historical methods of doing so.

Programming post-1968 adopted some of the same methods and interests of sociological studies of deviance that held sway right before and during this political moment of sexual, gay, and women's liberation movements. Whether as a means to repackage films in continual repertory circulation or to communicate a political position vis-à-vis sexuality and gender, or both, programming found ways to resculpt as well as entirely invent film genres to make their deviant qualities more pronounced. By positioning programming as an apparatus that classifies and reclassifies, this chapter speculates the ways film curating of this era wedged open a still-unrealized space for a radical deviant politics. This political imaginary entails owning—even celebrating—sexual and gender deviance, and conversely, disavowing regimes of pathology, stigma, and shame on which sexual knowledge has traditionally turned. In the process, programming, as Laura Marks has also argued, becomes an ethico-political practice of transformation that takes place on (inter)textual and spectatorial registers.

Defining Deviance

In the introduction, I explain why I opt for the term *deviance* over *queer* to better describe the sexual and gender representations found in much urban repertory and art house programming from the late 1960s to late 1980s. The work of filmmakers such as John Waters, Ken Russell, Pier Paolo Pasolini, Lucino Visconti, Bernardo Bertolucci, and Rainer Werner Fassbinder were but a few telling narratives of distasteful desires and practices that certainly included LGBT experience but more broadly amassed all kinds of perversions and, to a bourgeois sensibility, unsavory predilections.

Steeped in pathologizing clinical, medical, academic, and legal knowledges and histories, *deviance* wields broad application as a classification of social estrangement from the norm. Deviance bears many of the same structural and affective linkages of *queer* to formations of shame and repression, especially given that *queer* has sought to interrogate systems of compulsory normativity that relegate to a lower caste of society those who are unable or unwilling to capitulate to sterile standards of decency and respectability. In interrogating structures of sexual and gender oppression as well as studying sites of counterpublic pleasure and resistance to those structures, queer studies has theorized an array of objects and experiences that are not always limited to LGBT. Take, for instance, canonical works by Lauren Berlant, Michael Warner, Judith Butler, José Esteban Muñoz, and Eve Kosofsky Sedgwick that seek to rethink the terms of relationality, identity, and sociality that run counter to sexual and gender normativity at large. Butler's meditation on queer kinship and Berlant and Warner's on sex in public have cast a wide net in ideating against the codes of respectability that serve hetero- and homonormativity, thereby forging an outsider ethos of societal reconfiguration.

Although queer theory and queer film studies have successfully theorized sexual and gender estrangement, they have elided the particularities of non-LGBT exiles, especially those with institutionally and legally thornier standing; at an empirical level, these discourses still center LGBT subjectivities.[5] Deviance studies, as a still-imperfect alternative, better accounts for an underclass of types in name, from the sex worker to the pederast to the fetishist. Further, deviance readjusts our focus to think more structurally and systemically, to better heed Foucault's proposition that sexual oppression tends to get consolidated into specified types or groups. The concept of deviance might force us to better attend to interlocking histories of social outsiders, further fulfilling queer theory's promise to interrogate formations of sexual and gender oppression and seek out alternate liberatory imaginaries.

If programming aggregates a range of types, practices, behaviors, and desires of those subjects disqualified on grounds of sexual and gender expression—not just LGBT people—then what analytical procedures might we employ to do justice to that range? Part of the issue is that the classification of sexual and gender deviance may not as coherently constitute a genre such as "queer cinema," given the many guises deviance might take. Its expansiveness might indeed be too expansive, too multidirectional, and therefore risk diminishing political and social use value.

Heather Love expresses this concern through her analysis of the "underdog," writer Philip Toynbee's capacious deviant archetype, which serves as a metonymic object of study for postwar deviance studies at large. Love suggests *underdog*, like sociologist Erving Goffman's structural category of stigma, "always carries the risk of blurring the difference between greater and lesser forms of adversity, or even blurring out any concrete meaning for the term." In its sociological usage, the stigmatized person or *underdog* can describe virtually anyone from the convict to drug user to pedophile to disabled person to multiracial person to prostitute, and, of course, any combination thereof.[6]

Further, what might be considered deviant at one time or in one place might not be deviant in another. As Love indicates, the "system of stratification is in flux," as contemporary (especially white) gays and lesbians enjoy political and representational viability and visibility "with increasing success against other marginalized groups."[7] Love continues, those privileges and rights are "provisional, both in the sense that they can be withdrawn as the political climates shift, but also in the sense that they require a form of queerness that is purged of its associations with other stigmatized categories."[8] Deviance as a critical category, for all its social and political use value, is not without its taxonomical, temporal, and geographical complications. Is the concept worth all the trouble, we might ask?

There is still no denying that art house programming of the 1970s and 1980s produced a cinema of the underdog or outsider in which stories of those who were socially disqualified inhabited the screens in major cities across the country. For example, Paul Morrissey's trilogy featured hunk of the underground, Joe Dallesandro, as a drug addict and sex worker, and his partners were trans women, older women, and older men. Even classical Hollywood films such as *Member of the Wedding* (dir. Fred Zinnemann, 1952) and *Rebel Without a Cause*, which were repeatedly programmed on their own and at least once as a double feature at the Carnegie Hall Cinema in June 1976, depicted tomboys and pansies, characters at odds with the gender identity foisted on them at birth.[9] Patricia White beautifully suggests that *Member of the Wedding* "enacts a fantasy of autonomy and difference. Three outsiders—an adult Black woman, a sissy white boy, and his preteen tomboy cousin—figure the gap between hegemonic representation (the idealized picture of happiness that is the white wedding) and those who are disposed of the image."[10] These outsiders produced "chosen families," or as Judith Butler would have it, kinship configurations that course outside statutes of state legitimation, alternatives to the traditional families that rejected them. Perhaps spectators also found refuge, both in the depictions on-screen and with their fellow maladjusted outcasts in the audience. Thus, rather than give up on the political potential offered by an unwieldy category such as *deviance* or a genre such as "deviant cinema," we might think through what these offer, at times, in lieu of and, at other times, as an extension of *queer*. It consolidates the downtrodden "miscellany"—the "far-flung collection of outsiders and rebels in revolt against social norms," as Love puts it.[11]

Queer theory, in fact, has borrowed some of its most important tenets from deviance theory of 1960s sociology. Championing the act of social transgression and wielding systemic critiques of identity-based oppression, queer theory overtly politicized what had been stated "coldly," or at an "unbiased" remove, in 1960s deviance studies. Expounding on queer theory's detachment from 1960s sociology, Love explains that sociology's observational and objectifying methods (associated with power techniques and forms of social control) were anathema to queer theory's favor for poststructuralist theories of deconstruction and performativity. This leads Love to wonder if queer theory has reproduced, without acknowledging it, some of the same ambitions and blind spots as the 1960s movement, and to consider the ways queer theory might build from ideas of stigma and social alienation to address its blind spots.[12] Love tentatively recommends restoring description and observation as approaches to the "microdynamics" of social deviance—methodologies lost in queer theory's brassy activist ethos of transgression and disruption. Description holds a power, Love argues, that "makes space for marginal worlds and in cataloging injustices" without "anticipating [their] transformation, or wishing [them] away."[13]

One way of locating, observing, describing, organizing, and thus making visible the existence of varied people and things in the world is through classification. Love does not spend much time on sociology's taxonomies, but they would seem an important linkage to the discourse of coalition that Love advocates.[14] If classification is the process of grouping constituents whose characteristics correspond, deviance, though quite broad, constitutes a class in itself, as does the metonym of stigma. Through a method of consolidation and convergence, these classifications make possible an intersectional politics that isolate structural asymmetries and commonalities in the experience of those asymmetries. Film curating offered its own unique intertextual classification system, which delineate into the following: identity-based model, congruency model, and homology model.

Congruencies and Homologies

Generally, art houses fell into three different trends for organizing social outsiderness or deviance in filmic terms. Moving from most to least politically viable, the first programmatic mode corresponds with legible and represented identities, abiding by a rather strict identitarian logic. This model can be seen in double bills oriented around LGBT identity, for example, Bleecker Street Cinema's 1981 "Gay Perspectives" series, where they showed an array of lesbian and gay classics, from Dorothy Arzner's *Dance, Girl, Dance* (1940) to Ron Peck's liberationist-inflected *Nighthawks* (1978).[15] LGBT film festivals are particularly branded by this curatorial focus. Although some of these films are central to chapter 5's discussion of queer "bad objects," I am not particularly interested in this type of program here.

More curious and challenging here are the implications of two other modes of deviant programming. The second programmatic type correlates with unrepresented, what Stuart Hall calls "weak, emergent, marginal minorities," who nevertheless have identifiable class membership.[16] This curation adheres to a more cohesive logic of congruency or similitude, such as a program or double bill that incorporates intergenerational desire (or *chronophilia*), BDSM, interracial desire, or sex work, to name a few. This program tends to be schematized by way of dwelling on the same deviant theme across texts, even if its dramatization and characterization differs. These represented phenomena lack strong sociopolitical representation, even as they come with charged social views for and against. Despite their unviability within the political public sphere, such scheduling brings this category to the fore, the programming capitalizing on their provocation as they simultaneously share the mediated and fictionalized experiences of a demographic (such as sex workers) or relationship (such as interracial desire). We might call this the "congruency model" of programming deviant films.

The third is the loosest codification of the three, with a conspicuous lack of focus; this form of deviant programming makes up more a cosmos of perverse and anti-normative practices, acts, types, behaviors, and so forth that rely on their collisional implication. A looser syntagmatic mode than the former, akin to what anthropologist Gayle Rubin calls the "outer limits" of "bad, abnormal, unnatural, damned sexuality," this third category is heterogeneous to the point of seeming random, ostensibly devoid of any obvious connective tissue that ties one film to another. However, programming serves an adhesive role in mapping out this cosmos.

Intertextually, it links those narratives of stigmatized subjects and taboo acts; politically, it provides an undercommons of the societal rejects who might come together in pain or pleasure, to share in their particular forms of marginalization. This mode of programming reveals structural, experiential, and affective homologies otherwise eclipsed in the lived world; we might consider it the "homology model."

I consider these models also *modes* because they are separable but rarely autonomous; they often cross into one another, even if one displays dominance over another in the span of a series or calendar. Most of the programs I will go on to discuss here have elements of both, with connecting threads that crisscross and overlap across a calendar. For example, in Los Angeles, the Nuart Theatre's 1981 ten-week series called "Outlaw Cinema Thursdays" featured female sadism in the films of *Bad* (dir. Jed Johnson, 1977) and *Female Trouble*, as well as intergenerational desire in *Heat* and *Salò*. "Outlaw Cinema" (which I will discuss in more depth shortly) united this aggregate of heterogeneous perverse depictions and themes, even as there might be clear subcategories within it that connect a number of the films. Differing classification modes can coexist within the same programmatic space (series or calendar), and this can happen in name, by a series heading or name (e.g., "Outlaw Cinema"), or subtly, by their copresence in the calendar, with the canny spectator further stitching together their interrelations and making meaning out of their assembly.

New York Film Festival, 1967

Cinema 16 programmer Amos Vogel's landmark book *Film as a Subversive Art* presents a curious, if not charged, case of codifying deviance into loose homologies. Vogel published *Film as a Subversive Art*, a must-have companion for cinephiles at the time, in 1974 after leaving his post as head programmer at the New York Film Festival (NYFF).[17] The book, with its irresistibly suggestive title, sought to catalog the long history of controversial films that shocked audiences with their "taboo" and "forbidden subjects." In structure and look, *Film as a Subversive Art* was akin to a coffee table book, filled with stills from obscure films that would have been difficult to come by at the time.[18] Under a broad definition of "subversive" that is not always celebratory or liberatory, Vogel covers topics from socialist realism to Nazi propaganda to political satire to new wave cinema to what he called Third World cinema. In many ways, Vogel, who had not been formally programming for years, was now "programming on the page," if you will. Even if Vogel could not make the varied themes or categories that make up "subversive" come to life on the screen, the book offers an unparalleled look into how Vogel might have programmed if he had been actively curating in the mid-1970s.

Following sections on nudity and erotic or pornographic cinema, Vogel turns his attention to a classification he calls "The End of Sexual Taboos: Homosexuality and Other Variants." In it, Vogel includes a range from the most explicit self-identified gay examples (e.g., Rosa Von Praunheim's *It Is Not the Homosexual Who Is Perverse but the Society in Which He Lives* [1971]) to those coded texts that the gay community had adopted into their canon (e.g., *Some Like It Hot*). But mixed in—the "other variants"—were films that dealt with other culturally forbidden topics such as child sexuality (e.g., Shuji Terayama's *Emperor Tomato Ketchup* [1971]), necrophilia (e.g., Buñuel's *Viridiana* [1961]), and sex work (e.g., Buñuel's *Belle de Jour* and Paul Morrissey's *Trash*), among a dozen others.

By way of categorical conflation, Vogel risks eliding those many sexual "variants" and elevating the political viability of homosexuality in the process. But the catchall theme of "and Other Variants"—itself somewhat of a microcosm for the book's omnibus method—seems to use *homosexuality* not as a synonym coterminous with *variants* but as a way to pull in a presumed liberal reader who, in 1974, might have been coming around to the idea of accepting homosexuality. Hence Vogel eases his reader into other more marginal deviant forms (even zoophilia, a.k.a. "bestiality") by selecting films about homosexuality of a seedier variety. Vogel cites Paul Morrissey's films as well as *Un Chant D'Amour* (1950), Jean Genet's experimental ode to queer prison life teeming with BDSM and voyeuristic imagery, as well as *Death in Venice*, Visconti's rendition of Thomas Mann's 1912 novella about a dying composer who follows an adolescent boy (played by then sixteen-year-old Swedish actor Björn Andrésen) around Venice.[19] Vogel creates a layered version of homosexuality that is laced with other deviant styles (such as BDSM and chronophilia) with clear affinities to other practices on the "outer limits."

"And Other Variants" might be read as code for *deviance*, a term that 1960s sociology was redefining to think differences together as structurally meaningful and with parallel sociopolitical implications. We might imagine Vogel programming a series out of this category of what I would consider to be a homologizing logic. Homosexuality might hold a schematic place within the classification, but it is the highly assorted "and Other Variants" part of the heading that turns the reader's gaze to the problem of sexual oppression and repression and the social structures that they produce rather than the singular oppression of homosexuality. In an era in which gay liberationists labored to disarticulate homosexuality from the stigma of other sexual perversions or paraphilias and thus legitimate itself as a natural, inoffensive identity category, Vogel indeed seemed to be intentionally keeping these linkages alive by speaking of "homosexuality, sadomasochism, masturbation, bestiality, oral sex, [and] coprophilia" together as yoked phenomena.[20]

One film Vogel discusses stands out in its layered deviance vis-à-vis race and performance: Shirley Clarke's documentary *Portrait of Jason* (fig. 2.1). The film has been called a kind of long "screen test" in which Black gay prostitute Jason Holliday monologs and gesticulates about hustling in New York and taking advantage of rich white people, before he himself becomes the target of Clarke and her boyfriend's ridicule (as retribution; for what exactly, we still don't know).[21] The film is a remarkable audiovisual record of Black queer existence pre-Stonewall. It also, critically, indexes layers of difference that in some ways make Vogel's election of the term *variants* all the more warranted: as Holliday starts the film, "I am Black. I am gay. I am a prostitute. I am Jason." Jason's own words suggest no neat taxonomy will do—a "denizen of the sexual and racial undercommons," "triply criminal as he spoke," as Tavia Nyong'o puts it.[22]

In its exhibition, the film fits within a complex and shifting network of texts through the years. Crucially, Vogel and his team had programmed *Portrait of Jason* for its world premiere at the 1967 NYFF. (Shirley Clarke was also friends with Vogel and a regular attendee of Cinema 16.) That same year, the festival featured Claude Chabrol's *Les Biches* (1967), a film about the romantic tensions between two bisexual women who, separately, have relationships with the same man. On the surface, the two films seem to have little in common beyond the fact that the subject of the documentary and the characters in Charbol's drama share nonnormative sexual desires and identities at the time, and of course, that they were coinciding releases by two established art house directors. Perhaps Vogel, together with program director Richard Roud and possibly selection committee members that included Susan Sontag, recognized these films as on the precipice of a transitional moment, with gay liberation around the corner. *Les Biches* especially might seem caught between the coded, ambiguous representation of homosexuality and other nonnormative desire and the moment of its explicit characterization and dramatization by the 1970s.

2.1 Jason Holliday camping it up in *Portrait of Jason* (dir. Shirley Clarke, 1967).

The relationship of class (and for *Portrait of Jason*, race, too) to sexuality in large part motivates the films' arcs. Both films belong to stories' "subs": Jason and Why. Jason spends the majority of the film discussing his employment by rich older women as a "houseboy," and Why spends the majority of the narrative financially reliant on the wealthier and older Frédérique. Though they may be in relegated roles to an extent, the two films offer paradoxical, or at least oscillating, strategies in which the "sub" role gets flipped and becomes a "dom." Jason talks about how he was able to dupe the oblivious aristocrats who employed him over the years but he also holds power in deciding how he wants to perform for the camera; in *Les Biches*, we witness Why find strategies in stolen moments demanding things of and resisting Frédérique.

Further, both films carry temporal ellipses driven by an inscrutability that heightens their queerness. In *Les Biches*, the two women's physical relationship remains ambiguous, with a shared room arrangement and looking relations indicating a nonplatonic relationship; the lead characters Why (played by Jacqueline Sassard) and Frédérique (played by Stéphane Audran) are portrayed in an erotically cool, removed performance style that invites, if not requires, close speculation on the part of the viewer. Jason in Clarke's documentary invites speculation, too, but in regard to the degree of truth in Jason's grandiose autobiographical stories, formalized in the visual lacunae of the black screen, blurred lens, and jump cuts. In fact, the film lives on through debate around its elusive indexicality, shifting between an at-face-value reception of Jason's accounts to one that understands his fabulations to be historically generative, anchored by a bare or austere documentary approach that marks an imprint of the "triply criminal" life Nyong'o describes. As opposed to the affective inscrutability in *Les Biches*, which has an erotic dimension to it, the enigma that is Jason is almost negated by a charm and wit seductive in its presentation. Rather than be knowable, Clarke and her boyfriend's laughter heard behind the camera throughout the film are off-screen indications of Jason's captivating persona that viewers might also find themselves drawn to.

This is arguably this dyad's queerest or most deviant offering: that their joint potential to seduce the viewer is predicated on a deficit of knowledge and information that only enlarges the role of imagination and fantasy.[23] This imagination in some ways outsizes both the diegetic and real-world circumstances of the time, an off-ramp to a different time and place (though not necessarily one to come). In *Les Biches*, after Frédérique seduces Why's lover Paul Thomas (potentially as an act of revenge), Why attempts to unite all three of them. Her inability to transmute their dynamic into what today would be called a "throuple" is the real tragedy of the film, not Why's initial loss of Paul Thomas, nor even Frédérique's death at the end (fig. 2.2). Why longs for a life for all three of them that lacks societal and institutional backing—a utopian bisexual arrangement that cannot be realized. Jason's, too, is an impossible life of fugitivity, to again invoke Nyong'o's rich description, that thrives in the interstices of the legible shot.

If the act of longing for a world otherwise is to be found in the formal and narrative gaps in the texts, it is also in the space of camp—in *excess*—that is integral to Jason's documentary performativity. Richard Peña, who would go on to program the NYFF and the Film Society of Lincoln Center years later, along with his colleague Barbara Scharres, chose to exhibit *Portrait of Jason* in his summer 1983 series at the Chicago Art Institute.[24] Jason Holliday mingles with a different kind of queer company this time, playing one day after gay auteur George Cukor's Hollywood musical *Les Girls* (1957) (with the music by fellow deviant Cole Porter). The film is framed by a libel case in which two women take the stand in the courtroom to tell differing accounts about their relationships with their choreographer and a fellow dancer, played by Gene Kelly. With its *Rashomon*-like structure, the film plays with truth and fabulation, recalling the dubiousness of truth

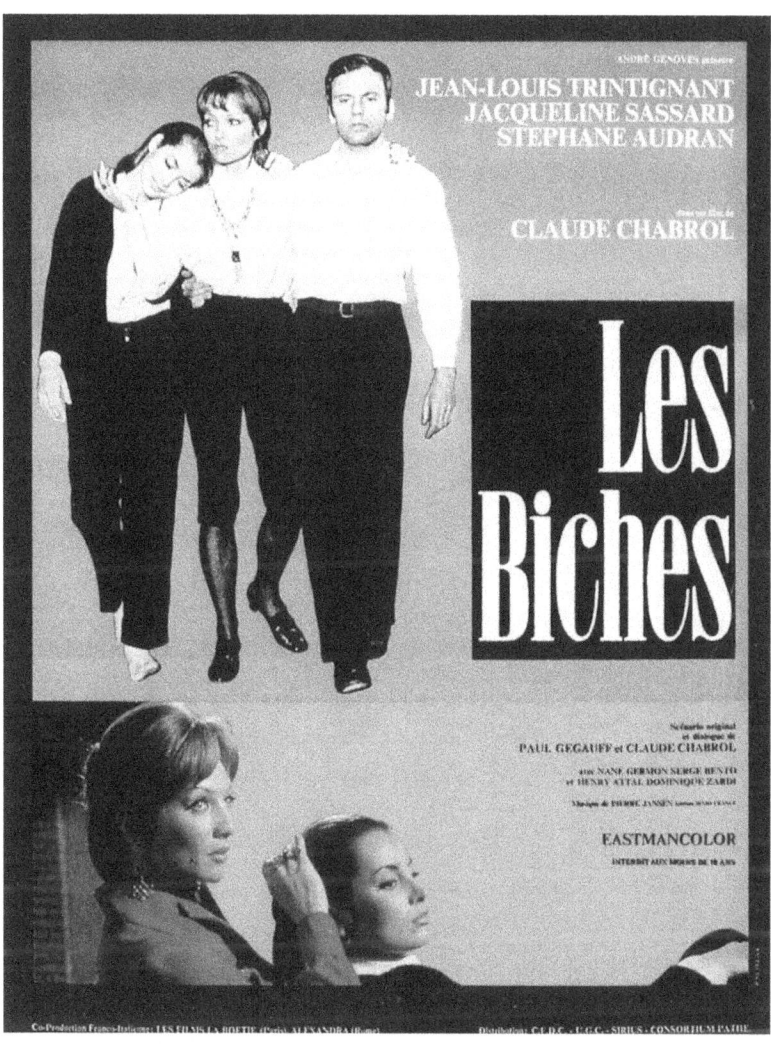

2.2 Aspiring to throupledom in *Les Biches* (dir. Claude Chabrol, 1968).

in *Portrait of Jason*. But what does truth matter when there is song and dance? As Jason does impressions of Mae West and sings as Fanny Brice in *Funny Girl* (the stage version, that is, because the movie was released in 1968), he seems to see his own life as a musical of sorts. Camp is Jason's language, then, as it was Cole Porter's and George Cukor's. If Jason's camp, then, is a way of speaking to his lived experience, it is simultaneously a way of denaturalizing it by drawing inspiration from the aesthetics and sensibilities of postwar musical performance.[25]

A day before *Les Girls* and two days before *Portrait of Jason* screened, the Art Institute showed the Tod Browning classic *The Unknown* (1927). Bringing us back to Vogel's framing in *Film as a Subversive Art*, *The Unknown* stars Joan Crawford as a circus assistant named Nanon in love with an escaped convict who is pretending to be armless (to perform knife throwing with his feet). Nanon cannot stand the touch of men's hands, so she finds refuge in Alonso (played by Lon Chaney), unaware he is an impostor. In the film's last act, Alonso forces a doctor to permanently remove his arms so that he can marry Nanon, only he returns to the circus to find Nanon has overcome her fears and married one of their circus mates (with arms!). Though not *precisely* about it, the film approximates dramatizing what John Money (along with Gregg Furth) identified as "apotemnophilia"—a form of body integrity dysphoria in which able-bodied people desire limb amputation or paralysis. Nanon might be seen close to an "acrotomophile" or "amelotatist," or one who is sexually aroused by amputees in any strict definitions of the term. The adjacency of *The Unknown* to *Portrait of Jason* and *Les Girls* shows the unpredictable reach of the homology model of deviance in which outsider affinities are created across disparate character/subject typologies and styles. Jason belongs to an undercommons with the circus freaks as well as gay camp. The fact that the films were all part of different series that month—*Portrait of Jason* in "The American New Wave," *Les Girls* in "The Gene Kelly Musical," and *The Unknown* in "The Members' Series"—speaks to the fact that these films in certain codifications exist in different corners of American film history, but, in their programming, find connective tissue that binds them under the banner of deviance.

Portrait of Jason is not a sedentary object fixed only in its production mythos and sociological significance. The film's ability to roam, to shift meaning depending on the texts that it collides with—from the sensual to the campy and performative to the feminist—extends the film's deviant implications beyond typology. Jason in many ways embodies a proto-poster child for queer theory's poststructuralist affection for the blurring of truth and fiction, of merging flamboyant fabulation with the dismal "reality" of history. Jason's disidentification with his assigned roles fuels his hyperbolic and embellished performance, demonstrating that deviance has a style, form, and tone to it. He is in good company with *Les Biches* and *Les Girls*, all relishing and mocking through their diachronic intertextuality the excess (if not stereotyping) of queer typology.

Jason's status as a criminal or fugitive subject also exceeds and defies his own representability, making him deviant not only in his layered typologies but also as a disorderly documentary subject willfully deviating from his interviewee protocol. He oscillates extravagantly in tonality: at once creating a comedy out of his testimonial and a melodrama out of Clarke's attacks, Jason is a figure to be championed for his elusiveness even as Clarke seeks to corner and interpellate him. Jason's intersecting deviances—Black, gay, and sex worker—are the sources of delicious insubordination that get amplified by the film's queer programming through the years. Although Jason might be isolated in the frame of the "screen test" documentary, he breaks through the frame and makes contact with other queer figures and tones, charming when he shouldn't, and seducing against the film's will.

Where is Jason Holliday placed in Vogel's "Homosexuality and Other Variants"? Is he the homosexual or the variant? The slipperiness of this codification is not its shortcoming; it is an imaginative opening. Programmers made classifications mutable and mobile, their deviant subjects mirroring attempts to deviate from the procedures of taxonomy itself. Programming's organizing principles and modes might shift across venues, different programmers, monthly calendars, and even days, but post-1968 programming forged relationality among ostensible incommensurable typologies, assembling a deviant coalitional front in the form of cinematic and programmatic expression.

"Fascinating Fetishism"

There is no way to speak about the institutional knowledge production of deviance without considering the social sciences. Psychology (and particularly early psychoanalysis) has garnered the most scholarly and theoretical attention and use in the humanities' study of sexual otherness. Less has been said about sexology and sociology as two disciplines that have been instrumental in producing a number of taxonomies by which sexual and gender peculiarities can be studied. Before bridging these fields and their discourses, there are crucial distinctions to be made: Sexology generally seeks to explain the *internal* conditions of a person or group's libidinal drives by way of biometrics, behavioral observation, and interviews with subjects, whereas sociology commonly studies the *external* conditions of sociocultural structures that determine relationships and hierarchies with the help of observation, data, and other empirical means of study.[26] Both fields importantly give us a multidimensional scope on cinematic deviance;

sexology teaches us about libidinal variety and sociology teaches us about the social dynamics of stigma and prejudice. Despite their divergences, the two areas of study clearly share a teratological interest in sexuality and gender's role in social deviation from the established norm. And they heavily rely on methods of observation and taxonomy to do so.

Even for sexology, where, unlike sociology, deviance is not a core concept, an understanding of sexual deviation from the "norm" compelled sexologists from the nineteenth and twentieth centuries, from Richard von Kraft Ebbing to John Money, to come up with terms, definitions, and explanations for sexual deviance. Sexology's notion of paraphilia offers the best analog to sociology's capacious concept of sexual deviance because it catalogs a list of phenomena that deviate from the path of normative sexuality.[27] Lisa Downing explains that *paraphilia* was introduced into the English language in 1934 to "free psychiatric terminology from its proximity to psychoanalytic concepts and to reject the originally religious implications of 'perversion' as a moral 'turning aside' from the path of righteousness."[28] Terminologically distancing itself from *perversion*, *paraphilia* still bears undeniable likeness to *perversion* in definition in that it suggests attraction or arousal to "socially unacceptable stimulus, either perceptually or in fantasy."[29] The list of paraphilias that has accumulated over a century's worth of research is over a hundred entries long. Such a glossary encompasses desires that range from the nearly ubiquitous and unremarkable—for example, pictophilia, or arousal by erotic pictures or moving images, and heterophilia, or heterosexual desire—to obscure, largely unthinkable classes such as taphophilia, or attraction to cemeteries, and formicophilia, a subcategory of a zoophilia in which someone is aroused by small creatures, ants, insects, or snails crawling on their genitalia, or autoassassinophilia, arousal at the idea of being hunted or at risk of being killed.

Your average urban repertory and art house cinema in the 1970s and 1980s was likely to serve up a menu of sexology's -philias and -isms through its programming. From US cult and exploitation to highbrow international, quickly canonical films by John Waters, Luciano Visconti, Ken Russell, Kenneth Anger, and Radley Metzger opened up a cabinet of sexual curiosities that included hebephilia (attraction of an adult to an adolescent eleven to fourteen) and ephebophilia (adult attraction to an older adolescent over fifteen) (e.g., *Death in Venice*), mixoscopia (arousal at the sight of a loved one having sex with another person, i.e., "swinging") (e.g., *Score* [dir. Radley Metzger, 1974] and *Bob & Carol & Ted & Alice* [dir. Paul Mazursky, 1969]), and hyphenophilia (arousal at touching and feeling skin, fur, leather, or fabric) (e.g., Kenneth Anger's shorts such as *Kustom Kar Kommandos* and *Scorpio Rising*).

Paraphilia has been organized into a number of taxonomies over the years. It was removed from the DSM's list of disorders and revised instead as *paraphilic disorder* when abnormal desire becomes harmful to others or oneself.[30] John Money, the controversial sexologist credited with coining the term *gender* and discredited for his traumatizing experiments with child sexuality and gender identity, developed six subdivisions for paraphilias, all predicated on the interplay of virtue and sin.[31] For instance, masochism and sadism belong to the class of "sacrificial paraphilias" (which he likens to the religious ritual of sacrifice, either of the self or another), and the old psychoanalytic notion of fetish is preserved in the class of "fetish paraphilias," which include erotic fixation on inanimate objects, smells, body parts (such as the foot), and other material "tokens."

A Marlene Dietrich and Josef von Sternberg retrospective at the Roxie in 1988 bleeds these two paraphilic categories together, undergirded as well as by a lesbian subtext that goes unnamed. The Roxie's triple bill including Josef von Sternberg's *The Blue Angel* (1930), *The Scarlet Empress* (1934), and *Shanghai Express* (1932) was titled "Fascinating Fetishism," which played for three days in a row (fig. 2.3).[32] (A couple days later, the Dietrich–von Sternberg series continued with two days in a row of *Morocco* and then about a week later, two days in a row of a double bill of *Devil Is a Woman* and *Blonde Venus*.) Dietrich's queer aesthetic appeal might be delineated along affective and materialist lines. The film's description in the calendar gives a hint at Dietrich's affective appeal. It quotes an unnamed critic from a 1930 Berlin publication: "She sings without involvement, unemotionally. But this sensual lack of emotion is stimulating. She's vulgar without acting."[33] Dietrich in this excerpt recalls Leopold von Sacher-Masoch's *Venus in Furs*, in which the cold master withholds affective legibility from her masochistic slave. Extending the films' baroque displays of male suffering, prominent most in *The Blue Angel*, Dietrich withholds from the audience as well, trapping spectators of all persuasions in her inscrutability. Multiple scenes from *The Scarlett Empress* involving close-ups of Dietrich's face behind netted or sheer fabric, separating the camera (and the viewer) from the star to tantalizingly opaque effect. This affective register resonates strongly with the "sacrificial paraphilias" of sadism and masochism, but at the same time the films invite Money's "fetish paraphilias" as well. A vivid material sensuality stretches across the triple bill, featuring revealing costuming, fabrics grazed, flesh rubbed. The Dietrich–von Sternberg films form congruencies not just for

Marlene Dietrich and Josef von Sternberg

OCT/NOV 1988

We are delighted to present the seven visually stunning, extraordinary collaborations between Marlene Dietrich and Josef von Sternberg.

☐ **Fri-Sun • Oct 28-30**

Fascinating Fetishism

THE BLUE ANGEL
(Der Blaue Engel)
One of the cinema's most startling tales of masochism, in which a puritanical school teacher finds himself desperately enthralled by a cabaret singer named Lola Lola. Hired by Ufa, Sternberg went to Germany as a prophet of the new sound film—but it was Dietrich who created the bigger sensation. "She sings and acts almost without involvement, unemotionally. But this sensual lack of emotion is stimulating. She's vulgar without acting. It's pure cinema, nothing is theatrical. For the first time in talking pictures a female voice comes across with timbre, tonal color, expression. Extraordinary." —*Berliner Borsen-Courier*, 1930. This is the film that launched the Dietrich phenomenon—and a thousand moralists. Produced by Erich Pommer. Photographed by Gunther Rittau, Hans Schneeberger. With Emil Jannings and Kurt Gerron. In German. Paramount/Ufa. 109 mins. 1930.
☐ FRI 8:00
☐ SAT, SUN 2:15, 8:00

THE SCARLET EMPRESS
The next-to-last Dietrich-Sternberg collaboration, and one of Sternberg's most bizarre and lavish spectacles, with Dietrich as a neurotic Catherine the Great. The script is nonsense but the cinematography is truly inspired, and the sets and costumes must be seen to be believed. Decadent and indulgent, this film is a sort of kitsch masterpiece. Script by Manuel Komroff, from a diary by Catherine the Great. Photographed by Bert Glennon. With Dietrich, John Lodge, Sam Laffe, Louis Dresser. Paramount. 109 mins. 1934.
☐ FRI 10:00
☐ SAT, SUN 4:15, 10:00

SHANGHAI EXPRESS
"Of all of them, *Shanghai Express* is undoubtedly the most remarkable, a film in which von Sternberg creates an entire universe to justify the actions of his star." —John Baxter. "It took more than one man to change my name to Shanghai Lily," drawls Dietrich as she embarks on a train journey from Peking to Shanghai. Lee Garmes' camera work is at its lushest, and Anna May Wong her sultriest. Photographed by Lee Garmes (for which he won an Academy Award). With Dietrich, Clive Brook, Anna May Wong, Warner Oland. Paramount. 80 mins. 1932.
☐ FRI 6:15
☐ SAT, SUN 6:15

2.3 Converging fetishes in Dietrich's star image. Courtesy of University of California, Berkeley, BAMPFA Film Library and Study Center.

their masochistic persuasion, but for a haptic fetishistic invitation that deserves deeper exploration.

Books and essays have been devoted to reading the masochism in Dietrich and von Sternberg's collaborations (among other pre-code features), but less attention has been paid to what Gaylyn Studlar, in her mostly psychoanalytic readings of these films, calls von Sternberg's "emphasis on surface texture."[34] Rather than connect these fetishistic surfaces, textures, fabrics, and accoutrements to the related psychoanalytic equivalences of lack, castration anxiety, and substitution, we might return material fetish to its early sexological roots, specifically the writing of Richard von Krafft-Ebing, a name often invoked as a metonym for the field's proclivity for pernicious pathologization, with critiques of him dating all the way back to his contemporary Sigmund Freud.[35]

In his seminal encyclopedic study of sexual pathologies, *Psychopathia Sexualis*, Krafft-Ebing offers numerous case studies of fetishism (*fetichism*) that involve articles of clothing that neither reveal nor accentuate "secondary sexual characteristics (bosom, waist, hips)."[36] Testimonies by fur, silk, shoe, and even handkerchief fetishists instead highlight tactile pleasures over genital stimulation. Dietrich's costuming in *Shanghai Express* and *The Scarlett Empress* enacts just that; her outfits and soft props tend toward ruffles, feathers, bows, fur lining, and other decorative frills that are framed by close-ups and medium close-ups. Cinematic scale, cinematographic framing, Dietrich's performative gestures and poses all assist in transforming ordinary fabric into the source for paraphilic—and cinephilic—worship. The flowing fabrics that surround, if not engulf, Dietrich are meant to haptically graze the repertory spectator, simulating a tactility that Vivian Sobchack might describe as "sensual catachresis," in which a spectator "fills in the gap in its sensual grasp of the figural world on-screen by turning back on itself to reciprocally (albeit not sufficiently) 'flesh it out' into literal physicalized sense."[37] Dietrich and von Sternberg's deployment of mise-en-scène encourages desire that eschews normative genital stimulation in favor of perverse ones of rather genital-indifferent tactile sensations.

Krafft-Ebing describes accessories and fabrics as "mnemonic symbols"; feathers that tickle and perfume that lingers on a silk handkerchief carry the trace of the body that donned it. For Krafft-Ebing, it is within the spectral that fetishistic desire emerges. For example, a handkerchief carries "warmth from the person and specific odors," attributes retained in the wake of its separation from the body. Material fetishes are thereby marked by an intimate distance, as traces or corporeal inscriptions that are proximate to yet detachable from the body. Herein lies a potent analogy to moving-image technology in that, like material fetishes, cinema offers the same kind of remove—a temporal and geographical leap from the profilmic to what exists on-screen—that promises optical and tactile contiguity. Marlene Dietrich endures in *rep*eated screenings at *rep*ertory houses not just in the entirety of her on-screen presence but in the details, in the frills that move with and independent of her body in the frames flickering on the screen.[38]

The Roxie's effort to organize their Dietrich–von Sternberg retrospective via congruencies in object-based fetishism and masochism risks eclipsing Dietrich's lesbianism (a topic on which, luckily, there has been a considerable quantity of scholarship in the years since). On the one hand, this is characteristic of art house programming's tendency to eschew LGBT identity as a potential programmatic framing device. By doing so, curators frequently sidestepped the struggles fought in women's and gay liberation. Programmers—many of whom, we should not forget, would have identified as heterosexual, male, and white—may appear to us now as backward or out-of-sync with the times, for they did not alter their practice to accommodate a gay and lesbian social and filmic consciousness. (Such a concurrent consciousness would be furnished in lesbian and gay film festivals such as Frameline in San Francisco or Reeling in Chicago.[39]) On the other hand, "Fascinating Fetishism," among other deviant series, does not necessarily *disinvite* a lesbian gaze—especially not a lesbian fetishistic one—as much as it seeks to broaden its address via the fetish form. The program grants space for a multitude of viewers to cognize, historicize, and sense the aestheticization of material fetish within the realm of the moving image—a political gesture in a public sphere that has rendered such a form of desire unspeakable, but by submerging identity positions also in need of recognition.

"Sexuality in Cinema"

"Sexuality in Cinema," a series at the Film Center at the School of the Art Institute of Chicago (with Richard Peña at the helm, supported by the Film Center's future director of programming, Barbara Scharres) in 1984, attests to a model both potentially utopian in its capaciousness and discriminatory in its avoidance of difference. In "Sexuality in Cinema," films with trans protagonists as far ranging as Fassbinder's *In a Year of 13 Moons* (1978) and the then more recent Ulrike Ottinger film *The Image of Dorian Gray in the Yellow Press* (1984) played with the classic *Cat People* (dir. Jacques Tourneur, 1942), a film also about another kind of metamorphosis and transition, one that has attracted readings of its racial and lesbian otherness, along with Marlene Gorris's *A Question of Silence* (1982), which has become a staple of European feminist cinema.[40] Generically titled, "Sexuality in Cinema" is surprising in its troubling of heterosexual and binary gender norms. In fact, the series' ambiguous title seems to smuggle in a rather queer politics, one that the *Film Center Gazette* makes clearer in its program description: "Heterosexual sexuality, as interpreted by male directors, long comprised the norm in cinema.... Contemporary directors, particularly women directors, have increasingly dealt with sexuality as a varied force, often at the root of individual's conflict with society at large."[41] Perhaps oversimplifying

2.4 Veruschka von Lehndorff's androgyny in Ulrike Ottinger's *The Image of Dorian Gray in the Yellow Press* (1984).

in its presentism, still, the series sought to elevate the work of women and non-heterosexual male directors whose perspectives on sexuality might be considered "varied."

The New German Cinema films in the series that focus on trans protagonists speak to this point. *The Image of Dorian Gray in the Yellow Press* and *In a Year of 13 Moons* both spectacularize the trans body intradiegetically. In Ottinger's film, female model Veruschka von Lehndorff struts around as the dandy Dorian Gray (fig. 2.4). Gray's narcissism in this version (versus Oscar Wilde's novella, *The Picture of Dorian Gray*) is reflected by the tabloid's obsession with him; a news mogul named Dr. Mabuse (played by Delphine Seyrig) catapults Gray into stardom by crafting a love affair between him and an opera singer. As Alice Kuzniar points out, Gray's gender ambiguity or androgyny implicitly drives the public's intradiegetic fixation. The artifice of Dorian's gender ambiguity, Kuzniar suggests, also invites a scopophilia that for the audience of the film is ultimately occluded because they are denied full visible access to Dorian's body. The trans body's simultaneous magnification and opacity is thematized through the narrative as well as performed by the film itself for its spectators.

By contrast, *In a Year of 13 Moons* expresses trans spectacularization not through the fetishization of the trans body but by its abjection. The film follows a trans woman named Elvira on her last days as she attempts to connect with former loved ones before committing suicide. Fassbinder's rendering of a trans protagonist fails the test of "good" representation, even against Vito Russo's measurement as early as the 1970s. Not only is Elvira yet another lonely and tragic trans character punished for veering from the mandates of a binary gender system; the film explains her impulsive transition as a means to attain a male heterosexual love interest, not as a product of "gender dysphoria." Despite these representational issues, Elvira's dissociation from her surroundings—what Lauren Berlant might call a "life in ellipsis"—can be explained by her inability to pass (fig. 2.5).[42] The film opens with Elvira getting transbashed for "falsely advertising" her gender, and other characters are constantly hounding her about her looks and figure. Using lingering shots that underscore Elvira's alienation, Fassbinder's heroine continues to unravel, and as a result, withdraws from the world, while she simultaneously observes and becomes porous to the world and her past. *In a Year of 13 Moons*, like *Dorian Gray*, thus thematizes its representation of an unassimilable trans character whose body is the troubling cathected site of social and psychic anxiety, though drawing distinct conclusions from Ottinger's meditation on techno-simulated modern life.

"Sexuality in Cinema" invited spectators to take in deviant forms and practices largely unavailable or still coded within mainstream cinema of the 1980s when the program was presented. *Cat People* channels this convergent spirit in its narrative of a Serbian-born woman who fears her suppressed desires. The film is read by Alexander Doty as an allegory about the fear of the exoticized ethnic other's sexuality and, alternatively, by Harry Benshoff, as a coded narrative about closeted lesbians who hold a "terrible secret or [belong to] a group of odd fellows."[43] In one scene, the protagonist Irena is approached by a mysterious woman who, in a thick Serbian accent, refers to her as her "sister," a fellow feline underneath. Both Doty's and Bensoff's exegeses explain Irena's unease with her feline lineage as one linked to her "aberrant sexuality," as Peña phrased it in an interview, be it because of her ethnicity or queer desire.[44] Just as Irena and the mysterious woman meet in a bonded sisterhood of deviance, Irena and Fassbinder's Elvira convene as social strays in the space of the program, fetishized and repudiated by those that surround them, and therefore alien to their social worlds.

2.5 A spatially isolated Elvira in Fassbinder's *In a Year of 13 Moons* (1978).

"Fascinating Fetishism" and "Sexuality in Cinema" arrange the films into contact zones of clashing eras and marginalized sexual and gender types that nevertheless find a vague commonality in their gender and sexual alterity. Putting these series side-by-side also moves us across disciplinary boundaries, even if those boundaries are blurred or overlapped (insofar as both engage sexual alterity as a unifying principle). "Fascinating Fetishism" draws from a sexological tradition, blending in lay Freudian psychoanalysis. "Sexuality in Cinema," however, is more akin to sociology's emphasis on social typology (rather than pathological conditions or disorders) and experience (rather than internal trauma), an aggregate of the stigmatized who share what sociologist William Simon might have called "sexual scripts."[45] Fittingly, the program description of "Sexuality in Cinema" mentions that the series was done in "conjunction with the School of the Art Institute's lecture series, 'Sexuality in Art and Media.'"[46] By cleverly collaborating and cross-promoting, Peña and Scharres intimately joined traditional forms of knowledge production with the more sensorial and affective experience of cinema. This conflux of academic study of deviance and its programmatic creative treatment demonstrate the ways in which the two are dynamically enmeshed and beckon multiple media, forms, outlets, and registers for their dissemination.

This underclass, which here marshals a broad range—from the trans to lesbian to racially exoticized other—implies the social forces of stigma, shame, failure, and disappointment are prevalent and constitute structures of feeling that cut across these types. Heather Love, in analyzing Erving Goffman's concept of stigma, proposes this is both a weakness and strength of what she calls the "universalizing" inclination of such a category.[47] Like deviance itself, the tremendous prevalence of stigma—or "spoiled identity," as Goffman also puts it—that would include virtually anyone not white, male, heterosexual, Protestant, good looking, and middle to upper class, could undermine its critical effectiveness while also expanding beyond embedded classifications of politically viable groups. Despite its downsides, this approach to loosely classifying a "stigmatized majority," as Love puts it, might kindle a model for ethical and political relationality and engagement—a mutual recognition of failure in the face of mythical normative ideals.[48]

For Gayle Rubin, a (near-)universalizing model of sexual stigma is foundational to her radical (one might say, today, "abolitionist") politics of sex, which "must identify, describe, explain, and denounce erotic injustice and sexual oppression."[49] Failure, stigma, persecution, repression, and criminality are key indicators of what subordinates groups to a low rank in the hierarchical or caste system of sexual value Rubin diagrams. Rubin's method is radical (and thus fundamental to 1990s queer theory), in part, because it opts out of a default appeal to identitarian or factional logics, and instead takes an intersectional and structural perspective on the history, operations, and effects of sex-phobia. In so doing, Rubin maps out what she considers the "most despised sexual castes currently [which] include transsexuals, transvestites, fetishists, sadomasochists, sex workers such as prostitutes and porn models, and the lowliest of all, those whose eroticism transgresses generational boundaries," all exiled to the "outer limits" of social thinkability and respectability (fig. 2.6).[50]

Audaciously written during the virulent debates about porn taking place among feminists in the 1980s, Rubin's 1984 essay "Thinking Sex: Notes for a Radical Theory of the Politics of Sexuality" consolidated disparate types into a distinct class in order to demonstrate the extent of American sexual puritanism, be it in the dubious, if not spurious, name of religious morality or protection of vulnerable populations (e.g., women and children). In fact, as a means to cultivate coalition, Rubin advocates for the continual development of sexological taxonomies that would track the "emergence of new kinds of erotic individuals and their aggregation into ru-

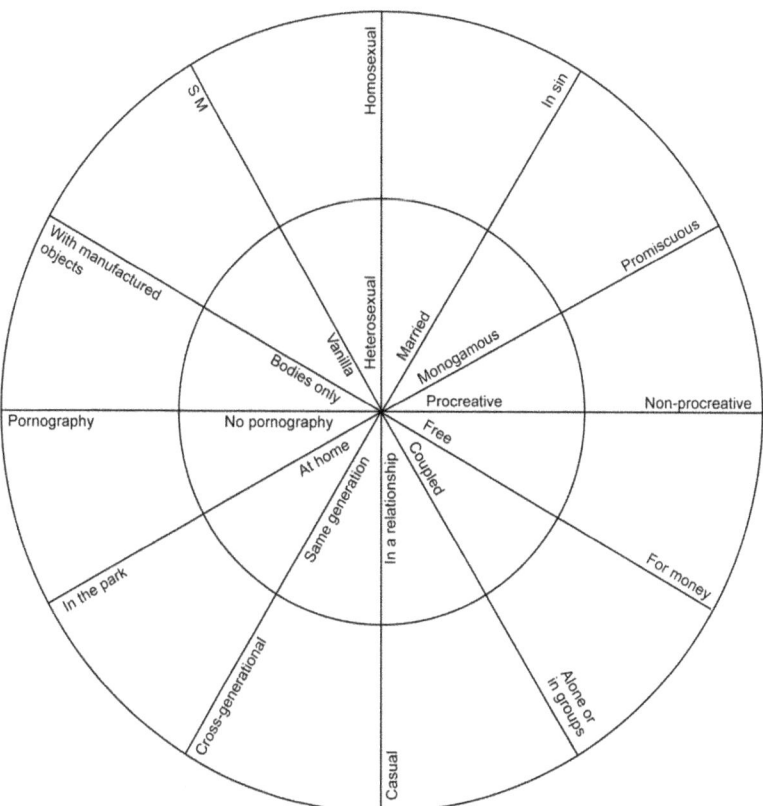

2.6 Gayle Rubin's diagram of "the charmed circle" ("good, normal, natural, blessed sexuality") vs. "the outer limits" ("bad, abnormal, unnatural, damned sexuality").

dimentary communities."[51] Rubin implores her reader to "reconceptualize" contemporary sexual politics through politicized organizational systems such as the one she proposes, thereby overtly politicizing traditional social science approaches that encompass sexology, sociology, and anthropology for radical, utopian inclusion.

Rubin's separation of the "charmed circle" of married, heterosexual, monogamous, and reproductive subjects from virtually everyone else, which also created "major areas of contest" for practices and types (including gays and lesbians), illustrates the productiveness of the universalizing model to which Heather Love points. This caste system binds and consolidates sexualities typically treated as discrete and random in their difference, in a fashion not unlike the Chicago Art Institute's "Sexuality in Cinema" series. In expanding the rationale for who belongs to the sexual and gender underclass and why, programming makes sensible and visible the protean relations that connect one type to another, one desire to another, and one behavior to another, in a chain of associations. Like Rubin's "outer limits," "Sexuality in Cinema" gives shape to deviance as a category of productive nonsovereign relationality.[52] The trans characters in the New German Cinema films and the exotic other in *Cat People* are contingent parts of a whole whose oppressions make legible a system favoring normative and white existence, and their contingence in the program gives them mutual support and viability in their particular struggles. Further, the structural and experiential resonances that bind together these societal underdogs create contingence in other ways, evoking for viewers intense feelings of affirmation, shame, outrage, and so forth, or even "softer" affects of curiosity and ambivalence, depending on the representation and how a spectator might see their own circumstances or desires reflected in it or not.

Taxonomania

Deviant film programs consist of the kind of sociological (or, in Rubin's case, anthropological) grouping of social pariahs, but within them are the motley of sexological types enumerated in the lists of -philias and -isms formed in the late nineteenth century all the way through the end of the twentieth century, creating an interdisciplinary mixture that draws from the collisional logics of their heterogeneous traditions and methodologies. To applaud the social sciences for providing a base for coalitional politics might seem banal on the surface, but this idea is intensely controversial in critical theory. (Even Rubin's highly distributive sexual politics marks an anomaly in queer theory's canon.) Dominated by philosophical and literary traditions, the humanities' criticism of the scientific rationality in the social sciences abounds, most salient in feminist and queer interventions that argue against sexology's and sociology's complicity in state and biopower and its postulated apoliticism.

Historians of sexology Janice Irvine, Lisa Downing, Iain Morland, and Nikki Sullivan have persuasively argued that the field has historically been torn between two poles: between biological and constructivist explanations for sexual "dysfunction," and between conservative efforts to legitimate the field through its rehabilitative promises and a progressivist view that might transfer pathology from an individual's failings to harmful social structures of repression and puritanism.[53] Like sexology, sociology has at times fortified discriminatory hegemonic views of minoritized groups when it intended to or could have done the opposite. As an example, Roderick Ferguson charges sociology with making white racialized assumptions of normativity to help distinguish itself from black deviance. Ferguson's queer-of-color critique diametrically opposes what he calls canonical American sociology, which "imagined African American culture as a site of polymorphous gender and sexual perversions and associated those perversions with moral failings typically."[54] These citations only scratch the surface of well-argued, warranted concerns over ways the social sciences (e.g., sociology, anthropology/ethnography, sexology, and psychology) have objectified supposedly unruly subjects and reinforced the racialized and gendered status quo, claiming neutrality, objectivity, and rigorous empiricism in the process.

Many of these critiques have their basis in Michel Foucault's philosophical analyses of institutions and the discourses they generate.[55] Studying sexuality alongside criminality and madness, Foucault demonstrates that the modern sexual subject was produced discursively through regimes of truth and knowledge based in religion, science, and medicine. Forming the social constructivist basis for queer theory, theorists have tended to emphasize one side of Foucault's thesis, that discursive power circumscribes the self, leashing one's identity and behavior to the dispositifs that make subjectivity legible and intelligible. The other side of this formation, that power relations are also productive, is often noted yet underexplored. These readings reiterate the circular logic that discursive productiveness is yet another circumscription, empowering the self through language (e.g., self-identifying as gay or lesbian) only to limit the extent to which the ego might otherwise develop into its sexuality. In the end, repression and its presumed opposite, productiveness, both constitute straitjackets in their own way.

Foucault, however, leaves some breadcrumbs for a different way to read the productiveness of *scientia sexualis*. Striking down the repressive hypothesis that sex was absent from Western cultures of the nineteenth century, Foucault insists, "There was no deficiency, but rather an excess, a redoubling, too much rather than not enough discourse."[56] Discourses of sexuality—sexology being the most instructive here—were indeed *overproductive*, bordering on anarchy, Foucault implies. Immediately following his oft-quoted assertion that the homosexual became a species, Foucault offers the reader a taste of these amassing "species": "Krafft-Ebbing's zoophiles and zooerasts, Rohleder's auto-monosexualists; and later mixoscopophiles, gynecomasts, presbyophiles, sexoesthetic inverts, and dyspareunist women."[57] Foucault's argumentation, as well as the classificatory act itself, cleaves in two here: on the one hand, taxonomizing transforms phenomena into species, producing a truth regime via "specification, the regional solidification" that would make "natural order of disorder." Classification, in this light, is an instrument of scientific rationality and objectification; by producing a nomenclature with attendant traits, it seeks to make the subject intelligible to various medical and state apparatuses.[58]

On the other hand, these classification protocols gesture toward their own absurd inexhaustibility; stuck in an unending marathon to capture the micro, to detect the most marginal of the marginal, classification measures get trapped in a Sisyphean cycle where they labor to keep up with multiplying phenomena as they surface and change with technological, social, and political conditions. Foucault even admits that these Victorian-era taxonomists continued to produce more species, "even when there was no order to fit them into."[59] As soon as deviance is apprehended, as soon as language for it gets invented, it simultaneously evades the process of apprehension itself, spinning out of control. The act of classifying gender and sexual typologies, in short, can easily collapse into a satire of itself. Within this double movement of apprehension and elusion exists a radical potential to appropriate the logic of scientific rationality under the umbrella of *deviance* while simultaneously undermining the authoritative power that it holds. This endless codification, for instance, is grounds for mockery or, more broadly, playfulness.

Programming, too, by presenting to the paying public a "cavalcade of perversions," to use a phrase from John Waters's *Multiple Maniacs*, was feeding an exhaustive and exhausting supply of deviant depictions. Indeed, John Waters emblematizes the irreverent reception of such a "cavalcade of perversions," as he is a product of the sexual and gender oddity in the exploitation and art films of Russ Meyer, William Castle, Luis Buñuel, George Kuchar and Mike Kuchar, and a host of others, as much as the clinical discourses of sexology popularized by the likes of Kinsey and Money.[60] Appropriately, Waters, ever the depraved polymath, provided a blurb for sexologist John Money's 1995 book, *Gendermaps*, calling him the "Duke of Dysfunction," no doubt with an overtone of irony.[61] So what to make of this endeavor to make functional sense, order, and knowledge of the disorder of human sexual life, only to turn it into the *dysfunction* of over-accumulated lists and categories? When the empirical strains to reach any coherent conclusion, when we become fatigued by the overwhelm of information about varied sexual practices, identities, and desires, what is on the other side of that fatigue?[62] What could be the objective of such a compulsion to comprehensive scientific observation and codification—what some have rightfully called "taxonomania"?[63] To seek causes and cures? To simply empirically catalog sexual phenomena for the specious neutral sake of knowledge production?

When these questions hit their logical limits, the only recourse we have is to recognize the innumerable variety of pleasures and desires in a world always trying to correct course away from their unwieldy immensity—that is, the whole repertory of human sexuality, as Parker Tyler and even sociologist William Simon put it.[64] The response is not to catalog all the forms of deviance that made their way onto art house screens of this era, as if to conduct a film studies equivalent of the empirical taxonomania of the sexologist or sociologist. Rather, we need to create and examine structural or organizing principles of cinematic deviance that make it possible not only to analyze the films in their programmatic context, but also to politicize the work of their curation—a film equivalent to Gayle Rubin's proposition, if you will. In this recognition, we are left with a Rubin-esque politics of sexual ethics that counteracts structures of repression and oppression, a coalitional model of protection and advocacy for those vulnerable to attack, censure, erasure, detainment, harassment, and other forms of violence and censorship. In this sense, the programming of deviant material bears direct weight on the social conditions of the lived world.

Programming of this era models a politics of sexual and gender deviance, which takes epistemic and definitional shape via discourses of deviance and takes ethical shape via Gayle Rubin, Michel Foucault, and the "new sociologists" (a term I will define in the next section). Whether by stitching together the fetishistic films of Marlene Dietrich or linking the experiences of trans misfits in New German Cinema, film programming directed audiences to the experience of stigma as something that operates under a number of guises, be it for the sexual acts one does in private or how one performs their gender in public, as Goffman demonstrated in the 1960s.

"Outlaw Cinema"

Poring over thousands of film programs in my archival research, the Nuart Theatre's 1981 series "Outlaw Cinema" was among the clearest attempts to create a new cinematic category or genre akin to deviance theory (fig. 2.7).

Each Thursday between July and October, the Nuart would play a double bill of films directed by a director-provocateur, reflecting, according to the series' calendar description, "anti-social filmmaking attitudes from John Waters to Herschell Gordon Lewis, Kenneth Anger to Paul Morrissey, Pier Pasolini to Rainer Werner Fassbinder, Andy Warhol to Roman Polanski."[65] Though certainly these filmmakers had been programmed contiguously countless times, and some were linked by critics in their creative genealogies (e.g., John Waters to Herschell Gordon Lewis), "Outlaw Cinema" marked a rare instance in which curators overtly created a category within which this range of disobedient films properly fit.

Even this calendar's design made a nod to the series' unruliness, to its unwillingness to fit in with the rest of the month's programming. In juxtaposition to the neat grid of orthogonal boxes containing the names of films and their respective graphics, the Outlaw Cinema boxes are arranged at alternating angles, spilling onto the margins of the page and disrupting the continuity and flow of the calendar's perpendicular axes. In each box are images of the films' stars, such as Joe Dallesandro, Edith Massey, and John Waters, their eyes covered by overlaying blindfolds to signify the forbidden nature of the material. John Waters's muse and frequent leading lady, Divine, is even pictured on the top right, appearing to preside over the wayward films, commanding them to do her bidding as she would in her "dom" roles in Waters's films. The layout suggests that these films (and Divine) pose a threat to the month's entire programmatic order, perhaps even to the organizing principles of coherence and alignment that structure programming at large—"anti-social" indeed.

These films, varying in genre, taste strata, and nation, are united also in their revolt against old traditions in film curating that persist even to this day, directed at one genre in particular: the Western. The Western, among the most popular and even valorized of masculinist film genres, found its cult of adoration in the auteur theory of Andrew Sarris and the curation of its many incarnations as the Hollywood Western, the Spaghetti Western, and later the revisionist Western. The Nuart's definition of "outlaw" here sheds this usual machismo image of the cowboy or gangster, a long-cherished figure among cinephiles for whom action and nostalgia came together in a perfect blend. *Outlaw* might to an extent also invoke the history of criminalized LGBT people, with several of the program's films involving trans, homosexual, and bisexual men and women. Still, the notion of the outlaw travels beyond these histories and typologies, incorporating a throng of sexual and gender outcasts into its stock.

2.7 "Gender Outlaw Thursdays" in Nuart's summer 1981 calendar.

In 1983, two years after the Nuart series, film critic David Chute wrote in *Film Comment* about a genre he identified as "Outlaw Cinema." It is unclear to what extent the term *outlaw cinema* was in casual circulation at this time, or if Chute attended or knew about the Nuart's series (it seems he moved to LA from New York in 1983), but the resemblances are more than salient: among its staple figures, Chute names directors Hershell Gordon Lewis, Rainer Werner Fassbinder, Russ Meyer, George Romero, and, most importantly, John Waters, the "Patron Saint and Theoretical Genius of Outlaw Cinema."[66] Speaking of identification with the films' monstrosity, Chute writes in a radical, punkish voice that echoes the Nuart's program description: Outlaw Cinema "doesn't want to *alter* social norms, it wants to annihilate them."[67]

Chute's article is mainly a revisionist response to Hoberman and Rosenbaum's book *Midnight Movies* published that same year. "Outlaw Cinema produced that stunted offspring known as the Midnight Movie," Chute laments.[68] Unlike Hoberman and Rosenbaum, Chute adopts an elegiac tone when discussing this group of "flagrant" films, "whose crucial social function is to overstep the limits of established taste."[69] According to Chute, the death knell had sounded for this body of cult films when its depravity had lost its bite; *Pink Flamingos* and *Blood Feast* (dir. Hershell Gordon Lewis, 1963) were now part of an accepted ritual and institution known as the "midnight movie."

And yet the Nuart's series in 1981 and art house programming at large throughout the 1980s suggest this supposedly moribund genre of obscene films was alive and well, sustaining public interest and excitement for years well beyond its supposed institutionalization. If they had truly been assimilated into the mainstream, wouldn't they have lost their perverse luster? To assume, as Chute does, that "there are no social taboos left for these films to violate" is to conflate widening representation and public interest with social acceptance.[70] In fact, the ritual and institution of the midnight movie does not eclipse the ongoing ideological work of those films to test cultural status-quo boundaries and resonate with outsider and underdog viewers. Further, writing in 1983, Chute perhaps couldn't predict the rise of the Moral Majority with Reaganite politics and HIV/AIDS, which would confer on these debased films a robust subtext that might become strategies for survival in a hostile anti-queer world.

Chute maps onto Outlaw Cinema a universalized reception in which these often violent and disturbing films strike at what he calls a "primitive" and "pre-aesthetic" level for fans. Films that "embody the world view of the dog, the beast, the sociopath who lurks in each of us," dispense with a generalized spectator's reflection of their own outsider perspective—the sense of *feeling* like a freak—consonant with the taste status of the "bad object" itself.[71] Such abstract appeals to the freak or outsider risk retaining or sidestepping the privileges that come with being cis, straight, white, and male. It does little to nothing to harness a politicized generality like the one described through 1960s sociology, or a queer theory to come, that would identify the marginalia of society in its grounded lived experience.

Within ten years of the series, queer theory would claim the figure of the "outlaw" and grant some specificity and political force to its mythos. Trans performer and activist Kate Bornstein's usage in her book *Gender Outlaw* seems to resonate with Divine and Fassbinder's protagonist in *In a Year of 13 Moons*, playing in the same series in quite literal fashion. For Bornstein, an outlaw is someone who "subscribes to a dynamic of change, outside any given dichotomy," and "regularly walks along a forbidden boundary or border."[72] Art historian Richard Meyer uses the term *outlaw representation* to describe the ways gay artists from Andy Warhol to Robert Mapplethorpe to Holly Hughes leveraged their brazen perverse approaches in order to radically dislocate the codes of acceptable artistic practice persisting in their profession. In both Bornstein's and Meyer's usages, the figure of the outlaw as transgressor was prized and positioned as the ultimate challenge to rigid structures of gender and sexual propriety. For Bornstein especially, the outlaw is someone who confounds social categorizations that, as Foucault theorized, had become taxonomized, administered, and policed in the name of modern social order and regulation.

If Divine wonderfully fits Bornstein's definition of the gender outlaw, John Waters might be seen as an easy addition to Richard Meyer's list of artists producing outlaw representation. (Moreover, three of Paul Morrissey's Warhol-produced films are also in the Outlaw Cinema program, further linking the program to Meyer's examples.) Waters is perhaps the most popular filmmaker on the Nuart's deviant roster, as he was able to cross over into Hollywood starting in the late 1980s with hits *Hairspray* (1988) and *Cry Baby* (1990), and has since become an icon as a stand-up comedian, writer, and even exhibited artist. It is easy to forget, then, where Waters got his start. Waters, along with Morrissey (who came around slightly earlier), symbolized a disavowal of and therefore a departure from the aesthetic sobriety of queer underground auteurs that came before them.[73] His midnight cult films such as *Female Trouble* and *Pink Flamingos* celebrated a visual style invoking home movies more than anything that was regularly screened at the art house cinema. The films' antisocial and subversive content, however, made them akin to a lineage of banned and censored films. They could fit within the programming of the art house not because they had nowhere else to be screened but because they defied the codes of morality that had for so long kept certain films on the margins or even largely unseen. Urban art house programmers and exhibitors prided themselves on bringing rare films and other obscure moving-image media out of the shadows and into view for inquisitive audiences. Programmatically, this content allowed art house theaters to position themselves as sites of revelation and discovery, granting visibility to social pariahs and unseemly acts otherwise obstructed from view. Waters's early films thus provocatively flaunted the antisocial and obscene, at which the paying public, comprising both queers and straights, could gawk.

In fact, his film *Multiple Maniacs*, which appeared in the Outlaw Cinema series in a double feature with his silent first feature, *Mondo Trasho* (1969), includes a showman who effectively serves as a proxy or surrogate for Waters himself. The opening scene is illustrative: A group of suburbanite spectators is slowly lured into the carnival tent in the middle of a forest and exposed to a range of distasteful exhibitions: puke eaters, fiendish fetishists who lick bicycle seats and armpits, and exhibitionist pornographers documenting their sexual indiscretions. The straitlaced attendees serving as proxies for a mainstream movie audience look on in horror at what the attraction's showman calls "assorted sluts, fags, dykes and pimps," all part of "Lady Divine's Cavalcade of Perversions." Note that the identifiers that the showman uses are quite broad; in a sense, this is enough to provoke titillation and fear in the minds and bodies of the white suburban spectators. The terms' broad application also might imply a collectivity of those deemed undesirable, an umbrella under which deviants can huddle, whether it be for their object choices, their behavioral characteristics, or their sordid professions. It is entirely fair to argue that both John Waters and his diegetic showman are both playing the role of pimp here, "pimping out" Divine and her cavalcade of perverts to an excitable filmgoing public.[74]

Waters, then, magnified the weird and twisted examples one would find in exploitation films and "shockumentaries," mediating for the public extreme examples of what one could find in the social science research of fields such as sexology or sociology. He unleashed these depraved figures into the diegetic suburbs of Baltimore, delighting in fantasies of terrorizing middle Americans whose mythic fears of homosexuals, vagrants, and fetishists kept them up at night. It is no wonder Waters was in such awe of the work of John Money—Money was, after all, one of his source materials. By extension, programmers were doing in the space of a calendar or series what Waters does in the space of his films, bringing to life onscreen an array of social deviants. Beyond John Waters's role as proxy for the showman in *Multiple Maniacs*, the film in general, if not Waters's body of work during the 1970s, might be regarded as a metonym for urban art house programming of this era at large.

Multiple Maniacs followed Waters's *Mondo Trasho*, his first feature, in the Nuart's double bill that evening. *Mondo Trasho*, not unlike *Multiple Maniacs*, uses Divine as a vehicle to showcase lewd fetishistic performances. But while *Multiple Maniacs* only obliquely speaks to this question of sexual identity and classification through the showman's enunciative act—a gesture at grouping deviants together—*Mondo Trasho* directly references and is inspired by the *Mondo* cycle of exploitation films popular in the 1960s. This Italian series of pseudo-scientific "shockumentaries," initiated by *Monde Cane* (dir. Gualtiero Jacopetti, Paolo Cavara, and Franco E. Prosperi, 1962), would often explore a wide range of so-called exotic topics—from cannibalism to nudism—as a kind of cinematic cabinet of curiosities. *Mondo Trasho*'s closest source material might be *Mondo Freudo* (1966), which focused particularly on sexual peculiarities, most of which involve some kind of sex work. As scholars have argued, the *Mondo* films give the (perhaps faint) impression of being rooted in scientific fact through the expository device of voiceover narration, a voice—often male—performing as a social scientist guiding the viewer through strange social practices around the world.[75] It is no coincidence they are often racist and xenophobic in their depiction of the "exotic" and "erotic," the pseudo-science present in them both capitalizing on and amplifying preexisting racialized scientific knowledges.

Waters was captivated by, if not himself wanting to capitalize on, this wave of what Chuck Kleinhans calls "sleazy documentaries." This cycle of documentaries was not limited to the *Mondo* series, instead stretching into a whole subgenre of sexploitation films. According to Elena Gorfinkel, sex exposé films such as *Files X for Sex* (dir. C. Davis Smith, 1967), *The Abnormal Female* (dir. George Rodgers, 1969), and *The Lusting Hours* (dir. John Amero and Lem Amero, 1967) thematize a "cultural voyeurism," in which a faux-scientific framing was employed to cloak the titillated viewer's voyeurism in sociological curiosity. The films follow a standard case-study template in which a "male narrator purported to be an expert tells a story of evidentiary deviance, erotically charged criminality, or sexual pathology that accompanies illustrative footage that claims a documentary facticity."[76]

According to Gorfinkel, these vignette-structured films operate as guided tours through spectacular dioramas of deviance, using the pretext of scientific inquiry to grant the prurient viewer audiovisual access to clandestine and taboo "practices of prostitution, transvestism, sadomasochism, and male hustling."[77]

Used as both alibi for and source of taboo arousal, the sociological and sexological conceit of these lewd films might be seen as more than a marketing ploy, thinly veiled disguise, or even pleasurable erotic conceit, especially given the backdrop of this cultural moment. Rather, sexology and sociology joined psychology as fields that occupied a central role in the laymen scientific comprehension of everyday postwar life. Janice Irvine has historicized the ways that the work of prominent sexologists Alfred Kinsey, William Masters and Virginia Johnson, and Wilhelm Reich tracked apace with the decades of the 1950s through 1970s and seeped into the popular domain, driving ordinary Americans' curiosity about the unspoken subject of sex—who was doing it, how they were doing it, and how often. This "marketplace of ideas" joined with exposé films and other sleazy faux-documentaries exploiting this larger cultural consumption by virtually billing themselves as tie-ins, visual companions to, or depictions of, the sexologists' published studies. The public was wild about sexology, but they also happened to be interested in sociology. Chuck Kleinhans notes parenthetically that in "1960s America . . . the favorite sociology course on many campuses was Sociology of Deviance, often known by campus slang as 'Nuts and Sluts.'"[78] Cinema was not only an extension of this cultural enthrallment, but also occasion to feed the libido audiovisually and sensorially, to animate for the senses what otherwise was isolated to circulating in academic or pseudo-academic written texts.

At this time, late 1960s and early 1970s sociology took a sharp turn away from the emotionally removed and cold approaches of the discipline's founding fathers and even some of the earlier 1960s methods, moving more toward Marxist-influenced methodologies in which researchers explicitly aligned their projects with the social "underdog" or "outsider." *Time* did a story on these young—some might say "radical"—academics in January 1970, dubbing them the "new sociologists."[79] Positioning Irving Horowitz and David Gottlieb as the movement's vanguard, the profile of this new cohort of social scientists explains that chief among their political goals was to trouble the idea that social alienation was a result or symptom of personal failure. Rather, according to this new school of thought, larger social structures and institutions had failed these marginalized subjects, and so hegemonic understandings of social failure or deficiency were in need of serious revision.

That the new sociologists were featured in *Time* magazine suggests that they were able to bridge the oft-regarded "insular" operations of the academe with that of at least the intellectual public, if not the public at large. The *Time* article even makes an argument for the popularity of the field's new phase; *Trans-action*, a regular publication new sociologist and surveyor of deviance Irving Horowitz helped found, boasts that "only 10% of its 70,000 circulation goes to social scientists." While the circulation of sexological findings remains much more on the forefront of cultural memory, I am arguing, in part, that the ideas of the new sociology and, particularly within it, deviance studies, also made their way into the consciousness of the general public, vitalizing a figure like the outlaw. In fact, one might say that the new sociology is an academic expression of a post-1968 shift in studies of culture, politically commensurate with the many political aspirations of minoritized groups during this era focused on liberation and freedom. Moreover, the new sociologists encouraged the public to use intersecting nodal points in thinking difference together structurally, in consolidating difference to help achieve utopian coalitional aims.

Deviance studies and popularized sexology had ramified into the public sphere to produce a series such as "Outlaw Cinema," generating similar knowledges in the realm of film exhibition and spectatorship as it had in readers of its literature.[80] Akin to *underdog* in sociology, the term *outlaw* in and of itself becomes a meaningful category, one, as I suggested, with social purpose (i.e., in terms of trans and queer theories to come) and filmic relevance (i.e., undermining the masculinist valorization of the Western and thereby elevating its queer valences). It implies a general discontent with the respectable and routine protocols of normative sexuality, and a call to deviate and disorient, to delight in the perverse stylings of acts unappetizing to what Gayle Rubin calls the "charmed circle" of subjects who regularly perform identities deemed straight, decent, and legitimate.

"Outlaw Cinema" sticks out in programming history as an unambiguous and pointed instance in which programmers directed audience attention toward an eclectic group of disparate texts, all unified under *outlaw* as its central concept. Filled with sex work and drugs, the films of the Paul Morrissey trilogy—*Heat, Flesh,* and *Trash*—converge here in a deviant matrix with the "anti-social" queer typologies and forms of Pasolini's *Salò* (discussed in formal detail in the next chapter), Roman Polanski's *Repulsion* (1965) (discussed in the afterword), and Russ Meyer's *Vixen* (1968). Along with *Female Trouble* and other John Waters films, this series proposes *outlaw* as a categorial answer to the reigning humorless puritanism of American mass culture. With a howling jouissance of anarchy and destruction, *outlaw* takes the regular menu—boilerplate even—of 1970s and 1980s revival houses and creates an itinerary for those whose desires and identities run against the societal grain.

By nature, repertory houses cycle through content, so they must find ways to market it as fresh or novel to keep patrons returning to watch the same films. A heading such as "Outlaw Cinema" might indeed pique the audience's appetites, perhaps even giving them occasion to relish in their alternative tastes (typified by David Chute's formulation of Outlaw Cinema). At the same time, a framing device need not be reduced to a gimmick. Doesn't the framing and classification inform the audience's understanding of the content—offering a concept, if you will, just as Goffman does with stigma? Even if Outlaw Cinema might not in actuality be such an outlaw in the larger scheme of the Nuart's or many other repertory houses' programming, the theater's effort to carve out a new category of films with resonating sexual and gender styles, attitudes, and sensibilities gestures at an organization or system of deviant attachments in which misfits might find pleasure in their own and others' desires. It was in this skein of kinks (straight, gay, and trans), camp, and gore that audiences were invited to revel in or try out, at least audiovisually, desires considered unseemly.

Whether upholding the taxonomic methods of the social sciences, defying them, or remolding them playfully, programming consolidated vilified groups and demographics—those on the "outer limits"—as Gayle Rubin put it. Viewed through the lens of deviance rather than queerness, film programming covers much of the same terrain as the gathered miscellany of theories of deviance that interrogate structures, sources, and histories of sexual and gender oppression. Programming thus gives these typologies occasion for collective outcry, to represent the mistreatment of those socially discredited on the grounds of their sexuality and gender, and to express utopian hopes and fantasies of what alternate modes of living, loving, and fucking might look like. It is in these moments that programming reaches out to the historical spectator, not for them to be "seen" or somehow mirrored in the projected image, but to see a distributed version of their deviance in others whose stories divaricate from their own as they also overlap. On these grounds, deviants are recursively invited back to the cinema, to cruise the endless repertories of human sexuality put on spectacular display.

Erotic Intertextuality

ON THE PROGRAMMATIC FORMS
OF DESIRE

Much has been said about the moving image's display of the eroticized body, and how cinema segments, lights, edits, dresses (or undresses) it. These elements of style, critics and theorists attest, amplify movies' capacities to arouse spectators at the moment of as well as in the minutes, days, weeks, or months following an audiovisual encounter. Less has been said about cinema's eroticized forms *outside* the body. What if the form of moving image and sound itself can be thought of as the referent for desire rather than its ancillary? What textual processes might make this possible? This chapter builds on as well as complicates discourses on cinematic eroticism by incorporating an overlooked historical source—the film program. I suggest that programming activates eroticism in formal ways that are dispersed and distributed across texts and time (i.e., across a film program).

What I am calling here the *erotic intertext*—a set of films programmed together to create an erotic cosmos—uniquely brings about orders of seeing, hearing, and sensation that a text alone might not elicit. In hurling films into a collision course we call a schedule or calendar, programming triggers a particular kind of semiotic-affective force between texts. As the Pacific Film Archive's (PFA) long-time head curator Edith Kramer has said, programming creates patterns, making things "reappear, [such as] fetishes or motifs."[1] I would contend that schedules are composed of patterns of editing, production design, performance style, and frame composition that establish noncorporeal terms for desire. These patterns can easily overshadow the performed simulated or unsimulated acts of penetration, kissing, touching, and so on.

What does the intertext tell us? What new amorous knowledges might it produce? Programming does peculiar things to texts, otherwise seen as coherent, unified, consistent. I will be arguing in this chapter and the remainder of this book that films programmed together act on one another, applying pressure to each other and collaborating in ways that defy their individual unity. In this sense, Laurent Jenny's comments on surrealist texts can be extended to the organization of a film program: "As attention is concentrated on the handling of forms and techniques their importance is exaggerated, the story becomes secondary and falls into tatters... The narrative framework becomes a 'pre-text' onto which all sorts of parasitic discourses are grafted. Intertextuality is then used as a weapon to disorganize the narrative order and destroy the realism of the account."[2] Following Jenny, I suggest that programming dismembers films, extracting formal devices, performance styles, climactic or heightened moments, and defining scenes from their narrative locations. These elements team up with one another, fragmenting and splintering texts into discrete parts that yoke, synthesize, and find tensions across a program. These aspects are altered by what films they come in contact with—as I will discuss in greater depth in the next chapter on double bills—producing vastly different meanings contingent on their arrangement.

Crucially, the erotics exhibited in the programmed intertext can look quite different from those arousing features in a single text. Consider, briefly, how a film such as Oshima Nagisa's *In the Realm of the Senses* produces a divergent erotic intertext when screened in a double feature with Bertolucci's *Last Tango in Paris* at San Francisco's Strand Theater in June 1980 than with Alain Resnais's *Hiroshima, Mon Amour* (1959) at another Bay Area cinema, the Camera One in San Jose, in December 1978.[3] These two diptychs elicit different arousal points in regard to themes of mortality, race, gender, nation, sadomasochism, and the kinds of sexual experimentation that divaricate from those categories. Film form does more here than aid the bodies on-screen to evoke highly erotic scenarios; form is what makes them erotic.

In *The Forms of the Affects*, Eugenie Brinkema argues that affect is locatable in the contours of form that take shape in the visual, acoustic, and narrative life of the moving image. Similarly, I propose that a sexual dynamism exists in the formal interstices of the programmed texts, as they collide and assemble new definitions of and associations with sex, rather than solely in the spectator watching the film. The film program—a cluster of homologous and clashing forms—can make cinematic style itself the eroticized object, not necessarily the body that it supposedly showcases.

The turn to form does not and cannot eclipse the body. Certainly the body houses form and, in the term's other ontologies, *is* a form.[4] But given the preoccupation in film theory with the meeting of the on-screen body with the spectatorial body, I want to temporarily put aside the body even in its formal conception for the rhetorical sake of making space for other forms, especially in the rich context of art house cinema (a term that, like *erotic*, is also plastic and ever-morphing, discussed in chapter 1). Too many studies have positioned cinematic style as an auxiliary enhancing the lure of the represented body, but what happens when the body is recast as form's auxiliary? What gets pushed to the foreground? We might see the body here as what Charles Sanders Peirce called a "degenerate index," that is, a subordinated signifier that orients a person toward a proximate subject that takes focus (a pointing finger or weathercock, for example).[5] The eroticized body points to the contiguous elements that then, through their programmed repetition themselves, become the sources of "degenerate" erotic delight.

In these examples as well as the others I will more closely read in this chapter, desire gets mapped onto filmic style and sensibility; programs' arousing capacities cannot be reduced to the presence or encoding of an eroticized body or sex act on-screen. Instead, homomorphic patterns of editing, production design, performance style, and frame composition emerge out of the intertext, establishing noncorporeal terms for desire. The on-screen eroticized body—nude, engaged in a sex act, encoded with sexual innuendo and subtext (such as in Production Code–era films)—is deprioritized, sometimes displaced altogether, as the potential site of spectatorial cathexis.

In the pages that follow, I will take a closer look at programming's abilities to agglutinate stylistic patterns across multiple texts, departing from the theoretical frameworks of mimesis and affect that tend to dominate discussions of cinematic eroticism. I will provide examples of audiovisual elements that can be assembled across a program, consigning the body to one element among many that moving images offer. I begin with a double bill of canonical art house hits (at the time), *Performance* and *The Devils*, that together merge instances of erotic feminist laughter to jointly produce an acoustic form of simultaneous jouissance and resistance. The second half of the chapter considers my central case study. Using the December 1978 through February 1979 calendar of the Nuart Theatre, then a repertory house (now mostly a first-run cinema) located in West Los Angeles, I propose three new categories for erotic intertexts that are inspired by the formal traits of these constellated art house and repertory films: (1) editing's erotic thrust, (2) cinematic spaces of debauchery, and (3) duration and stasis in BDSM. Although the intertextual organization of the films takes analytical precedence, I take into account the theater's location, audience demographics, relation to other local theaters, and general exhibition style in my taxonomy and analyses. Through this selective typology, I do not seek to exhaust the many erotic intertextual forms that cinema can produce. Rather, the goal is to begin to expand the terms of what aspects of the cinema we might find sexually arousing.

It Starts with a Laugh

Film curating makes moments of transgression and deviance more possible because of its ability to establish intertextual dialogue and patterns for new ways to desire. Part of my argument in chapter 2 was about how programmers of the 1970s and 1980s functioned as lay sexologists-cum-sociologists by making legible (sometimes ad hoc) classes of deviance that trouble usual boundaries and structures of sexual and gender identities. Operating similarly here, programmers—whether intentionally or unintentionally—can produce deviant erotic categories that spectators then make use of, again, in a deviant fashion that might undermine textual coherence or corporeal emphasis on desire.

The Elgin Theater's programming of a double bill of *Performance* (dir. Donald Cammell and Nicolas Roeg, 1970) and *The Devils* is one such occasion in which constellating erotic forms coalesced into a provisional genre. An art house repertory cinema sitting on the corner of 8th Avenue and 19th Street in a pre-gentrified Chelsea, New York, the Elgin played *Performance* and *The Devils* for repeated screenings every day for a striking five days in January 1973. Both films fit congruently together in rotation in that they share a general scorn for sexual repression—*Performance* by envisioning a drug- and rock-induced sex den of hedonistic remove, and *The Devils* by showing the hysterical violence that ensues in a medieval provincial state of ecclesiastical oppression. Both Warner releases (thus likely packaged together by the distributor) and united under a broad banner of anti-repression politics, these two films also feature intriguing visual and acoustic moments that resonate with one another: they are conjoined by the modality of erotic feminist laughter.

The Devils tells the real-life story of a seventeenth-century priest, Urbain Grandier, who was burned at the stake after being convicted of witchcraft by nuns. Vanessa Redgrave plays Jeanne des Anges, the humpback mother superior of a convent who is irresistibly and torturously infatuated with Grandier. Fast forwarding three hundred or so years in the double bill, *Performance* is about a gangster named Chas (James Fox) who is on the run for shooting a man. Eccentric, androgynous rocker Turner (Mick Jagger) and his housemate Pherber (Anita Pallenberg) take Chas into their London flat after he poses as a friend. While hiding, Chas undergoes multiple outward transformations, first to disguise himself from his enemies, and then more playfully, while in a psychedelic state Pherber induces.

There are several instances of laughter—some erotic and some not—in these films, but there is a scene in each film that is most illustrative of the form of erotic laughter. In *Performance*, Chas and Pherber, high and horny, find themselves naked rolling around in bed (fig. 3.1). Chas, at this point having undergone his psychedelic ego transformation, wears a long-haired wig and makeup. Straddling Chas, Pherber asks if he's ever been in touch with his femininity. She holds a mirror to his chest, reflecting one of her breasts to make him appear as if he is part female. Chas denies such an insinuation and yells "I'm normal!" to which Pherber lets out a piercing laugh, mocking Chas and the model of machismo to which he clings.

Sister Jeanne's laughter—alternating between maniacal, mocking, and erotic—fills the soundscape in *The Devils*, so much so that today she might be diagnosed with Pseudobulbar affect, a disorder characterized by a person laughing at arbitrary or inappropriate moments (fig. 3.2). Her laughter often reads as disturbed, but importantly only around sexual matters, such as when she scolds the nuns for lusting after Father Grandier, or when she accuses a prospective member—Grandier's lover—of being a whore. Jeanne's laugh also brushes up against the erotic later in the film, taking the form of a cackle when she officially accuses Grandier of being an incubus who seduced her during slumber. Blurting out the word *cock*, Jeanne laughs sharply, like a child when they are forced to say a prohibited word. Arguably Jeanne's most erotic scene takes place around the film's midpoint. Upon writing a letter to Grandier, Jeanne is thrown into a horny frenzy, masturbating frantically. Her ecstatic trills ring through the convent's passages. Her

3.1 Anita Pallenberg and James Fox play with gender transposition in *Performance* (dir. Donald Cammell and Nicolas Roeg, 1970).

sounds of arousal resemble a tickling laughter—spurts of pleasure—that spread across her moans.

Based on these descriptions, how is laughter erotic? Textually speaking, resonant laughter in these scenes takes place in the context of expressly sexual acts—straddling and masturbating. More broadly, laughter bears many resemblances to orgasm. Both offer the body a release that is at once consciously incited yet unfolds involuntarily. Nina K. Martin frames both as "excessive bodily responses," borrowing (and expanding) the terms of Linda Williams's conception of body genres. Drawing also from theories of sex and humor, Martin underscores that orgasm and laughter "share both the building of tension and the body convulsed," leading to a "form of defenselessness and physical vulnerability."[6] At the risk of stating the obvious, I would add that the mouth also plays a central function in the production of both laugh and orgasm. Acoustic vibrations emanating from the mouth communicate to another (or others) that an uncontainable pleasure has been reached, a climax of either humor or arousal (or both) that cannot be muted.[7]

Feminist media scholars B. Ruby Rich, Kathleen Rowe Karlyn, Anca Parvulescu, and Maggie Hennefeld have picked up on the power of feminist laughter, an idea that can be attributed to French feminist theorist

3.2 Vanessa Redgrave as the Medusan Sister Jeanne in Ken Russell's *The Devils* (1971).

Hélène Cixous.[8] Most notable is her manifesto on women's writing and voice, "The Laugh of Medusa," which has become foundational to feminist theory. Hennefeld insightfully observes a tension in the famous essay between "anti-symbolic laughter and analysis-defiling hysteria" that is key to understanding Cixous's subversion of patriarchal legacies of knowledge and power. Hennefeld writes that the productive clash of laughter and hysteria "broaches the threshold of jouissance—endless enjoyment for its own sake. Without the other's libidinal recognition, there is no limit to where enjoyment can go, so it intensifies beyond pleasure to anxiety, violence, mortal death throes, and so forth."[9] Cixous's laugh is one of annihilation, the laughing Medusa a gleeful Shiva, destroying to re-create.

We might think of Cixous's feminist laughter, existing on the "threshold of jouissance," as offering a funny twist on Bataille's erotic thesis. Bataille frames the orgasm as a moment of maximized pleasure in which life swells, but, paradoxically, this pleasure overwhelms the body and exceeds life, pushing one close to death. Contra Bataille, Cixous's feminist laughter, in Parvulescu's as well as Hennefeld's readings, does not threaten the laugher's body, but instead threatens the superego, the superstructure, the maintenance of social life—in this case, the patriarchal order that demands of women discipline, docility, and, for Cixous, silence. This is precisely why Cixous reclaims the figure of the witch, a heretic who later, with the arrival of modernity, becomes the psychological and medical problem of the hysteric. (Consider, for instance, Freud's patient "Dora," whom he failed to cure.) The witch and hysteric both openly flout, if not taunt, prohibitive institutions of religion and science and their institutional efforts to eradicate the threat that such feminine unruliness poses to the social order they impose. In a sense, Jeanne in *The Devils* resembles this witch-turned-hysteric, metonymic, perhaps, for the film's interest in France's transitional early modern period (dramatized in the film as a power struggle between the monarchy and Catholic church).

The Elgin's double bill of *The Devils* and *Performance* and Cixous's "The Laugh of Medusa" nearly coincide in the mid-1970s around the arguable peak of the women's liberation movement, an intersection perhaps not lost on theater attendees of the time. The theater's former programmers told Mubi's podcast on the Elgin that the cinema's owner and head programmer Ben Barenholtz (like Amos Vogel, also a European Jewish émigré who fled the Nazis) slanted his selections toward a "young hipster target demo-[graphic]." Leveraging its hip baby boomer audience, the Elgin turned the already existing phenomenon of the midnight screening into a cultural event—a cult gathering for nocturnal outsiders and weirdos—first with *El Topo* (Alejandro Jodorowsky, 1970) and later *Pink Flamingos*.[10] In this exhibition environment and cultural moment in New York City—the epicenter of social movements at the time—filmgoers expanded their consciousness by way of a range of media (which included art films) and controlled substances (such as marijuana and LSD) in the company of other spectators.[11]

Without attributing to these films a feminist intentionality akin to Cixous's writing, we can note that these filmgoers witnessed in one sitting films that enunciate shifting attitudes about women's identities and desires as they converged with sexual liberation. *The Devils* and *Performance* are not texts with clear feminist messages in their entirety, but nestled in them are brief performative gestures that align with second-wave feminism's concerns about women's bodies, sexual agency, and the history of their pathologizing. The laugh, a fleeting detail or character tic, is used in these films to signify renunciations of the old order in which heterosexual men determined the conditions for female sexuality.

In keeping with this liberation ethos, Pherber's and Jeanne's Medusan laughs directly undermine masculinist heterosexuality, mocking institutions with which the characters are at odds. Pherber's reaction is in keeping with a countercultural sexual ideal of free love, whereas Jeanne's laughter defies the compulsory physical confinement and regimentation that mandates any libidinal energy be quelled, or at least redirected in devotion to Christ. Their laughs, which channel pleasure and mockery simultaneously, interrupt the flows of male supremacy that structure the films' narratives.

When Jeanne is questioned by a priest about her possession, she quite pointedly interrupts him with a sinister laugh. In *Performance*, Pherber's laugh initiates a jump cut from a medium shot of the two lovers in bed to a close-up of Anita Pallenberg's face as she releases her hysterical laugh with her mouth open wide. In a shot that might in pornography translate to supposed evidence of the women's orgasm or, in a romantic comedy, signify a whimsical or charming response affirming successful and virile manhood, the laugh here threatens heterosexual masculinity—itself but another "performance" yet this time taking place in the bedroom. Chas's sexual security in his masculinity is precisely the thing that Pherber (along with her androgynous roommate) seeks to dismantle. Jeanne's and Pherber's laughs, their stakes for sexual freedom centuries and, in many ways, worlds apart, penetrate the repressive force of male-directed action that propels the films' narrative trajectories.

Laughter, as the bromide goes, is contagious and infectious. But is laughter's mimetic disposition an appropriate way to frame the dramatic action and relation of this intertext to a posited historical spectator? Perhaps corroborating recognition, identification or vicariousness, which all necessitate the meeting of the on-screen body and spectatorial body, are of less significance here. Paramount here is that laughter materializes as a haptic erotic form in and of itself that adds aural textures to *as well as exceeds* the baroque visual style of both films. These acute aural registers gel with the drug-induced editing style of *Performance* and the carnivalesque set design (by a young Derek Jarman!) and character blocking of *The Devils*, at the same time that they nearly break from the dieges. It is as if in laughter's piercing peaks in pitch the films themselves are in the throes of a jouissance that helps tip the diegetic worlds off their axes.

Further, the laugh has its source in the on-screen body only to an extent. In its annihilative authority, the hysterical laugh escalates to a position in which its meaning is isolated as an aural form unto itself, a metaphoric punch that outsizes the body from which it emanates.[12] Sound studies generally holds that a voice that comes from an on-screen bodily presence has an unambiguous material source and diegetic status. This claim, however, loses its ontological grip when there is more than one object under consideration, when the text becomes the intertext, by which the sound becomes loosened and unmoored from its source—the body and even the text. Laughter, in its nonlinguistic signification, disperses across the program, reverberating into other films, and turning it into a symbol of its own excess. The laugh thus does not belong to Pherber's or Jeanne's body; it is women's laughter, that Medusan, "analysis-defiling," unbridled, mocking, and potentially threatening guffaw titillated by its undoing of the sexist social hierarchy.

The masturbation scene in *The Devils* emblematizes laughter's programmatic traversal. Jeanne's body remains obstructed as she laugh-moans, the viewer offered a glimpse of her bare leg in a shot that visually only suggests she is stimulating herself. In lieu of a shot of Jeanne, the audience is offered a clear close-up view of the nun who is watching and listening to her, mouth quivering, that then leads to outright laughter in her own queer expression of hysterical titillation. The voyeuristic nun's laughter grows sadistically as Jeanne, post masturbation, beats herself for having sinned by way of lust and masturbation. Rather than depend on the visual composition of the actor's body, the laugh as the erotic referent belongs to and travels outside of the woman's on-screen body, a swelling jouissance of destruction that overwhelms the laws of on-screen bodily signification. The laugh, between madness and reason, on-screen body and acousmatic space, thus grants the audience an opportunity to take in an erotic feminist pleasure akin to that which Cixous describes, and it does so by casting some doubt on the ideal of the indexed haptic on-screen body. In this sense, programming does not morph the erotic into an abstraction even as the intertext challenges us to rethink the transparency of the erotic as inscribed on or dwelling in the body; rather eros is still very much bound to form—the material and legible existence of form—and form here is unavoidably yoked to the politics of gender.

Reverberating together in a chorus of sensuous disdain, laughter in these texts amplifies beyond the double bill by way of programming's diachronic extension, constituting almost a mini genre. The Elgin, the theater that showed *The Devils* and *Performance*, three months later, in the week of April 5, would screen another two films that further echoed women's defiant laughter, *The Killing of Sister George* and *Pink Flamingos*. Divine's signature maniacal laugh became iconic in *Pink Flamingos* (among other John Waters films), as she proclaimed "Filth are my politics!" (Recall the Elgin was also the theater that put *Pink Flamingos* on the map as a midnight movie sensation.) George's laughter in the opening to *The Killing of Sister George* has a more overly erotic dimension to it than Divine's in *Pink Flamingos*. George, becoming inebriated after receiving news about her termination, jumps in a cab with two stunned nuns (yes, more nuns!). She then flirtatiously puts her arms around the nuns and lets out a drunken laugh of delighted disregard for the veil. George's queer rejection of the closeted performance of heterosexuality, as well as the institutions that seek to protect it, is encapsulated by her laugh, a howl banding together with other laughs of feminist spite. This formal repetition is a programmatic realization of one of Parvalescu's terrific insights: in thinking alongside Teresa de Lauretis and Cixous, she observes, "We will come face to face with Medusa when we have learned to hear *echoes* of her laughter." Medusa's transmission here percolates through and proliferates in various forms and media to exert a lasting feminist force.

These instances of laughter are brief, fleeting, and seemingly insignificant in the larger scheme of an individual film, but when made proximate to one another by way of curation, these fleeting moments accrue stylistic and cultural significance. The coherence of the individual film is weakened in the move from text to intertext, and what is deemed erotic becomes more pliable and unpredictable. A text becomes an assembly of pieces that can be rearranged to produce wild intertextual classifications. The case, then, of the Elgin's double bill of *Performance* and *The Devils* demonstrates that by way of textual fragmentation, if not atomization, programming during this period established new erotic categories and even perhaps sensoria. The laugh—a puncturing, vibrating spasm of jouissance—is an example of one erotic intertextual form made possible by curation.

By coursing outside representational questions of bodies or even sexual acts, attending to form might lead to richer interpretations, concepts, and language for eroticism distinct from the ones based in individual reception or experience. Form can take on a life of its own, communicating to us the expanse of desires that exist in the world via the moving image and mediated sound's unique capacities. Intertextually speaking, laughter, in this case, travels from bodies through a series of texts, shifting in the specifics of its signification, and crescendoing into a chorus of tickling rage and pleasure. By historicizing film programming, we can see just how much Medusa's spirit was alive and well in 1970s art cinema, her delirious laughter resounding through the halls of repertory theaters across the country, if not the world, with no end in sight.

From Mimesis to Form

At the time of this writing, it has become difficult to think arousal and the moving image beyond theories of mimesis and affect. The collective yet diachronic intervention of scholars such as Laura Marks, Vivian Sobchack, Linda Williams, Ara Osterweil, Jennifer Barker, and Steven Shaviro has aimed to trouble any sense of mastery or command that exists within the viewing subject or viewed object, instead opting for what Sobchack might call "inter-objective" dynamics of the material viewing body to the material screen body.[13] Contributions to and redefinitions of theories of mimesis and affect effectively, and often lyrically, lend nuance to how we position sensory perception in the face of monolithic and reductive notions of spectatorship recycled in a range of discourses, from apparatus theory to pro-censorship arguments. For instance, according to Williams (via Miriam Hansen and Walter Benjamin), films gushing with erotic energy become the raw material for libidinal exploration rather than sources to be merely mimicked.[14] However, while this writing has deepened our lexicon for and understanding of mimetic processes, it tends to fall back on the primacy of the represented body and its relation to the theorist's own subjective body in discussions of the erotic. As an example, note the first-person positioning in Shaviro's important book, *The Cinematic Body*: "Cinema allows me and forces me to see what I cannot assimilate or grasp. It assaults the eye and ear, it touches and it wounds. It foregrounds the body, apart from the comforting representations that I use to keep it at a distance. This touch, this contact, is excessive: it threatens my very sense of self. Is my body ever truly 'my own'? I am my body, and for that very reason it resists my intelligence, I am unable to possess it."[15] Writing about the distinct experience of spectatorial masochism, Shaviro is representative of a subjective mode of theorizing about cinema and affect in which the body within the moving image acts on the spectatorial body in layered, even paradoxical, ways. This method and reading practice leads to confession-like moments in which the author pinpoints their own corporeal vulnerability and uses it as both evidence and case study.

Eugenie Brinkema is an especially enjoyable cantankerous reader of this body of work on affect. For her, such theorization results in "mild rhetorical force of summary and paraphrase, intoned synonyms, and thematic generalizations" that belie its own solipsism.[16] Brinkema accuses affect theory of a limited methodological range and "thematic generalizations," neglecting "textual particularities" and the "very ideological, aesthetic, and theoretical problems it claimed to confront."[17] Insisting instead on the "formal dimension of affect," Brinkema charts what she calls a "radical formalism" that would account for the kind of specificity and complexity that opens up a text's wild semiotic "fecundities."[18] Brinkema's method for close reading wedges open a hermeneutic expanse untethered to spectators' "real world" desires.[19]

Erotic intertextuality is a process that allows the interactions of forms to speak absent of full corporeal substantiation. Where I diverge from Brinkema is in our projects; Brinkema is explicitly working from a philosophical tradition that distances her from the kinds of ideological and cultural questions that compel my work. (She gets worryingly close to suggesting that reading form for politics "instrumentalizes" form.[20]) Although I pursue Brinkema's call for textual (or, in my case, intertextual) specificity, I do not position my thinking as a "de-contribution to spectatorship studies, an attempt to dethrone the subject and the spectator" altogether.[21] I find it impossible to think of programming and exhibition without theorizing historical modes of spectatorship and thus film culture at large. Programming provides a speculative affective entrance into historical spectatorship without resorting to or falling back on subjective testimony. To restate this in Brinkema's terms, programs contain affects in their forms, but differently; these forms are historically situated and have implications for how bodies in those theaters were guided through their viewing experiences.

Erotic Forms

In regard to sexuality and film, pornography tends to be treated as the mimetic genre par excellence because the viewing body is aroused and activated to states commensurate with on-screen scenes of desire and lust. Linda Williams famously identified pornography as a "body genre," that, along with melodrama and horror, narrows, if not collapses, the affective space between viewer and screen. Because of their visceral impact, body genres produce material, mimetic effects: in melodrama, the viewer will cry; in horror, the viewer will scream; and in porn, the viewer will cum, all at the sight of abject fluids (i.e., tears, blood, or cum, respectively).[22] In fact, a film's success rests on this direct mimetic response. Porn especially serves an ancillary function, aiding someone to "get off," "get hard," or "get wet," either in the act of watching or as they might recall watching in a future moment (alone or with company).

By and large, porn's raison d'être is to expose the on-screen body, even in milder soft-core versions that emphasize their seductive storylines over carnal visibility. The "art film," although it often uses its genre identity to get away with or sneak in risqué content, operates on a different logic vis-à-vis the body. More often than with pornography, prurience is grafted onto its stylistic qualities, reconfiguring how we should discuss desiring at the cinema. Repertory and art houses certainly showed hard- and soft-core (artful) porn like *Boys in the Sand* (dir. Wakefield Poole, 1971), *In the Realm of the Senses*, Radley Metzger's and Russ Meyer's films, but generally the films shown in these spaces stitched eroticism into their visual and narrative economies much more obliquely, by way of layered character motivation, eyeline matches or looking relations, open-ended or ambiguous narration, and so on. Examples of this range from the lowbrow to high tiers of the taste strata—from Russ Meyer's *Beyond the Valley of the Dolls* to Pier Paolo Pasolini's *Teorema* (1968) or Liliana Cavani's *The Night Porter*. Arousal, when removed from the telos of orgasm—the "money shot" in filmic terms—adheres to different aesthetic and temporal principles.[23] These differing principles call for a divergent model of formal eroticism to consider the many aspects of style that also account for art cinema's prestige.

Not just anything can be erotic; there must be some kind of proximity of the eroticized form to represented, embodied, or clearly repressed sexuality or sensuality. By "erotic," I mean quite plainly content and form that is meant to or has the capacity to arouse spectators. This corporeal stirring need not be solely genital in nature, as Freud demonstrated with his theories of polymorphous perversion. It can emerge from other areas of the body. BDSM provides an excellent illustration because many of its practices displace normative modes of sexual gratification onto other parts of the body or fetishistic accouterments and also make use of setting, lighting, and décor. These facets all surround or cloak the body; they all establish the scene of eroticism beyond reproductive and genital-based contact. Similarly, film form establishes aesthetics of mood, environment, atmosphere, rhythm, and duration that, in collaboration, might even subordinate the on-screen body.

Consider, for instance, the possibility that a gay-identified cisgender male, with no direct sexual attraction to women or heterosexual sex, could become aroused or excited witnessing the straight BDSM play in *Maîtresse* because of the design of the dominatrix's dungeon, or the lesbian BDSM in *Seduction: The Cruel Woman* (dir. Elfi Mikesch and Monika Treut, 1985) through Mechthild Grossmann's playful yet stern performance style as the film's dominatrix. The on-screen body is, of course, part of these erotic aspects, but arousal is not predicated on it.[24]

This noncorporeal, de-personalized erotic allure of form provides the groundwork for all kinds of deviant implications. For starters, in the context of exhibition, it raises the question: To what extent is the practice of cinephilia also that of paraphilia? *Paraphilia*, as I explained in the previous chapter, is a sexual fetish or desire that is classified as "strange" or "abnormal," outside of normative genital interaction between two adult partners. Paraphilia does not elude sexual and gender identities, but it does complicate their centrality and stability in the constitution of erotic desire. There might be a temptation to further diagnose eroticized form as a kind of animism or "objectophilia" in which the humans on-screen become sexually incidental. I want to avoid making such a wholesale (and rather literal) claim. Less reductive, I am proposing that erotic intertextual forms open up paraphilic avenues that elude correspondences between spectatorial identities and those belonging to the characters and/or actors on-screen, making room for oblique lines of desire and arousal. Erotic intertextuality does not fully negate those subjectivities represented on-screen or present in the audience, but it might compromise entrenched and divided subject positions supposedly qualifying what is erotic and for whom.

Though programming does not always entail the meeting of homologous objects (for example, it can also have a more dialectical or oppositional pattern, or be more open-ended), the erotic intertext functions in part through a pattern of repetition, of intellectual and somatic semiosis, that emerges from the calendar's iterative assembly. Interestingly, signification, fetishization, desire, and genre all congeal around a process of repetition that is fitting to the programmatic. Repetition, psychoanalysis tells us, is how we come into our sexuality (even if supposedly by way of loss or lack); it is how we form attachments; and importantly, it is how perversion, fetishes, and desire at large get folded into the ego.[25] Genre, like desire, is constructed through repetition, leveraging familiar codes of style to produce a body of interrelated work. Programs operate in a similar vein, disparate films finding parallel techniques in performance, framing, design, and rhythm that constitute even transient genres, smaller and more idiosyncratic than even a cycle. The film program also points spectators toward erotic features, and then repeats them in other objects, leading to a process of signification.[26] The iterative structures of semiosis, genre, and desire work together to yield an erotic intertext, an accretion of fetishistic forms that become legible through processes of recursivity.

Nuart 1978/1979: A Case Study in Erotic Intertextuality

The Nuart Theatre is a single-screen cinema built in 1929, located in West Los Angeles on the corner of Santa Monica Boulevard and Sawtelle Boulevard, feet from the 405 highway. In 1974, Steve Gilula purchased the Nuart as part of what would become the Landmark Theaters, now the largest art house chain in the United States. The Nuart is today primarily a first-run cinema, showing new releases with midnight screenings and occasional screenings of remastered or rereleased prints and Digital Cinema Packages. As a repertory house, the Nuart was unlike most other revival theaters in that it did not do continuous performances of films throughout the day, which meant it did not rotate films or double bills on a back-to-back schedule to maximize profits, nor did it have regular matinees. The theater held evening screenings only, surely a sign of a younger, "cooler" patronage.

In order to understand its history, I interviewed Mark Valen, the Nuart's current head programmer and its manager during the 1970s. Valen is the theater's unofficial historian, living and breathing its exhibition and curatorial history. According to Valen, who managed the Nuart from 1973 to 1977 (and later headed programming from 1997 to 2023), the theater at the time catered to mostly University of California, Los Angeles (UCLA) students and gay men, no doubt due to the cinema's proximity to UCLA's campus and LA's gay neighborhood, West Hollywood, both less than five miles away. (Curiously, West Hollywood proper had no repertory cinemas, and doesn't to this day.) Keenly aware of its patronage, the Nuart's programming team, led by Kim Jorgensen, tended toward the more outlandish and eccentric side of the art house canon of the time. It was at this intersection of queer and youth taste that the Nuart found a sweet spot, garnering a reputation for its rather eclectic, outré offerings.[27] Catering to its audience, the Nuart hosted the West Coast premiere of John Waters's *Pink Flamingos*. The film would go on to play at the theater weekly for nearly a decade.[28]

The Nuart was among a community of repertory theaters and screening series (e.g., LACMA's film program) and festivals (e.g., the Los Angeles Film Exposition, or "Filmex") that came and went through the years.[29] Among the repertory houses was the Encore, located across the street from Paramount Studios on the east side of Los Angeles, known for exhibiting the classics. The Silent Movie Theater, true to its name, showed only silent films to the period's aficionados. Compared to these other venues, the Nuart's curatorial style stuck out as hip, even baroque, in its heterogeneity and promiscuity.

The nearby Fox Venice and the Nuart had the most overlap in their programming. In fact, Valen recalls the Fox Venice accused the Nuart of repeatedly copying their programming. The Fox Venice had a more lighthearted (if not silly) approach. The *Los Angeles Times* noted in a profile of local repertory cinemas, "the theater's recorded messages are filled with outrageous puns, funny one-liners and assortment of news."[30] Unlike the Nuart, which was strictly used for screenings, the Fox Venice hosted concerts and other community events. Co-owner Rol Murrow told the *Los Angeles Times* that the Fox "wanted to be a forum, not be crassly commercial and avoid exploitation material unless it was in the spirit of high camp."[31] Jorgensen marketed the Nuart with a similar approach, showing "alternative" films; Jorgensen told the *LA Times*, "We take chances [and] experiment more." Both theaters' programming aligned in a way that stood out against many of the other revival houses, whose curatorial dispositions might be a bit more conservative or focused.

The years that Valen managed the theater from 1973 to 1977, the Nuart had a devoted crowd of regular patrons who would attend the cinema's double features on a weekly basis. The frequency of recurring attendance, mixed with the Nuart's eclectic menu, makes the Nuart a perfect historical case study for intertextual analysis. Further, Valen spoke of a rather canny audience in attendance, students of the 1970s and 1980s sharply aware of, influenced by, and/or involved in feminist, LGBT, Black, Third World, indigenous, anti-war, and other political movements of the time. Gay men from West Hollywood, some of whom were surely also part of liberationist struggles, and UCLA students had overlap in their tastes, the programming indicates, from tawdry sexploitation (some with direct LGBT themes) to classic Hollywood films, starring screen divas such as Marilyn Monroe, Liza Minnelli, and Josephine Baker.[32] These affinities in taste might be distilled down to an orientation toward a history of pushing the envelope of bourgeois respectability.

Over the course of two months, I watched sixteen double bills and one triple bill from the Nuart's December 1978 to February 1979 winter calendar, trying to simulate to the best of my abilities what it would have been like to have watched the calendar's deviant films in the order in which they were exhibited (fig. 3.3). Table 3.1 contains my full watch list, chosen from a packed calendar profuse with socially deviant themes and/or queer appeal.

On the one hand, the winter calendar brims with deviant and erotic content. I chose the calendar because the films depict homosexuality or garner gay and lesbian audiences (e.g., a Marlon Brando retrospective, *Bilitis*, *Therese and Isabelle*, *Outrageous!*, *A Star Is Born*, and *Auntie Mame*) neighbor films that depict BDSM (*Salon Kitty*, *The Night Porter*, and *Maîtresse*), sex work (*Cathy Tippel*, *Exhibition*), bi- and pansexuality (*Satyricon* and *Sunday Bloody Sunday*). On the other hand, the Nuart is by no

3.1 Nuart calendar selections, December 1978–February 1979

Fri **December 29**	*Salon Kitty* Tinto Brass, 1976	*The Night Porter* Liliana Cavani, 1974
Tues **January 2**	*Keetje Tippel* Paul Verhoeven, 1975	*Women In Love* Ken Russell, 1969
Fri **January 5**	*Satyricon* Federico Fellini, 1969	*Roma* Federico Fellini, 1972
Wed **January 10**	*Exhibition* Jean-François Davy, 1975	*A Labor of Love* Robert Flaxman and Daniel Goldman, 1976
Wed **January 17**	*A Streetcar Named Desire* Elia Kazan, 1951	*The Men* Fred Zinnemann, 1950
Fri **January 19**	*Andy Warhol's L'Amour* Paul Morrissey and Andy Warhol, 1973	*Bad* Jed Johnson, 1977
Mon **January 22**	*Outrageous* Richard Benner, 1977	*Sunday, Bloody Sunday* John Schlesinger, 1971
Tues **January 23**	*Sebastiane* Derek Jarman and Paul Humfress, 1976	*Maîtresse* Barbet Schroeder, 1975
Wed **January 24**	*Julius Caesar* Joseph L. Mankiewicz, 1953	*Mutiny on the Bounty* Lewis Milestone and Carol Reed, 1962
Thurs **January 25**	*A Star Is Born* George Cukor, 1954	*Auntie Mame* Morton DaCosta, 1958

continued

3.1 Nuart calendar selections, December 1978–February 1979 (*continued*)

Sat January 27 TRIPLE BILL	*Beyond the Valley of the Dolls* Russ Meyer, 1970	*Faster, Pussycat! Kill! Kill! / Supervixens* Russ Meyer, 1965 / 1975
Mon January 29	*Salò, or the 120 Days of Sodom* Pier Paolo Pasolini, 1975	*The Decameron* Pier Paolo Pasolini, 1971
Wed January 31	*Reflections in a Golden Eye* John Huston, 1967	*The Fugitive Kind* Sidney Lumet, 1960
Tues February 6	*A Slave of Love* Nikita Mikhalkov, 1976	*The Conformist* Bernardo Bertolucci, 1970
Wed February 7	*Last Tango in Paris* Bernardo Bertolucci, 1972	*Burn!* Gillo Pontecorvo, 1969
Wed February 14	*On the Waterfront* Elia Kazan, 1954	*The Wild One* Laslo Benedek, 1953
Thurs February 22	*Bilitis* David Hamilton, 1977	*Therese and Isabelle* Radley Metzger, 1968

means exceptional or unusual in its volume of deviant content. The Nuart's calendar typifies regular, even boilerplate, urban programming at revival houses across the country (and in such places as Canada, Japan, and parts of Western Europe) at this time (fig. 3.3).[33] Even the Marlon Brando retrospective was common; such series devoted to classical Hollywood queer icons were standard programming at repertory theaters, art house cinemas, and film festivals. This program is therefore ordinary by criteria of its time while extraordinary against the backdrop of today's queer politics and art house sensibilities. Though I could have chosen from dozens of programs

3.3 Nuart calendar, December 1978–February 1979, standard but still delicious fare.

a representative of the deviant fare exhibited in this era, I chose to analyze this calendar for its particular range, and the suggestive ways it clusters films into thematized double bills.

In what follows, I codify my viewing experience of the particularly deviant erotic content that was shown. In my viewing, a programmatic schema began to emerge—an intertextual organization that coalesced around questions of erotic form. The categories of scale, texture, and duration that surfaced, like those expounded upon in chapter 2, are meant to be experimental, provisional, and playful propositions, illustrations of the intertextual agglutination programming proffers and invitations to augment the list of potential classes of erotic form.

- **Category 1: The Frenzy, Revisited**

In the book's introduction, I alluded to director Ken Russell's repertoire in terms of its relation to religious, scientific, and pseudo-scientific discourses of sexual depravity. These films were incredibly popular in art house and repertory cinemas of the 1970s and 1980s, even though Russell's work has since been marginalized in the art house canon.[34] Russell's films from the late 1960s and early 1970s—*Women in Love*, *The Devils*, *The Music Lovers*, and *The Savage Messiah* (1972)—are spectacular indictments of sexual repression, replete with frenzied sequences of uninhibited libidinal release. Including Ken Russell's *Women in Love* in the same month as a Russ Meyer triple bill, the Nuart's winter calendar illuminates cinematic techniques that render the sensation of the orgasm as a frenzied state of disarray and disorientation.

Russell perhaps agreed to take up the adaptation of D. H. Lawrence's *Women in Love* about two sisters seeking companionship in 1910s England to reflect on the shifting mores of the 1960s England and United States.[35] Both Brangwen sisters, Gundrun and Ursula, begin cumbersome, even turbulent, relationships in which their sexual desires brush up against dictates of propriety foisted upon women of the time. To add to it, the sisters' love interests, Rupert and Gerald, are locked in a beyond-platonic attraction to each other that provides an underlying homoerotic tension throughout the film. When Gerald's sister and newlywed husband—a couple constantly kissing throughout the film, and thus serving as foils of sorts for the sisters' relationships—drown, the central characters go into a tailspin. Ursula and her love interest Rupert, witnessing the ordeal, go for a walk in the woods to discuss love and death. No longer able to resist one another, the two

3.4 Postcoital exhaustion and messiness in the wake of frenzied sex in Ken Russell's *Women in Love* (1969).

begin kissing and then drop to their knees into the dirty grass to consummate their relationship (fig. 3.4).

The sex scene is strikingly frenetic, featuring rapid jump cuts and shaky handheld camera techniques in a film that otherwise has a smooth tracking and framing pattern. As they roll around in the dirt, undressing themselves and one another, the camera almost struggles to stay on the two bodies enveloped in the rapture of coitus. Moving around in a frenzy, the camera itself gyrates, mimicking the pelvises of Ursula and Rupert in motion. The edits, quick and random, are not meant to just segment the bodies and coital act; the cuts themselves thrust and penetrate, turning the jump cut into an erotic form. This cinematographic and editing style is repeated two scenes later when the two men, Rupert and Gerald, wrestle naked in one of the film's most famous scenes. Ken Russell biographer Joesph Lanza acknowledges the similarities between the two scenes, yet holds them in juxtaposition: the aftermath of Ursula and Rupert's intercourse appears "flaccid and unsatisfying" compared to the sexier and more evocative (and more widely discussed) wrestling scene.[36] But the editing in particular tells a different story, one that compromises the identitarian and gendered hierarchy Lanza establishes. In the company of *Beyond the Valley of the Dolls*, the overcharged, spasmodic editing and cinematographic patterns are more indicative of the film's relationships to the late 1960s project of sexual liberation overall than of the particularities of sexual orientation.

This use of editing is quite a deviation from the way the cut is habitually articulated: as absence, ellipsis, gap, shift in time and space, a blink that can migrate us across a room or a galaxy. The eroticized edit is indifferent to the film's narrative economy, like the jump cuts in the New Wave films of Godard or early Oshima, only without a centrally modernist conceit. They are here erotic in their textured propulsion. Vivian Sobchack might attribute this to the "film's body."[37] Like the spectator, the film too feels, senses, expresses, behaves, desires, and moves. The film's body is not synonymous with or reducible to the representable on-screen body. Sobchack stresses that it is not even anthropomorphic.[38] Formally speaking, the film's body does not have a literal pelvis to thrust with, but it has the tools of visual and audio editing, camera movement, and shot composition at its fingertips in translating to screen coital movement and sensation.

We might see this "frenzy of the visible," to borrow Linda Williams's important Foucaldian concept, as a redirection of the "hard-core knowledge-pleasure" Williams locates in pornography. According to Williams, photographic and filmic technologies have consolidated "truths" about sexual pleasure by way of the recorded body, which becomes an anxious site for visualizing the orgasm as evidence of pleasure.[39] But what if the "frenzy" here, extracted from its hardcore location and repositioned within erotic art house cinema, does not seek to produce or encapsulate anxiety about supposed knowledges of erotic pleasure, but is the erotic pleasure itself? What if camera movement and editing together, as in the sex scene from *Women in Love*, unleash a visual frenzy that is untethered to the genital knowledge of the bodies on-screen? Such a frenzy thereby courses outside the realm of representation; it cannot evade appearing mediated (which, for Williams, porn and its reception can run the risk of) because its mode is mediation itself—the cinematic technique and form inextricable from the technology, resonant with corporeality yet isolatable from it.[40]

The Nuart calendar produces a knowledge of an erotic paradigm by way of intertextual practice. Though by no means suggesting direct influence, Russ Meyer's frenetic montages in films such as *Beyond the Valley of the Dolls* and *Supervixens* (in the latter case styled with disturbing violence) perform an analogous formal function as the spastic editing in *Women in Love*. *Beyond the Valley of the Dolls*, written by a young Roger Ebert, was Meyer's biggest commercial success. It tells the story of a girl rock group who move from their small town to Los Angeles with big dreams. One by one they fall prey to the big city's lascivious and greedy influences, which tear them apart.

The film culminates in a dizzying final act in which three of the lead characters end up at a mansion in the palisades owned by Ronnie "Z-man" Barzell, the film's dandy (revealed in the end to be trans) who has been lusting after the film's (mostly) straight hunk. Ronnie's mansion is a cross between an opium den and a medieval palace. It is a site of release and restraint—release because the characters are given a space to sexually explore, enabling the two lesbian characters to finally consummate their relationship, and restraint because Ronnie always controls his guests' experiences through psychological manipulation and mind-altering substances.[41] The film, like much of Meyer's oeuvre, showcases a version of sex busting at the limits of bodily experience. For Meyer, sex includes several restless dualities: transformative yet combustible, exciting yet depraved, liberating yet dangerous.

Toward the end, Ronnie and his three guests gather on the floor around a hookah table to consume drinks laced with what we learn to be the psychoactive drug peyote. The shots shorten and tighten in on their faces as the psychedelics set in. The gelled lighting mimics Technicolor greens, purples, and reds, drenching the characters' faces, while the music is a whirling symphony befitting a circus of clowns entering the ring. The group's deepening trip leads to growing caresses and kissing, building to the approaching orgy (fig. 3.5). The jump cuts accelerate the suspense of what's to come as well as simulate their drug trip for the viewer. The cuts are overexcited caresses themselves, frantically massaging and fondling the characters into seduction. Resonating with *Women in Love*, the edits suggest a reading of late 1960s sexual liberation that has become overripe and over-seasoned. Rather than a smooth transition to reclaiming a pent-up sexual freedom in the wake of the Cold War era, the scene's edits reveal a messier leap into bed, like an oversexed adolescent. The soothing sensuality and unmediated pleasure promised by sexual liberation transmogrifies into a blitz of drug-induced agitation, disorientation, and over-exhilaration, not unlike the frenetic editing in Ken Russell's sex scene in *Women in Love*.

I revisit *Beyond the Valley of the Dolls* and other Russ Meyer films in the next two chapters (first about carnivalesque double features and then queer "bad objects"), expanding on Meyer's ostensibly paradoxical views of sex, but here I want to focus on the editing styles of the sex scenes in *Beyond the Valley of the Dolls* and *Women in Love* to show how they reassign the category of the frenzied jump cut as an erotic form.[42] Further, these jump cuts lead to erotic forms that differ from other kinds of jump cuts in sequences or scenes that also blend sexuality and violence.

3.5 Drugs accelerate the libidinal drive in Russ Meyer's *Beyond the Valley of the Dolls* (1970).

As I have already indicated in my descriptions, there is something volatile, if not violent, within these erotic scenes. The fast cuts are thrusts—libidinal deliverance—and they are also heaving thrashes, caught in a fever-pitch rhythm that could prove destructive. That *Beyond the Valley of the Dolls* was programmed with *Supervixens* at the Nuart only seems to strengthen its sexualized violent finish. Critics deemed *Supervixens* among Russ Meyer's darkest and most humorless films, featuring scenes of violent death, such as a woman's graphic electrocution in a bathtub, and deeply uncomfortable suspense, such as when one female character is tied up with burning dynamite positioned inside her crotch. *Beyond the Valley of the Dolls* ends with Ronnie having a psychotic break and massacring all his guests. He is wrestled to the ground by the virtuous characters who have attempted to rescue their now deceased friends, but they are too late.

The muddy sex scene between Gundrun and Gerald in *Women in Love* is also bookended by quietus. The two find themselves alone in the forest in the first place as part of a search party looking for two lovers who have gone missing in the water. The sex scene ends with a cut to the drowned lovers washed ashore in an embrace that then transitions back, in a perfect match cut, to Gundrun and Gerald also entwined. These sequences resulting in demise return us to and literalize the Batallian understanding of eroticism—jouissance that exceeds the body's capacity for life and pushes it close to death. Leo Bersani describes this fatal threshold as a "self-shattering," by which lovers lose themselves in the radical self-negation of coitus.[43] The jump cuts, seen in death-drenched hindsight, then don't just thrust and thrash; they shatter in the name of reclaimed yet combustible pleasure.

This rapid editing technique—particularly mimicking thrusting and thrashing—harkens back to Alfred Hitchcock's horror classics *Psycho* (1960) and *The Birds* (1963). Disorienting jump cuts are used to heighten the violence during Janet Leigh's shower scene in *Psycho* and the final bird attack on Tippi Hedren in *The Birds*. The quick cuts that appear almost random are synthesized by framing techniques of varying angles and assorted close-ups on different parts of the body and the weapons themselves (the knife in *Psycho* and the beaks in *The Birds*) to amplify the horror. The assaultive edits slice, jab, and ultimately kill in scenes that have become routinely formalized in the slasher genre. That it is the female characters in particular that are brutalized in such formal detail is foundational to charges of Hitchcock's sadistic misogyny. Between the segmentation of Leigh's naked body in *Psycho* and Hedren's gasps in *The Birds*, which sound more like moans than anything resembling screams, montage subtends death and sexuality, uniting them under the sign of the woman's physical and aural body under assault.

The frenzied jump cut, undergirded by opposing drives toward pleasure and death, would seem to close the gap, even if only for a scene or two, between the body genres of horror and porn. Certainly Meyer and Russell and their editors are indebted to Hitchcock and his long-term editor, George Tomasini (and before that, Sergei Eisenstein, among other masters of the montage). Ken Russell's editor and collaborator on numerous films, Michael Bradsell, should share the credit here, deploying what Adam Powell calls a "staccato" jump-cut montage style.[44] Russ Meyer famously edited a good portion of his own films, at times working with different editors over the years.

Meyer's and Russell's works mark a departure in the history of this highly expressive editing style. This departure becomes legible via the very definition of a body genre, which works in service of both the on-screen and viewer's bodies. Mimesis activates when the two meet and form a sensorial bond. In porn, the nude body, and the acts they might perform, is the viewer's tie to the screen. *Beyond the Valley of the Dolls* and *Women in Love*, however, do not grant this pornographic visibility to the viewer; it does not purport to provide any "truth" about sex or orgasm or even just the body, as Linda Williams explains of hard-core porn specifically. The frenzied cuts need the bodies on-screen to make erotic sense, so they are not fully disembodied, but rather *obliquely* bodied. Corporeality is rendered an auxiliary component to the main attraction that is the form.

Like feminist erotic laughter, the frenzied jump cut rippled outward into the larger field of programming at the time. Even just staying with Meyer's and Russell's bodies of work, those UCLA students and gay men who frequented the Nuart and other local cinemas would have caught other films that deploy the same formal devices for the same reasons. Ken Russell uses the device to dramatic effect in *The Music Lovers* when the closeted Tchaikovsky tries to make love to his new wife, Nina, played by Glenda Jackson. The bouncy, turbulent train car within which the fraught and failed act is attempted provides diegetic reason for the shaky camera, but it also externalizes the couple's crescendoing anxieties about their sex life. Russ Meyer's *Cherry, Harry & Raquel!* (1969), made only one year before *Beyond the Valley of the Dolls*, begins with a long textual declaration against censorship that scrolls over a manic montage of street shots of iconic LA locations such as the Watts towers, the Cinerama dome, and LAX airport, intercut with bare-breasted women. The frenzied montages in the winter Nuart calendar thus reach into past and future screenings, enabling spectators to collect homologous forms through their viewing practices.

- **Category 2: Cinematic Spaces of Debauchery**

Cinema, from its inception, has been a site in which audiences could watch sinful acts, turning what was once sequestered to the private sphere into reproducible public fantasy and spectacle.[45] Shifting from the "cinema of attractions" to early Hollywood, displays of decadent, hedonistic acts became common among work by pioneers D. W. Griffith, Cecil B. DeMille, and Erich Von Stroheim, who masterfully wove compelling narratives with images of extravagant sexual display, rebuking carnal capitulation while profiting from its large-scale presentation. Film historians such as Parker Tyler and Foster Hirsch describe how pre-Code films such as *Intolerance* (dir. D. W. Griffith, 1916) and *Cabiria* (dir. Giovanni Pastrone, 1914) imagined the excesses of antiquity, bacchanals of bodies lounging and consuming platters of overflowing food, carafes of wine, and, of course, each other. Hirsch writes, "The faithless are traditionally associated with luxurious dissipation and they are typically observed in the banquet hall or the arena. The scenes of pagan revelry are overloaded, as in *Intolerance*; the frame is filled with swirling activity, with (in later films) splashes of reds and purples."[46] Tyler draws a direct genealogical line between films set against these ancient banquets and those that depict the "moral decay" of the roaring twenties. Von Stroheim's *The Merry Widow* (1925) and DeMille's *Manslaughter* (1930) contained orgies—both figurative and literal—of "frantic body-contortions and limb flinging and much hard liquor."[47] Sewn into cinema's DNA was an impulse toward the Dionysian pursuit of pleasure and self-indulgence, an impulse that the Motion Picture Production Code would repress for decades but clearly not fully defeat.

These excessive scenes of consumption could be described by the sybarites' acts—drinking, dancing, fucking—as much as by the filmic production of space that surrounds the performing bodies. The Nuart's printed winter calendar highlights this erotic use of scenic architecture, one that contemporaneous films inherited from the pre-Code era. The Nuart's programmed films marshaled style aspects of production and set design, and the camera's movement through the decorative space, to suggest scenic design itself can be an erotic object. Though not limited to them, the films *Salò, or the 120 Days of Sodom*, *The Conformist*, *Salon Kitty*, *The Night Porter*, *Satyricon*, and *A Streetcar Named Desire* (dir. Elia Kazan, 1951) make erotic use of production design, deploying aesthetic conventions of scale, proportion, angularity, perspective, and density.

Several deviant design motifs emerge within the intertextual schema of the December 1978 to February 1979 Nuart calendar: decaying, ruined buildings; stripped classical style and architecture; banquet halls and other large-scale interiors; sculpture and artwork styles of centuries past. Signifiers of opulence and riches in several of the films offer material reflections of libidinal overindulgence; signifiers of decay reflect a desire gone askew, an irrevocable loss of innocence better indulged than rectified.

Prominent within the above list of films is a theme of fascism and Nazism that cuts across texts including *Salò, or the 120 Days of Sodom*, *The Conformist*, *Salon Kitty*, and *The Night Porter*. Several explanations for this cycle of films exist. In postwar European cinema, a generation of filmmakers who came of age during or in the wake of WWII were drawn to fascism as the ultimate taboo, a transgressive symbol of a social system gone array. Susan Sontag was among the first to identify this trend, which she dubbed "fascinating fascism." These films presented "fascism as an amalgam of decadent images," Kriss Ravetto suggests, to create moral distance between the contemporary moment of their production and the atrocities of the past.[48]

Laura Frost submits a compelling explanation for the cycle's existence, one less damning of sexual appetites for what Marcus Stiglegger calls the *sadiconazista*, or "Nazi sadistic," genre and its Axis-powers relatives.[49] Frost observes that "heterosexuality founded on equality, respect, and nonviolence" was meant to reflect the democratic ideals of Allied nations. In these countries, then, outré sexual practices that did not align with this national imaginary, such as sadomasochism, became, in the popular imagination, associated with fascism (and later, in the McCarthy-era United States, communism), correlating them with "oppression and domination."[50] In a strangely or counterintuitively reparative extension of this argument, we might then see the subject matter of fascism in films such as *The Night Porter* and *Salon Kitty* as outlets to explore BDSM and other paraphilia that were (and still are) censored or repudiated in democratic political contexts that demand "palatable" representations of sexuality.[51]

The Nuart and a plethora of other revival houses at the time exploited this trend in art and exploitation cinema. On December 29, 1978, the Nuart played *The Night Porter* with *Salon Kitty* in a double bill. While *The Night Porter* tried to be taken seriously as an art film (a point still debated), *Salon Kitty* was clearly Nazi exploitation, or what became known as "Nazisploitation," with sexploitation motifs interwoven.[52] A month after the "Nazisploitation" double feature, *Salò, or the 120 Days of Sodom* screened in a Pasolini double bill with *Decameron* (surely resulting in tonal dissonance, if not stupefying confusion at a strictly interdiegetic level). A theme of eroticized fascism that had clearly emerged within the Nuart's calendar was also layered with implication of what desiring at the cinema entails.

Salò, *Salon Kitty*, and *The Night Porter* are unified not only in their theme of fascism but also in their framing devices. All three contain performances within their performances (sexual, nonsexual, and mixed), their tableaux figurative or literal theater prosceniums through which to watch the sadistic spectacles. Reusing the device famously deployed in *Cabaret*, these films use the proscenium view to remind viewers of the power relations that exist between the vulnerability of the performers and Nazi viewers' sadistic gazes. The Nazis and Italian fascists command the look that objectifies and dehumanizes the subjugated performers. This theatrical framing also thematizes the films' spatial relationship to that of the cinema spectator to the screen frame, reflexively involving them in the spectacle. The films' spatial organization governs and is governed by the performance of the erotic, delineated along axes of power and desire.

Salò and *Salon Kitty*, films that seem worlds apart in their politics, in fact share many of these narrative and aesthetic properties. First, each contain orgiastic scenes of grouped bodies performing sex acts to the gaze of state and military officials. Structurally, they are, at their base, strung-together sequences that enact a range of paraphilia, from sadism and masochism to coprophilia to incest to acrotomophilia (sexual attraction to amputees or physical disability).[53] Positioned similarly for the fascist officer and the film's audience, the two films exploit the sexologist's long list of -philias discussed in the previous chapter.

Salò allegorizes the oppressive tactics of the Mussolini regime by staging a fictional scenario in which fascist officials take a group of adolescents to a vacant mansion, subjecting them to different forms of abuse, torture, and humiliation. Criticism and scholarship on *Salò* have tended to focus on how Pasolini transposes Marquis de Sade's violent erotica to a contemporary milieu in order to censure the use of state-sanctioned violence. Given Pasolini's own comments on the film, and his Marxist, antifascist views, the film is rightfully taken seriously as a grave allegory of fascism as itself a certain kind of sociopolitical perversion. Although part of the same cycle of fascist-fetishistic films by "Visconti, Fosse, and Bertolucci" that Kriss Ravetto calls "neodecadent ([marked by] kitsch and camp)," Pasolini's film employs, according to Ravetto, a "radical politics of entropy."[54] However, programming, as I stated via Laurent Jenny's quote, can pervert the meaning of a text by way of intertextual contact and transformation.[55] In the company of *Salon Kitty* and *The Night Porter*, *Salò* might resemble less a European art film than a "roughie," the sexploitation subcycle from the 1960s that Elena Gorfinkel describes as distinct for its blunt depictions of extreme sexual violence and paraphilic mania.[56] Could fascism serve as the optimum context for the Sadean fantasy, the ultimate perversion of postwar trauma, and thus mutate an art film into a "roughie"? Even a film as dark and unsettling as *Salò*, therefore, can wield an erotic formal dimension that makes libertine fascism the apotheosis of an attractive Sadean fantasy.

Salò and *Salon Kitty* in particular play with proportion of bodies to space, refocusing attention from body to scenic design. Unlike *Salò*, *Salon Kitty* is based on the true story of a Nazi-frequented brothel that was commandeered by the SS to spy on its own. The SS recruited Aryan women to play prostitutes and report on their findings. The scene of the recruitment and testing process, in which the women are assessed for their sexual performance, is a prime example of how eroticism gets grafted onto the production of cinematic space. The sequence begins with a parade of over a dozen naked men and women marching into an auditorium. Commandant Helmut Wallenberg, portrayed by Helmut Berger, watches as the group performs a sort of sexual gymnastics, in a nod and wink to

3.6 Architectural grandeur designed for fucking in *Salon Kitty* (dir. Tinto Brass, 1976).

Leni Riefenstahl's *Olympia*. The shots alternate between zoomed medium shots of orgy participants sucking and fucking, close-ups of the Nazi officials watching, and long shots of the choreography of bodies, panning and zooming the immense auditorium (fig. 3.6). *Salò*'s sex scene with the film's two virgins intercuts between varying scales as well, associating the bodily acts with the disciplined opulence of the architecture (fig. 3.7). Scale and proportion here are not only produced through the imbalance of body to the surrounding composition (populated with sets or negative space), but also through duration, the editing compromising how much close attention is given to the bodies as opposed to the surrounding space, inanimate or oversaturated with other bodies.

This choreography of bodies engaged in sex acts in imperial spaces runs the risk of being upstaged, almost swallowed up, by the surrounding production space by way of editing technique, cinematography (framing and composition), and, of course, production design. The production design simulates a grand sense of scale that is characteristic of what is called "stripped classicism," an interwar fascist aesthetic that fused design principles of classicism with modernism. For these architects and designers, classicism expressed the prestige, purity, and strength of empires past, and the modernist elements heralded an orientation toward the future. *Salò* and *Salon Kitty* mostly take place in locations with high ceilings, in open halls

3.7 Stripped classicism frequently overshadow human bodies in Pasolini's *Salò, or the 120 Days of Sodom* (1975).

with little to no furniture, producing negative space reserved for bodies to fondle one another and imbibe.

Writing about production design, C. S. Tashiro asserts that space and objects can overwhelm narrative function and focus. "Once placed in a narrative, objects and spaces acquire meaning specific to the film. While the overriding goal of the use of these objects is to serve story and character, these narrational elements frequently can work at cross-purposes. These (and other) conflicts of intention, while not part of design's stated purpose, nonetheless affect the associations we take away from a film."[57] Tashiro's wonderful point, inflected with a poststructuralist undertone, can easily be extended to the programmatic scenario in which design as form takes on a life outside of its narrative or thematic trappings. Tashiro's insight might encourage us to rethink corporal focus within the frame, with an element such as production design working at "cross-purposes" with the on-screen body.

Through set design and frame composition, *Salò* and *Salon Kitty* produce grand deep-space perspectives reminiscent of nineteenth-century paintings such as Thomas Couture's *The Romans in Their Decadence* or Mato Celestin Medović's *Bacchanal*, which imagined ancient feasts (fig. 3.8).[58] Harkening back to silent films like *Cabiria*, these banquet halls and their design became the signifier of a hedonistic Greco-Roman

3.8 Thomas Couture's *The Romans of the Decadence* (1847), a clear inspiration for orgiastic profligacy on film.

past. Taking on erotic qualities itself, design and space might pull the eye away from the bodies within the frame engaging in deviant acts. Through a chain of aesthetic and historical associations—fascism with ancient civilization with decadent sexuality—the space itself becomes eroticized.

The Night Porter also makes use of its design to erotic ends, though oftentimes in tighter and crumbling, rather than majestic, spaces. Because *The Night Porter* takes place partially in the memory of the Holocaust, specifically that of a traumatized survivor and her Nazi captor-lover, the decay is a symbol of their spiraling psyches, dually supporting the fantasy of secret underground sites that the Nazis appropriated to play out their sadistic fantasies.[59] In the film's most famous scene, a shirtless Rampling dons suspenders and a peaked cap as she performs Marlene Dietrich's "Wenn Ich Mir Was Wünschen Dürfte" to a crowd of Nazi officers (fig. 3.9). Every surface in these flashback scenes contains chipped paint, cracked walls, and large swaths of naked infrastructure; a rusted, moldy color palette of greens, grays, and blacks permeates the gloomy interior. A palette and sensibility that, Gaetana Marrone suggests, "evokes such artists as Munch, Klimt, and Schiele," impresses upon Rampling's skin a grayish tint, the lighting bringing out somber hues against backdrops of disrepair.[60]

EROTIC INTERTEXTUALITY 129

3.9 Crumbling infrastructure in desire and memory in
The Night Porter (dir. Liliana Cavani, 1974).

The Night Porter certainly overlaps with *Salò* and *Salon Kitty*; all three present sadistic prosceniums within which fascist officials play out their fantasies. Strangely, however, *The Night Porter* finds its closest partner in space and form in *A Streetcar Named Desire*, also on the same Nuart calendar. The walls in *Streetcar* sweat, wallpaper fading and peeling away from the Delta's humidity. The New Orleans apartment that Stella and Stanley share lays itself bare through holes in the walls. Like the structural carnage as a product of shots fired from Nazi pistols in *The Night Porter*, Stella and Stanley's apartment is ravaged by years of Stanley's rage, scars of domestic abuse that are inscribed onto the walls and furniture (fig. 3.10). In a play and film that are drenched in allegory (typified by the title itself), these visual metaphors of decay, in scenes of characters' psychological ruination, are erotic indexes to clandestine and underground caverns of taboo play. Rather than being about scale, as with the other examples, decay here within production design has an eroticized texture, rough and seedy.

The Conformist, which the Nuart played a day before Bertolucci's bigger hit *Last Tango in Paris*, also puts in collision the question of desire and fascism, but in a dramatically differing fashion than *Salò*, *Salon Kitty*, or *The Night Porter*. The image of decay that links *The Conformist* with *The Night Porter* also signals a departure; at the conclusion of *The Conformist*, the protagonist Marcello is not paralyzed by it like the lovers in *The Night*

3.10 Set design in *A Streetcar Named Desire* (dir. Elia Kazan, 1951) reflects Stanley's rage and abuse.

Porter, but rather freed to act on his homosexual desire. The entire last sequence of the film takes place after Mussolini has resigned. Marcello walks the streets of a chaotic Rome, a city and nation in search of future direction. In the film's last moment, Marcello finds himself in a cavernous space, steps away from a homeless boy who lies stomach-down naked in bed, his butt reflecting the ambient street light. The boy plays the gramophone, an object that links back to Marcello's earlier love interest, the bisexual Anna, whom he helped kill. The film ends with the boy and Marcello exchanging looks, the final shot of Marcello behind a gate (figuratively imprisoned) staring at the boy. Although the film does not indicate whether Marcello follows though, it is in the ruins of fascist ideology, a broken city, and a false life that his queer desire becomes available. This stands in stark contrast to *The Night Porter*, which posits a perverse space of decay within the presence of fascism. Although the decadence permeates both action and space in both films, *The Night Porter* sees deviance within the fascist past, whereas *The Conformist* spots its opening in fascism's retreat.

Departing from the fascist theme, Fellini's *Satyricon* purposes aspects of scale and texture to reflect on history and desire. *Satyricon* establishes a more dialectical relation to debauchery through its production of space. Encolpius's journeys through ancient Rome, in a search for his male slave-lover Gitón, shift between cavernous dwellings to open-air locations such as a villa and a ship at sea. The film's many episodes are united by little more than Encolpius's queer encounters, a bold decision for Fellini in his adaptation of the Latin satire.[61] Encolpius, while looking for his boyfriend, ends up becoming lovers with his rival, Ascyltos. The two become travel companions, sharing sexual adventures such as having a threesome with a freed Black slave at an abandoned villa and, later, transporting an intersex demigod across the desert. These transitions through space and time function as a kind of queer chronotope of journey and voyage; their transience lubricates sexual exploration and causes deviant affinities to emerge. Interestingly, the Nuart that evening exhibited *Satyricon* with Fellini's *Roma*, another of the director's reflections on Italy's history, albeit seemingly much straighter. Still, in *Roma*, a crotchety older man expresses his disappointment in how much Italy has changed in the post-Mussolini era, lamenting it is now full of "perverts," "transvestites," and "street walkers." *Satyricon*, a canonical work about the Roman empire, confirms the opposite: the perverts have always been there.

Salò, *The Conformist*, *Salon Kitty*, *The Night Porter*, *Streetcar Named Desire*, and *Satyricon* range in their diegetic time and space from Ancient Rome to Nazi Germany and fascist Italy to the post–World War II New Orleans French Quarter. Through their range, they find uneven commonalities, giving physical shape to debauchery and hedonism. The erotic intertext here provides spatial fantasies of temples devoted to sexual depravity and sinful acts. Programming maps this cosmos of deviance and decadence by way of production and set design. Tropes of spatial textures—cracking decay, majestic decor, stripped classicist architecture—get positioned as erotic forms, displacing the body as the object of focus. Space, not the body, sweats, pulsates, seduces, and teases. It recalls eras of hedonisms past, inviting the viewer—whoever they are—to the orgiastic feast for the eyes.

- **Category 3: Stasis in BDSM**

Extending and intersecting with the "fascinating fascism" of films like *The Night Porter*, *Salò*, and *Salon Kitty*, the Nuart winter schedule offered several films with sadomasochism as their common theme. The double bill of Paul Humfress and Derek Jarman's *Sebastiane* and Barbet Schroeder's *Maîtresse* puts a fine point on this, collapsing space and time between 300 AD

Rome and 1976 Paris, to construct a paraphilic matrix of BDSM. BDSM is more than an act, a bodily sensation, or a practice, but also a form, mood, style, and aesthetic. As Elliott Stein observes of *Maîtresse*, "S&M is about mise-en-scène."[62] Perhaps this is no better illustrated than in the film's early scene of the two thieves exploring the dominatrix's apartment. As they sift through the woman's closet in the dark with their flashlights, in a kinky throwback to the opening of *The Earrings of Madame De . . .* (dir. Max Ophüls, 1953), they graze with their hands the owner's rubber suits, spiked leather accoutrement, chains, whips, and even a baby bottle. In *Sebastiane*, Sebastian is put in the pigsty to extend his punishment beyond the flagellation that precedes it. In both cases, prop and setting establish the BDSM mise-en-scène and suffuse the scenes with the respective glamour and filth of suffering and infliction of pain.

But even more than an aesthetic or mood, BDSM in *Sebastiane* and *Maîtresse* has a specific temporality stitched into it. Antithetical to a commonsense understanding of BDSM as dramatic, severe, and disquieting, these films find quiet and stasis within the power dynamic that emerges. This leitmotif extends into other films in the series as well, including *Last Tango in Paris* and *The Night Porter*. Stasis in these films holds an ambiguous status in relation to BDSM, opening onto a horizon of potential meanings, connotations, and sensations: it can create suspenseful withholding leading up to the surprise of a lash, slap, piercing verbal command, or insult; the quiet can provide a counterintuitive kind of tranquility or calm—a satisfying relief—between BDSM actions or after their climax; it can also serve as an interval within which the two characters in a BDSM relation assess or negotiate with one another and the situation, in hopes of an alignment of both positions that may or may not come. Stasis in the present (rather than evaluated in hindsight or premeditated beforehand in an agreement between participants) is therefore erotic in its ambiguity and contingency—a floating signifier of elusiveness and inscrutability.

We might consider these films as part of a filmic tradition of what Linda Williams calls "aesthetic sadomasochism." Although Williams is speaking generally of work produced and distributed within the porn industry, her definition is helpful: "high production values, professional acting, literary sources, and complex psychological narratives in which characters become self-aware" constitute this subgenre with which these erotic art house films share traits.[63] The art house examples in the Nuart calendar go a step further in their aesthetic incorporation of BDSM by also translating it into form. The durations of long shots, scarce dialogue or sound, static framing, and the slowness of on-screen activity lend to this feeling of stasis that films such as *Sebastiane*, *The Night Porter*, and *Maîtresse* link to BDSM pleasure.

It may be odd to think of stasis in this instance as somehow pleasurable. In fact, the word *ecstasy* is its etymological opposite, emanating from the Greek *ekstasis*—to be or stand outside of oneself. If ecstatic pleasure means that one is outside of a stable spatiotemporal coordinate—or stasis—and is engulfed in a pleasure that makes one feel as if outside their own body, or outside stasis, BDSM reverses course by *restoring* stasis—to be arrested in space—to the scene of pleasure or *ecstasy*. Stasis, an ingredient within the BDSM interplay that these films make indispensable, temporalizes the pleasure and thickens the present. Halts to narrative action that reflect states of relief, suspense, or assessment can be found across sadomasochistic forms, even dating back to the writings of Marquis de Sade and Leopold von Sacher-Masoch, who give sadism and masochism their names.

Gilles Deleuze, in his study of masochism via Sacher-Masoch, observes that waiting and suspense are key to the temporality of masochistic fantasy.[64] For Deleuze, it is important to separate masochism from sadism—contra its common compound of *sadomasochism*—given that the two adhere to differing, if not sometimes opposing, principles. Following Linda Williams's rebuttal to Deleuze that the two can in fact slide into each other, at least in the realm of cinematic representation, we might see that sadism also makes principled use of suspense, at least in diegetic terms.[65] Within the two positions of sadist and masochist, which might be inadequately reduced to the binary of dominant/active and submissive/passive, stasis functions on multiple sides of the BDSM action—before and after, as well as in the middle as an interval, a link from pleasurable injury to injury—that is essential to the repetitive structures of sadomasochistic gratification.

Barbet Schroeder has said in interviews that he resisted moralizing the practices depicted in *Maîtresse*, and that he attempted to film BDSM matter-of-factly and without judgment.[66] Schroeder's avoidance of gratuitousness translates the scenes of domination and masochism into serene tableaux. Though one might argue that this rather distant directorial approach has the effect of a cold, deadpan flatness, it could also be seen as a pleasure nearer to transcendence. The film features three main sequences depicting the dominatrix, Ariane, torturing paying (mostly male) clients, some of whom were real-life practitioners hired by the production to act out the scenes. In all three scenes, the framing remains rather static, with occasional slow pans or tracks and minimal dialogue. The soundtrack is usually a soothing, quiet church organ or chamber music that juxtaposes

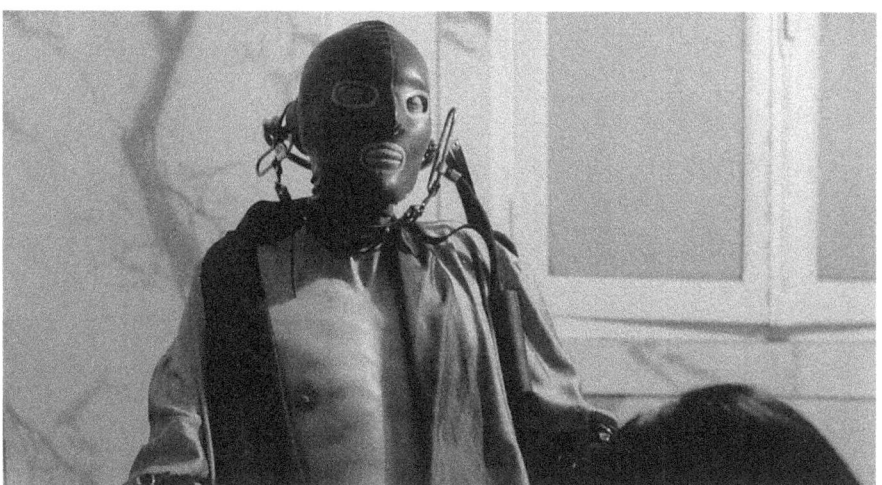

3.11 In *Maîtresse* (dir. Barbet Schroeder, 1975), a real-life dominatrix had to be hired as a stunt double to nail a real-life masochist's foreskin to a wooden board, perhaps documentary evidence of the scene's tranquility.

the severe action taking place. In one scene, Ariane (or rather the real-life dominatrix stunt double hired for the scene) sedately nails a client's foreskin to a wooden board (fig. 3.11). No music plays nor is any dialogue spoken while the client lets out subtle moans in frames that barely entail camera movement. The stillness here seems to reflect the client's experience of converting pain into serenity.[67]

Paul Humfress and Derek Jarman's *Sebastiane*, programmed in the Nuart's double feature before *Maîtresse*, depicts what may be the urtext of gay masochism: the scene of St. Sebastian's body being pierced with arrows. The image of the masochistic boy-saint being penetrated to the point of what cultural historian Richard A. Kaye calls "visibly triumphant bliss" has become iconic in gay male art and literature, a shifting signifier of "mischievous appropriation" and decadent androgyny.[68] Humfress and Jarman's rendition of *Sebastiane* is a quiet meditation, saturated with transcendent imagery of natural landscapes and wildlife and slow-motion sequences of men wrestling in the water, in what might read as an artful version of a softcore male physique film.[69] The film ends with the familiar staging of the martyr tied to a post as his commanding officers and comrades shoot him with bows and arrows (fig. 3.12). As in *Maîtresse*, there is no dialogue. Only the sound of the wind is heard, setting an almost tranquil (or ominous)

3.12 Hurts so good in *Sebastiane* (dir. Derek Jarman and Paul Humfress, 1976).

tone. The arrows are shot in a strikingly unaggressive manner, repeated with pauses in between the action, to create tableaux seen in paintings such as Il Sodoma's *Martyrdom of Saint Sebastian* or Peter Paul Rubens's *St Sebastian*.[70] Kaye calls this ending a "gang rape, in which a homosexual identity is forced on Sebastian metaphorically as Sebastian's tormentors become the necessary instruments of the martyr's homosexualization."[71] If so, it might be the most visually static and aurally quiet gang rape to ever be depicted on-screen, curiously joining sadomasochism with stasis.

In film theory and criticism, stasis has been linked to many filmmakers, movements, historical contexts, and philosophical perspectives. Paul Schrader, taking a cue from André Bazin, associates stasis in films by Yasujiro Ozu, Robert Bresson, and Carl Dreyer with a transcendental visual and narrative form that expresses the "inner-unity of all things."[72] For Schrader, transcendence is equated with an inner-peace or harmony—a Zen balance of one's being in relation to nature, others, and a larger religious or spiritual presence. For David Campany, Michelangelo Antonioni's "aesthetic of decelerated alienation" emerges from the "existential entropy of postwar modern life."[73] Long takes with slow moving or still actors (if any are present at all), often upstaged by their environments, have also been read as markers of death, a stillness antithetical to cinema's conceit as an animated moving-image medium associated with vitality.[74] For example, Jean Ma interprets the spectral presence in Tsai Ming-Liang's *Goodbye, Dragon Inn* (2003) as an allegory for the decline of public spaces for filmgoing and cruising.[75] Scholars of slow cinema bring any number of these interpretations, along with ruminations on structures of perception and attention, into their analyses of the contemporary global current of slow films.

Yet stasis functions differently within the context of the "aesthetic sadomasochism" of these art house films. Stasis unbinds itself from any state of harmony, death, or alienation to which it has been linked because the stillness cannot be ascertained in the moment of its unfolding. The narrative and aesthetic contexts that surround these moments of stasis provide no firm answers. The absence of a fluid exegesis creates conditions for the sensuality of the stillness to be precisely in its ambiguity, in the question of how the dynamic will transpire, begin, continue, or end. Stasis as suspense, relief, or interval of "gathering information," if you will, presents characters with a set of erotic vectors suspended in time and space within the intervening stillness they find themselves.

This gap between the characters and caesura in physical (and narrative) action may be as torturous as it is sexy. Questions fill the void of narrative action and audiovisual activity: In *Night Porter*, will another shot be fired at Lucia (i.e., *suspense*)? In *Salò*, is the stasis *relief* from the unrelenting torture or an unbearable *suspense* of more to come? Even in *Sebastiane*, in which suspense might be foregone, for anyone familiar with the story knows that another arrow and another arrow after that is to come, its reading is still indeterminate: Is the interval between shot arrows the space of Catholic *transcendence*, through which Sebastian's suffering brings him closer to god?[76] Is it a moment of *relief*? Or is there an erotic negotiation underway between Sebastian and his sadistic assailants? The erotic inscrutability of these moments creates a tension of an agonizing pleasure, amplified by potential narrative unpredictability.

The Night Porter and *Last Tango in Paris*, exhibited about a month apart at the Nuart that winter, take stasis into a slightly different direction that adheres to the spatiotemporal conditions of their narratives. Less ambiguous than the other BDSM examples in the program, these two films use stasis to convey a sense of what we might consider sadomasochistic mutuality. Within this repeated beat, participants quickly reverse roles in an attempt to share in each other's extreme subject positions. These scenes of intensified intersubjectivity inevitably reach an unbearable threshold for the characters who can no longer bear their lover's trauma. But before they do, time thickens and the recognition of meeting as willing participants saturates the space between them. Extended pauses in which characters stare at one another, arrested in place without utterance, serve as intervals within which the participants negotiate and renegotiate the terms of their BDSM relationship.[77]

Consider a scene from *The Night Porter* in the latter half of the film. Lucia and Max have confined themselves to Lucia's Vienna hotel room. Shown in flashbacks, as well as described by Max himself, he treated Lucia as a little girl, a plaything that he exploited. As an adult, Lucia begins to play the game, too, and turns the tables on him. While ducking from sight in a hide-and-seek moment, Lucia breaks a perfume bottle on the floor as if acting like a petulant child. Max then enters the room and steps on the broken glass barefoot. No words are spoken between the two; they smile slightly, if not grimly, at one another as Lucia slowly places her hand under Max's foot, Max now pressing firmer against the broken glass, to share with Lucia his physical pain. The slowness and quietness of the moment resolves in a mutual exchange, recognizing their co-participation in the present iteration of their longstanding BDSM bond.

Both *Last Tango in Paris* and *The Night Porter* exist in a perilous relation to time and space, making them static in their very narrative structure. In *The Night Porter*, the characters are stuck in a loop of their own trauma, repeating cycles that result in a self-administered pain. Dramatizing an eroticized version of Stockholm Syndrome, the film suggests that the two are shackled to their pasts, which prevent them from having the will to move on. The past oversaturates the present in *The Night Porter*, illustrated not only through the heavy use of flashbacks that weave fluidly into the tone and action in the present, but also in their present-day power dynamic, which replays (even while it attempts to rewrite) history. This chance encounter of former prisoner and guard, it seems, has proven that Lucia and Max are permanently chained to one another and their shared memories. In *Last Tango in Paris*, Paul demands that he and Jeanne's recurring encounters at the apartment exist outside of time and place, barring (without success) mention of their pasts. This also sets in motion a cyclical structure in which the two repeat sadomasochistic play, quarantined in the removed apartment location. *The Night Porter* and *Last Tango in Paris* suggest that the only way out of these confined spaces is through death, the sole solution to an unbearable, unsustainable love that was doomed from the outset.

It is no coincidence that both *The Night Porter* and *Last Tango in Paris* take place in confined chronotopes to which the characters isolate their fantasies. In fact, the production of cinematic space plays a pivotal role in all the examples of BDSM that I've described, connecting questions of BDSM form to my thoughts on hedonistic production design and location discussed earlier. Max and Lucia in *The Night Porter* contain their relationship to her hotel room, and as their circumstances grow more desperate, leading to starvation, the space begins to look and feel more like the decrepit rooms their affair played out in during the war. Paul in *Last Tango in Paris* attempts to figuratively barricade the apartment they share against the outside world. Intertextually, the apartment performs a similar function to the apartment from another Marlon Brando film in the Nuart's star retrospective—*A Streetcar Named Desire*. But unlike the scars on the furniture and walls of the New Orleans apartment, the flat in *Last Tango*, with its covered furnishings and bare mattress at the center, looks more like a haunted house. The apartment is out of joint with time (Has it been sitting there for a month or years?), unaware of life outside of it, just as Paul and Jeanne aim to be. The static enclosure of space for these lovers mirrors the extended pauses in dialogue, bodily movement, editing, camera movement, and narrative action that punctuate the cruelty at the center of their relationships.

Coda

I want to return to where we began: with the body. In *Hard Core*, Linda Williams makes the claim that, in sadomasochistic porn, there is no guarantee that a spectator's identification corresponds with the gendered subjectivity of a character. Provocative for 1980s feminist film theory, Williams argued that identification may shift between beater and the one beaten, using Freudian psychoanalysis and feminist theories of bisexuality in vogue at the time to support her point. This general intervention about gendered identification has by now become accepted in theories of spectatorship, no longer determinant about the structures or teleologies of identification so core to apparatus theory. At the same time, while gender and racial positions have been destabilized and de-essentialized, theories of mimesis in spectatorship theory still lean on the body as *the* qualifying, affecting referent that defines a film's erotic character.[78]

Some queer film and media studies have turned toward form in a way to circumvent the analytical dependence on representation, specifically the body in apparent representational terms. Nick Davis's Deleuzian conception of the "desiring-image," Cael Keegan's trans readings of the Wachowskis' oeuvre, and Eliza Steinbock's theoretical framework of the trans "shimmering" image all point to a new scholarly horizon that engages with form, gender, and sexuality. These theorists attribute to cinema's form and technology a medium-specific source of desiring or imagining queer and trans experience. Defining the "desiring-image" through Gilles Deleuze's writing, Davis notes that "sexuality orients itself toward people but equally toward objects, ideas, or sensations, or to no stable site whatsoever."[79] Davis gestures at a rhizomatic view of sexuality that courses along multiple axes, undoing a normative orientation ill-suited to cinema's techno-formal properties. Such thinking destabilizes the body as just a representation on the screen to make a case instead for its distributive percolation through what Sobchack would call, in phenomenological terms, "the film's body." I have tried here to add formal specificity to this gesture at what might be thought of as a kind of paraphilic cinephilia (perhaps even a tautology if cinephilia tends to hide paraphilic proclivities).

To be clear, I am not endorsing a fully posthuman method for studying erotic film forms that entirely casts off the place of the human or the human body. At this historical juncture, I am unsure that the erotic can exist without some form of human perception to deem it erotic, which is partly why I can only go so far with Eugenie Brinkema's radical critique in which the perceiver disappears entirely from the analytical scene. Still, inspired by Brinkema's emphasis on form, I have aimed more to expand the epistemic possibilities for what we constitute as erotic. Not just anything can be erotic; there must be some kind of proximity of the eroticized form to represented and embodied sexuality or sensuality, anchored by some rational legibility that the context is indeed sexual. In place of the body (and its forms), textures, rhythms, movements, acoustics, and scales are the erotic geometries and forms that compose mood and sensibility. They also elude traditional sexual signifiers that suggest a certain orientation of a person or a work toward legible identity or even bodily fixture. Rather, erotic forms are deviant in their indiscrimination. They can be dangerously seductive because they transgress secure, seemingly intractable demarcations in sexual identity and desire.

Film programming crafts deviant connections across texts that unmake and remake films' erotic connotations by way of textual fragmentation. In assembling classes of deviant films by way of programming, I demonstrated that while the body is not entirely erased within either the on-screen space or the site of its perception (i.e., the spectator), arousing attributes of the moving image can course outside the represented body. The Medusan laugh of feminist destruction is an aural object that I used as an example of how erotic forms can move outside of and beyond the indexed body. Erotic forms, as sewn into the text, bear no correlation to the orientation or embodied desires of a spectator. Losing the body, eros goes on a wayward drift, accruing all kinds of deviant modalities on its course.

The phenomenon of erotic intertextuality has wild implications for spectators. In these moments, programming encourages spectators to become undisciplined in their hermeneutic training; as the film's many components slip from the text's grasp, they start to take on new meanings, evading a film's narrative organization and logic. Critical to this pivot is the historical consideration that spectators experienced multiple films in one sitting or short spans of time for most of film's twentieth-century history, roughly from the 1910s to the 1980s. This is especially significant for the decades that this book covers, from the 1960s to the 1980s—a period that overflowed with erotic content in pornography, art house, and even some "mainstream" cinema. Spectators' viewing practices were already intertextual, stretched across the span of a double bill, triple bill, ongoing screenings throughout the day or week, or even just regular attendance at their neighborhood cinema. These historical viewing conditions beckon for a theory that accounts for eroticism's distribution across time, bringing to bear the temporality of spectatorial practices.

Such curation produces what Janet Staiger calls "perverse spectators," viewers prone to transgress a film's dominant reading through embodied viewing practices and paratextual interaction.[80] A film's programming is yet another catalyst for spectatorial transgression—despite its ongoing omission in spectatorship theories; it's a spectator's pass to not toe the line of exegesis, to think and feel in ways that deviate from normative and disciplined protocols of respectable reception. The programming of what I consider deviant films thus trains spectators to be deviants, finding stimulating and arousing material where they shouldn't—or wouldn't if they were seeing a film by itself without any perverse objects to collaborate with.

Although I have focused on form and programming in this chapter, they are but one way that spectators are trained to be deviant. The next chapter will turn toward the ritual of double-feature filmgoing as a communal practice where films concatenate only to lose their textual unity and further fragment. Through what I will identify as *repertory time*, double and triple bills foster the conditions for a deviant time and place in which erotic forms coalesce. Whether the discussion is of textual form or spectatorial time, the common thread remains programming's ability to alter texts entirely by way of intertextuality.

Repertory Time

4

DOUBLE FEATURES AND THE TEMPORALITY OF QUEER SPECTATORSHIP

Few opening shots are as iconic as those rose-colored lips, growing with size and luminosity as they launch toward the audience from out of a black abyss. These are, of course, *The Rocky Horror Picture Show*'s unmistakable first frames. In its opening number, "Science Fiction/Double Feature," this giant pair of red lips appears on-screen and nostalgically sings about times at the "late-night double-feature picture show," in which tawdry horror and science fiction films, with their gimmicky plot points, campy heroes, and even campier villains and monsters, flickered across movie screens. *The Rocky Horror Picture Show* is perhaps one of the few films to enshrine the double-feature phenomenon, to celebrate it as a decades-long trademark of exploitation, grindhouse, and repertory houses.

Those lips would implant themselves indelibly into spectators' memories; the opening credits would later prove to serve a mimetic and meta function, encouraging its audiences to sing along during midnight screenings as viewers invoke their own nostalgia for a time in which the movie theater was a singular space, unrivaled by video or television, where one could bear witness to towering robots and giant tarantulas terrorizing the streets. *The Rocky Horror Picture Show*, a midnight sensation that has endured to this day, has done much to fasten "trashy" genre films (e.g., science fiction and horror B movies) to the dyadic exhibition model in which programmers would show films back-to-back at a low admission price. *The Rocky Horror Picture Show* would go beyond monumentalizing the double bill; in its supreme self-reflexivity, it would be crowned the king—or rather, queen—of all trash films: *the* midnight movie.

Counter the double bill's cultural mythos, however, cinephiles who can remember the time of original grindhouse, exploitation, and B movies might recall that, in actuality, double features were not limited to these lowbrow genres; they were nearly ubiquitous. Less an event, unique attraction, or small subset, they were part and parcel of the repertory and second-run moviegoing experience. In fact, they were the dominant repertory exhibition mode for most of the latter half of the twentieth century. If one went to the repertory cinema anytime between the 1950s and 1980s, it would be unusual to find a repertory house that did not regularly show double bills. Photographer Nan Goldin mentioned once in an interview, "I grew up on double features—I'm still not used to the single feature. We would also go to all-night screenings."[1]

Double features (alternatively called "double bills," "twin bills," "dual bills," and "double programs") have had a long life in cinematic history and were not originally restricted to the repertory house. By 1931, 90 percent of Chicago theaters overall, for instance, showed double features.[2] Theater owners learned fast that it was a smart business model. Audience members would be charged for the price of one admission, and even if it meant more for print rental costs, the increased ticket and concessions sales would make it worth the exhibitors' while. Theaters' efforts to capitalize on this did not go without contention, and the history of the double feature is laden with legal struggles between local theaters, distributors, and the studios.

Scholars have adequately captured these battles in exhibition studies. However, very few have dwelled on the ideological implications of a filmgoing experience that was framed as plural, that is, a dyad of two films shown back-to-back. The fact that the historical phenomenon was so pervasive might have caused scholars to take it for granted, effectively leaving it in a theoretical blind spot. This inquiry is especially significant within the art house milieu, where programmers might consider taste and aesthetics alongside, if not above, commercial gain. How did art house programmers negotiate satisfying audiences with what they already knew and delighting or challenging them through exposure to content that might surprise them? What kinds of interplays of signification were formed out of these double feature arrangements?

Double bills, I propose, are excellent microcosms for programmatic multivalence overall; highly concentrated exercises in intertextual cross-pollination and juxtaposition, they generate meaning within the minds and bodies of spectators. I claim that double features could leave deep impression upon spectators, and this assertion hinges on the fact that moviegoers would stay for both films (as was intended). Admittedly, I was surprised to hear from many older colleagues and friends that this was indeed the norm. Even if one had seen either the first or second film to screen in a double bill, it was typical to stay for both, especially because this would be the only way to see films prior to the proliferation of Video Home Systems (VHS) and video stores (which would then trigger a different kind of cinephilia), unless one could catch a film with highly degraded quality on television in its set time slot. I call this ritual of going to the repertory cinema for extended periods of time—sometimes even triple bills or all-night marathons of films shown in succession—*repertory time*.[3] Double bills effectively structure repertory time because they are its modus operandi. Repertory time could be described as immersive viewing in that, while spectators would usually be given a brief intermission between films, they remained in the theater for three to four hours (but again, sometimes longer) at a time, fluctuating in states of focus and distraction, reflection and captivation, engrossment and alienation.

*Re*pertory time is also one of *re*petition. Cinephiles and frequent spectators were likely to reencounter over and over again films that they loved, that posed intellectual challenges, or were simply paired well with co-features they longed to see. Repertory time, in this sense, would seem to embody Peter Wollen's description of cinephilia as an "infatuation with film, to the point of letting it dominate your life . . . as the symptom of a desire to remain within the child's view of the world, always outside, always fascinated by a mysterious parental drama, always seeking to master's one's anxiety by compulsive repetition."[4] Wollen's lyrical (albeit totalizing) description of a religious devotion to cinema—one that is consuming, compulsive, but also world-expanding—is a behavioral or habitual effect that is integral to the repertory time that I explicate here. In what follows, I postulate that these long stretches of time spent at the cinema in front of a projected image could, with the right fare, maximize queer thought and feeling, beyond what any single screening could achieve.

I have thus far argued that film programming made, by way of textual propinquity, deviant classes and coalitions of sexual and gender expression, and merged diegeses to make film form itself a deviant erotic object. This chapter is meant to more tightly zoom in on the spectatorial experience of being plunged into long-duration viewing. My archival research has led me to assemble here my own slate of found double bills that are salient, suggestive, or recurring throughout the years, and across various repertory venues. These double bills invoke intertextual and dyadic mutuality, commonality, tension, ambiguity, and undecidability. The durational intensity of repertory time yields a mutable dynamic of semiotic and affective regeneration with each occurrence.

A History and an Education

Nickelodeon theaters as far back as 1908 began advertising something they called *double features*, comprising two or more films or illustrated songs.[5] By the 1910s and 1920s, as moving pictures became longer and integrated more intricate narratives, the "double feature" grew into the phenomenon of two feature-length films shown back-to-back. Exhibitors used this idea as a promotional strategy and to increase competition with movie houses that only showed one feature per price of admission. By the early 1930s, it was clear that double features benefited discount theater exhibitors more than others in the distribution circuit. Given that audiences consumed films at twice the rate they otherwise would have, studios could not keep up unless they turned out a faster product. This resulted in the production of what became referred to as *B movies*, which would often play after the A movie, or spotlighted feature. B movies became synonymous with lower-quality pictures, a term that is still used today, though out of its original context.[6] With studios struggling to keep up and audiences displeased with poor options, distributors and studios called for government regulations, citing mostly the unfair competition leveraged by the discount theaters over their more distinguished counterparts.[7] To add to it, theater employees complained that the increase in double features led to increased hours.

Despite these tensions within the industry, moviegoers returned time and time again to cinemas with package deals. This invokes an image of endless consumption, an insatiable spectator willing to watch anything and everything just to be granted time in front of the big screen. Further, this invokes the archetype of the Depression-era spectator who compulsively attends the cinema to escape his or her daily troubles. The cinema, as a wish-fulfilling machine, offers fantasy not only through weekly rotations but also through its durational capacity to relieve people of their daily burdens for elongated periods of time.

Robert Hayden's 1980 poem "Double Feature" conjures up the kind of immersive fantasy that the double bill offered. Describing his wonder as a young Black child going to Detroit theaters in the 1920s, Hayden writes, "At Dunbar, Castle or Arcade / we rode with the exotic sheik / through deserts of erotic flowers; held in the siren's madonna arms / were safe from the bill-collector's power." Hayden describes the escapism that a double bill promised. By referencing the bill collector, he suggests that the double feature offered relief from disenfranchisement and even poverty. His allusion to the "exotic sheik" also obliquely recalls a racial fantasy that would have been further sustained by the "double fantasy" of the twin bill. By the end of the poem, Hayden appears to extinguish this fantasy. He ponders, "What mattered then the false, the true / at Dunbar, Castle or Arcade, / where we were other for an hour or two?" The use of "other" is curious here, both alluding to a sense of absorption where one can forget one's own Black identity within the prospect of escape while maintaining a sense of self-recognition, reminded perhaps by the racist theater policies and atmosphere common to US cinemas at this time.[8]

Hayden's poem vividly describes a profound scene of subjectivization prompted by a double feature. It not only epitomizes film's ideological suturing capacities but also amplifies them through its durational quality. I assume Hayden as a child attended a 1920s for-profit cinema inclined to show commercially robust fare and was exposed to the likes of Rudolph Valentino playing a sheik or Al Jolson in blackface. Problematic and decontextualized representations such as these help to distinguish, though not without complication, mainstream commercial time from repertory time. Even fast forwarding thirty or so years, mainstream cinemas would have had no interest or obligation to stimulate reflection upon the films they exhibited. These spaces, one could assert, would not likely have sought to disrupt the status quo but rather capitalize on it. Although the art house context should by no means be regarded as a fully emancipatory and progressive space, still, we might see the double feature doing other work in a repertory context than in one of commercial novelty. Surely repertory houses were profit-driven, but repertory time could, and even capitalized on ways to, immerse spectators in the unfamiliar, in what was deemed foreign, strange, and idiosyncratic, to encourage comparative reflection rather than simply escape.

Programmers continually strategized ways to expose patrons to films beyond their immediate interest, all the while staying mindful of the ticket sales needed to keep their theaters in operation. Ben Davis cites several approaches that New York City programmers took, mobilizing their keen awareness of intellectually hungry city slickers.[9] First, programmers would oftentimes base one of their selections in a double feature on the guarantee that it would attract an audience. Whether the film already had a following (sometimes a cult one), had been a box-office success in the past, or was a rarely screened print of a famous film, programmers could then take a risk in selecting the film's partner. At times this was another hit or canonical film, but there were instances when programmers would exhibit an obscure or rarely shown title to go with it. Some even took a chance by screening a film that in the past had been a flop but now merited reconsideration. Dan Talbot, the longtime programmer of the New Yorker Theater, was famous for putting together two disparate films from completely different traditions, countries, time periods, and so on.[10] He called this "fragmenting a bill," as opposed to creating shows with "thematic" continuity.[11] He did this to wrest spectators of their comfort zones and expose them to content that they might otherwise overlook or willfully avoid.

The ordering of the films exhibited in a double bill might matter when only one double feature performance would take place per day. Programmers would try to show the main attraction at a prime time in order to draw the biggest audience. Frequently, however, double bills screened in what were called "continuous performances," with films playing all day long on a loop. Because patrons expected films to replay, they might come late or in the middle of one film, watch the entire co-feature that followed, and stay for the beginning of the film they had walked into partway through. For this reason, scheduled order was often enough not of major concern for programmers.[12]

Davis explains that double bills could come as part of a larger series or festival (organized around a star, director, genre, theme, national cinema, movement, etc.) or be randomly scheduled and change day-to-day. They also might be part of a festival or series that shows on a certain day of the week for a period of time (e.g., pornography exhibited on "Blue Mondays") or one that takes up an entire week or several weeks (e.g., a weeklong film noir series). These festivals and double features, Davis stresses, provided an "invaluable educational function" before or outside of university settings offering film production or studies courses.[13] Sitting and watching two Busby Berkeley films or Hollywood musicals from the 1930s, for instance, increased spectator awareness of style, trends, and paradigms within a historical moment and, of course, in the spirit of *Cahiers du Cinéma* and Andrew Sarris, of different auteurs' artful predilections.[14] Repertory cinemas of the 1950s and 1960s were training grounds, instructing the public on the medium's aesthetic and even, at times, its social power.

As Haidee Wasson has shown, MoMA's first film curator and archivist Iris Barry, within the atmosphere of progressivism, began this practice some thirty years prior, by way of integrating the then middle brow medium of cinema into the institution's museology. Barry, Wasson underscores, did not bow to the "ascendant Eurocentric critiques of film" but instead treated "film's role in aesthetic and social critique more as a question than as a forgone conclusion."[15] Barry's work lay the groundwork for those later programmers who aimed to use the cinema as a kind of classroom—though free from its didactic procedures—for learning about film history.

If indeed repertory time could be considered educational time, programmers conceived of a different kind of education than one of straightforward art appreciation, especially in the turn toward eclecticism that took hold by the 1970s. Contra the art house cinema's dull cerebral connotation, here is a model predicated on surprise, defamiliarization, and even destabilization. Promiscuous programming, I proposed in chapter 1, is not just about decentering the purported masters or disrupting and thus reestablishing new so-called artful taste arrangements, but also about endeavoring to find out what epistemic and affective connections might form by putting in dialogue disparate texts from divergent traditions, genres, strata of the entertainment industry, and so on. The double bill, itself a textual assemblage, asks of texts what they can do, that is, what political imaginaries they make available for spectators who make meaning out of the ostensible randomness.

Despite the fact that double bills had been part of the repertory programming practice for some time, its deployment at the Bleecker Street Cinema offers insights into how a cinema could make use of textual mutability. Marshall Lewis, who was the Bleecker Street Cinema's programmer in the early to mid-1960s, was known for turning necessity into ingenuity. Due to austere budgetary restraints, the cinema would rent a limited group of films for the year and recycle them into different combinations. Ben Davis cites the examples of Ingmar Bergman's *Naked Night* (1953) being paired with Kenji Mizoguchi's *Ugetsu* (1953), and then *Ugetsu* with Jean Renoir's *La Grande Illusion* (1937).[16] This rotation of films might appear financial suicide to a contemporary viewer, who, beset by an onslaught of online streaming options, might assume that spectators would grow bored with the selection and go to another cinema. In reality, the Bleecker had packed houses. Lewis's method yielded a successful and sustainable business model. Its success implies that devoted and repeated audience members did not avoid seeing a film again, or several times over, when paired with a film that may have not seen.

In celebrating Lewis's approach, Dan Talbot noted that "it was like going to a film academy."[17] Given the double bill's ability to immerse spectators as well as disrupt pleasures, attachments, assumptions, and predilections, Talbot's comment deeming the Bleecker Street Cinema a "film academy" more deeply invites the question of a repertory education. Many art house and repertory programmers, it should be noted, were averse to academic studies of the moving image. Their chosen reception was steeped in a pleasure that was jargon-free and immune to rigorous explication and critical justification.[18] But in Talbot's formulation, the double-feature paradigm is a quasi-institutional twin to the film academy, which enacts a certain didacticism through repetition and duration. For example, within a film course, one would likely not only watch an Alfred Hitchcock or Yasujirō Ozu film, but dissect it scene-by-scene, shot-by-shot, to more deeply understand and come to appreciate the stylistic components of artful filmmaking. Repertory time could indeed perform a similar function through prolonged exposure to a text or series of texts within the same director's oeuvre, a national movement, genre formation, or historical moment. Programming, in this sense, similarly facilitates repetition as a mode of analysis. It encourages dissection and appreciation through recursive viewing.

If one were to approach Talbot's compliment as more a simile or point of comparison, that going to the Bleecker Street Cinema was *like* going to a film academy, instead of *actually going* to a film academy, its didacticism could look more like heuristic experimentation in meaning production than disciplined (if not compulsory) methods in film loving. In other words, far from the protocol of doing deep and close analysis in a space such as a classroom, these double features could move spectators to feel and think through interactions between texts in less structured fashion. The Bleecker Street Cinema thus offered, through recycled yet reshuffled double features, opportunities to encounter chains or relays of signification. Semiosis in this sense is less a product of regimented imperatives to love the object and either aspire to reproduce it or revere its aesthetic value than it is a testing ground in which to probe the conditions of relationality and connection of text to text and text to world. These programmatic processes do not simply entail thematic yoking or parallelism, but dynamic epistemic reconfiguration and affective collision.[19]

Davis's historical account implies that double bills were not random. While the programming's theme might change day-to-day, the pairing on a particular afternoon or evening had to correlate in some way, even if it remained a mystery to the curious audience until they witnessed or felt a schema emerge, sometimes even hours to days after a screening. At the same time, the relationships between co-features should not be regarded as inevitably symbiotic. There were many times when double bills thrived on radical discontinuity or dialectical opposition. There were also times when it might have been difficult to distinguish the symbiotic from the antagonistic. While two films may appear thematically, stylistically, or contextually commensurate, they may in fact be affectively incongruous. Or two films could equally be at tension with one another or find compatibility based on the angle or lens through which a spectator perceives them. In what follows, I provide a protean schema of semiotic engagement with double features that will purposefully oscillate between these two poles of symbiosis and tension. With the help of some central films—*The Lovers* (Louis Malle, 1958), *Last Tango in Paris, Beyond the Valley of the Dolls, Cruising* (dir. William Friedkin, 1980), *Klute* (dir. Alan J. Pakula, 1971), and *Looking for Mr. Goodbar* (dir. Richard Brooks, 1977)—I traverse their different readings to illustrate that these texts were and are in continual semiosis, shifting in meaning due to their arrangement and context. Parallelism and incommensurability, and the sliding of one into the other, offer audiences multiple strategies for interpreting and putting to ideological use the texts they receive over time.

Fantasy, Interrupted

Louis Malle's French classic *The Lovers* was repeatedly screened at art house cinemas throughout the 1970s. Audiences of the time would likely have been familiar with the film's backstory: Around the time of the film's initial US release in 1959, a theater owner in Ohio was fined for showing the film because the county and then the state deemed it "obscene." The case went to the Supreme Court in *Jacobellis v. Ohio*, and in 1964, the film was finally exonerated.[20] Supreme Court Justice Potter Stewart famously asserted that the film did not contain obscenity worthy of censorship, for, he stated, "I know it when I see it." The film was purported to be obscene because the protagonist, a wealthy housewife, makes the decision to leave her husband for a young archaeologist, still virtually a stranger, who picks her up off the side of the road when her car breaks down (fig. 4.1). Linda

4.1 The fantasy of tabula rasa for the impulsive couple driving off together at the end of *The Lovers* (dir. Louis Malle, 1958).

Williams takes note of the "long scene of adulterous lovemaking that was so intrinsic to the film that it could not . . . be cut without doing extreme violence to the narrative."[21] Although the film might have appeared sexually restrained at this point to a young urban art house crowd of the 1970s, its reputation for challenging US obscenity laws would have been of historical interest to cinephiles.

More can be said about the film's ongoing appeal than first meets the eye. Its position in relation to the other films with which it was programmed lends nuance to the film's enduring legacy. On August 25, 1974, the Elgin Theater in Manhattan screened *The Lovers* with Agnès Varda's *Happiness* (1965) on an all-day loop.[22] Agnès Varda was already a venerated "Left Bank" director within the art house scene and larger French New Wave movement, most famous for her film *Cleo from 5 to 7* (1962). Besides being a historical artifact, *The Lovers* would have likewise had auteurist appeal, given Louis Malle's place in the pantheon of beloved European directors. In light of these factors, it can be difficult to determine precisely what might have attracted spectators to a double bill such as this one. Was it Malle's canonical status? Varda's unique perspective as a woman filmmaker? The novelty of a critical film screened less often (and perhaps unseen) or the comforts of one that many find sublimely romantic?

On the surface, the messages of the two films—*The Lovers* and *Happiness*—could not be further apart. While *The Lovers* appears to advocate for the pursuit of love as the pursuit of freedom and joy, Varda's film reveals the gendered asymmetry of these aspirations. In *Happiness*, a

4.2 Replication of the nuclear family in Varda's *Happiness* (1965).

housewife drowns herself after discovering that her husband has been having an affair, which he refuses to dissolve. Rather than deciding to end with the protagonist's death, the film follows the widower as he pleads with his mistress to marry him and help parent his now motherless children. The film ends hauntingly with the new family enjoying a daytrip to what appears to be the same location where the wife had committed suicide (fig. 4.2). In contradistinction to *The Lovers*, *Happiness* does not welcome freedom in love, suggesting instead that women's roles are as replaceable as normativity is replicable. In both cases, the endings are meant to shock, but to disparate ends. Where Malle seems to use narrative surprise to accentuate the spontaneity of love and its ability to remedy crippling ennui, Varda depicts love that does not find relief from the mundane. In fact, the cyclical workings of heterosexual mundanity—in its promise of romantic *happiness*—conceals the sexism that structures it. The last shots of these two films perfectly capture their narratives' stark contrast: one set of lovers driving off together, filled with euphoria and hope for the future; the other set, now part of the recalibrated family, walking off together in chilling amnesia, and into the recursive patterning of heteronormativity.

The juxtaposition of these two films—united, of course, by the fact they are both French and interested in women's points of view—would not have been lost on the room. For this reason, the exhibition context of this double bill is important to understanding these potential exegeses. Davis describes the Elgin, where this double feature played, as a Spartan theater housed in a rundown building in the middle of pre-gentrified Chelsea. The audience, Davis notes, was primarily young and intellectual. *Happiness*, for a politically and intellectually aware audience, provides a corrective of sorts to the fantasy *The Lovers* proposes, familiar in its bromidic love-conquers-all message. Even if the audience was not made up of young activists, their knowledge of or ideological alignment with second-wave feminism could easily make the intervention in *Happiness* all the more legible. Seen alone, *Happiness* makes a clear case against heteronormativity and sexism. Seen with *The Lovers*, suddenly the film is anchored in and works to counter a textual and mediated history that positions romance as the cure for all ills. *Happiness* in this case is disruptive and disjunctive, historically, textually, intellectually, and affectively. The film might be seen as a *lever*, as Jacques Derrida and Gayatri Chakravorty Spivak describe the device, prying open and exposing the naturalized ideology that its co-feature reproduces.[23]

On the surface, the great tonal, stylistic, and narrative gulf between *The Lovers* and *Happiness* might appear to ensure greater dialectical thinking and feeling on the part of the spectator. The billing of *The Lovers* in continuous performances with *Last Tango in Paris* at the Carnegie Hall Cinema in September 1976 might appear to have a similar effect.[24] Pauline Kael, in her famous rave review of *Last Tango in Paris*, noted that there was "something like fear in the atmosphere of the party in the lobby that followed the screening" she attended.[25] The fear that Kael sensed may be a product of what Linda Williams identifies as a film about sex—a practice often associated with life affirmation, whether through reproduction or jouissance—that is here driven toward death, specifically murder.[26] *The Lovers*—a credo that advocates one surrender to love in order to right all wrongs, heal all wounds—would thus appear in diametric opposition to *Last Tango in Paris*, tonally, narratively, and ideologically.

But look closer and *The Lovers*'s ending might appear ironic when set against *Last Tango in Paris*. Consider a reading of *The Lovers* as a text that comments on the implausible and even ridiculous euphoric pursuit of reparative love, a trope intrinsic to sustaining heteronormativity. After all, the lovers fall in love within twelve hours of knowing each other, having only sparse conversation, resulting in the protagonist suddenly leaving behind her husband and daughter in the hopes of romantic liberation. From this angle, the nihilism of *Last Tango in Paris* might infect the idealism of *The*

Lovers, rendering it a delusion or impossible romance. In this sense, *The Lovers*'s abrupt ending—read as a desire to circumvent memory and history through the spontaneous fantasy of futurity and reciprocity—is reframed as a critique of manufactured love masquerading as transcendental.[27] *Last Tango in Paris* does not so much undercut *The Lovers*'s ostensibly inherent optimism here as it unearths the criticality that dwells in an alternate reading of its narrative structure, found perhaps in "reading against the grain."[28] Reading *The Lovers* from this angle might be commensurate rather than in tension with Varda's *Happiness*; within these assemblages, all three films—*The Lovers, Happiness,* and *Last Tango in Paris*—whether one might be compelled to deem them queer or feminist, are suddenly available for the feminist and queer modes of critique ignited by, crucially, repertory time.[29]

These double features offer spectators a space to feel through divergent ideological production, inciting queer reflection upon the constructs that make certain desires thinkable and acceptable and others unsavory and alien. These double bills confirm what Laura Marks positions as "ethical" programming in that they seem to contain arguments that invite "agreement, qualification, or dissent" through both ideation and sensation.[30] They offer queer-feminist points and counterpoints on which their audiences are encouraged to ruminate, giving them space to foster generous readings of nonnormative pleasure as opposed to its admonishment.

Repertory time occasions hermeneutic revision. Programming double bills can entirely revise films' connotations and the decoding strategies of spectators who aim to understand arcane forms of signification common to art house screens. By virtue of spending concentrated amounts of time watching films, spectators are asked to make connections and locate disjunctions between films and their meanings. In the cases just described, double features catapult films into unpredictable affective associations that at times might result in the unease of conflicting messaging. Caroline Bem, framing the double feature as a kind of diptych, posits that "diametrically opposed" readings introduce a "third space" within which "competing political or ethical positions *coexist* with equal validity."[31] Co-features then can carve out a space in which the spectator must "'sit with' irreconcilable tensions."[32] This unease might also help illuminate, in the tradition of dialectical materialism, the world's hegemonic structuring. As Marks writes, "The curator is responsible for synthesizing meanings that emerge from the dialogue between the work and the world."[33] Repertory time is therefore not isolated from the lived world but provides a heuristic to help face it, interpret it, reimagine it, and even rescript it.

My intention here is not to exhaust all possible readings, but rather to show that in these dyadic formations, that which appears dialectical and conflicting on the surface cannot be trusted to be the conclusive reading. Each relay generates new points of contact where new continuities and discontinuities can form.[34] In the case of *The Lovers*, its repertory life as experienced in repertory time keeps it in semiotic motion and therefore irreducible in its polysemy and affective capacities. In his elaboration on Charles Peirce's notion of unlimited semiosis, philosopher and semiotician Umberto Eco writes, "from a sign which is taken as a type, it is possible to penetrate, from the center to the farthest periphery, the whole universe of cultural units, each of which can in turn become the center and create infinite peripheries."[35] *The Lovers*, taken as representative of all films put back into repertory circulation over and over again, creates new centers and new peripheries that expand in meaning and repurpose the film for eras past and eras to come.

Repertory time, in this formulation, is definitively anti-absorptive even as it is immersive. To do their dialectical work, these double features rely on the prolonged attention of spectators, and by way of a dialectical logic, resist absorption typically attributed to classically made films' diegetic fantasies. These examples contrast Hayden's description of his experiences as a child going to the commercial cinemas. The intertextual design of repertory time dislodges a critical preoccupation with monotextual form—that it facilitates a passive viewing experience through deployments of continuity editing, verisimilar mise-en-scène, and naturalistic acting. Instead, *The Lovers* and its shifting companion texts are turned on their heads, encouraging reflection upon the sexual and romantic conventionality and normativity on which these films appear to place a premium (when viewed solo, outside their programming). However, as I will explain, double bills can also favor pleasurable critique or critical pleasure, not only to decode or lay bare the hegemony lurking beneath representation, but also to help imagine worlds beyond the immediate and dominant ones with which spectators are all too accustomed outside the cinema.

Other Feminist-Queer Crossings

It is common for double features to be premised on themes considered topical or timely. The circulating and cross-pollinating ideas of various liberation movements can be detected in many exhibitive pairings, especially in contemporaneous films speaking to or questioning current cultural attitudes. Sexual liberation is one movement that stemmed from and extended its tentacles into multiple other movements, emerging in some ways from the anti-war and counterculture movement, and dovetailing with Black empowerment and other anti-racist struggles, as well as, most notably, women's and gay liberation. As Ramzi Fawaz writes of these interconnections, the women's and gay liberation projects "identified patriarchy as a type of structural domination that arbitrarily enforces hierarchies of gender and sexual normativity to render women and queers inferior subjects," and so aimed to "wholly reimagine what women and queers could be or become when the categories that traditionally constricted them ... were questioned or defiantly refused."[36] Programmers responded to these social confluences by putting films such as *Cruising*, *American Gigolo* (dir. Paul Schrader, 1980), *Looking for Mr. Goodbar*, and *Klute* in double-bill rotation; they sought to cultivate comparative frames for films with closely coinciding releases as well as explore the diachronicity of women's and gay liberation, and how Hollywood mediated and meditated on their budding gender and sexual consciousnesses.

Cruising and *Looking for Mr. Goodbar* are two provocative texts from the era that have in recent years experienced renewed critical interest and been compared to one another—and for good reason. Seen as two of the most controversial wide-release films of the late 1970s (*Cruising* was technically released in February 1980) to deal with sexuality, they were positioned as products of the newfound freedoms afforded in the post–Production Code era of Hollywood filmmaking as well as a backlash against the social movements running parallel to it, most notably gay liberation and second-wave feminism. For these reasons, they were typically regarded as "bad objects" in the history of queer and feminist filmic representation. (See the next chapter for a more in-depth theorizing of queer "bad objects.") Both films featured major stars at the time—Al Pacino and Diane Keaton—cruising in bars late at night, immersing themselves in worlds unthinkable until the baby boomers came of age.

Given the two films' many correlations, one might assume their pairing in double bill exhibition. In fact, I found no such case of it in my research. Perhaps this is because their mixture might be combustible. Gay activists hated the representation of gays as psychopaths and fetishists in *Cruising*; feminists (and the general public as well) despised that Keaton's character in *Looking for Mr. Goodbar* is senselessly and without warning killed at the end, an ostensible punishment for sexually asserting herself. These films' heated responses lingered following their releases. Programmers might in turn avoid patron grumbling or, worse, financial risk—both in the short- and long-term—that might be too much for smaller cinemas to handle. While avoiding their direct interactions, programmers did exhibit these films through the years, carefully profiting from their controversy, but also carving out new paths for their reevaluation and reconsideration. For instance, *Looking for Mr. Goodbar* was screened alongside the Jane Fonda hit *Klute* in 1978 in a double feature at two Bay Area theaters, the UC Theater and the Strand Theatre, a textual pairing that yields striking feminist overlaps and tensions that I will tease out momentarily.

Another dynamic pairing was *Cruising* with *American Gigolo* at the Strand Theatre in April 1981—the latter film being regarded as artistic, "sexy," and palatable in contradistinction to the response to the former.[37] It is likely that the films were exhibited together in part because of their thematic ties—both films, as well as *Looking for Mr. Goodbar*, feature straight characters traversing the debauchery of commercialized urban sexual pleasure. (And with a similar tie, *Looking for Mr. Goodbar* was exhibited in a double bill with *American Gigolo* at the Nuart in June 1982.) While *Cruising* galvanized the gay and lesbian community to protest its production and distribution (and also, crucially, the participation of real-life gay men playing extras), *American Gigolo* garnered little to no criticism from the community for its own brand of homophobia. Activists were likely too distracted by the more publicized depiction of the supposedly lascivious gay lifestyle depicted at length in *Cruising* (fig. 4.3). The question might become: Is this double feature intended to create continuity and connect the two films in their homophobic depictions? Or is there another way to read their coupling?

I here quote Robin Wood at length, both in his remark on the community's oversight in its response to *American Gigolo*, as well as his reading of the film itself:

> Homophobia is central to *American Gigolo*. It was playing without protest in the same Toronto theater complex where gay activists were picketing *Cruising*; I find it incomparably the more offensive of the two films, and would argue that its social effect is probably far more harmful, being covert and insidious (in addition to the fact of the film's trendy commercial success). The entire progress of the protagonist, Julian (Richard Gere), is posited on the simple identification of gayness with degradation. Julian, the gigolo of the title, is accorded the status of Existential Hero because he takes pride

in bringing frustrated middle-aged women to orgasm (for suitable monetary compensation). He is trying to forget a past when he used to "trick with fags," and is threatened with having to return to it, coerced by a black homosexual pimp and criminal. . . . The fact that the ultimate Schrader villain is both black and homosexual can scarcely be regarded, in the general context of his work, as coincidental.[38]

The fact that Wood finds *American Gigolo* "incomparably . . . more offensive" than *Cruising* (the latter of which, for Wood, is productively incoherent and renders the cause of queer villainy too undefined to locate) suggests that it is working in the same vein of *The Lovers/Happiness* double feature. *Cruising* is what exposes the repressive and ultimately heinous characterization of gayness in *American Gigolo*. What in *Cruising* can be perceived as ambiguous, confused and confusing, even campy, *American Gigolo* employs as narrative device, a deeper reviled queerness against which the male heterosexual protagonist is redeemed.

Programming here also constellates representations of sex work, underground sex cultures, and promiscuity, themes that at the time channeled circulating questions and challenges being posed to postwar normative reproductive sexuality. Following in the footsteps of *Midnight Cowboy*, *American Gigolo* would also become a mainstream hit about male sex work, and augured the sleek materialism of the 1980s. Before this, the late 1960s and 1970s saw a number of art and mainstream films about sex work, most famously *Belle de Jour* and *In the Realm of the Senses*. Jane Fonda's performance as a call girl in *Klute* stands out in its attempt to bring a sense of layered interiority to the archetype of the female prostitute, here taking the form of deep ambivalence to the profession (fig. 4.4). In *Klute*, Fonda's character, Bree Daniels, is asked to help a detective named John Klute (played by an aloof Donald Sutherland) find a missing executive from Pennsylvania who appears to be stalking Bree via letters and phone calls. Bree has been in what we might call a dissociative state, unable to be in tune with herself and her desires, and her difficulty with vulnerability only becomes compounded by the romantic and sexual relationship she begins with Klute.[39]

Bree's characterization recycles clichés about fallen women being desensitized by sex—a sex worker who has turned off her real desires in order to perform a role for her male sexual partner. Her numbness and emotional distance—a clichéd irony that a sex worker emotionally shuts down at the same time that they provide intimate labor—becomes the psychological

4.3 Masculinity and gay desire in *Cruising* (dir. William Friedkin, 1980) are wildly multivalent.

obstacle to overcome as Klute's investigation works to free her from the stalker's hold. Despite the film's reductive assumptions around sex workers' psyches, *Klute* endures as a landmark feminist achievement for several reasons. In fact, Fonda took the role in part because the male screenwriters and director Alan J. Pakula had given her room to build upon the character's scripted psychological depth. For instance, Fonda transformed Bree's therapy scenes, first, by insisting her therapist be a woman, and second, by improvising in those fictional sessions and producing over ninety minutes of almost only monologue (with six being used in the finished film).[40] Fonda's burgeoning feminist consciousness (mixed with field research she had conducted spending time with actual sex workers) shines through here and becomes diffracted through Bree's psychological development.

Klute is full of antinomies articulated by the film's neo-noir tone and style. In the film's famous sex scene, it is Bree who makes the first move on Klute, no doubt a gesture toward second-wave feminists claiming their own bodies and sexuality (a point that will, in a moment, unite *Klute* and *Looking for Mr. Goodbar* as a telling double bill). At the same time, Bree finds a new vulnerability and sensitivity by leaning into Klute's paternal protection and masculine stature, which is conveyed through Sutherland's

4.4 Poster for *Klute* (dir. Alan J. Pakula, 1971).

stoic performance and in shots that linger on the bewitched lovers. Bree's corresponding ambivalence toward love and men might be read less as representative of the sex worker's psyche, and more as a microcosm for the larger dilemma many heterosexual women at the time faced as they attempted to recalibrate their relationships to men and masculinity with their newfound self-worth and empowerment.

This ambivalence toward masculinity is seen also in the ways that Klute is a stalker of sorts himself. Aligning him with the film's anonymous villain, Klute, too, lurks and follows Bree for a good portion of the film's first half. This resonant theme of men surveilling women's bodies connects *Klute* to another box-office success of the time, *Looking for Mr. Goodbar*, the latter of which would become a "bad object" that stands in stark contrast to *Klute*'s

4.5 Diane Keaton cruises at bars in *Looking for Mr. Goodbar* (dir. Richard Brooks, 1977).

canonization. Based on a quasi-biographical novel of the same name, Diane Keaton plays Theresa Dunn, a twentysomething who spends her days as a teacher at a deaf school and her nights cruising at bars, casually dating and having sex with men (fig. 4.5). *Looking for Mr. Goodbar* chronicles Theresa's sexual awakening by way of spontaneous encounters, punctuated by intermittent flashbacks of her complicated religious upbringing and childhood battle with scoliosis. Things begin to spiral out of control for Theresa when several of her lovers (one played by a young Richard Gere, the star of *American Gigolo*) turn into obsessive and insecure stalkers. Both *Klute* and *Looking for Mr. Goodbar* frame male characters as destructive forces in the female protagonists' lives, threatening women's sense of personal security and thus their ability to thrive in the world on their own terms.

Looking for Mr. Goodbar was subject to a deluge of feminist analysis and criticism upon its release because of its ending. Without clear warning or indication, Theresa dies at the hands of a closeted gay man she brings home for a one-night stand.[41] Feminists read this ending as a backlash against their call for sexual equality, a reinforcement of the double standard that permitted men promiscuity yet shamed women for open sexual expression. The ending, which follows a series of scenes where Theresa fails to strike a balance between her professional life (read: responsibilities) and her party life (read: pleasures), was interpreted as Theresa's price to pay for cruising in bars and sleeping with strangers.

Not unlike *Cruising*, critics and historians over the years have asked whether the ending punishes the protagonist and thus moralizes to or cautions its female audience, or if it indicts the culture that enables or perpetuates such sexist views, in turn punishing its audience who are presumably complicit in stratified social norms.[42] There is diegetic support for this latter argument, as the audience is taken closer into the frenetic energy of Theresa's life, in close-ups of Keaton's face as she orgasms, or through flashbacks to her childhood. This leads us back to the question of blame for Theresa's murder, but this time posed through pleasure-seeking that is not strictly sexual in the private sense but social and public, and it is a public dominated by men that abruptly halts Theresa's flourishing.[43]

That the UC Theater and the Strand Theatre screened *Looking for Mr. Goodbar* with *Klute* in 1978 offered a chance for viewers to take stock of two representations of sexual women with complicated psychic lives at very different flashpoints in feminist consciousness, even if the two films were only seven years apart.[44] If *Klute* was attempting to dramatize ambivalence toward domestic life, largely via internal conflicts (vulnerability/stability vs. solitude/mistrust), with oblique relation to external causality, *Looking for Mr. Goodbar* bluntly presents an external conflict—that is, a woman who has very much come into her sexual identity in a world hostile to its carnal realization. Further, I would suggest that Theresa's attempts to live out the aspirations of sexual liberation were heavily influenced by the practices of gay male cruising and promiscuity. The UC Theater, literally steps from the activist hub of UC Berkeley at the time, and the Strand, blocks from the Castro and Haight Ashbury districts in San Francisco, presented to audiences in the midst of their own gay and women's liberation, snapshots of two distinct moments in feminist sexual consciousness: the identification of the problem of a kind of woman's double consciousness and its inchoate remediation, followed by a parable (not necessary a cautionary tale) about the impossibility of living in a state of pure sexual autonomy.

As with *The Lovers* and *Happiness*, these juxtaposed endings, one where the protagonist is coldly mutilated and the other where she tries to surrender to the humdrum domestic good life, might contain their own feminist critiques in that they underscore the problem of heterosexual women's limited sexual options: women are often either rebuked for pursuing pleasure on their own terms or they must learn to contain and channel them into healthy, heterosexual, and monogamous coupledom. Neither offers a satisfying answer, parallel to a certain reading of *The Lovers*/*Happiness* pairing. Because these two films come close to bookending a decade of second-wave feminist thought, there might be an impulse to read in the dual bill a narrative of progress in feminist consciousness from 1970 to 1977. Is *Looking for Mr. Goodbar* more ideologically "evolved" than *Klute*? There is reason to believe so. *Looking for Mr. Goodbar* takes the audience directly inside of Theresa's psyche (i.e., her memories and desires), whereas *Klute* keeps Bree at a distance, (arguably) unknowable to the audience and herself. But beyond understanding the distinct aim of each film, this compare-and-contrast exercise might also reveal the diachronic and persistent difficulties of integrating lessons from therapy (*Klute*) or attempts at self-actualization (*Looking for Mr. Goodbar*) into a lived experience consonant with one's surrounding social world. In this sense, a double bill can occasion its audience to observe the historical distance between two paralleled texts as well as, painfully, their historical collapse.[45]

Double bills, as intertexts that foster reparative sensoria alongside new forms of apprehension, epitomize that, as Kathleen Stewart might put it, "thought is not the kind of thing that flows inevitably from a given 'way of life,' but rather something that takes off with the potential trajectories in which it finds itself in the middle."[46] A given double bill, a film series, or a calendar's larger programming schema are some of these potential trajectories for this cognitive-affective reparative work. Multiple hermeneutic trajectories exist within these operations, intersecting and diverging through time. The textual forces that films exert on one another can thus ignite *re*petitive opportunities for *re*parative longing. Double features, especially within the idiom of promiscuous programming, become the source material for regeneration out of the ultimately unlimited resource we might call something like the past.

Queer Diegeses

Inversely and alternatively, the double feature can offer a more exuberant queer kind of immersion than those just discussed. I have already argued that double features were not at all exclusively made up of cult fare. Certain cult film double bills were nonetheless uniquely able to plunge spectators into queer universes. Cult films emblematize the ways that repertory time serves as a radical departure in sensibility and taste from the codes of propriety governing everyday public life. These double features—often comprising exploitation and B movies—offered highly concentrated periods in which a range of spectators could experience ruptures of heteronorms.

No doubt there exists a wealth of cult films with a queer charge and appeal to them. Some of the most salient examples, films by Ed Wood (e.g., *Glen or Glenda* [1953]) and John Waters (e.g., *Pink Flamingos*) as well as *The Rocky Horror Picture Show*, have tended to hold symbolic value for the rebellion against the dictates of taste for straight culture rather than bear much weight on sexual politics. By wresting queer cult films from the stronghold of heterosexist cinephilia, it is here I want to gesture to the ways in which they reorganized normative sensibilities and did so through repertory time. Russ Meyer's *Beyond the Valley of the Dolls*—a film that is not necessarily centralized in gay film history but is noted for its campiness—is a prime example of this kind of work. It joined other films in double features that, as Susan Sontag posits about camp, spring "from an irrepressible, a virtually uncontrolled sensibility."[47]

This prolonged exposure to queerness through camp might suggest that double features operated as safety valves for their straight fans (who cannot or do not live out those transgressive fantasies) and queer audiences (who find relief in liberated worlds where they can picture being themselves openly).[48] Such a reading might assume the theater to be an enclosure, an exception to the world outside of it. I insist, contra such a limiting reading, an immersive repertory queer experience forms not only a temporal but also an epistemological and affective break from the normative propulsion of quotidian life. Cinema might be a place of "sense-making," in the way that Vivian Sobchack describes it, but in its queerest moments, it is also a space of *nonsense-making*.[49] Queer double features do more than offer glimpses into absurd worlds of base desire and humor; they drench the sensorium with an irreverence that must then rebound and grapple with the normative world outside the theater.

Take *Beyond the Valley of the Dolls*, released in 1970 in the midst of the counterculture movements in the United States and elsewhere. Fans of Russ Meyer who went to see the film would have been well aware of his idiosyncratic, if not ostensibly contradictory, attitudes toward sex and morality, which are reiterated in the film. Its ideological incoherence—on the one hand, damning a culture consumed by sex and fame, and, on the other, mocking one of piety, righteousness, and censorship—helps to foster readings that highlight the film's uneven tone, which swings between melodrama, comedy, horror, and, of course, softcore pornography. Meyer's feverish montages of sex- and rock 'n' roll-obsessed teenagers—an apparent product of a corrupted culture—ironizes the moralism that was employed to attack his sleazy pictures. On its own, the film satirizes a widespread belief that counterculture was dismantling the fundaments of a civil society through permissive drug use and promiscuity.

Beyond the Valley of the Dolls screened several times with another tale of debauchery and rebellion: *Myra Breckinridge*, based on the popular book by queer author Gore Vidal. To say the least, the two films are indeed *beyond* the pale. They also sprang from the same studio, 20th Century Fox, which made them easier to package together.[50] In *Myra Breckinridge*, the titular trans character played by Raquel Welsh goes to Hollywood to try to inherit her uncle's acting school and destroy the values of the repressed and idealistic students who attend it. Both films equally mock hippie subculture and the larger repressed culture it intends to defy. They are steeped in a camp logic and sensibility that knowingly confounds classical conventions of narrative economy and coherence. In this sense, both films, while immersing spectators in worlds that turn on inflated sentimentality punctuated by sudden montage-induced ruptures, are "gloriously" incoherent in the way Umberto Eco describes cult films.[51] Similarly, Eve Kosofsky Sedgwick identifies camp excess as "waste products"; repertory time provides the spatiotemporal coordinates for spectators to remold these wacky aspects into reframing devices for receiving the world as camp instead of camp as representative of one exceptional version of the world.

The two films' play with excess invokes a Bakhtinian notion of the "carnivalesque." As Robert Stam has explained it, "The carnivalesque principle abolishes hierarchies, levels social classes, and creates another life free from conventional rules and restrictions."[52] The "carnivalesque" echoes the carnival time of the Middle Ages by incorporating into its aesthetics a loosening of social codes that must at other times be blindly obeyed.[53] Laughter, Stam points out via Bakhtin's writings on François Rabelais, is a central component of the carnivalesque. It "becomes the form of a free and critical consciousness that mocks dogmatism and fanaticism."[54] I underscore this particular point because it conveys the subversive parody that the *Beyond the Valley of the Dolls/Myra Breckinridge* double bill channels. The communal aspect of the theater parallels the carnival in this sense in that an audience responds audibly to, even at times competes with, the images and sounds supposedly centralized by the big screen they share in front of them.⁵⁵ What double feature embodies this more than *The Rocky Horror Picture Show* and *Myra Breckinridge*, programmed together at the UC Theater down the block from UC Berkeley in August 1977 and May 1978?⁵⁶

The carnivalesque tends to be marked by its limits, and similarly, here there looms a question about the spatiotemporal boundaries of repertory time. Can such queer fantastical imagining bleed into quotidian life, even political life? Several scholars have noted, for instance, the carnivalesque quality of *The Rocky Horror Picture Show* midnight screenings.⁵⁷ At these highly participatory shows in which audience members act out and respond audibly and physically to the film, participants of various gender identities also cross-dress, sport outrageous makeup, and disrobe to golden underwear and lace garter belts. But by Monday they are back to their proper gender-conforming attire as they rush off to their nine-to-fives without a trace of the weekend's degeneracy. Within this model, where the topsy-turvy practice of gender ambiguity and reversal is coupled to the unfastening of gender's correspondence to object choices, there is an imperative to return to productive life. Productive life (of labor, reproductive futurity, and consumerism), as Jack Halberstam and Elizabeth Freeman have emphasized, is enmeshed, if not synonymous, with normative time.⁵⁸ It must forget that of queer repertory time. The closure that marks the completion of the show is the enclosure of queer potentiality. There is no ripple, only momentary relief.

This narrative of the contained carnivalesque implies that the immersion double bills provide does not leave lasting impressions on spectators and operates mostly as a kind of safety valve to momentarily break from heteronorms. Little, however, can be fully determined about the reverberated impact such a double bill as *Beyond the Valley of the Dolls* and *Myra Breckinridge* (fig. 4.6) might have on the body. In comparing Bakhtin's carnival to Nietzsche's Dionysian fete, Stam offers that "both celebrate the body not as a self-contained system delineated by the ego but rather as the site of dispersion and multiplicity."⁵⁹ This "excessive body that outstrips its own limits and transgresses the norms of decency," I would claim, is not one that retreats once it exits the doors of the cinema. The vestiges of the filmgoing experience remain within the bodies of spectators. Taking *The Rocky Horror Picture Show* as the most popular and obvious example, consider the ways that fans and cinephiles begin to orient their lives around the ritualistic practices of not just watching but also participating in or even merging with the diegesis. Spectators build entire queer communities, kinships, and lifestyles as outgrowths of these texts. Such phenomena should

4.6 Myra Breckinridge, played by Raquel Welch, straps one of her students to a table before sodomizing him.

not be taken for granted or relegated to the place of epiphenomenon; these are evidence of the extended branches of repertory time.

The dispersion and multiplicity of which Stam speaks sounds similar to the dismantling and subjective experience of cult films that Umberto Eco discusses in his writing on the topic. This similitude suggests that spectatorial interplay with cult texts is framed by destabilized and fractured versions of the world that counteract otherwise normative conceptions of the world that operate on pretenses of consistency, normality, order, equilibrium, and rationality. The queer delight in the pairing of a double feature such as *Beyond the Valley of the Dolls* and *Myra Breckinridge* or *The Rocky Horror Picture Show* and *Myra Breckinridge* is a surrender to a fragmented existence, not where social bonds and self-sovereignty are broken and must be mended (in the Marxian tradition of renewed sociality), but where a panoply of desires and fantasies undercut the fantasy of social coherence and amicability.[60] Further, these double bills, while immersing spectators into queer worlds that celebrate disjunction, spotlight the artifice of desires rather than naturalize them. Perversion within this scene of spectatorship can be reduced neither to a Freudian return to some original site of trauma nor to an instance of pre-oedipal or pre-symbolic release, but rather is a product of (inter)textual mediation that constructs erotic, queer, anti-verisimilar, and unruly imaginaries.

Texts and lived experience press against one another in a generative dialectical play that is a defining characteristic of the queerness that can be discovered (psychically, affectively, and intellectually) within the space of certain double features. Using *Beyond the Valley of the Dolls* as an index for deviant nonsense-making, we might take its screening with *Mandingo* (dir. Richard Fleischer, 1975) at the Nuart Theatre in August 1979 as an example of the perverse enjoyment of sexploitation in a highly mediated sense.[61] *Mandingo* (serving also as inspiration for Tarantino's 2012 *Django Unchained*) is set on a plantation where torrid affairs take place between white masters and Black slaves, the latter of whom are used in slave fighting matches. Linda Williams situates the film's release historically in a "moment in American culture when mainstream audiences, black and white, began to find titillation—not just danger—in depictions of interracial lust."[62] Williams goes on to demonstrate how the historical interracial taboo (especially between Black men and white women) plays out later in hardcore pornography as a potentially fetishized remnant of a formerly consuming racist threat that still haunts, though arguably doesn't consume, the present.

The threat of stereotyped Black hypersexual masculinity, for example, is in part attenuated (but by no means eradicated) due to temporal (post–civil rights era) and stylistic (the campiness of sexploitation) distance, but this attenuation is also programmatic. Given that the film was programmed with *Beyond the Valley of the Dolls*, Meyer's extreme camp—itself not contingent upon temporal remove but legible upon the film's release—makes the taboo of interracial desire safer for audiences to enjoy. *Beyond the Valley of the Dolls* serves as both a relaxant and a stimulant. It complements *Mandingo*, itself tawdry because it is part sexploitation and part cheap melodrama, by establishing a tone of what we might call "veri-dissimilitude," where what is represented on-screen does not aim to mirror the real, and should be read accordingly. *Mandingo* certainly doesn't celebrate antebellum interracial sexual dynamics, which are riddled with reprehensible power asymmetries and violence; however, the film uses such devices as "overacting," discordant scoring, and other stylistic cues—such as filming one bedroom scene between a slave owner and his mistress slave entirely through a mosquito net (fig. 4.7)—as simultaneously playful, erotic, and distancing strategies. Here the campiness and the solemnity cohabitate and oscillate in their tensions and compatibilities, with *Beyond the Valley of the Dolls* helping to tip *Mandingo* over into a third space of historical fantasy with contemporaneous resonances vis-à-vis the shifts in interracial desire Williams observes.

This promiscuous sensibility throws into crisis any temptation to frame these double features (or much repertory programming of this time, for the matter) as what semiotics regards as a syntagm, a conglomerate of parts that together build a lucid system.[63] Where a syntagm strives for clear

4.7 Fraught interracial desire in *Mandingo* (dir. Richard Fleischer, 1975).

intelligibility and coherence, here the repertory programming, though certainly including some thematic programs that are indeed coherent, thrives on unpredictable and bizarre combinations. The titillating appeal of films such as *Mandingo* or *Beyond the Valley of the Dolls* might thus be better seen as a result of an agglutinative process that builds a constellation of associative worlds and sensibilities.[64] In this interdiegetic space, certain features of the films' narratives and style latch onto one another, even becoming unmoored from a totalizing ideological schema of a given text. Signifiers of gender and sexual nonconformity (including interracial desire) are extracted and isolated from their sources and then reconfigured along with their contextual residue to produce new intellectual and affective configurations that alter the connotations of the objects themselves. In this sense, the films become different texts depending on their programmatic and viewing contexts, with altering emphases, resonances, and relevancies.

All the while, they retain traces of their narrative locations. Here identities and experiences cross-pollinate and cross-pollute while also maintaining distinct narrative and stylistic characteristics, production contexts, and social issues and types. This is most palpable in the June 1981 example of the double feature of *In the Realm of the Senses* and *Last Tango in Paris* screened at the Strand Theatre in San Francisco.[65] Emanating from disparate cultural and national contexts, the two films unite in their Bataillian take on

4.8 Eros and death united in a publicity still from Oshima's
In the Realm of the Senses (1976).

sexuality and kinky sexuality.[66] *In the Realm of the Senses*, a 1976 Japanese art-porn film based on real events, also ends in murder, in this case, with a geisha castrating and murdering her beloved customer (fig. 4.8). Further, *In the Realm of the Senses* and *Last Tango in Paris* unite in their portrayals of unsustainable sexual obsession in that the main characters isolate themselves from the outside world to create utopias of continual pleasure—an unsustainable fantasy that short-circuits and ends in tragedy.

Such unbearable and uncontainable concupiscence becomes the thing of inflated pathos and extensive coital duration. In this case, however, improbable love looks and feels different from what one might see in *The Lovers/Last Tango in Paris* double bill. *In the Realm of the Senses* and *Last Tango in Paris*, whether read through high-art camp or earnestness, offer consolation for spectators' own relegated and inconceivable desires, and feed the imagination of those whose desires are stuck within a normative sensorium. The style and narrative events diverge and converge, weaving in and out of the detailed, verisimilar sex acts they depict and the hyperbolic form in which they are couched. The parceling out of these films'

REPERTORY TIME   171

attributes becomes the raw material for agglutination. It allows the films to retain their distinctions at the same time that it encourages their corresponding kinks to intermingle and to even lose, under certain circumstances, their textual grip.

Queer and deviant spectators might come to identify with or recognize these aspects because so much of queer love, belonging, intimacy, and desire was at the time—and remains to an extent—impossible, invisible, and unthinkable in the public sphere. These films, despite their blatant heterosexuality, might actually have queer affinities with affects and effects of shame, concealment, and alienation that become legible within the immersive deviant universes pieced together by repertory time.[67] By bringing silenced desires out of the shadows, a deviant double feature such as *In the Realm of the Senses* and *Last Tango in Paris* salvages these representations for viewers who know this erasure, censor, or censure all too well.

There are limits to how much these two films can be used for deviant erotic empowerment. *In the Realm of the Senses*, not unlike Ken Russell's *The Devils*, reinscribes the stereotype of the hysterical woman who compulsively craves orgasms. The film's unsimulated sex, which functions as a visceral visual metaphor for the deeply penetrating lust that the two characters have for one another, might help justify the protagonist's extreme actions in the end to castrate her lover and carry his severed penis with her around town. Even more fraught is the information that came out more recently about the infamous "butter" scene in *Last Tango in Paris* in which Maria Schneider is anally raped by Marlon Brando. All parties—Schneider, Brando, and Bertloucci—attest to the fact that the sex was simulated, yet the scene was not in the script and a nineteen-year-old Schneider was coerced by the director and Brando (the one who allegedly came up with the idea that day on set) into doing it.[68]

This production backstory, which surfaced years after the film's release, does not necessarily negate spectators' or programmers' uses of the film in the 1970s and 1980s, when it was still part of the repertory cycle and thus its canon. Repertory time carved out prolonged contact with this deviant content, allowing spectators' imaginations to run wild. But this information, along with a more critical view of *In the Realm of the Senses* as having sexist implications, does complicate their individual legacies. Perhaps it reins in a romanticized view of repertory time as totally freeing from social constraints and realities. These canonical films are thus potent examples that show we cannot simply ignore history in the name of celebrating timeless allegories of kink as deviant. Additionally, spectatorial strategies of fragmentation are that much more necessary as an alternative to lauding an entire text for its transgression and, as a result, ignoring its relation to vexed power structures.

The Bisexual "Menace"

Between the late 1960s and mid-1970s, a host of films with unambiguously bisexual characters cropped up in art and then Hollywood films. *Les Biches, Score, The Conformist, Daughters of Darkness, Satyricon, Reflections in a Golden Eye, Sunday Bloody Sunday, Teorema, Cabaret, Flesh,* and the mostly forgotten dark comedy *Something for Everyone* (dir. Harold Prince, 1970)—just to name some—appeared across repertory house calendars and were featured on the pages of *The Village Voice* and other urban local newspaper listings.[69] Queer film criticism and scholarship has explained the commercial viability of bisexuality in a number of ways: cinema leveraged bisexuality to expeditiously achieve narrative and psychological complexity (consider here the prevalence of the love triangle); bisexuality might also help to bridge gay and straight audience interest; and, last, it served as a passage en route to overt representations of homosexuality, which would come to experience a newly public visibility that could simultaneously feed general social curiosity while capitalizing on a new viable lesbian and gay market. If bisexuality could also be an effective metonym for the bohemian waywardness of sexual liberation at large, programmers were certain to keep films with bi appeal in frequent and recursive exhibition as a way to boost repertory cinema's opportuneness—ironic, perhaps, because it did so by way of recycled texts.

Vito Russo, in identifying Hollywood's effort to profit from gay liberation, saw the double bill as an effective ideological vehicle for propagating phobic myths about LGBT people. He writes, "The gay [sic] cult film *Something for Everyone*, often shown on a double bill with *The Boys in the Band*, is a good example of the way in which a gay audience is lured into supporting a negative image of itself in response to an attractively homoerotic but ultimately destructive sensibility."[70] Putting aside questions of whether the protagonist, Konrad, in *Something for Everyone* is gay or actually bi, it is important that Russo suggests the double feature functions in part to have one film reinforce the phobic logic of the other by literally doubling down on an ideological position.

Maria San Filippo's scholarship on bisexuality in film draws heavily from these historical critiques, noting the ways "bisexuality always risks becoming either sensationalized . . . or diluted and assimilatory."[71] The bisexual within these narrative scenarios is shifty by nature; she or he tends to be a schemer, opportunist, user, careerist, manipulator, deceiver, con artist; or alternatively, she or he is immature, directionless, confused, noncommittal, transient, and indifferent. In either formulation, the bisexual tends to be egocentric and uncaring. At first blush, *Something for Everyone* appears to conform to this paradigm. Its star, Michael York, would only a few years later play another bisexual character in *Cabaret*, only this time less shady and, perhaps, just appearing fickle.

One can find several instances of the *Something for Everyone* and *The Boys in the Band* double bill that Russo had observed.[72] In my research, I found two examples in the San Francisco Bay Area alone. The films were shown together at the Castro Theatre in September 1978 and the UC Theater in February 1978 (the same exact theaters and year as *Klute* and *Looking for Mr. Goodbar*).[73] At the same time, I found a host of other cases in which the films were paired with other queer films, especially ones that centralize bisexual characters, if not the theme of bisexuality. For instance, *Something for Everyone* was also shown repeatedly with *Cabaret* in cities and theaters throughout the Bay Area across nearly an entire decade: the UC Theater on August 16, 1976; Richelieu Cinema on September 26–28, 1976; Gateway Cinema on November 24–30, 1976; and the Castro Theatre on September 22, 1979, July 25, 1980, and July 29–30, 1984. Surely York's stardom and diegetic bisexuality serve as the double bill's adhesive and appeal, but its repetition sets off a deeper set of questions about the films' interdiegesis that might trouble the "good" vs. "bad" object binary that queer representational politics has established (perhaps with the aid of some double bills!).

Something for Everyone (fig. 4.9) is a class farce that almost reads as a mainstream retelling of Pasolini's overtly Marxist *Teorema*, which was released only two years prior. (Note that *Something for Everyone* was in fact based on Harry Kressing's 1965 novel *The Cook*, with echoes more of Patricia Highsmith's Ripley archetype.) Konrad (whose name invokes "con," as in "con man"), played by York, is a mysterious figure who bicycles into a German country town and sets his sights on the castle on the hilltop, a residence owned by the aristocratic Orstein family. After becoming their butler, Konrad schemes and kills to climb the social ladder, shifting tactics when plans go awry, and by the end, seduces multiple family members including the Orstein matriarch, played by Angela Lansbury, and her son, a shy, closeted homosexual teen. By contrast, York's character, Brian,

Conrad the butler.
If he doesn't kill you, he'll have an
affair with your wife. Or your son.
Or your daughter. If he doesn't commit
any of those delightful old
sins, he'll think of...
Something for Everyone.

The butler did it...to everyone!

The Countess

Her Son

Her Daughter

Her Daughter-in-Law

Angela Lansbury • Michael York
"Something for Everyone"
...a comedy of evil.

A CINEMA CENTER FILMS PRESENTATION
co-starring John Gill • Heidelinde Weis • Jane Carr • Eva Maria Meineke
introducing Anthony Corlan • screenplay by HUGH WHEELER • produced by JOHN FLAXMAN
from the novel "THE COOK" written by HARRY KRESSING • directed by HAROLD PRINCE • in COLOR
A MEDIA PRODUCTION • A NATIONAL GENERAL PICTURES RELEASE [R]

4.9 The poster for *Something for Everyone* (dir. Hal Prince, 1970) belies the fact that everyone—not just the bisexual—is a schemer.

in *Cabaret* is sensitive and caring, embracing the openly capricious Sally Bowles (famously played by Liza Minnelli), whose preoccupation with life's pleasures deflects life's problems as well as the escalating sociopolitical turbulence of early 1930s Germany. The two enter into a love affair with a charismatic and rich playboy who abandons them both. A b-plot involves their friend Fritz, a German Jew masquerading as a protestant, who is in love with a Jewish heiress.

On the surface, the two films offer opposing bi types (one conniving and the other stray), but on a deeper level, the double bill puts to a test bisexuality's narrative function and its relation to the social bonds among the films' characters. Maria San Filippo's playful concept of "bi-textuality" is helpful here. By deploying a kind of ideological double layering, bi-textuality "attempts to work through bisexuality . . . by reading it through another discourse pertaining to economic class, cultural heritage, ethnicity, gender roles, mental health, or psychological states."[74] Such a movement between text/signifier (bisexual persons and/or acts) and the subtext/signified (its proxy or symbolic meaning production) offers a constructive pathway for interpreting sexuality's allegorical operation within these films' (inter)diegetic structures.[75]

Cabaret and *Something for Everyone* invoke a device that involves two registers that formalize their bi-textuality—that of background and foreground (fig. 4.10). Typage (e.g., stereotypes and archetypes) often tends to occupy the foreground in critical analyses of bisexuality, which then pushes all the constitutive elements of narrative and frame to the back. This background often works either in service of the problematic representation or as extraneous refuse that can be ignored or even negated. In *Cabaret* and *Something for Everyone*, however, diegetic context and ensemble characters compose a backdrop that reframes the bisexual's status and function, thereby altering the dual bill's entire exegesis.

In *Something for Everyone*, there is no virtue against which to measure Konrad's wicked behavior because, typical of many black comedies, all the characters lack a moral compass and act out of self-interest. Subterfuge is diffuse across the cast, and indeed Konrad's stealth is pitted against the old-world strategies of marrying for or into money as a means of sustaining or attaining wealth. The gentry, *Something for Everyone* stresses, is just as petty and superficial, desperately driven by their own ambitions. The Orstein matriarch, played by Lansbury with an ironic blend of resolve and resignation, monologues in multiple scenes about her family's dissipating finances. This sentiment culminates in a long tracking shot toward the end of the film in which she melancholically strolls past the castle's paintings, photographs, and other relics of her family's legacy, speaking of her diminishing societal relevance. Set against this dissipation and decay, *Something for Everyone* is a class farce that indicts everyone, especially a waning and anachronistic aristocracy in post-socialist Europe, who must scheme to preserve their social status.[76]

Something for Everyone pushes a background of opportunistic supporting characters into the foreground, equating them with what might otherwise

4.10 A *Cabaret* (dir. Bob Fosse, 1972) publicity still stresses tensions between foreground and background.

be perceived as an immoral bisexual menace. *Cabaret*, too, figuratively racks focus, but does so by refusing to segregate the characters from their sociopolitical backdrop, which continues to bleed into, if not disrupt, the narrative flow (fig. 4.10). Both the a-plot love triangle and b-plot romance between one closeted Jew and an open Jew operate in tandem to presage the Nazis' aspiration for a future ethnically and sexually "purified" Germany in which neither relationship can exist. Totalitarianism and genocide loom for both the characters grappling with the changing tide as well as the historically aware audience dreading what is to come. This double feature therefore incites a to-and-fro "bi-textual" motion within and across the texts—doubling and layering within the double feature structure itself—intradiegetically and interdiegetically, with York's bisexual a locus through which background and foreground pass into each other, thereby altering and alternating perceptions of what and who matters within a given narrative space.

Before the release of *Cabaret*, when it would become a regular double-bill companion to *Something for Everyone*, the Times Theater in San Francisco showed *Something for Everyone* with *Flesh* on November 19–20, 1973.[77] The double bill offers two distinct definitions of male bisexual hustling:

one a sex worker and the other hustling his way to the top. In *Flesh*, Joe Dallesandro is a street hustler who drifts from one sexual encounter to another, sometimes for work and other times out of boredom.[78] As with York, the star paratext in part informs the cinephilic and critical interest in *Flesh*, as there is a documentary slippage to Dallesandro, who, in his real life before becoming the hunky poster boy for Warhol's Factory, was a bisexual nude model and hustler himself. *Flesh*'s shaky handheld camera capturing extended, uneventful—meandering even—conversations in a mix of long takes and jump cuts, and its casual inclusion of male and female frontal nudity, makes it in many ways a stylistic inverse of the polished and classically styled *Something for Everyone*.

If a historical spectator wanted to read the two films for any moralizing stance on hustling (and bisexuality as a kind of social hustle), they would quickly run into trouble. Primarily, the dual bill eludes a simple opposition of commercial/mainstream vs. independent/art house representation. The open-ended observational style of *Flesh* does not necessarily redeem or demonize bisexuality; it leaves judgment largely up to the viewer, though negative preconceptions about sex work would have been common, compounded by potential knowledge that Morrissey himself claimed his films were tales of America's declining values. As a formal mismatch that lacks clear dialectical or parallel relation, this double bill exemplifies the limits of typage in analytical procedures. In lieu of clear representational politics, the several double bills that include *Something for Everyone* ask much more compelling and open-ended questions about, for instance, the many meanings and guises of hustling, and how bisexuality gets centralized within those discourses and representations. Repertory time helps to elucidate the theme of doubling here, generating from it "infinite peripheries" that span laterally across multiple texts, and also move medially between a text's many surfaces and depths. This itinerant intra- and intertextual movement helps free bisexuality of its cultural and critical fixity.

Coda

Repertory time, as I have conceptualized it in this chapter, virtually comes to an end by the 1980s and early 1990s due to the proliferation of VHS. The rise of Blockbuster Video and niche independent video stores meant that people no longer needed to go to the repertory cinema to see old classics, cult films, obscure foreign features, or even semi-recent releases on their second run. Repertory houses thereafter went into decline, with only a few lasting through the years. Within what might be called VHS *time*, one can watch on one's own schedule, stop, rewind, fast-forward, pause, and watch the movie over and over again. This practice might magnify the compulsive and recursive cinephilic habits of repertory time, but it also curtails the ritual of communal viewing and potential for spectatorial surprise.[79]

Long-duration viewing has more recently taken the form of *binge-watching*, a term that emerged in the 1990s and grew exponentially in the first decades of the 2000s alongside the expansion of DVD, DVR, as well as what scholars and critics call "quality" or "prestige" TV.[80] Netflix helped usher binge-watching into the age of streaming in 2008 when they began offering high-quality streaming of films and TV shows on their website.[81] In the years since, the use of algorithms to predict taste has undergone ongoing scrutiny, consumers often remarking on their ineffectiveness and media scholars and critics sounding the alarms on media companies' control and surveillance tactics. Despite these concerns, most streaming consumers continue to habitually devour the heaps of scripted and unscripted content released each week on platforms such as Amazon, Hulu, Netflix, Peacock, HBO Max, and so on.

This glut of content production and distribution has led to a fatigue, for both the audience and the entertainment industry's financial structures. Caetlin Benson-Allott observes that streaming's overabundance of content induces what she calls the "ennui of the scroll," that is, a common consumer experience of numbingly and aimlessly browsing the plethora of film and TV options on platform catalogues.[82] Like Neta Alexander, Benson-Allott reveals that streaming, though appearing to offer a utopian picture of plenitude, pushes the consumer into an anxious and directionless state.[83] In this sense, the grid of the streaming interface offers a divergent experience from the grid of the repertory calendar; binge-watching looks little like repertory time. The ennui of the scroll is a nightmarish symptom of not just surplus but also little to no filtration, that is, proper (human) curation.[84]

Film festivals—all which range from the high-profile international markets to moderately sized, quasi-indie cinephile gatherings to retrospective sites of worship of silent or rare film prints to microcinema-style local happenings of less than a hundred people—have preserved and protected the classic filmgoing model of being in a dark space full of strangers all watching the same film or media (when they are not virtual, that is).[85] However, festival time is not repertory time, even when its fare is akin to the repertory house (and when it isn't cost prohibitive for the average patron, either). Even at Il Cinema Ritrovato in Bologna, spectators rush to get to screenings, attendance is often limited, and attendees are forced into a daze from all the watching.[86] Historically, repertory cinemas did offer marathon viewing, but that was by no means their modus operandi. In contrast to the festival, repertory time has quotidian intervals, is punctuated by lived experience, and includes an ever-changing audience of strangers, dependent upon the day and time.[87]

Throughout this chapter I have tried not to make steadfast or deterministic claims about what effects queer or deviant double bills have on spectators, but instead to pry open the multivalence and polyvocality that such viewing phenomena engender. If anything, double features disrupt a logic of a stable text that entails secured analysis or interpretation. This is in large part because the double bill is predicated on intertextuality that is immediate, in the span of a single sitting. As I have demonstrated, these chains or relays of signification enabled spectators to think and feel through different versions of what only in title appears in the same film.

In an age before the software-engineered programming of taste done by algorithms, human programmers and spectators had to consciously and non-consciously work reciprocally with one another. Arguably, some double bills were meant to fulfill audiences' fantasies of nostalgia or social harmony, but there are enough instances where programmers set out to introduce audiences to unfamiliar or even uncomfortable content, as the example of *Happiness* being shown with *The Lovers* illustrates. Even when double bills seemed aimed at making profits off salacious content, there existed a powerful potential for spectators to be transformed by these films' configurations.

Repertory programmers, whether intentionally or not, prompted hermeneutic exercises in spectators who were asked to think and feel within the space of a dyadic viewing rather than one of singularity. As I have indicated, audiences were frequently asked to hold conflicting thoughts and affects together, urging them toward new openings for critique and pleasure both with their given objects and the world beyond the cinema. What in part made filmgoing so exciting at this time, besides its collective experience in a pre-VHS and digital world, was discovering what new knowledges and sensations might emerge from unexpected curatorial permutations. While theorists have elaborated on the important contextual aspects of screening environments and architectures, type of audiences, and image and sound quality, it is my hope that this chapter—or, rather, this project overall—has put into the conversation the aspect of programming. This constellating practice puts films in dialogue with other films, constituting and reconstituting their affective and cultural meanings, which reverberate into pasts and futures already felt and futures still to come.

5

For Shame!

ON THE HISTORY OF PROGRAMMING
QUEER "BAD OBJECTS"

In 1990, as film festivals across North America and Europe were looking toward the future of indie cinema with what would become known as New Queer Cinema, San Francisco's fourteenth annual Frameline Film Festival for gay and lesbian cinema was also reassessing the past.[1] That year, the festival programmed a retrospective series on women-in-prison films including *Caged* (dir. John Cromwell, 1950), *Prisonnières* (dir. Charlotte Silvera, 1988), and *Scrubbers* (dir. Mai Zetterling, 1982).[2] The accompanying description in the Frameline program states the series' purpose: it was part investigation of the heterosexual male fixation on lesbian desire and part exploration of female empowerment and lesbian spectatorial looking relations that could be gleaned from the genre. Given that this genre was among the most disdained by feminists throughout the 1970s, clearly Frameline's programming had signaled a sea change.[3] Had lesbian feminists left behind their critiques of sexploitation films, with their excessive displays of bare breasts and stereotypical depictions of hysterical and prurient women? What had transpired in the 1980s, perhaps even earlier, to encourage such a reconsideration? Even if it was not a complete reclamation, a spectatorial positioning that had been unthinkable a decade prior had manifested in the form of an institutionally supported and tangible phenomenon: the film series.

Film programming and curation, a key facet of film exhibition often overlooked in film theory and scholarship, I would argue, played a pivotal role in this shift toward queers loving queer "bad objects" that had long been accused of producing homophobic and transphobic injury, shame, self-loathing, and stigma. Programming, which I have defined as intertextuality put into practice, was over time able to change the meanings and affective associations of once offensive texts. Although there are several queer examples of this phenomenon, it is perhaps the ongoing programming of lesbian "bad objects" that presents the most complex of case studies, given the intersection of gender and sexual oppression, and the illuminating feminist reading strategies that became especially prominent by the 1990s.[4] This chapter therefore tracks the reevaluation of women-in-prison films, lesbian vampire films, and Russ Meyer's "skin flicks," dwelling at times on specific canonical lesbian films: *Daughters of Darkness, Caged, The Big Doll House* (dir. Jack Hill, 1971), and *Faster, Pussycat! Kill! Kill!* (dir. Russ Meyer, 1965).

This chapter pursues two interconnected propositions related to the programming of "bad objects," the first of which is meant to be a methodological intervention and the second more descriptive.[5] First, I tackle queer film criticism's difficulty historicizing spectatorial pleasure for and, crucially, *with* mainstream cinema.[6] I here bring to bear multiple ways to narrate this history, throwing into crisis a unilineal telling that positions trauma at the center, as is the case in many histories, and pleasure at the margins, of queer spectatorship.[7] I suggest that programming might direct film historians toward intertextual readings of filmic assemblages that encourage what I consider *reparative historicizing*. Within this methodology, the historian forges a relationship to the past that does not presuppose loss, deficiency, and pain but rather is open to various positions that one can have to a past context.

Second, I zero in on several specific programs to demonstrate how *repertory programming*, by way of *repetition*, leads to *rep*arative relationships with individual films by continually putting them in relation to other films. As I will explain, this comes with time's passing, as texts lose their relevance and intensity, but repeated programming and viewing also weakens a text's unity or rigidity, making films riper to be treated by audiences as what Eve Kosofsky Sedgwick refers to as "part-objects," or what Richard X. Feng deems "scavenged bits and pieces," those shards or fragments of texts that can unmake and remake attachments.[8] The examples that follow help tell the story or explain how troublesome texts were "reclaimed," but the programming of films such as *Daughters of Darkness* or *Faster, Pussycat! Kill! Kill!* also lends nuance to theoretical definitions of *reparativity*. The later relationships that lesbian feminist audiences forged with these films reveal the reparative position entails more than a simple reversal of the paranoid one.

Reparativity is a less reactive and more robust framework for approaching these questions than the notion of *reclamation*, which suggests some kind of cultural ownership, or "negotiation," which tends to be framed by wins and losses. "Reparative reading" has become a popular practice adopted by queer theorists of affect since Eve Kosofsky Sedgwick first employed Melanie Klein's psychoanalytic concept in her essay "Paranoid Reading and Reparative Reading, Or, You're so Paranoid, You Probably Think This Essay Is About You." This essay, which urges critical theory to integrate joy, pleasure, and healing into its analyses of culture, has also made some cameos in film and media studies.[9] Strangely, however, no one has considered it in relation to those films that have been maligned in the past but then later exonerated. Reparativity, in my conception of the paradigm, is not meant to simply explain a kind of unadulterated pleasure that takes the place of negative feelings. It is not simply about "feeling good." Reparativity, instead, leaves room for a plenitude of simultaneous spectatorial psychological and emotional states, of which empowerment, ambivalence, and shame are but a few. Like Patricia White's use of the psychoanalytic term *representability* instead of *representation*, *reparativity* over *reparation* here attempts to gesture at what is available and apprehensible—as an open question or proposition—to a spectator, as an option that may prove enriching *or* insufficient in the end.[10]

Reparativity is full of productive contradiction and imaginative incommensurability. As Sedgwick argues, it is "possible in turn to use one's own resources to assemble or 'repair' the murderous part-objects into something like a whole—though, I would emphasize, *not necessarily like any preexisting whole*."[11] In lieu of hoping to find a wholly satisfying object for attachment, implicit here is a sense that marginalized subjects produce alternate practices for seeking out those nourishing "part-objects" in popular culture. Invoking a kind of disidentification, Sedgwick regards pleasure as already contaminated—it is a mixture of tropes, attachments, fantasies, and disavowals that can be revised and reworked. I would suggest that this conception might lead us to a more ethically inclined politics of pleasure that enables the cohabitation of critique, fantasy, recognition, identification, curiosity, and ambivalence, sometimes simultaneously. My definition of *reparativity*, therefore, emphasizes a loosening of the text's grip—a repudiation of the text as authoritative and monologic—in order to make room for more dynamic forms of processing texts collectively and diachronically.

Literary and media theorists tend to use *reparative reading* in terms of attachment to the object, that is, to the text. In order to seek out pleasure, these theories hinge on a notion that subjects are not at the mercy of the external object but can find modes of adjustment or coping in order to change the attachment to the object.[12] But this chapter takes a step back from this by not presupposing that it is first and foremost the relation to the text-as-object that is being repaired. Programming, as anchored in a viewing context and history, makes clear that besides the relation to the text, one's relationship to the communal, that is, the public and counterpublic, can oftentimes undergo repair. There is also one's relation to history itself, which might be conterminous with an imagined community. And then there is the possibility of repairing or healing the relation to the self, and the self as part of a community or several communities, or the self as part of the historical present.[13] In short, the object may shift, even moment to moment, and these objects (history, community, identity, and text) are usually composites of one another, and charged with meaning.

Programming thereby illuminates the ways that reparativity courses along several vectors, many of which are intersecting. It advances the Barthesian stance that the power of readers' subjectivities can undermine the role of the author even one degree further by suggesting that the embodied viewing context sometimes competes with, if not wholly shapes, the text itself to produce counter-readings and rereadings.[14] I contend that programming problematic queer texts engenders pleasure for *and* with "bad objects" that comes as a result of moving through, not simply displacing, a layered affective repertoire. As Lauren Berlant writes, "The very shifting of the subject in response to its own threat to its self-attachment can be the source of an affective creativity that is not just a fantasmatic toupée, but also the possibility of a recalibrated sensorium."[15]

In many historical cases, programming is a diachronic process of mapping and remapping spectatorial sensoria. Communal responses and awareness of historical modes of representation are therefore central to reparativity. The camp reading is one much-discussed queer reparative strategy that requires the affective work of community interaction. One might even say that camp readings are programmed—learned and recycled, and passed on from one queer generation to another. In the pages that follow, I use camp readings to exemplify and highlight the communal and diachronic aspects of reparativity. Camp readings necessitate the dialectical nearness *and* distance that come with insider recognition and enjoyment of recycled tropes and clichés. This knowledge accrues over time and through communal interaction (such as laughter), in turn resignifying queer objects. In this sense, programming, through repetition and iteration, can make clichés and tropes identifiable and locatable, and thus useful for parodic ways to not only approach the text but also reimagine worlds.

Trauma Trouble

In queer film criticism, mainstream cinema has long stood as the culprit of distasteful depictions of LGBT people. To many critical and scholarly accounts, its history is laden with ruthless Hollywood directors and executives sensationalizing or censoring sexuality and gender variance. Accordingly, Hollywood and other mainstream industries made films littered with vilified stereotypes of the helpless pansy, the prurient lesbian vampire, the self-loathing and confused closet case, the insatiable bisexual, and the depraved transsexual. And as one might assume, their narrative outcomes were almost always bleak.[16] This is, of course, if the film could even get away with explicitly representing queerness instead of just alluding to or encoding it, as was the case during the Hays Code years. For critics and scholars, these texts reflected an oppressive culture determined to malign queers. The result of these depictions, it has been argued, is to help construct or reinforce inimical ideas, and also, for queer spectators, to produce feelings of self-disgust and inadequacy. It is in this way that trauma and harm—both self-inflicted and motivating hate in others—get centralized in queer film scholarship that charts non-avant-garde, pre–New Queer Cinema histories.

The main force, figure, and teller of this convincing traumatic narrative is Vito Russo, whose book *The Celluloid Closet* may have seemed just the antidote. Stemming from a leftist gay liberation ethos, Russo's view was that Hollywood, as the great generator of cultural myths, had perpetuated homophobia by monopolizing the hearts and minds of American spectators. Russo tended to stick to the party line: a good queer film had to be anti-escapist and anti-fantasy (ironically, he deemed *Rocky Horror Picture Show* an "expert satire"); depict the effects of homophobia (a little self-loathing was fine, but not too much); treat queer characters with compassion; emphasize dimensionality over stereotyping; give authentic glimpses into the lived experience of (white and middle-class) gays and lesbians; and, crucially, provide characters with a chance to pursue a future of self-acceptance. This telling privileges "positive representation," with affirmation leading us on the righteous path to healing and (self-)respect.[17]

The Celluloid Closet might now read as a time capsule of an important moment in gay rights history, one that bears little resemblance or relevance to the present. Professors teaching queer cinema courses have indeed phased out Russo's groundbreaking anti-Hollywood treatise; however, the narrative has seemed to stick.[18] The idea that mainstream media had to render queerness invisible or encode it keeps the text feeling relevant to this day, especially as righteous politics come back in vogue. (Consider the attacks on the 2017 indie hit about male intergenerational desire *Call Me by Your Name* for supposedly sanitizing its homosexual sex scenes.[19]) Further, from gender studies to film studies courses, Rob Epstein and Jeffrey Friedman's 1995 documentary of the same name continues to be a mainstay of queer film pedagogy. The film version, similar to the book, enjoins its readers to adopt a certain kind of interrogative practice that takes representation at face value. This becomes a teachable narrative with a cogent argument and streamlined thesis about queer film history.

Epstein and Friedman's documentary, Heather Love suggests, echoes Russo's aim to chart what she provisionally calls the "trauma of queer spectatorship."[20] However, Love shrewdly observes that something felicitous happens in translation. Though following the same overall structure as the book, the documentary version of *The Celluloid Closet* (1995) supplements Russo's narration with a polyphony of voices—ranging from scholarly expertise to personal anecdote—from critics, actors, and directors who all have close relationships to the queer films cited. Love writes, "The use of interviews creates the atmosphere of a group screening, in which knowing subjects speak over and against the images we see on the screen and also drain them of their pathologizing force."[21] Love here pinpoints how the documentary functions as a (conscious or not) reparative modifier to Russo's severe approach, lending other viewpoints and positions to a queer spectatorial past. Such voices, I would agree, mitigate the perceived trauma of queer spectatorship by giving necessary voice to negative affects as well as by restoring the place of pleasure, awkward and shameful as it may be at times.[22] Take, for example, Harvey Fierstein's proclaimed love for and identification with the stereotype of the sissy, or Susie Bright reveling in Mrs. Danvers's fur fetishism in *Rebecca* (Alfred Hitchcock, 1940). By including clips from and romantic montages of different queer films, or even films with sparse queer moments, the documentary tacitly sidesteps Russo's line of argumentation, thereby enacting a form of reparative historicizing that subordinates—in moments—trauma to pleasure. It brings to bear the alternate histories, where structures of *multiple* feelings are brought to the fore.

From a reparative vantage point, much scholarly queer film historiography begins to look, as Sedgwick would put it, quite "paranoid." After all, the narrators of this history meet Sedgwick's criteria for paranoid readings: to anticipate an object's harm; to have faith in the ideological exposure, demystification, and decryption of its harm; and to generate others' analogous participation by way of making paranoia teachable and mimetic. I want to stress that Russo is not the only paranoid reader in this historiography, despite his resounding influence.[23] Reading queer cinema scholarship through the years, pleasure is too often taken as suspect. The default critical starting point is frequently homophobia, heteronormativity, and heterosexism, the scholar then positing how these problematically structure desire and identification.[24]

Reparative historicizing, in contrast, might first require for the subject some affective space from historical objects; this might serve as a precursor to seeking out sources for alternate experiences, for instance, where pleasure dared to exist not just in experimental and avant-garde cinema, but also in Hollywood, independent, and world cinema as it was programmed recurrently in art houses. I invoke Sedgwick to emphasize that pursuing reparativity allows a reader to "entertain such profoundly painful, profoundly relieving, ethically crucial possibilities as that the past, in turn, could have happened differently from the way it actually did."[25]

So how to produce a reparative counternarrative? One could argue that such a reparative approach to history already exists in queer film studies. Alexander Doty's theoretical inquiries into popular culture and the film canon, for instance, reveal the ways that close reading and autobiography can work in tandem to locate queerness *within* the text, not grafted onto it, as heterosexist views might dictate. *Pee Wee's Playhouse* (1986–1990) and *The Wizard of Oz* (dir. Victor Fleming, King Vidor, George Cukor, Richard Thorpe, Norman Taurog, 1939) are but a number of "heterosexual" texts Doty seeks to decode as containing LGBT characters and narratives. Doty's mission, after all, is to explore what pleasure or critiques can be discerned on the part of queer viewers who have been historically sidelined.[26]

As poignant and, at times, uplifting as his work has been, Doty's textual analyses are meant to channel the history of queer spectatorship, not locate it. Doty tended to forgo embodied historical viewing conditions for the sake of psychoanalytic or intertextual readings with vague cultural contexts. Alternately, programming, as a tool for reparative historicizing, can better serve to support but also complicate Doty's readings.[27] As an exhibition practice that works in a feedback loop to cater to spectators' desires at the same time that it disrupts and redirects those desires, programming challenges taken-for-granted notions about queer spectatorship, in turn lending insight into the conditions through which new sensations and new understandings of old sensations can emerge.

Oddly enough, one need not stray too far from Russo's biography to detect a counternarrative that is historically situated in the programming of his time. The November/December 1978 program from the Roxie Cinema (fig. 5.1), located in the Mission District of San Francisco, provides a fascinating wormhole into a reparative kind of affective intermingling. Nestled in the middle of the calendar grid is a box that reads "THE CELLULOID CLOSET" in bold capital letters. The event is described as follows:

> Combining his interest in films with gay activism, Vito Russo has spent a great deal of effort in documenting, analyzing, and criticizing the portrayal of homosexuality in the cinema. His forthcoming book *The Celluloid Closet* looks at the stereotypes and role models that the silver screen has presented of and to the homosexual. His lecture will document the changing image of gays in film with excerpts from several dozen films, including *The Children's Hour, Advise and Consent, Victim, Broadway Melody, The Boys in the Band, Call Her Savage, Tea and Sympathy,* and *Sunday, Bloody, Sunday.*[28]

One might expect the month's other programming to move along the same grain as Russo's thesis, but on the contrary, and not unlike the documentary adaptation of his book, the program reveals a different story. Strung across the calendar are double bills of significant queer films, many of which get but brief mention in Russo's text: a weekend exploring Italy's perverse sexual history with the help of Pasolini's *Decameron* and Fellini's *Satyricon*; another weekend of what the programmers called "camping out," enlisting the film *Outrageous!*, which tells the story of an aspiring drag queen, programmed with the documentary cult classic *Grey Gardens*, where aspirations go to die and then are immortalized in the text itself; just below is a John Waters double bill of *Desperate Living* (1977) and *Female Trouble*; the calendar even gives a peek into the programming for the first week of January 1979, which includes a "Decodada" pairing of *Salome* (dir. Charles Bryant, 1923), starring the film's producer and lesbian actress Alla

5.1 One locked closet and a whole lot of open doors in the Roxie's winter 1978 calendar. Courtesy of University of California, Berkeley, BAMPFA Film Library and Study Center.

Nazimova, and Jean Cocteau's *Blood of a Poet* (1932), which has garnered queer readings through the years due in part to its maker's open bisexuality.

This group of queer double bills creates what I call in chapter 4 *repertory time*, a concept that denotes extended and immersive viewing hours spent at the repertory cinema. Double bills, which structure repertory time, have the ability to plunge spectators into novel modes of criticality or submerge them in interdiegetic worlds of perverse, deviant delight. Repertory time, in allowing texts to promiscuously mingle with other texts across time, also proliferates ramified meanings that morph diachronically depending on intertextual arrangements and the cultural moments of their multiple revivals. In this sense, repertory time here is also reparative time. In their ongoing circulation and recurring exhibition, these espoused queer classics find renewed energy not only symbiotically by finding each other in a deviant cosmos, but also frictionally by scratching up against disparate joyless portrayals.

This 1978 calendar lends intertextual evidence to queer film history's multi-narrativity. The Roxie program assembles films made by queer auteurs and amateurs, straight documentarians, and collaborations among the sexually ambiguous and sexually resolute. As suggested in my abbreviated descriptions of the films, a fantastical cosmos of decadence cuts across many of these selections, whether couched in the extravagant failures of *Grey Gardens* or *Desperate Living*, or in the nostalgia for queer mythology in the perverse Italian double feature and "Decodada" evenings. In this instance, reparativity therefore does not hinge upon a total rereading of the films in and of themselves, but is an effect of reading through a program's assemblage. It challenges Russo's thesis because it makes clear in an empirical sense that, alongside the vexed representations manufactured by Hollywood, there also existed a counternarrative highly accessible to urban audiences. I read this calendar as a history where pleasure dared to exist, an exercise in reparative historicizing that leaves room to retrofit a multifaceted queer history ripe for recuperation to queer theory's explicit affection for decadence, camp, insouciance, and resilience.

Calendars such as this one could be positioned as *contact zones*, which are, as Donna Haraway aptly defines them, "material–semiotic nodes or knots in which diverse bodies and meanings coshape one another."[29] For Haraway and many other affect theorists, contact zones are spaces of possibility, contingency, reflection, and productive tension. Programs embody these kinds of contact zones where different objects meet to foster new connections among themselves and new knowledges on the part of spectators. Films converge with and diverge from one another, congeal and fail to meet, form dialectics and parallels, cross-pollinate and cross-pollute.

We might see the meeting ground of the double bill "Camping Out," in which *Outrageous!* and *Grey Gardens* were paired together, as a contact zone that further cultivated queer reading practices. The Maysles brothers' 1975 documentary *Grey Gardens*, about mother and daughter fallen socialites living in their dilapidated East Hampton mansion, contains but one supporting LGBT character. But by the programmatic framing device of "camping out," spectators were encouraged to look at the entire film through a queer lens, just as its co-feature demands. The film's camp factor is felt strongest in Little Edie, presenting to the camera her bizarre musical numbers and makeshift outfits; for some, she might resemble a drag queen on her last leg. This would in part explain how the film has been treated as a queer allegory for outsiderness and endurance in the face of social ruin. Here the contact zone of the calendar meets the contact zone of the theater, where we might assume many spectators had an awareness of *Grey Gardens'* queer sensibility in this instance, especially given the cinema's neighborhood adjacency to the Castro in San Francisco. In this sense, "camping out" is a framing device that reinforces the representational codes of queerness by producing for those just discovering the film, or perhaps validating for those more familiar with it, queer ways of feeling like a social outlier, misfit, or freak.

This Roxie calendar also exemplifies the ways that histories themselves clash within their own kinds of contact zones. Russo's formulation of injurious representation as dominant meets the dominance of its pleasure-inducing counter-history within the exact same schedule. These, however, might be received as competing strategies for reparativity that emerge from discordant or asynchronous temporalities, as Elizabeth Freeman might call them.[30] After all, one could argue that finding solidarity in critique of the queer clichés and stereotypes that populate film history is a reparative move in the communal sense. This is akin to what bell hooks describes as the "oppositional gaze" that finds a "pleasure in interrogation."[31] At the same time, this form of collective comfort still keeps a paranoid view of objects—they set out to injure. An alternate history of pleasure is one that must be discovered elsewhere, perhaps not in historicity itself but by discerning how we, as Richard Dyer puts it, "feel the historicity of our feelings."[32] Programming provides such an outlet.

The contact zone of the program reveals what Raymond Williams calls "structures of feeling" that brim underneath the surface of what appears a fixed or finished history. Williams writes that "even where form and response can be found to agree, without apparent difficulty, there can be qualifications, reservations, indications elsewhere."[33] Those "exceptions," Williams suggests, also crucially structure history, despite the fact that they often go unnamed, overlooked, unarticulated, or silenced. Perhaps the queer structures of feeling created in this Roxie calendar have been sidelined because they do not register as commensurate with or illustrative of the political identity formations of the time. In other words, the calendar's intertext perhaps did not read as political because it did not exemplify a legible liberation ethos that would have been popular at this point in San Francisco and other US cities. At the same time, the intertext indexes a silent yet salient position that cannot be simply reduced in presentist terms to one of pride or empowerment (notions that can thinly cloak liberal respectability politics). Here we might discard an idea of pleasure as simply "feeling good," or more specifically, finding resolution within that satisfaction. This history indicates thornier, and again, more contaminated forms of pleasure.

Cohabitation of affects here parallels the cohabitation of histories at tension with one another. Confronting knotty and knotted relationships to so-called dated texts, Ramzi Fawaz muses, "What might happen if we treated cultural representations *as if* they were our friends . . . in the sense of someone with whom we engage in a meaningful dialogue and action . . . And we might learn to forgive these forms when they fail us."[34] Doing so might open us up to a nexus of muddier affective engagement that traverses uncertainty, curiosity, incredulity, critique, and identification, which can together form the reparative scene, for the historian as well as for the viewer at the time. Reparative historicizing is in part a process of speaking to or orienting us toward both pre-emergent and manifest desires and critiques that did not in their present find narration or description. They must be sought out in marginal sources of affect such as programming.

Across Time

Recognizing and activating the coexistence of multiple histories is more easily done from the vantage point of temporal removal than in the present. It is worth noting that this is not equivalent to the progressivist notion and slogan that "it gets better." Oppression thrives in forms too covert and invisible to warrant such a hasty claim. At the same time, one is more likely to form a reparative relationship to a problematic film when one acknowledges that they are in a different moment than when the film was first released. This is precisely the kind of "temporal awareness" that Meira Likierman, in analyzing Melanie Klein's concept of reparation, says orients a person toward making good with his or her objects.[35]

The camp reading is a perfect example of how this operates. As Susan Sontag claims, "Things are campy, not when they become old—but when we become less involved in them, and can enjoy, instead of be frustrated by, the failure of the attempt."[36] For Sontag, a reparative reading of camp might be most rewarding for a spectator when the camp is unintentional. By this account, earnest representations, or better, representations *perceived as earnest* at the moment of their release, age to become pleasurably ironic, inflated, and mannerist, and therefore fail to be taken seriously in contemporary encounters. We might consider films such as *Cruising* and *The Killing of Sister George* as optimal examples of camp "bad objects" because their tropes and stereotypes of gays and lesbians as perverse fetishists become that much more obvious with time. Their repetition can now be so effortlessly detected that the retrograde depictions become amusing.[37]

Repertory programming—the name itself suggestive of *repetition*—can incite these forms of camp recognition. As Andy Ditzler proposes, programming reveals that cinema is "not just an art of time, but of *relation across time*." Repertory programming thus offers increasing opportunities for spectators to reencounter "bad objects" outside of their original historical contexts.[38] It is crucial to note that these forms of revision do not happen in isolation but among other people, including strangers and friends. The discernment of camp is especially contingent upon communal affective responses. Consider the concordant laughter that might permeate a room, a potential sign of knowing irony or incredulity. Celine Shimizu vividly describes this spectatorial scene when she recounts her experience seeing the stage musical *Miss Saigon* with fellow Asian and Asian American girlfriends, all of whom jeered and laughed at the show's fantasy of the docile Asian woman.[39] This communal response served to loosen the object's racist grasp, and therefore to create distance from it. At the same time, as Shimizu notes, this distance does not undo the attachment as much as create a disobedient relation to it. We might call this insubordinate relation a "camp reading." Repertory programming facilitates reading practices such as these, which help to reorient pleasure as a way to grapple with, not necessarily counteract, the retrograde.

I would suggest that the theater in this case is what Deborah Gould calls via Pierre Bourdieu an "emotional habitus," a contact zone that provides clusters of bodies with a set of parameters and expectations for how to think and feel, guiding desires and ruminations without fully determining or dictating them.[40] The cinema allows audiences in the dark to move affectively together with the potential of the current changing direction, yielding new sensoria and ideologies often simmering beneath the surface, or at times brimming over. This meeting ground of subjectivities and bodies might also yield a felt dissidence, one that Shimizu describes in her discussion of the post-show confrontation with other Asian(-American) female spectators who felt that the group's mockery extinguished the power of the performance's pathos. The contact zone here is also a contested zone where difference is sensed and might then be confronted.

Similarly, Vito Russo reported that at the Frameline Film Festival in 1988, "a screening of the 1936 classic *Dracula's Daughter* (dir. Lambert Hillyer) was marred by audience members' mindless knee-jerk booing of sexist remarks, which," he adds, "prevented more sophisticated audience members from hearing all the dialogue."[41] Whether Russo's quarrel is with the audience's lack of decorum, or with their rigid attitudes, the latter of which suggests he himself experienced a reparative shift during the 1980s in his views of old Hollywood films, is debatable. But more relevant here is the fact that there existed concurrent and clashing relations to *Dracula's Daughter* that caused a felt friction in the theater. Did the programmers foresee this reaction? Did they think *Dracula's Daughter* had camp value, and therefore the audience would find the "bad object" amusing? Did they regard it as a worthy artifact of historical curiosity? Or was it meant to force audiences to take stock of what had and had not changed in queer representation in the passing of time?

The Frameline programming from a year prior provides some clues. In 1987, one year before *Dracula's Daughter* had its spotlight screening and three years before the women-in-prison series with which this chapter opens, curator, filmmaker, and critic Andrea Weiss gave a presentation at Frameline on the lesbian vampire film and, similar to Russo, used clips from films such as *Dracula's Daughter* and *The Hunger* (dir. Tony Scott, 1983) to probe the question of queer representation.[42] The description of Weiss's presentation in the program is welcoming of debate but goes as far as "to explore what possibilities, if any, these films hold for subversive reinterpretations by gay and lesbian audiences."[43] Immediately following Weiss's presentation was a screening of *Daughters of Darkness* at the same venue, the Castro Theatre. Why *Daughters of Darkness* and not another lesbian vampire film? A strict historical logic *might* position the reparative readings

New Castro Midnight Series!
Daughters of Darkness
Beginning Saturday, August 2, and continuing every Saturday midnight until further notice during our Summer Festival, the Castro will present **Daughters of Darkness,** an elegant, surreal vampire story starring the honey-voiced, etherally beautiful Delphine Seyrig as a countess from Transylvania, who haunts a nearly desolate luxury hotel at Ostand on the Belgian coast where she meets a newly-wed couple and is immediately taken with the bride. At this point, it becomes clear that we are in for a vampire film of a very special nature—bizarre and compelling—dominated by the sophisticated, tongue-in-cheek portrayal of the exquisite Delphine. "A **satanic Auntie Mame, all cheek-bones, patent-leather and feather boas. A bit like seeing the devil in drag."**—Variety "**Quite flatly one of the most elegant horror pictures ever made. It is an ultra-sophisticated, utterly daring triumph of style and mood."**—Kevin Thomas, L.A. Times   Separate admission is required.

5.2 "A Satanic *Auntie Mame,*" *Daughters of Darkness* plays at the Castro "every Saturday midnight until further notice." Courtesy of University of California, Berkeley, BAMPFA Film Library and Study Center.

of the lesbian vampire film—with its themes of sexualized contagion—as evidence of queer defiance against the sex-phobia brought on by Reaganism and AIDS. While this may in part provide a synchronic explanation, it does little to account for the diachronic workings of programming *across time*, which cultivated contact zones of colliding meanings and feelings that reverberate into this later moment of the genre's reassessment.

Seven years prior to this presentation, in the summer of 1980, the Castro had decided to continually screen *Daughters of Darkness* as part of their summer midnight series "until further notice" (fig. 5.2). Even nine years after its initial release, *Daughters of Darkness* had clearly left its mark on queer spectators. Alone *Daughters of Darkness* is fairly homoerotic and even feminist. In her book *Vampires and Violets: Lesbians in Film*, Andrea Weiss notes that the film "tends deliberatively to subvert the lesbian vampire genre" by making heterosexuality "frighteningly abnormal and nightmarish" and queer desire a "welcome alternative."[44] In the same Castro Theatre calendar from 1980, several other films with lesbian themes or appeal played alongside *Daughters of Darkness*. These included *Pandora's Box* (dir. G. W. Pabst, 1929), *The Bitter Tears of Petra von Kant* (dir. Rainer Werner Fassbinder, 1972), and *Ninotchka* (dir. Ernst Lubitsch, 1939).[45] For lesbian regulars at the Castro, exposure to these other representations might spur comparative thinking. A queer female viewer might see *The Bitter Tears of Petra von Kant* and *Daughters of Darkness* only and be aroused by the sadomasochism in both films' depictions of master-slave scenarios. Or she might see the contrast between depictions of sadistic lesbians in such films as *Pandora's Box* and *The Bitter Tears of Petra von Kant* and that in *Daughters of Darkness*, favoring instead the otherworldly version Delphine Seyrig's vampiric character offers.

The extra diegetic, or what Gerard Genette calls the *paratextual* (such as audience knowledge of Louise Brooks's and Greta Garbo's queer sexualities or Seyrig's unabashed feminism), here might also team up with the intertextual to strengthen queer spectatorial associations.[46] In these situations, which are but a few in a multitude of possibility, *Daughters of Darkness*, because it was repeatedly programmed, is given opportunities to incite reparative readings. These arrangements illustrate what Patricia White, among other queer film historians, has argued: "reading formations evolve in relation to extra-cinematic practices such as gossip and subcultural codes as well as [promotional] intertextual matrices."[47] In this case, the program is another one of those intertextual matrices. *Daughters of Darkness*, far from a lone lesbian text, is infected by the others that surround it, endowing it with multiple associations and meanings that echo in its later reception.

Russo's observation at Frameline one year after Weiss's presentation attests to the fact that reparativity is a communal experience that seldom happens fluidly. The simultaneity of these discordant affective economies demonstrates a divide not just in reading practices but also in what programming is meant to do. Andrea Weiss, I would argue, frames the space of the cinema as one of proposition, of reconsidering visual objects whose modes of reception and therefore signification did, or at least could, shift. Repertory programs and series including "bad objects," in this light, might be seen as cinematic laboratories that leave room for spectatorial reflection and revision, not as tools to segregate the past and present, but to put them within each other's shifting orbits.

Weiss's programming of the lesbian vampire film series might be best engaged with through Judith Butler's (via Michel Foucault's) definition of *critique*. A practice that is distinct from judgment, critique is best understood as a reflexive mode by which one acknowledges one's subjectivization through a text and thereby "risks one's very formation as a subject."[48] For Butler, critique is an insecure "juncture where social norms intersect with ethical demands."[49] In other words, it is the ethical exercise of working through one's relation to a text as one reencounters the world beyond it. Critique might therefore open up a door to pleasure, but a pleasure that invites labile affective interaction in lieu of or before the ossification of opinion. These programs thus mark an opportunity for spectators to develop a critical practice out of rumination, which might indeed lead them to develop several positions on any given text simultaneously, to interpret the texts' interpellative power, and to respond to them anew. Programming could very well be seen as a form of critique that opens the door for thinking "critical" more capaciously.

Picking up the Pieces

When critique is treated as such a vulnerable exercise, as Butler suggests, the reparative process is likely to start with hesitation. The 1990 women-in-prison series at Frameline, with which this chapter starts, speaks to this point. Note the ambivalence in this excerpt of the series' description: "The punishment of female criminals has provided fodder for the male gaze and generated B-movie fare for decades. What happens between women when they are locked up together has pandered to the misogynist and prurient point-of-view; scratching and hair-pulling usually ensues. On the other end of the scale, the survival of women within a patriarchal justice system (albeit administered by other women) is a worthy and necessary subject to explore."[50] The description goes on to say that *Caged*, *Prisonnières*, and *Scrubbers* represent "different points within this continuum." The blurb is forthright in its critique and then tentative in its pleasurable recuperation of the women-in-prison genre. The parenthetical note, which demonstrates suspicion for a women-based power structure, qualifies the series' ability to be a "necessary subject to explore." However, this prose reveals only part of the story. Across the program's binding is a frame enlargement from *Caged* featuring Hope Emerson as the cruel matron and Eleanor Parker as her prisoner prey (fig. 5.3). The image of the two women takes up the entire page, and across the middle of it in large bold letters reads, **"lusty and lawless: the lesbian prison picture."** There exists a split between the program's two marketing strategies, one couched in feminist ambivalence, and the other appearing as if it was lifted from the cover and tagline of a lesbian pulp paperback, and thus meant to appeal precisely to viewers' "lusty" desires.

The ostensible dualism of this publicity—surely a product of contradictory readings—could be read as a sign that the festival organizers resigned

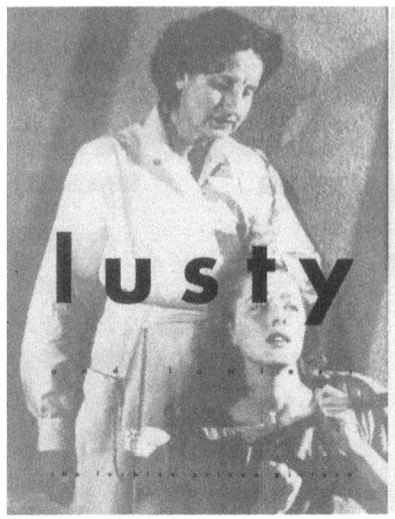

5.3 Dueling messages in Frameline's 1990 women-in-prison film series.

themselves to an affective impasse. However, we might also see this incongruence as an inchoate attempt to rethink the use value of camp within critical procedures. Judith Mayne's scholarship on the women-in-prison film is illuminating here in that she employs the genre to make room for what I consider a politics of pleasure. Admitting at the start that "there is much to love, and much to hate, about the women-in-prison film," Mayne writes that these films nevertheless offer "spectacles of female bonding, female rage, and female communities, with strong doses of camp and irony."[51]

Ironically, Mayne observes an earnest representation of female rebellion and empowerment in an otherwise campy style. This becomes a canny technique for Mayne to forge a reparative connection to the objects. Take, for example, Mayne's telling analysis of one scene from *The Big Doll House*, a Jack Hill women-in-prison film in which Pam Grier plays a dominant lesbian. Grier's character, who happens to be named "Grear," is left no choice but to perform unsavory sexual favors for the sleazy deliveryman in order to procure drugs for her addict girlfriend. When the deliveryman identifies her as a lesbian, Grear, in classic Pam *Grier* blaxploitation fashion, knowingly mocks his white straight masculinity with a cliché.[52] Mayne aptly recounts the scene: "'Strange desires creep up on you like a disease,' she says and tells him that her lesbianism is curable with a 'real' man—like him. One assumes that this is a performance, and it is certainly in keeping with the overall campy tone of the film."⁵³ Mayne here registers the scene's irony, a sardonic gesture at the homophobic (and here homosocially inflected) cliché that "she just needs the right man" to set her straight. In fact, one could say that this line of dialogue alone—which makes light of the myth of the lesbian contagion—sums up the camp pleasure of both women-in-prison films and lesbian vampire films programmed in retrospect, the idea of queer contagion and recruitment closer now to humorous than it was during the days of Anita Bryant.⁵⁴

In claiming that "it is precisely the coexistence of exploitation with feminism—sisterhood with attitude—that makes [them] so interesting," Mayne seems to be locating within her viewing experience the complex relationship between seriousness and camp, despite historical impulses to counterpose them.⁵⁵ Mayne's remark partially resonates with Jack Babuscio's suggestion that camp "allows us to witness 'serious' issues with temporary detachment, so that only later, after the event, are we struck by the emotional and moral implications of what we have almost passively absorbed."⁵⁶ But, crucially, rather than "detachment" serving as a measure to buffer or cushion inimical or thorny representation, which can then later facilitate reflection or analysis, Mayne frames the humor or risibility as precisely the thing that signposts the film's implications for lesbian feminist audiences. Camp and seriousness are thus adjoined in Mayne's reading of *The Big Doll House*, each co-animating the other, even as they represent distinct simultaneous registers.

Like the layout of the Frameline program, Mayne approaches the text, and by extension, the genre, as already fragmentary, a composite made of incongruous parts that require disparate reparative aims. Because the texts are recognized as "part-objects," as Sedgwick puts it, they allow room for a depressurized form of spectatorship that is not in pursuit of a total identification. By identification, I mean the idea that one feels present and recognized in the world of the text. When moments of identification happen in reparative camp readings of "bad objects," they may require spectators to recognize their own subject formation out of those shards, perhaps to even see their desires reflected in or produced by those fragments.⁵⁷ And by contrast, spectators might take pleasure in those disidentifactory moments that index stereotypes or simulacra that feel absurd and highly constructed. On yet another register, audiences might also derive pleasure from, as Racquel Gates observes, "negative texts precisely because of their distance from 'quality' and 'positivity,' if we understand these terms in quotes and presume that the audiences do as well."⁵⁸

Just as programming leads to reparative reading practices, as the Frameline programs on lesbian vampire and women-in-prison films exemplify, the inverse is also true: reparativity can be programmatic. I do not mean *programmatic* in the strict etymological sense of the word, *to write* ("-gram," from the Latin *graphein*) beforehand ("pro-"), but in the sense of having a durational build—an itinerary that can change course as it moves toward an elusive destination. These series are affective training grounds for how to unmake and remake attachment forms that do not overly invest in the object as whole or deterministic, just as reparativity itself tends not to be a unified process or fixed horizon to effortlessly glide toward. As Sedgwick stresses, "Hope, often a fracturing, even a traumatic thing to experience, is among the energies by which the reparatively positioned reader tries to organize the fragments and part-objects she encounters or creates."[59] Reparativity thus requires first a disposition of open willingness to transform objects and be transformed by them, and then from there, an elastic relation that keeps questions of style, temporality, sensibility, and fantasy in dynamic intertextual play.

Camp readings as critical practices that make use of excess—what Sedgwick affectionately calls "waste or leftover products"—are very much honed and inherited within queer cultures.[60] Pedagogies of camp retrain—reprogram, even—the sensorium, and disarticulate pleasure from simplistic notions of identification. Suddenly, identification might be found in the lowbrow codes of drag and freakishness in *Grey Gardens*. It is found in the female solidarity in a film such as *Caged*. Within queer modes of spectatorship that are learned, often passed on from generation to generation, there exist many other forms of attachment within the repertory milieu, such as humor that arises from spectators' recognition of clichés (*Les Biches*); the retrospective curiosity of imagined queer life (*Cruising*); the gratification derived from hyperbolic, unbelievable desire as it can only be realized on-screen (Russ Meyer's films).

I am describing here spectatorial scenes that are not so much "strategies for survival" as much as they are ways to learn pleasures that pivot on oscillatory processes of affective distance and nearness. Within these moments, one courses through relations to objects, histories, communities, and the self to produce healing in the most unlikely of places (i.e., "bad objects"). Rather than constructing a one-size-fits-all or righteous theory, reparativity necessitates complex understandings of the ways in which it is programmed and organized across time and across an assemblage of objects that cannot in and of themselves hold the mythic power of total redress.

As I have already described, reparative ties to "bad objects" are more likely to happen when time has passed between the film's release and its reevaluation. Repertory programming, as a practice that resuscitates texts time and time again for new contexts, puts films in diachronic contact with others, which in turn infects their meanings. Programming is therefore a praxis that strengthens intertextuality, that is, the connections among various texts put in contact with one another. Critics such as Vito Russo, for instance, came to expect certain double features, thus linking films to one another in their intertextual connectedness. But the reverse can also take place; because intertextuality implies continual semiotic and affective shifts, the intertextual tapestry frequently gets rewoven.

The programming and correlating reparative readings of Russ Meyer's sexploitation films provide evidence of this paradigm. The exhibition history of Meyer's work alone lends itself to an assorted trajectory that spans porn theaters, mainstream cinemas, and art houses.[61] Meyer's films, which went through numerous legal battles throughout the 1960s, made their way into art house cinemas and even museum spaces because they were interpreted as anti-establishment anthems against censorship and celebrations of pulp and camp made all the more artier by Andy Warhol in the preceding years.

Films such as *Vixen* and *Faster, Pussycat! Kill! Kill!* were repeatedly programmed at art house theaters across US cities such as New York, San Francisco, Chicago, and Los Angeles throughout the 1970s and onward. As early as 1971, the Museum of Modern Art (MoMA) in New York City exhibited Meyer's work, taking it out of the softcore pornography theaters and into the venerated museum space. This did not happen at random. *Vixen* and *Cherry, Harry, & Raquel!* were first shown in July 1971 as part of MoMA's "Cineprobe" series, which aimed to confront spectators with, as it was stated in a MoMA press release, "images that shock; ideas that are provocative; points of view that are controversial."[62] Meyer was invited back to Cineprobe in October to discuss the censorship of his sexploitation films throughout the 1960s. Unsurprisingly, censorship was a hot topic at this time in light of the recent reversal of the Production Code, now replaced by the ratings system. Partly a product of his prolific career, the censorship he experienced throughout it, and this recent turn in censorship history, retrospectives of Meyer's work could be found at art house cinemas throughout the 1970s, both within the United States and abroad.

Meyer was known for casting busty women and, in line with other sexploitation films, depicting lesbian desire. The lesbian desire serves to epitomize anarchic worlds where, as Kristen Hatch puts it, masculinity is in a "state of disarray."[63] Clearly intended to be salacious, the films' art house afterlives have also pulled focus away from the sexual content and more toward Meyer's ingenious use of editing, cinematography, and music, which both amplifies the films' pulpy conceits and pushes them in the direction of aesthetic veneration. These dual tracks (the prurient and the virtuosic), which sometimes converge and other times diverge in criticism of his films, suggest that programming fractured Meyer's work in that certain moments signify artfulness, while others highlight lowbrow humor or carnal lust.

B. Ruby Rich's 1995 rereading of *Faster, Pussycat! Kill! Kill!* embodies these cleavages in taste as they become part of a productive site for textual regeneration (fig. 5.4). In reencountering the film upon its rerelease twenty years after having first seen it, Rich noted that what at the time appeared "retrograde male-objectification of women's bodies and desires further embellished by a portrait of lesbianism as twisted and depraved," had morphed into a "celebration of bad-girl empowerment" and, for dykes, a "shit-kicking history" delivered in the form of "frenzied femmes whose approach to men lies halfway between Sharon Stone [from *Basic Instinct*] and Hothead Paisan."[64] Rich here revises the opinions of the film she held in the 1970s through fictional cultural icons of the 1990s. The intertext that Rich produces serves to further fragment the film, to parcel out its associations. Her reparative reading results in a destabilization of the text that both undermines a male gaze while it also underscores, textually, Meyer's penchant for overthrowing manhood and rendering a formidable portrait of femininity, a sentiment that Kristen Hatch echoes in her analysis of Meyer's oeuvre. I would venture to say that the aesthetic consideration, even reverence, in the art house scene carved out a path for Rich and Hatch to do feminist reparative work with the film, while at the same time, be able to affectively engage with it as a sensational object.

With their dizzying montages and paradoxical tonal mixes of moralism and rebellion, Meyer's films, including *Beyond the Valley of the Dolls* and *Cherry, Harry, & Raquel!*, are sites of bricolage, a sampling of cheap gimmicks and aesthetic talent. The temporal remove that fuels opportunities to reconsider his work seems to highlight these heterogeneous aspects of his corpus. We might therefore see this formal heterogeneity mirrored in the layout of Rich's article for *The Village Voice*. Below her review of *Faster, Pussycat! Kill! Kill!* is an ode to the film's star, Tura Santana. Implicitly critiquing a notion of directorial authorship, Rich cleverly reminds the reader that auteurism falters in the face of a film's collaborative tendency.[65] Rich,

5.4 The busty badasses of Russ Meyer's *Faster Pussycat! Kill! Kill!* (1965), Santana on the right.

aware of how a film's cult value can increase with time, uses its rerelease as a recuperative opportunity to spotlight Santana, who, she writes, "should now be eligible for cult status if not outright goddesshood."[66] And like that, Santana gets reinstated within the film's authorial history. Like Mayne's consideration of Pam Grier's recurring roles in Jack Hill's women-in-prison films, Rich uses the star to muddy the film's identity, here dominated by Russ Meyer as a cult auteur reigning over the sexploitation genre. Instead, she uses the reparative opportunity to demonstrate that the "bad object" does not belong to Meyer, nor even Santana, but that it is an assembly of its parts, which generate new meanings as the film resurfaces across time.

These rereadings demonstrate not just the range of evaluative criteria available to the canny spectator, but exemplify that this range expands as it becomes increasingly part of intertextual nexuses. This expansion opens up a space to love the clichés presented in mainstream representation as both comfortingly familiar and risibly fabricated, or even bathetic. What emerges is a simultaneous love of the object's affective distance and nearness, of its representational impossibility and sense that it may have, through cultural mythology and fantasy, also structured one's own desires. Although these readings are not always immediately available, they might emerge in a context that is much more hospitable to the idea of women's sexual agency.[67] They may require the temporal awareness and distance that come with programming's propensity for textual intermingling, which amplifies camp imaginaries.

Spectatorial Specters

In the film *Ghost Dance* (dir. Ken McMullen, 1983), Jacques Derrida states that cinema is an art of battling ghosts. As Akira Lippit points out, it is, for Derrida, also a medium of echoes and "narcissism adrift."[68] According to Lippit, a viewer is led into a series of feedback loops of reflection upon the self in relation to the other, and back again. Lippit describes an ethical spectatorship that can form out of Derrida's notion of "generous narcissism," which continually orients and reorients a spectator inward and outward, back and forth, between the self and other, and, in the examples I have given here, between self and history, history and community, self and text, and onward. Programming's diachronic power to repair lies in these endless loops across time and space. It is what forestalls any mastery over the reparative experience with the "bad object," itself subject to processes of endless fragmentation and therefore multitudinous resignification.

Programs that recover queer "bad objects," I have tried to argue, resist the calcification of meaning and affect because they produce intertexts that are in continual flux, moving with and against their cultural backdrop. For instance, the programming of *Daughters of Darkness*—how it brushes up against and is inflected by other lesbian texts; how it is resurrected throughout the decade; how it comes to be indicative of a kind of "guilty pleasure"—represents the manner in which films are but moving parts in intertextual networks that stretch across time. This is why any static definition of pleasure will not suffice. It cannot be captured in one mode of absorption or ecstasy, as it has been argued in the past, nor solely in the "interrogation" of retrograde and problematic imagery. This pleasure then is neither one of negating nor negotiating the trauma—as if pleasure and trauma could be neatly opposed—nor is it due to a process of compartmentalizing. Pleasure for *and* with the "bad object" is a movement between different relations and strategies made available through reparative opportunities. The critique, curiosity, wish fulfillment, fantasy, and identification commingle to produce the pleasure felt within the reparative reading, dialogically, as many repertory calendars or programs themselves are.

Camp readings put into crisis conservative views of identificatory practices and modes of recognition. Conversely, we saw readings of campy texts that do not rely solely on verisimilitudinous collapse to be their benchmark for pleasure. From Mayne to Rich, these thinkers index their fantasies in relation to historicity. Camp offers opportunities to discern and then gain distance from recycled tropes and clichés. Repertory programming especially as a practice that *rep*eats screenings of cult films makes legible these tropes through accretive means. This coupled with films' passages from low forms of trash to venerated objects in institutions such as museums make "bad objects" ripe for recovery. In acknowledging this, a scene for fantasy that values a politics of pleasure is able to be constructed out of the accessible fragments.

I have argued that repertory movie houses, where providing pleasure is as central to their business model as invoking nostalgia, helped to facilitate both subsequent and contemporaneous moments of reparative readings. As examples from the Roxie, the Castro, and Frameline demonstrate, programming fosters different modes of intertextual overlap, parallelism, and even dissidence, and these are continually up for grabs depending on the context, viewer, or moment. The examples of the women-in-prison and lesbian vampire film series explain how reparative gestures can come to be accompanied by other positions and sobering inquiries. Reparativity, therefore, demands a process of moving through various affective positions and coming out the other side transformed by the objects we should, hypothetically, just renounce.

In order to exemplify an overall attraction to these programs and their varied reiterations, however, trauma as an undergirding and binding principle of queer spectatorship has to be decentered, and pleasure reinstated as a potent rationale for spectatorial appeal. For me, it has been crucial to separate the past and the present—to take stock of the changes in queer identities and rights throughout the twentieth century—while resisting progressivist impulses to espouse a tidy history. Reparative historicizing is therefore necessary if queer subjectivities are to be done justice.

Despite the many queer scholarly and critical projects that refuse to admit to pleasure for *and* with "bad objects," perhaps queer film and media history has spoken for itself. In the 1990s, wicked gays and lesbians filled the screens in films such as *Swoon* (dir. Tom Kalin, 1992) and *Poison* (dir. Todd Haynes, 1991), both made by queer directors. Diachronic programming all the more explains how it came to be that New Queer Cinema filmmakers unabashedly incorporated the "low" taste of queer "bad objects" into their indie aesthetics, as is so often argued but without historical substantiation.[69] Although the call for sanitized and uplifting depictions subsided by the 1990s, little to no theorizing and historicizing has been done to explain how this effort dissipated. It is my hope that this chapter presents a way to better theorize and historicize the place of pleasure, in all its political incorrectness and messiness. Perhaps then we might be able to give ourselves the room to realize the uncomfortable intimacy between historicity and potentiality.[70]

Afterword

CURATING QUEER CINEMA
AFTER 1989

Toward the beginning of Cheryl Dunye's queer Black mockumentary, *The Watermelon Woman* (1996), we peer into a rare, if not singular, occurrence of watching someone curate films on-screen. Cheryl (Cheryl Dunye), the film's protagonist, meets her soon-to-be girlfriend, Diana (Guinevere Turner), at the video store where she clerks (fig. A.1). Cheryl spots Diana wandering the aisles and perusing the shelves, mulling over what to rent. Seeing Diana needs help, Cheryl approaches and informs Diana that there is a two-for-one special, implying that, effectively, Diana should make her rental a double feature. Deliberating with VHS sleeves in hand, Diana asks Cheryl, "*Cleopatra Jones, Jacob's Lyric,* or *Personal Best*?" In the end, Cheryl selects as her co-features the blaxploitation hit *Cleopatra Jones* (dir. Jack Starrett, 1973) and art horror classic *Repulsion* starring Catherine Deneuve, despite the fact that Diana's proposal of *Personal Best* serves as a coded way for her to make her sexuality abundantly clear to Cheryl.

What is Cheryl communicating back to Diana in her selections? And what exchanges might these films elicit for Diana, distinct from Cheryl's curatorial vision or intent? Cheryl's curation seems to suggest, "Yes, I'm a lesbian, but I'm not that kind of a lesbian, and maybe you aren't, too." The scene brims with a flirty subtext, playfully invoking retrospective cult titles from the 1960s and 1970s that lean toward the outlandish and encoded

A.1 Flirtation by way of double-bill VHS curation in Cheryl Dunye's *Watermelon Woman* (1996).

queer readings of women protagonists disinterested in—even *repulsed* by—heterosexuality. By choosing these two objects requiring decoding over *Personal Best* (dir. Robert Towne, 1982)—an explicitly lesbian but quite conventional film—Dunye constructs from the shelves a program that proposes a queer history that puts a premium on the films' dialogic capacity. *Cleopatra Jones* and *Repulsion*, the latter of which centers on a woman who has a hysterical aversion to men, it's implied, might invite the notion of expendable male presence and thus strengthen a lesbian gaze even better than a middlebrow melodrama like *Personal Best*.

Moreover, these two films belong to a constellation of lesbian intertextuality that expands outward and onward. The sequel to *Cleopatra Jones*, *Cleopatra Jones and the Gold Casino* (dir. Charles Bail, 1975), it has been argued, features a coded queer interracial relationship between its asskicking heroine and her female "sidekick" Mi Ling, and *The Hunger*, one of Catherine Deneuve's later films, is explicitly a lesbian vampire film.[1] Within this queer cosmos, in which verisimilitude is jettisoned, the indexed "real" of explicit lesbian desire is blown asunder, Dunye's political imaginaries are left ample room to roam, to entertain critical fantasies and scenarios unavailable in 1990s mainstream lesbian representation. Camp enjoyment inherited from 1970s and 1980s film programming (the topic of chapter 5) motivates a selection of *Cleopatra Jones* over *Personal Best*, possibly to the dismay of viewers invested in so-called realistic or authentic representations of queers. Dunye instead produces an intertext out of her disidentification, a compound of both existing texts and imagined ones, erased or forgotten, and coalescing into a scene of queer Black female pleasure.

Of course, the double bill that Cheryl has programmed for Diana is meant to be watched at home on VHS and not in the cinema. However, a double feature like *Cleopatra Jones* and *Repulsion*, with its anarchic interplay of feminist and lesbian camp sensibility, *could* very well have been found in art house and repertory cinemas of the 1970s and 1980s, screening alongside irreverent lesbian cult classics such as *Daughters of Darkness*, *The Killing of Sister George*, and *Les Diaboliques* (dir. Henri-Georges Clouzot, 1955). *Curating Deviance* has aimed to capture the spirit of these programming practices and imagine the spectatorial possibilities for encountering filmic intertexts such as these. We might wonder, in light of the case studies brought to the fore in this book, how queerness itself is not only programmatic but also intertextual, a relay of textual interplays and accumulations that result in a creative nonnormative reading practice for the world. Dunye's programming is both highly personalized (for her and her targeted audience of one) and generalized in the broader scheme of queer "bad object" programming. This moment in *The Watermelon Woman* expresses a keen understanding of the dyadic textual interaction of the double bill as well as the joys of textual promiscuity—programmatic attributes specific to post-1968 curatorial techniques and sensibilities.

The Watermelon Woman is often placed within the 1990s moment in independent queer film production and reception known as the New Queer Cinema (NQC).[2] One could argue that the NQC is a progeny of repertory and art house cinema of the decades that precede it. A generation of queer cinephiles, including Dunye, Gregg Araki, Tom Kalin, and Todd Haynes, would turn into that generation of queer filmmakers, their aesthetics and sensibilities sculpted by art house's deviant programming of the period under discussion in this book. Films such as *The Living End* (dir. Gregg Araki, 1992), *Swoon*, and *Poison* reclaimed and repurposed the politically incorrect and reviled stereotypes, playfully and critically, for a 1990s audience uninterested in sanitized depictions of LGBT people. Furthering these resonances, Marcus Hu, the founder of Strand Releasing, named his distribution company after the Strand Theater in San Francisco, where he had worked, watched queer films, and first acquired the US rights to Lino Brocka's *Macho Dancer* (1988) in the 1980s. The irreducible influence of post-1968 programming echoes into NQC and beyond in ways that cannot even be narrated or tracked.

There might be a temptation, then, to situate this book as a prehistory of NQC. While not incorrect per se, I have tried to avoid this teleology primarily because it runs the risk of centralizing NQC as an authenticating moment—*the* moment—in queer film history. It diminishes the power and distinct deviant politics of the 1970s and 1980s film programming, which at times runs counter to contemporaneous lesbian and gay liberationist projects. This book diverges from histories that claim facile continuities and advancements in the realms of queer politics; *Curating Deviance* rebuts the flawed logic that equates queer authorship with notions of aspirational progress, healthy identification, and even far-reaching inclusion. Moreover, the cinematic instances of queer coalitional and reparative possibility that I have historicized and theorized in this book are specific not to the films themselves (some of which long predate 1968) but to their post-1968 programming, with its own cultural and spectatorial conditions, which should not be reduced to the opening act for the main historical event of 1990s independent cinema. Instead, I would suggest, there is a benefit to this era's version of queerness that antedates its cinematic institutionalization; in the movie houses of the 1970s and 1980s, queerness was given the space to wander into a host of genres and styles, brushing up against and blending with other disorderly abnormalities that play havoc with the illusion of pleasant social cohesion.

Changing Technologies of Queerness (and Deviance)

One question lingers: Does the waning of repertory programming translate to a loss of deviant sensibility in non-mainstream film culture? By 1989, the endpoint of this book's chronology, art house cinema's presence in the cultural sphere was diminishing: urban repertory houses were in steep decline, most shuttering permanently in part due to the proliferation of VHS and increasing rent costs (in places like New York City); a generation standing for sexual revolution was now in the grips of or had capitulated to Reaganite neoliberal principles, which pervaded the US cultural sphere and helped decimate populations of gay men dying of HIV/AIDS; as a response to this devastating cultural shift, queer film history begins a new chapter with NQC.[3] More optimistically, the fading novelty of the movie theater yielded dynamic fandom in VHS and later DVD cultures, through bootleg tapes such as Todd Haynes's *Superstar* or the cult following of Kim's Video in NYC.[4] *The Watermelon Woman* attests to the fact that video stores had their own queer cultures, with their own codes for cruising and socializing. In addition, cable TV such as HBO offered rare Hollywood classics and cult films with growing frequency, allowing for more exposure to those who might not have easy access to queer classics at the repertory house or video store, all from the comforts of one's home. As a result, Ben Davis notes, some art house programmers "felt that a conservative programming policy was the insurance for survival."[5] By "conservative," Davis means programmers could not take as many risks, in turn exhibiting fewer films that might challenge or offend a spectator's worldview. Additionally, programmers were more likely to opt for themed series over ostensibly random and scattershot selections. As a result, films experience a more orderly arrangement, with the framing device of a series unambiguous in its intended audience consumption.

In chapter 2, I hinted at efforts by LGBT groups to codify and institutionalize knowledges of LGBT cinema through film festivals and scholarship. Into the 1990s, proliferating LGBT film festivals, taking place on an international scale, signal the category's deeper institutionalization; as a result, LGBT films are worthy of programming based on the sexual identity of the director and the extent to which the queer community welcomes the film as representative of its politics and worldviews—or fantasies thereof.[6] By the time of what B. Ruby Rich identifies as NQC's crossover moment in the late 1990s, queer films are no longer euphemistically referred to as "art," "European," "avant-garde," or "offbeat"; LGBT viewers comprise a viable market seeking reflections of idealized versions of themselves.[7] As a consequence, much queer and deviant art house representation, often treated as germane to LGBT and straight audiences alike in the context of post-1968 programming, gets segregated programmatically. Enter the age of the LGBT indie flick, the lesbian or gay rom-com, the AIDS melodrama, and other films with niche appeal. Just as with the late 1960s turn in art house cinema, which films get produced forms a feedback loop with how they are programmed, with one informing the other; only this time, the feedback loop tends to the more "conservative" in the ways Ben Davis describes. By the 1990s, the remaining repertory and art cinemas are more likely to do an LGBT-specific film series rather than one that channels the perverse sensibilities of films that beg for queer reading practices over queer representation in obvious terms. Intertextually speaking, there is less likelihood for surprising connections among deviant characterizations and kindred critiques of sexual and gender normativity that course outside the LGBT sphere.

Fast forwarding to the digital present, much has changed in the world of film and media curating since Diana rented those videocassette tapes from Cheryl's store in the mid-1990s. For one, the cinema is no longer the primary site for viewing high-quality versions of films, even obscure art films.[8] Cinephiles now collect DVDs and Blu-rays, or stream Criterion Collection classics, and even attend film festivals virtually (in the wake of COVID-19). In addition, *curation*, a once sacred term reserved for museums and fine arts spaces, has found its way into everyday parlance.[9] *The New York Times* in March 2020 published an article covering experts' irritation at the term's overuse; today anything that involves discernment and culling, "editing and refining," from restaurant menus to Instagram accounts, is "curated," the piece bemoans, as the word is used to elevate even the most effortless or perfunctory selection processes.[10]

The word's over-circulation coincides with the undervaluation of the kinds of laborious logistics and technical knowledge that a curatorial role requires. In May 2022, *IndieWire* reported the International Film Festival Rotterdam had laid off much of its programming staff, suggesting that even such elite and esteemed institutions as film festivals undervalue programming as labor. Compounding the issue, digital distribution has changed the landscape of how we view curation. The human curation of clever and timely series on such platforms as MUBI and Criterion Channel tends to be invisible, with no clear authorial presence or trace to accompany the work. Worse yet, predictive algorithms that drive much of the media consumption of streaming platforms such as Netflix, Amazon Prime, HBO Max, Hulu, and Disney Plus have automated the curatorial process, driving "personalized" modes of digital consumerism with the help of keywords and tracking mechanisms. This book enters an AI-dominated mediascape in which the human labor of programming is in a state of crisis, if not at risk of obsolescence, intensified by increasing neoliberal divestment of public and nonprofit institutions. As a response, *Curating Deviance* has endeavored to study the cultural and political implications of the strenuous and irreplaceable *human* work of film curating, serving as a corrective to its oversight.

In October 2021, *The Washington Post* reported that repertory houses were coming back full throttle post-pandemic.[11] Given that many are considered nonprofits, they were able to use government assistance programs to stay open during COVID lockdowns and, due to their community marketing strategies, have sustained a loyal clientele. As an LA local, I can attest to the sold-out shows and long lines of patrons vying for the best seats at repertory cinemas such as the American Cinematheque and the Tarantino-owned New Beverly Cinema. By 2024, *Indiewire* was reiterating the same sentiment: "How to Get Young Audiences in Theaters? Show Old Movies."[12]

As far as queer and deviant fare goes, one cannot ask them to return to the model of post-1968 programming, a disparate time in terms of mediascapes, costs of operation, and audience norms, to say the least. Queer or LGBT films tend to cluster in June for Pride month, with occasional programming at the American Cinematheque or Metrograph in NY reminding attendees of cinema's deviant history. In July 2017, the American Cinematheque programmed a series called "Rated X: Not for Children (But Not for Porn)" that almost exclusively included films, not-so-incidentally, released between 1968 and 1989, such as *Female Trouble*, *If...* (dir. Lindsay Anderson, 1968), *Performance*, *The Devils*, *Last Tango in Paris*, *The Decameron*, *Arabian Nights* (dir. Pier Paolo Pasolini, 1974), *Tie Me Up! Tie Me Down!* (dir. Pedro Almodovar, 1990), and *The Cook, The Thief, His Wife, and Her Lover* (dir. Peter Greenaway, 1989). In 2022, they arranged an Erotic Tuesday series, inspired by the *You Must Remember This* podcast on the "Erotic 80s," similarly seeking to awaken a retro perverse curiosity in a new generation of cinephiles.[13]

Moving beyond repertory exhibition and into the digital realm, perhaps we have more access than ever to deviant texts, an archival plethora of kinky shorts and features that span porn sites (some even have Russ Meyer and old sexploitation films on them such as Tube Porn Classics, X Videos, and Archive.org) and indie streaming apps such as Criterion Channel and MUBI. These websites and platforms offer a substantial portion of the films referenced here, or ones following in their deviant tradition. But the question of access can quickly transition into one of use: What do we do with this glut of content? How does it get to a consumer inundated with viewing options?

Curation has always been a filtering tool, one guided by honed knowledge and instincts; streaming necessitates methods of discernment and filtration. In light of this, I would venture to say that we don't need less human curation today but more, as a means to manage this excess of digital content. What forms of deviance and queerness might be filtered in and filtered out in its wake? Who might be granted visibility and who might be pushed into the margins? Media technologies come and go, but what seems perennial is our need to stay vigilant of repressive cultural forces and, as a response, to protect those subject to sexual and gender persecution who do not necessarily have the loudest voices in the room. I have tried my best to offer a remedy for the diffuse forms of erotophobia that remain present in American culture. *Curating Deviance* might be seen as a manual of sorts for training the ethical imagination, the films of art house and repertory cinema as ingredients for a lasting recipe to be feasted on by future generations.

Notes

Introduction

1. Tyler, *Screening the Sexes*, xxiii.
2. Film, video, and other media have influenced queer thought since their beginnings in the 1990s, and vice versa. Judith Butler, in the groundbreaking book *Gender Trouble*, explicitly cites the John Waters's film *Female Trouble* and its filthy heroine Divine as inspiration for their theory that all gender could be considered drag. Early volumes *Queer Looks: Perspectives on Lesbian and Gay Film and Video* (edited by Martha Gever, Pratibha Parmar, and John Greyson) and *How Do I Look? Queer Film and Video* (edited by Bad Object-Choices) on the topics of porn, documentary activism, and experimental video are cited in canonical writing by José Esteban Muñoz, Michael Warner, and Jack Halberstam, among others.
3. Or picking up on another dimension of queer heterosexuality, Cathy Cohen asks of queer theory, "For instance, how would queer activists understand politically the lives of women—in particular women on color—on welfare, who fit into the category of heterosexual, but whose sexual choices are not perceived as normal, moral, or worthy of state support?" ("Punks, Bulldaggers, and Welfare Queens," 442).
4. Along these lines, I further wonder: Is this a problem intractably lodged in the audiovisual medium, which is arguably dominated by linear narration? Are other art forms or media better suited to queer readings that

can eschew LGBT identity, ones that don't necessitate representational corroboration? As an exception, see David Church's excellent exegesis of *It Follows* for ways to read non-LGBT-related queerness in narrative and stylistic form in "Queer Ethics, Urban Spaces, and the Horrors of Monogamy in *It Follows*."

5. Recent queer film studies, including some trans work, has turned to questions of form and affect to move beyond reductive binaries of positive and negative representation, but this work still struggles to break from defining queer textual and spectatorial attributes in terms of LGBT identity and experience, that is, *queer lifeworld*. This book joins other recent writing, especially in Black film studies, in calls to disarticulate representational art forms from their reality effects, inviting a range of reading practices of the reparative flavor. Michael Gillespie's and Racquel Gates's scholarship in particular seek oblique lines of identification and formal openings that reveal dynamic cultural fantasies of difference. For Gates, Blackness might be thought of in its affective qualities, such as through the bad-object reception of "trashy television"; for Gillespie, "cinematic blackness" is a form that brings about insights, expansions, questions, pleasures, fantasies, and critiques that should be delineated from the Black lifeworld. I draw inspiration from these projects' methods, which tease out how cultural objects refract and diffract racial and social categories in ways that elude assignment as "good" or "bad" representations. See Gates, *Double Negative*, and Gillespie, *Film Blackness*.

6. Throughout the book, I use *programming* and *curation* interchangeably because this reflects the terms' usages in the practical field during this era of art house exhibition. More recently, scholars and practitioners have tried to separate one from the other. Laura U. Marks defines *programming* as "ongoing exhibition, such as for festivals or regular series in galleries and other venues"; *curating*, on the other hand, is the practice of "organizing thematic programs that are not necessarily linked to a regular venue" (36). See Marks, "The Ethical Presenter." One could argue that, in a contemporary context, *curation* is more appropriately applied to a museum or formal institutional space, whereas *programming* befits repertory and independent movie houses.

7. Programming has been an ongoing blind spot in the field of film studies. Even in exhibition studies, brief mention might be given to a significant film here and there as representative of a venue's general fare, but rarely do these studies survey a theater's scheduling in depth enough to speak to its programmatic vision, politics, and sensibility. Programming has been caught in a number of disciplinary splits: between textual reading and industrial/institutional analysis, text (consisting of form and content) and reception, history and theory. Studying programming in all these areas is a necessary historiographic expansion because it better

anchors cinema's intertextual history in its viewing contexts and thus engenders us to better speculate historical modes of reception. There has been a scattering of essays on the topic over the years, including one dossier coedited by Jan-Christopher Horak and Laura U. Marks, and a few important forays into the history of niche curation, such as Scott MacDonald's *Cinema 16: Documents Toward a History of Film Society*. These academic voices seem to all agree that film programming is meant to, first and foremost, as Chon Noriega puts it, "incite questions" in the audience. See Noriega, "On Curating," 297. Marks briefly describes scholar-programmers' differing approaches. Marks explains, "I could summarize them as: Scott [MacDonald], respect the work; Patty [Zimmerman], respect the audience; Robin [Curtis], use argument to respect work and audience." Marks, "The Ethical Presenter," 37. Under debate then is a rather binary opposition. The struggle appears to be between a loose educational model of programming in which spectators are allowed to heuristically explore and discover meanings on their own, and one in which they are more directly steered toward the programmer's intended meaning. For Curtis, Marks elaborates, "a curated program is an argument, a well-defined, defensible, pertinent statement. An argument needs a thesis. And a thesis needs a verb. Without these, a curated program is meaningless." Marks, "The Ethical Presenter," 39. Though helpful in parsing the pedagogical intent of some forms of cultural programming, I leave this debate to the side in the context of commercial and nonprofit art house spaces where questions of didacticism and pedagogy, if present, play out quite differently within the minds of curators and programmers.

To my knowledge, *Curating Deviance* is the first book to consider programming from a conceptual or theoretical angle (which tends to be viewed unfavorably in exhibition studies), and to generate from research on more than a thousand calendars a theory of programming based in intertextuality.

8. Balzer, *Curationism*, 33.
9. Balzer, *Curationism*, 33.
10. *Village Voice* film critic Melissa Anderson remembered sitting two rows in front of famous essayist Susan Sontag at a screening at the Quad in New York. See Anderson, "The Quad Relaunches," 28. A young Jonathan Demme was a regular at the Bleecker Street Cinema in the 1960s. See B. Davis, *Repertory Movie Theaters*, 47. In an interview, photographer Nan Goldin told Criterion Collection about her teenage years, "In Cambridge there was the Brattle Theatre and the Orson Welles Cinema, which showed three movies at a time." The continuation of this quote is featured in chapter 4. See Goldin, "Feeding the Appetites." On Albert Johnson, see Luckett, "The Black Film Ambassador."

11. For this reason, this book is hesitant to position the programmer as a kind of author or "auteur" in their own right, except for in chapter 1, where I use key historical figures such as Iris Barry and Amos Vogel to produce a genealogy of what I consider *promiscuous programming*.

12. Upon mentioning Jackie Raynal's filmmaking, B. Ruby Rich writes, "Sid Geffen was one of a series of men who made a huge difference in film history through their exhibition choices in New York City. Geffen, who ran the Bleecker Street Cinema in the crucial years of the late seventies and early eighties, along with Amos Vogel and Fabiano Canosa, significantly effected the course of film history." See Rich, *Chick Flicks*, 105.

13. Geritz, "Edith Kramer," 73.

14. Bosma, *Film Programming*, 44.

15. Eric Schaefer notes that "1968 marked the year in which media representations of sex were finally seen by large numbers of men and women in a public setting, the year it moved from 'under the counter' to 'over the top.'" Schaefer, "Introduction," 8.

16. Osterweil, *Flesh Cinema*, 15.

17. Young uses films such as *Barbarella* and Brigitte Bardot's oeuvre to identify the codification of the "liberal sexual subject" as fantasy of "autonomous, pleasure-seeking agent" nonetheless still moored by a "republican social contract" that universalizes compulsory normative sexuality. See Young, *Making Sex Public*, 8.

18. Tyler, *Screening the Sexes*, 314.

19. Though I tend to prefer the term *deviant* to *queer* in much of this study, I am not inclined to completely supplant *queer* with *deviant*, even in these contexts, given how much light queer theory has shed and still can shed on these intertexts. Throughout the book, these two terms will slide into one another; this is an implicit acknowledgment of their enmeshed genealogies, detailed by Love in *Underdogs*. It is worth noting that the two discourses emerge from capacious and pejorative uses, though only one has enjoyed full-scale reclamation.

20. Sekula, "The Body and the Archive," 7. For more on the topic, see Adams, *Sideshow U.S.A.*

21. See Ferguson, *Aberrations in Black*; and McRuer, *Crip Theory*.

22. Seitler, "Queer Physiognomies," 83.

23. Seitler, "Queer Physiognomies," 83. Italics in original text.

24. Dušan Makavejev's 1971 documentary *W. R.: Mysteries of the Organism* explores Reich's sexual theories. The film was programmed in New York City at the Carnegie Hall Cinema in July 1974 ("Carnegie Hall Cinema," Pacific Film Archive [BAMPFA], Berkeley, CA) and Bleecker Street Cinema in

March 1978 ("Bleecker Street Cinema," Pacific Film Archive [BAMPFA], Berkeley, CA). In the Bay Area, the film screened at the Times Theater at Wheeler Auditorium in 1974 and at the Clay Theatre in April 1974 as part of the "Radical Psychiatry Film Series with Speakers" ("filmcalendar," Pacific Film Archive [BAMPFA], Berkeley, CA). Its numerous screenings attest to the filmgoing public's interest in sexology. See also Kate Bush's song "Cloudbusting," inspired by Peter Reich's memoir about his father, Wilhelm Reich.

25. Scott, "Gender," 1055.

26. See Yacavone, "Towards a Theory of Film Worlds." In zooming in on its formal and narrative features, the "interdiegetic" also temporarily and necessarily eschews analytical considerations of extradiegetic factors such as star texts, production backstories, critical and cultural reception, and so forth.

27. Taylor, *The Archive and the Repertoire*. Taylor juxtaposes the archive's claim of stability and durability (coming from Greek *arkheia*, "public records," and *arkhē*, "government") to the changeability of the repertoire (20).

28. In chapter 4, I define this as *repertory time*, a long-duration and immersive form of spectatorship that leaves room for meanings to unfold and keep unfolding as films are encountered and reencountered in other intertextual arrangements. For example, repertory time can submerge a viewer into the carnivalesque, campy fantasies of a popular 1970s double bill like *Myra Breckinridge* and *Beyond the Valley of the Dolls* or, in the case I make in chapter 5, it can make a viewer read a "bad object" such as *Dracula's Daughter* in a new, even affirming light in the context of an LGBT film festival.

29. Geritz et al., "Film Culture."

30. They were programmed over six times in a span of three years in just the Bay Area's theaters alone: Surf Theatre (September 1975); the UC Theater (November 1977); Roxie (April 1978, June 1978, November 1978); Strand Theater (October 1978). "filmcalendar" and "Roxie Theater," Pacific Film Archive (BAMPFA), Berkeley, CA. They were also shown together in May 1974 at the Carnegie Hall Cinema in New York City.

31. Programmed at the Carnegie Hall Cinema (Summer 1974, Winter 1978). "Carnegie Hall Cinema," Pacific Film Archive (BAMPFA), Berkeley, CA.

32. Muñoz, *Cruising Utopia*, 4. Muñoz's main target is the "political impasse that characterizes the present," namely the unimaginative domain of heteronormative and homonormative white-centered politics that dominate the public sphere (e.g., marriage rights, a hot topic at the time of his book's publication), as well as Lee Edelman and others' calls to abandon the future as a normative promise embodied in the figure of the child.

33. See Ferguson, *One-Dimensional Queer*, and Fawaz, *Queer Forms*.

34. See North, "The Disturbing Story." Regarding the *Death in Venice* allegations, see Lang, "Björn Andrésen on His Tortured Relationship."

35. Lauren Berlant writes about the "failures" of the sexual revolution: "What 'went wrong' doesn't mean everything failed in the sexual politics/structural conjuncture. A specific political project did: the ha-penis problem [in reference to *Last Tango in Paris*], which I take to refer both to the attempted release of a white masculinity from its radical sixties' aspirational armors of invulnerability and superiority, along with the problem of sustaining and remaining with unfinished revolutions whose outcomes continue genuinely to be mixed." Berlant, *On the Inconvenience of Other People*, 32.

36. Muñoz, *Cruising Utopia*, 28. This reparative and utopian reading practice comes through strongest in chapter 5, where I discuss the historical programming of queer "bad objects" such as the lesbian vampire film and women-in-prison picture.

1. Promiscuous Programming

1. In June 1966, the Bleecker Street Cinema in the Village was screening double features of Fellini's *8½* (1963) and Godard's *Breathless* (1960). On the Upper West Side, the Thalia was showing a Bergman double bill of *Through a Glass Darkly* (1961) and *Winter Light* (1963). *Village Voice*, June 30, 1966, 20–21.

2. *Village Voice*, May 15, 1969, 46–47.

3. On this lusty subtext, see Wilinsky, *Sure Seaters*, 99.

4. Lee, "A Never-Ending Film Festival."

5. B. Davis, *Repertory Movie Theaters*, 86–87. Davis bases his periodization on the quantitative existence of repertory houses more than on a qualitative analysis of shifts in their practices. The key New York theaters that emerged and remained in operation between 1968 and the early 1990s that Davis discusses are also key examples in this book: the Elgin, Theater 80 St. Marks, First Avenue Screening Room, Carnegie Hall Cinema, Bleecker Street Cinema, and the Thalia. Importantly, Davis notes that art theaters were in decline during this period but repertory was going strong.

6. For a more comprehensive analysis of the ontological debate around the term *art cinema*, see Galt and Schoonover, *Global Art Cinema*. They seem to embrace its "definitional impurity," calling it an "elastically hybrid category" with a "mongrel identity" (3). Expanding on this, they write, "We find in these impurities the kernel of art cinema's significance: as a category of cinema, it brings categories into question and holds the potential to open up spaces between and outside of mainstream/avant-garde,

local/cosmopolitan, history/theory, and industrial/formal debates in film scholarship" (9).

7. Wilinsky asks, "Was the art film industry ever interested in being an alternative culture that was 'left alone,' or was it simply interested in its *image* of exclusivity? Did art house operators, perhaps, exploit the appeal of being part of an alternative culture detached from concerns about mass audience, yet market this distinction to as many people as possible? Since at least the 1940s, art cinema has balanced its desire for difference and its desire for maximum profits" (*Sure Seaters*, 5). And later, on the ontology of art cinema, she writes, "Rather than accepting a static notion of the art film as an abstract concept, we become aware of the instability of the notion of the art film and it becomes clear that the entire art film industry was needed to ground the art film, define the term, and determine the values of the growing art film phenomenon. As the exhibition sites for art films, art houses helped to establish art cinema's image as well as its qualities" (39).

8. The film society movement formed in Europe before it took off in the United States. See Richard Abel's account of 1920s cine clubs in Paris in *French Cinema*.

9. For an engaging discussion of MoMA's first director and curator, Alfred H. Barr, see Balzer, *Curationism*, 41–44.

10. See Wasson, *Museum Movies*, 195–208.

11. Wasson, *Museum Movies*, 2.

12. Wasson, *Museum Movies*, 133.

13. MacDonald and Stauffacher, *Art in Cinema*.

14. MacDonald, *Cinema 16*, 6.

15. See MacDonald, *Cinema 16*.

16. They may have been able to get around the high cost of union projectionists too, but Vogel—a leftist to the core—agreed they should go union. See MacDonald, *Cinema 16*, 43.

17. See Carroll, "The Future of Allusion."

18. Wollen, "Godard and Counter-Cinema," 500–508.

19. Bourdieu, *Distinction*, 1–2.

20. One might then assume the rest of Bourdieu's *Distinction* would confirm this thesis over and over again. Curiously, however, film scholars rarely note that Bourdieu finds many inconsistencies and complications in his case studies. The book is full of exceptions, instabilities, and instances of fluidity within the historically rigid and class-ridden system of taste. Unsurprisingly, Bourdieu conducted his research for his dizzyingly comprehensive study in 1963 and 1967–68. Major social changes were underway in

France—as well as much of the world—at this time (typified, of course, by the May 1968 riots). My point is that all of these factors magnify the futility in making steadfast claims about what high, middle, and low taste look like. See, for example, all the variations of the petite bourgeoisie that Bourdieu provides in *Distinction*. These forestall any overarching claims that can be made about taste and its direct and determined correspondence to class.

21. Bourdieu, *The Field of Cultural Production*, 35.

22. In *The Field of Cultural Production*, Bourdieu writes on the power of the art dealer: "he is the person who can proclaim the value of the author he defends (cf. the fiction of the catalogue or blurb) and above all 'invests his prestige' in the author's cause, acting as a 'symbolic banker' who offers as security all the symbolic capital he has accumulated (which he is liable to forfeit if he backs a 'loser')" (77).

23. Bourdieu, *The Field of Cultural Production*, 76.

24. There are limits to this analogy. Most prominently, cinema adheres to different industrial standards and protocols altogether than the "fine arts" (painting, drawing, printmaking, installation, and sculpture). Nonetheless, programmers do work to an extent as cinema's "art dealers," functioning as intermediaries or middlemen along the production-reception circuit, on the side of reception and consumption.

25. In a September–October 1960 program, Kael writes, "*Touch of Evil* is a flamboyant shocker which has something, but not very much, to do with drugs and police corruption in a border town. What it really has to do with is love of the film medium and all its stylistic possibilities; and if Welles can't resist the candy of shadows and angles and baroque décor, he turns it into stronger fare than most directors' solemn meat-and-potatoes" ("Cinema Guild," Pacific Film Archive [BAMPFA], Berkeley, CA).

26. Kellow, *Pauline Kael*, 51.

27. Based on conversations I had with queer filmmaker Steven Arnold's archivist, Vishnu Dass, Arnold and another queer artist named Jess (https://www.sfmoma.org/artist/Jess/) designed the programs.

28. Kael, "Trash, Art, and the Movies," 339.

29. For more on this point, see Sconce, "Introduction," 2.

30. Kael, "Trash, Art, and the Movies," 340.

31. In her contempt for the sober art house attitudes and reverence for the "brilliant" masters (which pitted her against Andrew Sarris, the US importer of French "auteurism"), Kael set out to not only displace taste demarcations but also reframe the art house cinema as a possible outlet for facetious and insouciant views of "art," not as a celebrated and protected category, but as a highly varied one. See Kael, "Circles and Squares."

32. One should also note a shift in European film festival culture during this time. At festivals such as Cannes and Berlinale, Thomas Elsaesser notes, "Sweeping changes were made by adding more sections for first-time filmmakers, the directors' fortnight (*Quinzaine des realisateurs*) as well as other showcase sidebars" (78). For more on this, see Elsaesser, "Film Festival Networks."
33. "Kaelite" is also used on occasion.
34. Fabiano Canosa spoke of Kael's influence on him in an interview I did with him in July 2015.
35. For more on *Funeral Parade of Roses*, see Francis, "Tokyo Unmasked."
36. J. Hoberman writes, "'Funeral Parade' did not reach New York until June 1973, opening for six days at the First Avenue Screening Room, a 220-seat art house in the shadow of the 59th Street Bridge" ("A Tale of a Tokyo Drag Queen"). *The Village Voice* ignored the film (even though it name-checks the *Voice* film critic Jonas Mekas); *New York Times* critic Vincent Canby was unimpressed, calling it "a mopey soap opera that might have been made for Bette Davis. Not likely—in addition to assimilating art movies like Alain Resnais's 'Hiroshima Mon Amour' and Kenneth Anger's 'Scorpio Rising,' 'Funeral Parade' seems steeped in the Japanese Kabuki theater tradition of the onnagata, or female impersonators." Hoberman, "A Tale of a Tokyo Drag Queen."
37. Canosa programmed Oshima's *Diary of a Shinjuku Thief* in July 1973 at First Avenue Screening Room, arguably before the director became a world-renowned auteur with his hit *In the Realm of the Senses*.
38. Stephen Soba in discussion with the author, July 2014.
39. Vogel, "Independents: Structures."
40. See also its Cinema Treasures web page, under Art East Cinema, http://cinematreasures.org/theaters/9502/.
41. In this historical moment, repertory programmers seem to diverge from art curators, at least by Balzer's account, when "custodianship *becomes* connoisseurship" (*Curationism*, 46). Balzer writes, "Curators no longer tended ground, but secured, organized and landscaped it. This emerged out of a real need: in the 1960s and 1970s, the art world increasingly yearned for a figure to make sense of things, to act as advocate for an ever more obtuse, factionalist art scene. Too many artists, too many movements, too many works in too many shows, too much discussion: who would parse them? The curator's new position entailed duties of ringleader, translator, mediator, diplomat, gatekeeper. It was a full-time job, and a completely new one" (46). As the art world longed for order, film programmers, by contrast, seemed to embrace the freeing eclecticism of the cinephilic zeitgeist.

42. See Gorfinkel, *Lewd Looks*.

43. See D'Emilio and Freedman, *Intimate Matters*, 327.

44. Young calls this consumer the "liberal sexual subject" who labors to break free of the bonds of sexual repression by way of the same democratic rationale that fortifies normativity. Young is far less romantic in his historical view of the time than other scholars of sexuality. Young stresses that the liberal sexual subject is one that will inevitably short circuit because it is caught irresolvably between democratic ideals of sexual freedom or autonomy and the burden of good, respectable citizenry (*Making Sex Public*, 7).

45. As Linda Williams says of her own experience seeing it at the time, "The film [was] at once too real, too hard-core, and too beautiful to fathom." See L. Williams, *Screening Sex*, 184.

46. Staiger, *Perverse Spectators*, 149.

47. Take the case of the Pacific Film Archive (PFA), located in Berkeley, California. PFA's founder, Sheldon Renan, has cited the Cinémathèque Française (helmed by famed programmer Henri Langlois) in Paris as the model for the institution; the PFA too wanted to be a dedicated space for serious cinematic viewing, reflection, and conversation. No doubt PFA's programming has been shaped by the academic and countercultural energies of the Berkeley area that surrounds it. For more on BAMPFA's history, visit "BAMPFA Mission and History," https://bampfa.org/about/history-mission; and see Amazonas, "Guerilla Cinematheque Comes of Age." See also the Special Focus devoted to the Pacific Film Archive's fiftieth anniversary in Geritz, "Edith Kramer."

48. Anthology Film Archive began in the Village and moved to Soho in 1974 and then moved to its current home in the East Village in 1979, according to its website on the "About / History" page, www.anthologyfilmarchives.org/about/history.

49. Wilinsky, *Sure Seaters*, 99. Parallel to this, Eric Schaefer has demonstrated that poster and marquee advertising were key to exploitation cinema's promotional strategies in his book *"Bold! Daring! Shocking! True!"*

50. Wilinsky, *Sure Seaters*, 124.

51. YouTube alone offers rich amateur documentary footage of Times Square marquees. See Zerkzeez, "Dirty Seedy Old Times Square and 42nd St. ('The Deuce') Before Gentrification," YouTube, March 2, 2009, www.youtube.com/watch?v=MS7Q3tcnHWM; and MyFootage.com, "1970s New York Adult Theaters Marquees Stock Footage HD," YouTube, January 9, 2017, www.youtube.com/watch?v=7PpoVoR2pPI.

52. Gorfinkel, *Lewd Looks*, 210.

53. Doerfler, "Radley Metzger," 16.

54. Gorfinkel, *Lewd Looks*, 219. I found documentation of Meyer's visits while conducting my own research at MoMA, but I learned about Metzger's appearance from Gorfinkel's book.
55. Gorfinkel, *Lewd Looks*, 219.
56. Zaeske, "The 'Promiscuous Audience' Controversy," 192–93.
57. D'Emilio and Freedman write, "For many, sexual promiscuity became part of the fabric of gay life, an essential element holding the community together. Yet the fact that such sex businesses [such as bathhouses, bars with back rooms, and porn shops] could operate in the 1970s relatively free of police harassment and that the media could spotlight them in discussions of gay life says as much about heterosexual norms as about those of gay men." D'Emilio and Freedman don't directly state that straight people adopted gay male norms, but they further intimate it with the following passage. "In the larger metropolitan areas, male homosexuals were no longer serving as symbols of sexual deviance, their eroticism no longer divided the good from the bad. Heterosexuals sustained vigorous singles nightlife, and advertised in magazines for partners; suburban couples engaged in mate-swapping; sex clubs were featuring male strippers with women in the role of voyeur. By the end of the decade, some 'straight' men and women were even patronizing a heterosexual equivalent of the gay bathhouse, as the success of places like Plato's Retreat in New York demonstrated. The experience of the urban gay subculture stood as one point along a widened spectrum of sexual possibilities that modern America now offered" (*Intimate Matters*, 340).
58. There are other examples of this as well. In January 1973, Carnegie Hall Cinema did double-bill performances of the "two best reviewed male films of 1972," *Left Handed* (dir. Jack Deveau) and *American Cream* (dir. Rob Simple). "Carnegie Hall Cinema," Pacific Film Archive (BAMPFA), Berkeley, CA.
59. See Patton, *L.A. Plays Itself/Boys in the Sand*; and Capino, "Seizing Moving Image Pornography," 122.
60. Bathhouses would also open up to the general public periodically for cabaret and variety shows. Heterosexuals would enter these spaces that otherwise were exclusively for gay sex. *Saturday Night at the Baths* (dir. David Buckley, 1975) contains wonderful documentary footage from one such evening of entertainment. Coincidentally, film exhibitor and programmer Jackie Raynal edited the film.
61. Delany, *Times Square Red, Times Square Blue*, 16–17. At the same time, Delany erroneously states, "By the early seventies the movie industry was already reeling under the advent of video home technology." This is a decade too early; VHS was still a new technology in the 1970s (in a format war with Betamax) and too costly for the average consumer. Other

factors leading to this mitosis are more likely: Times Square's increasing association with vice, and thus the decline of big movie palaces in the area, and the legalization of porn.

62. Delany, *Times Square Red, Times Square Blue*, 79.

63. B. Davis, *Repertory Movie Theaters*, 22.

64. Mark Valen (whom I discuss in more detail in chapter 3) recalled in conversations with me that the grindhouses by Times Square had been notorious for their balconies. We might then regard the repertory theater as a distant cousin to the grindhouse.

65. B. Davis, *Repertory Movie Theaters*, 171, 94.

66. B. Davis, *Repertory Movie Theaters*, 94. Conversely, the kitsch of the Theatre 80 St. Marks was almost tailor-made for queers, with its uniformed ushers in buttoned tailcoats (more reminiscent in design of a marching band than a movie palace) greeting patrons at the door. Davis calls Theatre 80 St. Marks the "Lower East Side version of Grauman's Chinese Theater" (117).

67. Galt and Schoonover note, "While early sociological studies of the art cinema audience suggested that it appealed primarily to men, art cinema has often been represented in the public eye as feminine, effete, or queer" (*Global Art Cinema*, 8), later adding, "even several decades after neorealism, art films continue to grant priority to the downtrodden, the underdog, and the abjected members of human communities" (15).

68. See Love, *Feeling Backward*; and Freeman, *Time Binds*.

69. The queerness of the repertory house is perhaps best personified in Tsai Ming-Liang's *Goodbye, Dragon Inn* (2003). The film follows the demise of a dilapidated repertory house on the eve of its closure. Buckets are scattered about the hallways to catch dripping water from the torrential rainfall, and patrons' bodies move slowly as they cruise one another in bathrooms and alleyways, as *Dragon Inn* (dir. King Hu, 1967) plays to an audience of both the emotionally disinterested and the emotionally shattered. The film anticipates with a heavy heart the ramifications of losing and then forgetting such a space as the repertory house, specifically as the phenomenological specificity of embodied space gets replaced by the easy accessibility of virtual ones. *Goodbye, Dragon Inn* is thus not so much an ode to old movies such as *Dragon Inn* as much as it is to the messy, inconvenient, distracting, and unpredictable communal experiences of watching them in repertory theaters. For a gorgeous exegesis, which incorporates Roland Barthes's essay "Leaving the Theater," see Ma, *Melancholy Drift*.

70. London and Berlin had theaters that perfectly fit the bill. In 1980s London, the Scala Theater was adjacent to a nightclub. Patrons of either venue

would use a staircase conjoining the two spaces to sneak between the dance floor and the repertory theater's all-night continuous screenings. Making interchangeable the partygoer and moviegoer, attendees could take a break from dancing to watch *Grease* (dir. Randal Kleiser, 1978) or *Performance* next door, just as moviegoers might be energized by the party next door in order to sustain their nocturnal marathon. See Giles, *Scala Cinema 1978–1993*; and Ali Catterall and Jane Giles's 2023 documentary *Scala!!!* At a screening of the documentary at the Metrograph I in New York City, I recall director Mary Harron saying how much the Scala had shaped her filmic tastes and called the boisterous environment a kind of "nightclub for cinephiles." In Berlin, the Kant Kino showed New German Wave films by Fassbinder and Wenders and was located alongside the Kant Kino Music Hall, where bands such as X-Ray Spex and Culture Club performed.

71. Lee, "A Never-Ending Film Festival."
72. Lee, "A Never-Ending Film Festival."
73. Hoberman and Rosenbaum, *Midnight Movies*, 311.
74. For more information, see the Fox Venice's memorial website, www.virtualvenice.info/media/fvt.htm.
75. Tent, *Midnight at the Palace*, 28.
76. Conflicting accounts of who started and ran the Nocturnal Dream Show exist. Steven Arnold's archivist Vishnu Dass attests that Steven ran it for several years, as do Cockettes members (such as Rumi), but that Sebastian claims full credit. See Eilers, "Sebastian's Nocturnal Dream Shows."
77. Characteristic of the time and place, there are conflicting stories about how their performances began. Though Arnold's story is mostly casual and vaguely uneventful, Pam Tent describes almost a coup of the stage, stealing the show from the Floating Lotus Opera Company who was the hired talent that night. See Tent, *Midnight at the Palace*, 34.
78. The Steven Arnold Museum and Archives, "Steven Arnold, the Nocturnal Dream Shows, and the Cockettes," YouTube, July 15, 2022, https://www.youtube.com/watch?v=vvo_O5lub3c.
79. Tent, *Midnight at the Palace*, 60.
80. Importantly, Hoberman and Rosenbaum discuss Divine's and John Waters's collaborations with the Cockettes: "Throughout the first half of 1971, *Multiple Maniacs* was the weekend midnight feature at the Palace Theater, a North Beach movie house whose main attraction was the stage show performed by the Cockettes, a local group of hippie-dopefiend-transvestites. Divine was invited out for an appearance that April, and Waters concocted a special live show. Introduced as 'the most beautiful woman in the world,' Divine sashayed out on the Palace stage in *Multiple*

Maniacs costume, pushing a shopping cart filled with dead mackerels. In between 'glamour fits' (defined by Waters as 'a combination of exhibitionist poses and temper tantrums'), she heaved the fish into the audience, strobe-lit by the continual detonation of flashbulbs. The happening climaxed with an actor dressed as a policeman running on stage and being strangled to death" (*Midnight Movies*, 147). See chapter 2 for more on *Multiple Maniacs*.

81. Taking a more aerial viewpoint of bricolage to describe the cultural conditions of the 1970s and 1980s would bring us close to Derrida's notion that discourse itself is a bricoleur, "borrowing one's concepts from the text of a heritage." Derrida's redefining of discourse itself as a site of bricolage is a response to Claude Lévi-Strauss's conception that mythical thought is not a product of deliberate engineering but rather bricolage: it uses the "debris of events" as its inventory to construct the logics and ethics that govern a given culture. See Derrida, *Writing and Difference*, 285. Derrida's effort to widen the application of bricolage (indeed to the point of deconstruction) and to make it a metaphor for discourse overall is useful in this historical-cultural context.

82. For a more direct link to curation, see Balzer, *Curationism*, 29–30.

83. Foster, "The 'Primitive' Unconscious of Modern Art," 64.

84. It may be tempting to position promiscuous programming as merely an early symptom of *postmodernism*, a stylistic movement that allegedly took hold by the 1980s. Historians and critics characterize the movement as having a disregard for cultural distinctions and thus as leading to hodgepodge aesthetics in which quotation, reference, pastiche, and appropriation signify globalized capitalism's tragic envelopment of society. Dick Hebdige situates teddy boys, mods, and punks in this framework as "*bricoleurs* [who] appropriated another range of commodities by placing them in a symbolic ensemble which served to erase or subvert their original straight meanings" (*Subculture*, 104). Quite cynically, Hebdige believes that subversion in these cases is mostly wishful thinking, because material and commodities are still tethered to capitalist modes of production regardless of whether efforts are made to resignify them. This is a tenet of the kind of thinking of postmodernism that would come to be affiliated with literary and cultural theorist Fredric Jameson. For Jameson, postmodernism's defining trait is the spatialization of time. When everything begins to cohabitate in the congestion of culture, when simultaneity takes the place of periodization, we lose the ability to think historically and to think through connections beyond what they mean at the moment of their encounter. Jameson's definition would seem to capture repertory and art house cinema's predilection for troubling the divisions between different histories, tastes, geographies, and genres, to the point where one could argue (albeit not without hyperbole) that it erases such distinctions

and creates a spatialized form of temporality within the parameters of the repertory program. And certainly postmodernism, as it has been periodized by Jameson and others, coincides with the period of promiscuous programming. See Jameson, *Postmodernism*. Such an application might be fine if postmodernism did not carry strong connotations of condemnation or celebration with it. Because postmodernism is so frequently subject to intense valuation, it is difficult to locate in it subject-object formations that do not evoke kneejerk responses. To some, postmodernism promises the freeing eradication of difference; to others, the lamentable desegregation and decontextualization of discourses that had hitherto made history and therefore human existence legible and distinct from mediation. See Eagleton, "Capitalism, Modernism, and Postmodernism." Postmodernism and its critiques therefore do not serve us in thinking about programming as a desire-inducing apparatus that profoundly altered spectators' awareness of sexuality during this period.

85. One could argue that films from India (e.g., Satyajit Ray) and Brazil (e.g., Cinema Novo), for example, were widely shown in art cinemas, but with far less regularity than films from the United States, Europe, and Japan. In terms of my own study, films from the Global South with provocative or deviant depictions of gender and sexuality would have been more difficult to come by. In an interview, Richard Peña, longtime programmer of the Film Center at the School of the Art Institute of Chicago and Film Society of Lincoln Center, spoke of his interest in gay Filipino director Lino Brocka's films, as well as Antonio Carlos da Fontoura's *The Devil Queen*, a 1974 Brazilian film based on the drag queen and gangster João Francisco dos Santos (later represented explicitly in Karim Aïnouz's *Madame Satã* [2002]). Peña explained that print accessibility prohibited him from being able to show these films in an analog era. Richard Peña in discussion with the author, December 2023.

86. See Galt and Schoonover, *Global Art Cinema*, 3–5.

87. B. Davis, *Repertory Movie Theaters*, 150.

88. "Ben Davis Collection: Thalia Calendars, 1977–1983," MoMA Archive, New York City. The Thalia had programmed "Fifties Melodrama: Post-War Auteurs and the Cinema of Hysteria" only seven months before, in September and October 1978. It was clearly popular, as were their "Film Noir" series, split into two parts in 1979. The Film Noir series follows the same pattern as the melodrama one, subdividing the genre by theme, director, star, and so on. According to James Harvey's tribute to Schwarz at Anthology Film Archives in 1996, *Village Voice* critic Tom Allen wrote lovingly that the Film Noir series confirmed that "the Thalia was not only honoring cinema, it was helping define it."

89. Schwarz and the team's curatorial subcategorization destabilized the genre's coherence in a manner that seems to emblematize the poststruc-

turalist angle of genre theorists such as Rick Altman, Christine Gledhill, and Steve Neale.

90. The Thalia's explicit remolding of an entrenched genre into smaller queer taxa is rather unique for this time. That the Thalia outright names subcategories for films that belong to a larger genre is illustrative of programming's ability to remold filmic classifications time and time again, but such explicit framing was not necessarily convention among other repertory houses of the time. Rarely did repertory houses reframe established genre in such an overt manner. Instead, they would either come up with a new category altogether or reframe from naming a framework, creating a contact zone or intertext of relationality that would leave it up to the spectator to interpret. For more, see chapter 2 on genre and taxonomy in film curating.

91. On the ways melodrama stages moral oppositions and acts as a corrective to those dualities, see Mulvey, "Notes on Sirk and Melodrama."

92. Anthropologist Claude Lévi-Strauss found the bricoleur a useful way to think about mythical production across cultures. Lévi-Strauss argued that myth tellers do not engineer their stories from scratch but take already-existing scraps and remnants to construct new myths out of them. "They make do with 'whatever is at hand,'" their repertoire consisting of materials both finite and heterogeneous. See Lévi-Strauss, *The Savage Mind*, 22. Lévi-Strauss writes, "Mythical thought, that 'bricoleur,' builds up structures by fitting together events, or rather the remains of events, while science, 'in operation' simply by virtue of coming into being, creates its means and results in the form of events, thanks to the structures which it is constantly elaborating and which are its hypotheses and theories" (22). Consider the parallels with programmers here, too: "his first practical step is retrospective. He has to turn back to an already existent set made up of tools and materials, to consider or reconsider what it contains and, finally and above all, to engage in a sort of dialogue with it and, before choosing between them, to index the possible answers which the whole set can offer to his problem" (18).

93. See Vogel's October 1950 shorts program in MacDonald, *Cinema 16*.

94. MacDonald, *Cinema 16*, 10.

95. Zaeske, "The 'Promiscuous Audience' Controversy," 192.

96. Lewis and Short, *A Latin Dictionary*; email exchange with classicist Todd Berzon, October 11, 2022.

97. Zaeske, "The 'Promiscuous Audience' Controversy," 192.

98. On *postmodernism*, see note 84.

99. Another way of situating the queerness of post-1968 programming is as a subsequent chapter in what Osterweil identifies as the "Flesh Cinema"

of underground queer filmmaking in 1960s New York City. Osterweil describes spectatorial scenes of haptic inundation, of viewers having "shattering encounters with desire, sex, pain, birth, and death," in the films of Jack Smith, Andy Warhol, and Barbara Rubin (*Flesh Cinema*, 14). This saturation of flesh and promiscuity displayed on-screen in those experimental shorts would find its narrative integration in the later art films I discuss in this book.

As Tom Gunning, Miriam Hansen, Kristen Whissel, Jacqueline Stewart, and others have demonstrated, cinema has been multisensory from its near origins, enmeshed with sensory-driven attractions that persist (from vaudeville at the turn of the century to the 1950s horror gimmicks of William Castle up through 3D and spectacularization devices). However, promiscuous programming incorporates "adult" forms of recreation such as drug use, concert going, and anonymous or casual sex into its sensibilities by virtue of its place alongside or within spaces of undisciplined experience. These attributes and the sensations and knowledges they produce had not been seen before on such a scale, and therefore this era marks an important shift in the production of modern sexuality as constitutive of social and bodily perception.

100. B. Davis, *Repertory Movie Theaters*, 90.
101. I would say this is catachrestic because "random" would suggest it is arbitrary. Even when programmers operate from their viscera over their purportedly rational thinking, their selections are not merely "random," despite the many factors such as print availability and costs that played a role. At the same time, I cannot find a better qualifier for this at the moment.
102. Barol et al., "The Last Picture Shows."
103. Ben Davis rightfully notes that both sides of this debate are "absolutist" (*Repertory Movie Theaters*, 218). Indeed, over the years, repertory programming often combined both thematized series (both over the span of a given week or month, or on a day of the week for a month, for instance) and eclectic mixtures of double-feature and single screenings.

2. Deviant Repertories

1. For writing on the relationship between early film curation and genre production, see Abel, *French Cinema*; Wasson, *Museum Movies*; and chapter 1 of this book.
2. Rubin was technically an anthropologist, but was very much influenced by sociologists of deviance. See Rubin's essay "Studying Sexual Subcultures: Excavating the Ethnography of Gay Communities in Urban North America" in *Deviations*, 310–46.

3. I underscore "figuratively" to distinguish between art films and nontheatrical films intended for clinical, medical, or industrial settings and purposes. A few fascinating titles blur those boundaries, especially in regard to trans subjects, such as Pat Rocco's short film *Changes* (1970) and Doris Wishman's *Let Me Die a Woman* (1977).

4. Bosma lists strategies programmers often use for assembling series and schedules, including pulling from "existing classifications [such as] genres, film movements, and film styles," as well as finding or creating themes to link films together (*Film Programming*, 57–59).

5. It is worth remembering that "queer cinema" embodies a classificatory contradiction that it inherited from New Queer Cinema (NQC). NQC had an ambivalent relationship to LGBT identity formations in that it problematized notions of identitarian stability and coherence while also clinging to and being organized by the lesbian and gay identities of a generation of filmmakers whose work was explicitly predicated on their identities. (This constituted a necessary tectonic shift in LGBT representation on and off the screen, both in terms of diegetic depictions and their authorship, when LGBT filmmakers of earlier generations wouldn't publicly address their sexualities.) Queer cinema, then, like NQC, struggles to escape the bind of identity in production and/or representation.

6. Erving Goffman writes, "If there is to be a field of inquiry called 'deviance,' it is deviants here defined that would presumably constitute its core. Prostitutes, drug addicts, delinquents, criminals, jazz musicians, bohemians, gypsies, carnival workers, hobos, winos, show people, full time gamblers, beach dwellers, homosexuals, and the urban unrepentant poor—these would be included. These are the folk who are considered to be engaged in some kind of collective denial of the social order" (*Stigma*, 144). Note that some of the terms in Goffman's list and mine have undergone lexical revision over the years, while others have been omitted from linguistic scrutiny and calls for timely revision.

7. Love, *Underdogs*, 165.

8. Love, *Underdogs*, 165.

9. Like *Member of the Wedding*, *Rebel Without a Cause* has also been seen as an allegory for queer youth, with extradiegetic knowledge of homo- and bisexual stars Sal Mineo and James Dean animating its subtext. Both films also render the normative familial unit a highly restrictive barrier to alternate forms of profound belonging.

10. White, *Uninvited*, xii.

11. See Butler, "Is Kinship Always Already Heterosexual?"; Love, *Underdogs*, 161.

12. Love writes, "Deviance studies shapes contemporary racial, gender, class, and geographical exclusions in queer studies, but it also shares its vision of collective liberation, characterized by coalitional thinking and an elevation of society's most stigmatized individuals, practices, and communities" (*Underdogs*, 15).

13. Love, *Underdogs*, 163.

14. About Eve Kosofsky Sedgwick's and Adam Frank's writings on Silvan Tomkins, Love writes, "While taxonomy might be used to stabilize identity, grouping traits to confirm the existence of determinate kinds of people, in their account it has the opposite effect, opening new possibilities for being and relation" (*Underdogs*, 10).

15. It began as a one-month series in October 1981 but was so popular that they extended it beyond October, stretching even into the new year. See "Ben Davis Collection: Focus on Public Cinema, Spring 1980–Jan. 1983," MoMA Archive, New York City.

16. Hall, "Deviance, Politics, and the Media," 66.

17. Vogel, *Film as a Subversive Art*.

18. Mark Betz writes, "The copy [of *Film as a Subversive Art*] in my university library was missing so many pages, as students had evidently taken scissors and razor blades in hand to excise from this copiously illustrated volume some of the more extreme and (usually sexually) explicit images for their own personal collections or use" ("High and Low and in Between," 513).

19. See the mention of Andrésen in the introduction.

20. Vogel, *Film as a Subversive Art*, 235.

21. For an excellent reading of the film through the genre of the screen test, see Gustafson, "Putting Things to the Test."

22. Nyong'o, *Afro-Fabulations*, 48, 52.

23. For a clever reading of the film with wordplay using *crush* in its many aesthetic, technological, and affective valences, see Nyong'o, *Afro-Fabulations*, 55.

24. That same year, Jason Holliday also found himself with unusual bedfellows in the Whitney Museum's women filmmakers series in May 1983. There Jason shared a schedule with Clarke's other films as well as with experimental queer work by Constance Beeson and Yvonne Rainer. I have not had the space to fully delve into the implications of this program.

25. As Jack Babuscio writes, "Theatricalization of experience, which is the key element to [Bette] Davis's camp, derives from the passing experience (wherein, paradoxically, we learn the value of the self while at the same time rejecting it) and from a heightened sensitivity to aspects of a

performance which others are likely to regard as routine or uncalculated (See Goffman)" ("The Cinema of Camp," 125). Babuscio is right to allude to Irving Goffman, who denaturalized everyday social interactions by likening them to the dramaturgical realm. This has been taken up in documentary studies about subjects performing for the camera.

26. Of course, there are times when sociology takes an interest in the psychological and behavioral, and times when sexology extends its analyses into the social conditions of the world. There is some overlap and flexibility in these definitions.

27. In fact, their relationship is more than analogous in psychology; the term *sexual deviation* in DSM-I and II was later replaced with *paraphilia* by DSM-III, published in 1980. See Milner et al., "Paraphilia Not Otherwise Specified."

28. Downing, "A Disavowed Inheritance," 45.

29. Francoeur, *A Descriptive Dictionary*, 463.

30. Importantly, paraphilia was introduced in DSM-III to replace "sexual deviation." DSM-5 redefined the term *paraphilia* to refer to a "persistent, intense, atypical sexual arousal pattern, independent of whether it causes any distress or impairment, which, by itself, would not be considered disordered." In de-pathologizing paraphilia, the DSM-5 replaced it instead with "paraphilic disorder" to describe scenarios in which "unusual" sexual appetites become destructive, either to the self or another person or multiple people. First, "DSM-5 and Paraphilic Disorders." See also Balon, *Practical Guide to Paraphilia and Paraphilic Disorders*.

31. See Money, *The Destroying Angel*.

32. "Roxie Cinema," Pacific Film Archive (BAMPFA), Berkeley, CA.

33. "Roxie Cinema," Pacific Film Archive (BAMPFA), Berkeley, CA. The only information given is that the excerpt comes from the *Berliner Börsen-Courier*, 1930.

34. Studlar, *In the Realm of Pleasure*, 107. For an engaging analysis of Erich von Stroheim's brand of masochism, see also Schlüpmann, "Queen Kelly."

35. Freud, *Three Essays on the Theory of Sexuality*.

36. Krafft-Ebing, *Psychopathia Sexualis*, 247.

37. Sobchack, *Carnal Thoughts*, 82.

38. Mary Ann Doane writes of *cinephilia* as "the intense and privileged relation to contingency, assured by photographic indexicality in the abstract, which can be loved again, this time as lost" (*The Emergence of Cinematic Time*, 229). Doane frames cinephilia as a love of contingency, an ironic blend of unpredictability or spontaneity and recursivity. Citing Paul Wil-

lemen's notion that cinephilia captures something "in excess of the film's register of performance, as potentially undesigned, unprogrammed," Doane observes that the search for contingency is intensified by cinema's precarity as a medium (226).

39. In 1977, San Francisco had its first *official* gay and lesbian film festival (followed by New York City in 1981 and Los Angeles in 1982). That same year, Richard Dyer's *Gays and Film* was published, carving out a legitimate academic space for the study of homosexuality and film. (A special section on "Lesbians and Film" in *Jump Cut* edited by Edith Becker, Michelle Citron, Julia Lesage, and B. Ruby Rich would follow in March 1981.) In the United States, there were occasional gay and lesbian series in art house cinemas.

40. "Chicago," MoMA Archive, New York City.

41. "Chicago," MoMA Archive, New York City.

42. For a description of *ellipsis*, see chapter 3 of Berlant's *On the Inconvenience of Other People*.

43. Doty and Ingham, "The 'Evil Medieval'"; Benshoff, *Monsters in the Closet*, 101.

44. Richard Peña in discussion with the author, December 2023.

45. Simon, "Deviance as History," 4.

46. "Chicago," MoMA Archive, New York City.

47. Predating the post-1968 work on deviance, Goffman's 1963 book established useful methods for looking at populations who resort to such maneuvers as passing and covering to subsume their status as other, or who, in claiming their status as other, must manage a spoiled identity that might entail seeking out others like them, although this could entail potentially being met with hostility or resentment among stigmatized people. Stigma as a binding "attribute," then, served as the pivot on which to describe an experience of social alienation not defined exclusively by race, class, gender, sexuality, disability, or ethnicity. These facets of identity absolutely guided Goffman's examples—all were discrete parts of a larger deviant system made legible, in part, through the structure of stigma. Such a conceptualization of everyday life enabled the new sociologists to develop new criteria for how people become and stay alienated or, in Goffman's terms, "discredited."

48. Jack Halberstam makes failure a central concept of queerness in *The Queer Art of Failure*.

49. Rubin, "Thinking Sex," 149.

50. Rubin, "Thinking Sex," 151.

51. Rubin, "Thinking Sex," 155.

52. On *nonsovereignty*, see Berlant and Edelman, *Sex, or the Unbearable*; and Davis and Sarlin, "'On the Risk of a New Relationality.'"
53. Irvine, *Disorders of Desire*, 7, 109. Famed sexologists Alfred Kinsey, William Masters and Virginia Johnson, and John Money are representative.
54. Ferguson, *Aberrations in Black*, 20.
55. David Halperin writes, Foucault's "books on the history of the insane asylum, of the clinic, of the prison, of the human sciences, and of sexual discourse constitute *political histories of the production of 'truth'*—scholarly attempts to historicize and defamiliarize, so as the better to sabotage, the technologies of a socially empowered rationality that phobically constructs, then scrupulously isolates and silences, the mad, the sick, the delinquent, and the perverse" (*Saint Foucault*, 51). More recently, Jack Halberstam in *Wild Things: The Disorder of Desire* summarizes Foucault's *The Order of Things*: "Scientists and humanists invented and explored the natural world in order to challenge or validate various man-made systems of morality and to create, by the end of that century, a new system of norms" (29). Clearly Foucault's critiques of scientific knowledge production remain germane to queer theory's analytical frameworks.
56. The sentence ends with "in any case an interference between two modes of production of truth: procedures of confession, and scientific discursivity." Foucault, *History of Sexuality*, 64.
57. Foucault, *History of Sexuality*, 43. Foucault is being as facetious as he is critical or analytical here, demonstrating that sexology was inventing its own language through bizarre terminology.
58. Trans studies have especially taken up this charge, demonstrating the violence to which medical, legal, educational, and state institutions subject people who do not fall in line within the binary codes of a male-female system. See Spade, *Normal Life*. Also, for earlier study, see Butler, "Doing Justice to Someone"; and Stone, "The Empire Strikes Back."
59. Foucault, *History of Sexuality*, 43.
60. Holmlund, "John Waters: *Multiple Maniacs* Relaunch," 99.
61. John Waters's blurb-turned-epigraph begins the book's introduction and reads, "Dr. John Money is the Duke of Dysfunction, a man who writes about 'unspeakable' human sexual problems with such dignity and ease that his case studies make me feel almost normal." Sullivan et al., "Introduction," 1.
62. Lisa Downing astutely remarks, "It becomes an apparently observable fact that abnormality, in taking so many forms, in being everything that is not the one thing that is 'correct,' appears to be everywhere, endlessly proliferating, and out of control. Thus, the hypothesis about human sociosexual life that the sexologists most feared appears to be true precisely

because of the premises upon which they construct their logic" ("A Disavowed Inheritance," 45).

63. See Schlib, "Future Historiographies." Downing also mentions the term in "A Disavowed Inheritance," 47.

64. See reference in the introduction and Simon, "Deviance as History," 11.

65. Quote from the calendar, Nuart Theatre's program archive, Los Angeles. "Anti-social" in this press release resonates strongly with what was dubbed the "anti-social turn" in queer theory, taking a hardline anti-assimilationist position against reproductive futurity. Lee Edelman, Leo Bersani, Jack Halberstam, and others' death drive–inspired approach figures a "brutal rejection of the comforting platitudes that we use to cushion our fall into mortality, incoherence and non-mastery," according to Halberstam in "The Anti-Social Turn in Queer Studies."

66. Chute, "Outlaw Cinema," 13.

67. Chute, "Outlaw Cinema," 11.

68. Chute, "Outlaw Cinema," 13.

69. Chute, "Outlaw Cinema," 10.

70. Chute, "Outlaw Cinema," 15.

71. See also Sconce, "'Trashing' the Academy."

72. Bornstein, *Gender Outlaw*, 97.

73. Consider the work of Gregory Markopoulos and Jean Cocteau. Kenneth Anger's work is not necessarily sober, but his experimental and nonlinear form aligns him with a highbrow tradition.

74. One can trace this back to Waters's love of exploitation movie showman William Castle, who would use gimmicks and marketing tactics to exploit exciting subjects. See Waters's interview segments in the 2007 documentary *Spine Tingler! The William Castle Story*, directed by Jeffrey Schwarz.

75. *Mondo Trasho* is mostly silent, however, without any "voice of god" or even intertitles (as in the case of the most famous silent expository documentary, *Nanook of the North*). Although it is aurally absent, the scientific presence remains intact in the film's prurient observing gaze; Waters might even be implying that sexological interest in sexual and gender deviants might all have some link to desire, be it out of curiosity or otherwise.

76. Gorfinkel, *Lewd Looks*, 167.

77. Gorfinkel, *Lewd Looks*, 171.

78. Kleinhans, "Pornography and Documentary," 100.

79. The *Time* piece focuses on sociologist Irving Horowitz. This passage from the article is worth quoting at length because it best summarizes the new

sociologists' effort to marshal maligned identities. The author writes, "In company with most of the new sociologists, Horowitz is bent on redefining the traditionally accepted symptoms of social deviance: divorce, homosexuality, crime and revolution. In a white-dominated society, for that matter, a man can be labeled deviant just because he is black. 'But how do we know what is and is not deviant?' asks Horowitz. 'When 41% of all marriages end in divorce, for example, must we still regard divorce as a social problem?' Instead of asking the question, 'What went wrong with the marriage?' he suggests, the sociologist should ask: 'What's wrong with the institution?'" *Time Magazine*, "The New Sociology."

80. Exemplified by Amos Vogel and Parker Tyler, it was not uncommon to find references to sexology and sociology in film criticism of the 1960s and 1970s dealing with sexuality and gender. Statistics about the actual frequency of ostensibly scarce and unusual practices and desires made it easier to dissuade the reader of sexual judgment, to naturalize their occurrence. Given Vogel's and Tyler's towering significance in art cinema, it is not a stretch to extrapolate that programmers read this criticism and might have come to understand systems of sexual valuation through such smart critical writing.

3. Erotic Intertextuality

1. Geritz, "Edith Kramer," 75–76.
2. Jenny, "The Strategy of Forms," 48.
3. "filmcalendar," Pacific Film Archive (BAMPFA), Berkeley, CA. See chapter 4 for a more in-depth reading of *Last Tango in Paris* and *In the Realm of the Senses*.
4. Brinkema, *The Forms of the Affects*, 40–41.
5. Only for Peirce the "degenerate index" is "contentless"; it is purely referential in nature and thus helps to chart designations. The difference here is that the body is not without information or content. It still carries meaning, even if that meaning is labile and shifts from foreground to background. For more on Peirce's degenerate index, see Peirce, *Collected Papers*.
6. Martin, "Never Laugh at a Man with His Pants Down," 190–91.
7. Analyzing Joris-Karl Huymans's description of Christ on the cross, Ellis Hanson notes, "As with the hysteric, sensation and meaning are perversely and painfully distributed along the body according to the dictates of an unknowable, unconscious language. The effect is erotic, though not necessarily genital or even pleasurable" (*Decadence and Catholicism*, 121). It is noteworthy that this definition of the erotic stresses convulsive sensation and epileptic paroxysm over an affirming pleasure.

8. Rich writes, "For Cixous, women are having the last laugh. And, to be sure, all the films in this camp deal with combinations of humor and sexuality" (*Chick Flicks*, 77). Rich references *Daisies* (dir. Věra Chytilová, 1966), *Celine and Julie Go Boating* (dir. Jacques Rivette, 1974), and *A Comedy in Six Unnatural Acts* (dir. Jan Oxenberg, 1975) as films that exemplify this paradigm.
9. Hennefeld, "Affect Theory in the Throat of Laughter," 129.
10. Hoberman and Rosenbaum, *Midnight Movies*, 154–57.
11. The programmers of the time remembered that attendees were allowed to smoke in the balcony and weed was commonly used, likely along with other mind-altering substances such as LSD. See Hoberman and Rosenbaum, *Midnight Movies*, 93. Critic Amy Nicholson added that Barenholtz's programming tended to lean toward "the surreal and absurd." See Gagliano, "The Elgin and EL TOPO."
12. In fact, the laugh is such a fascinating example precisely because of this liminal tension to both be part of the body and outside of it. Unlike dialogue, which often belongs to the body that speaks it, the laugh leaves its source (the body) as an abstraction, an effect of a sensation (e.g., tickling, arousal, humoring).
13. See Marks, *The Skin of the Film*, 152; Sobchack, *Carnal Thoughts*, 71; Shaviro, *The Cinematic Body*, 258. See also Sobchack, *Carnal Thoughts*, 56, for a list of related scholarship.
14. See L. Williams, *Screening Sex*, 18.
15. Shaviro, *The Cinematic Body*, 268.
16. Brinkema, *The Forms of the Affects*, xiii.
17. Brinkema, *The Forms of the Affects*, xiii–xiv.
18. Brinkema, *The Forms of the Affects*, xv.
19. Though I cannot be fully removed from the scene of analysis, I am not theorizing from the position of my own desires per se. My thinking here is by no means a kind of autotheory. I am engaging with the erotic forms that conspicuously shine through in the intertext.
20. Brinkema writes, "[Caroline] Levine's interest in *Forms*, for example, in how 'attending to the affordances of form opens up a generalizable understanding of political power,' urging literary critics to '*export* those practices, to take traditional skills to new objects—the social structures and institutions that are among the most crucial sites of political efficacy'—is an investment in reading forms insofar as they can be instrumentalized for the sake of something else, converted into confirming the logic of the political or social, which retroactively gets established as prior to and external to the formal; thus forms never themselves pose the question

of the political, of efficacy, of site, of export, of practice, &c." Brinkema, *Life-Destroying Diagrams*, 259.

21. Brinkema, *The Forms of the Affects*, 36.
22. L. Williams, "Film Bodies," 9.
23. L. Williams, *Hard Core*, 95.
24. D. A. Miller's naughty reading of *Cruising* hints at this; musing about the film's brash displays of dancefloor and orgiastic (s)exultation, he parenthetically remarks that the extras' naked "backsides (like the background in toto) insist on coming to the fore of our attention." The mise-en-scène of the club shifts to the foreground in its unavoidable eroticism, co-constitutive with the gyrating bodies. Miller's luscious descriptions might be a queer precursor to a Brinkema-esque affect-as-form and form-as-affect *as well as* the kind of affect theory Brinkema pushes against. See Miller, "Cruising."
25. For repetition in Freud and Lacan, see Krips, *Fetish*.
26. "Fantasy and the Origins of Sexuality," by Jean Laplanche and J.-B. Pontalis, has influenced feminist psychoanalytic theories of film spectatorship. They write, "Fantasy . . . is not the object of desire, but its setting. In fantasy the subject does not pursue the object or its sign: he appears caught up himself in the sequence of images. He forms no representation of the desired object, but is himself represented as participating in the scene although, in the earliest forms of fantasy, he cannot be assigned any fixed place in it (hence the danger, in treatment, of interpretations which claim to do so). As a result, the subject, although always present in the fantasy, may be so in a desubjectivized form—that is to say, in the very syntax of the sequence in question" (335). My thanks to Dolores McElroy for steering me toward this essay.
27. In a personal interview on July 23, 2024, Jorgensen mentioned that the *Los Angeles Times*' gay film critic, Kevin Thomas, frequently boosted the Nuart by reviewing films that no other local critics would watch. Jorgensen recalls Thomas was the only critic to show up to a screening of the Andy Warhol–produced film *Bad*, which I reference in this chapter.
28. In chapter 2, I analyze at length the Nuart's Outlaw Cinema series, which included films by Fassbinder, Pasolini, Gordon Lewis, Morrissey, and Waters.
29. It is significant to note that, compared with other local film institutions, the Nuart's cadre of programmers was rather heterosexual. Other local theaters and screening series were spearheaded by gay men: the Los Angeles International Film Exposition, also known as Filmex, was programmed by two gay men, Gary Essert and Gary Abrahams, from 1971 to 1983, before it morphed into the American Cinematheque. Ronald Haver was

the director of the film department at the Los Angeles County Museum of Art (LACMA) from its launch in 1970. Douglas Edwards programmed primarily at Academy of Motion Picture Arts and Sciences, and additionally programmed series at Filmex and LACMA. Haver and Edwards were instrumental in the 1983 restoration of *A Star Is Born* (1954), which tried to fill in, with music and production stills, chunks of missing footage that had been cut for its initial theatrical release. Essert, Abrahams, Haver, and Edwards all died of AIDS-related illnesses between 1992 and 1993. A devastating loss to the filmgoing community of the time, their deaths also figure an insuperable gap in exhibition histories that makes it difficult to understand the full extent to which queer men shaped film culture in Los Angeles and beyond.

For their obituaries, see Todd McCarthy, "Gary Essert, Founder of FilmEx, Dies," *Variety*, December 16, 1992, https://variety.com/1992/film/news/gary-essert-founder-of-filmex-dies-102146/; "Gary Abrahams; Co-Founder of Popular L.A. Film Festivals," *Los Angeles Times*, November 7, 1992, https://www.latimes.com/archives/la-xpm-1992-11-07-mn-1082-story.html; "Ronald Haver, 54; Was Film Restorer of 'A Star Is Born,'" *New York Times*, May 21, 1993, https://www.nytimes.com/1993/05/21/obituaries/ronald-haver-54-was-film-restorer-of-a-star-is-born.html; and Todd McCarthy, "Academy Administrator Edwards Dies," *Variety*, February 3, 1993, https://variety.com/1993/scene/people-news/academy-administrator-edwards-dies-103666/.

30. Lee, "A Never-Ending Film Festival."
31. Lee, "A Never-Ending Film Festival."
32. Josephine Baker retrospectives were not common during the 1970s and 1980s, perhaps due to print availability and/or racial bias in programming. However, the Nuart did program a double bill of *Princess Tam Tam* (1935) and *Zouzou* (1934) in April 1989. Nuart Theatre's program archive, Los Angeles.
33. Julian Ross, email message to author, December 5, 2022. Ross wrote, "I think these films screened in theatres managed by the Art Theatre Guild—distributor and exhibitor for international arthouse cinema. It might also be worth looking into Sogetsu Art Centre too (esp for Warhol). In Shinjuku, the Theatre Scorpio (Sasori-za) also screened such films. Pasolini, Warhol, Bertolucci and I think Ken Russell I've definitely seen in my research on the 1960s, but I'm pretty sure the other directors you mention too."
34. There has been some renewed interest on Criterion Channel and at the American Cinematheque in Los Angeles.
35. Russell biographer Joseph Lanza does not exactly pinpoint Russell's motivation for taking the project. See Lanza, *Phallic Frenzy*.

36. Lanza insists the film is really about the repressed love between Rupert and Gerald. Lanza even suggests the women in the film are mere "distractions" (*Phallic Frenzy*, 80). He does this to counterbalance the many readings of the film that downplay or subtract the men's homoerotic attraction. Note the opulent décor of the room in which Rupert and Gerald wrestle nude, which invokes the production of cinematic space I discuss in this chapter, with the debauchery of space in tension with the "gentlemanly decorum" of sport. See also L. Williams, "Bad Sex and Obscene Undertakings."

37. Sobchack, *The Address of the Eye*. The notion of the "film's body" could be more formally robust. Sobchack often likens the film-body's "organs" to the camera and the projector. Movement is key to her concept but there is little attention to aspects of style beyond point of view. There is a bit more attention to on-screen textures in her reading of *The Piano* in her later book *Carnal Thoughts*.

38. Sobchack, *Address of the Eye*, 167; Sobchack, *Carnal Thoughts*, 66n48.

39. L. Williams, *Hard Core*, 36, 50–51.

40. Valerie Orpen acknowledges the strange dearth of literature on editing in particular. She observes that "editing as an expressive technique is largely taken for granted. We all know that it is expressive, but it is more difficult, uncomfortable even, to explain why and how. The expressiveness of lighting, camera movements, colour, sound and so forth has been explored to a large extent. Editing is far more elusive. Editing can be equated with movement but unlike camera movement or movement within the frame, it is difficult to pin down, to freeze, to control. As it is, the medium of film is lengthy to describe verbally, but describing editing seems even more difficult since its crucial element, time, is particularly arduous to quantify. In fact, Noël Burch uses a word which is almost synaesthetic: he calls the plastic aspect of editing 'intangible'" (Orpen, *Film Editing*, 3).

41. Ronnie's fascist posturing is reflected by his German servant Otto's costuming in the final sequence. Otto sports a Nazi uniform and even salutes Ronnie with a "heil Hitler." This also invokes the fetishistic fascism (as an extension of Ronnie's depravity) that I go on to discuss in this chapter.

42. Russ Meyer's use of montage throughout his body of work is layered. In *Beyond the Valley of the Dolls* alone, the jump cuts are a return of what had come before and a foreboding of what is to come. Similar disorientation is produced in the first party scene at Ronnie's mansion when the girls arrive to town. The montage introduces the cast of personalities to the viewer in rapid succession while inducing a sense of countercultural exuberance facilitated by drugs and alcohol. The jump cuts then return in the action sequence that ends the film, when Ronnie murders everyone in the house. And they return later again in the epilogue when the

voiceover narration does a moral assessment of all the characters. This faux moralism is a signature of Meyer's use of irony, expressed through hyperbole apropos of exploitation. His awareness of censorship and the repressive society into which his films will be released informs sex scenes that usually "dial up" his female characters' anarchic libidos.

43. Bersani, "Is the Rectum a Grave?," 222.
44. Powell, "Nicolas Winding Refn and the Ken Russell Style," 262.
45. Although this has been suggested in many places, I'm borrowing this notion specifically from de Lauretis, "Popular Culture, Public and Private Fantasies" 314.
46. Hirsch, *The Hollywood Epic*, 32.
47. Tyler, *A Pictorial History of Sex in Films*, 77.
48. Kriss Ravetto writes, "Many such representations, whether historical, theoretical, or filmic, apply conventional (prefascist) aesthetic images of evil (sexual perversion, intoxication, madness, disease, decadence, and impurity) to fascism and nazism as a means of expelling them from the present . . . However, the images of perversity, obscenity, inhumanity, and horror that are attributed to fascism, nazism, and the 'Final Solution' cannot be exculpated from ideological discourses; they are, indeed, fastened to preexisting moral codes and sexual and racial theories (Darwinism, psychoanalysis, criminology, sexology, and sociology). Therefore, rather than unmake fascist aesthetics, the result of this retrofashioning of fascism and nazism (depicting fascism and nazism as decadent, camp, kitsch, sentimental, or aberrant) attests to the impossibility of disengaging visual and rhetorical constructions from political, ideological, and moral codes" (*The Unmaking of Fascist Aesthetics*, 5–6).
49. Stiglegger, *Sadiconazista*.
50. Frost, *Sex Drives*, 6–7.
51. Of course, this theory does not account for fascist mandates for sanitized heterosexuality, but given that none of this work actually comes from fascist contexts, it is not of concern in this study.
52. Both films share an intertext that does not appear in the program but extends the double bill's reach: Luchino Visconti's *The Damned*. Visconti's exploration of Nazism and homosexuality starred the Italian director's German boyfriend Helmut Berger, who also appeared in *Salon Kitty* as the sadistic officer, and Charlotte Rampling, the protagonist in *The Night Porter*. These films make up a cycle of art films that rode on the coattails of *Cabaret*'s success, and they replicate some of the same framing devices and tropes. On the question of taste and prestige, Mark Betz writes, "*Il portiere di notte / The Night Porter* is now positioned, and has been for some time, as the central node in the scholarly discussions of

what Sabine Hake in a recent article identified as 'the fascist imaginary in 1970s Italian cinema,' which would crystallize in its wake into one of the most disreputable exploitation film subgenres or cycles, Nazisploitation . . . Clear lines of division have tended to be drawn between the art and the exploitation films that fall into this category, with the latter marked as Nazisploitation films in a way that the former are not. Alongside *Salò*, then, *Pasqualino Settebellezze / Seven Beauties* (dir. Lina Wertmüller, 1975) and *The Night Porter* are frequently considered as standing apart from others circulating in the mid 1970s that nonetheless often similarly deal with the historical experience of fascism and of the Nazis in Europe, and especially in Italy" ("High and Low and in Between," 506).

53. See Francoeur, *A Descriptive Dictionary*.

54. Ravetto, *The Unmaking of Fascist Aesthetics*, 12, 5.

55. Daniel Magilow suggests *The Night Porter* and *Salò* could be read as exploitation films: "Detractors see them as pornography or pretentious 'Euro-trash', while proponents praise them as daring, taboo-breaking masterpieces that make sadomasochism, coprophagy and other forms of deviance into metaphors for fascism" ("Introduction: Nazisploitation!," 8–9).

56. Gorfinkel, *Lewd Looks*, 25, 93. See chapter 2 of *Lewd Looks*, "Peek Snatchers: Corporeal Spectacle and the Wages of Looking, 1960–1965," for a more detailed analysis.

57. Tashiro, *Pretty Pictures*, 9.

58. Hirsch in *Hollywood Epic* writes, "Hollywood's predilection for the grandiose was anticipated by the late Nineteenth-century academic paintings of classical scenes by artists like John Martin, Alma-Tadema, Gérome, and Bougoureau, who cleaned up history and overlaid it with a Victorian infatuation for a fussy detail. The ancient world as conceived by these Nineteenth-century artists is incredibly lavish—far grander, probably, than the original. Their huge, crowded, busting canvases have the overstuffed quality of a Victorian interior" (31).

59. In a rare show of spatial vastness, the film flashes back to Bert, a trained ballet dancer, who performed for the Nazis. Bert dances in the almost nude, flesh-tone spandex underwear barely covering him, in a room somewhere between industrial and institutional, performing on a stage as endless as he could have dreamed, for an audience of his torturers. In the present, Bert and his captor, Max, whom he shares with the protagonist, Lucia, have a quasi-homoerotic relationship that never seems to get realized or confirmed.

60. Marrone, "*The Night Porter*."

61. One of the film's posters reads: "Rome. Before Christ. After Fellini," with an image below of Encolpius and Ascyltos holding each other on horseback, their bare legs suggestively positioned. Another *Satyricon* poster can be found in the introduction.
62. Stein, "*Maîtresse.*"
63. L. Williams, *Hard Core*, 199. Williams elaborates, "The violence of [aesthetic sadomasochism] . . . is not real, nor does it aim at the effect of reality. Here the *effect* of violence—the slap, the whip lash, the flinch—is created through editing, acting, and sound effects; the 'frenzy of the visible' is not offered as hard core" (201). Likewise, the art house films do not seem to have an investment in the real, at least not like pornography.
64. Deleuze, *Masochism*, 72.
65. Despite Deleuze's cogent arguments to separate sadism and masochism, Linda Williams suggests cinema offers "play in oscillation between active and passive and male and female subject positions, rather than fixing one pole or the other as the essence of the viewer's experience" (*Hard Core*, 217).
66. Stein, "*Maîtresse.*"
67. Film distributor and curator Cornelius Moore talked about remembering this exact scene from the film many years after seeing it at the PFA. See Geritz et al., "Film Culture."
68. Kaye, "Losing His Religion."
69. See Waugh, *Hard to Imagine*.
70. Andrea Mantegna's portrait *St. Sebastian* (1480) happens to be the cover of Kaja Silverman's *Male Subjectivity at the Margins* (Routledge, 1992).
71. Kaye, "Losing His Religion," 98.
72. Schrader, *Transcendental Style in Film*, 77.
73. Campany, *Photography and Cinema*, 37.
74. See Brinkema engaging with Brigitte Peucker (*The Forms of the Affects*, 106–7). Brinkema suggests that stasis in Michael Haneke's *Funny Games* (1997) does not represent death itself but rather posits grief as a "representational problem." Brinkema writes, "The image labors to step forward, to re-find the smoothness of cinematic movement free from the heaviness of irreversible mortality" (109).
75. See Ma, *Melancholy Drift*, 101.
76. In *Decadence and Catholicism*, Hanson writes, "Catholicism has always been founded on a peculiar organization of sexuality, a certain deployment of sexual secrets and revelations, a system of repression, punishment, confession, sublimation, displacement, and fetishization. As we

might infer from the myriad psychoanalytic examinations of mysticism, of the spectacle of virgin motherhood or Christ's passion or Saint Sebastian run through with arrows, this libidinal organization might be described as perverse" (22).

77. One could argue that these techniques inspire the formal treatment of BDSM in Michael Haneke's *The Piano Teacher* (2001), in which Isabelle Huppert subjects her students, her lover, and herself to humiliation and pain. Note the ambiguous long takes and inscrutable close-ups throughout the film.

78. Why are we so fixated on the body? I find it curious that even as the post-human studies of animals and artificial intelligence steer scholars away from anthropocentricism, theories of spectatorship have fallen short of identifying noncorporeal sources of affect and desire.

79. N. Davis, *The Desiring-Image*, 15.

80. See Staiger, *Perverse Spectators*, 31–32.

4. Repertory Time

1. Goldin, "Feeding the Appetites."
2. Rhodes, "'The Double Feature Evil.'"
3. This may sound like a play on Mary Ann Doane's concept of "cinematic time," detailed in her book, *The Emergence of Cinematic Time*. For Doane, cinematic time condenses time, standardizes and mathematizes it, and keeps a record or archive of it. More invested in questions of modernity and the metrics of ordinary life, Doane is not so much interested in the question of immersion and prolonged exposure that I describe here. Repertory time then is a *version* of cinematic time, distinct from but not opposed to the implications Doane proposes. She does address cinephilia toward the end of the book, a point that seems to intersect with my interest. Primarily through the writing of Paul Willimen and Miriam Hansen, Doane frames cinephilia as a pleasure of contingency. It seeks out contingency in the accidental, the micro, the gesture, defined as that which "resists systematicity, rationalization, programming, and standardization" (229). Cinephilia is a site of particularity—"unique to the viewer"—and thus "unsharable and inarticulable" (228, 227). The spectator here is absorbed by the detail that is or, rather, *feels* like his or her own. Doane's account of contingency is predicated on the image. My interest in the contingent, however, is located in the viewing experience itself—that is, the physical conditions of the theater, one's mood, and the distinct mood diffused throughout the room, the films with which it is programmed, as well as those experiences outside the theater that make a person want to return to a text, or which shape a

text, such as critics' or friends' readings, or a change in world or local events.
4. Wollen, *Paris Hollywood*, 5.
5. Rhodes, "'The Double Feature Evil,'" 57.
6. Ohmer, "Speaking for the Audience."
7. See Rhodes, "'The Double Feature Evil.'"
8. See David Marriott's discussion of *Native Son* in *On Black Men*.
9. B. Davis, *Repertory Movie Theaters*, 30.
10. B. Davis, *Repertory Movie Theaters*, 30.
11. Talbot, *In Love with Movies*, 22.
12. And for the purposes of my study here, I do not put much stock in the order in which the films played because, in this recursive viewing environment, it would not have been uncommon for many spectators to have already seen one or both films in a double feature, perhaps even earlier that day (as part of a continuous performance). Despite the use value of Caroline Bem's theoretical framework of the diptych, the historical attention to exhibition in her piece is limited. Bem writes, "Double bills invited significant conceptual work from their viewers, who were required to keep the first film in mind while watching the second feature" ("Cinema | Diptych," 10). I am not being nitpicky about history here; this idea leads Bem to suggest "film pairings create coherent wholes to be contemplated, studied, and in some way perhaps, committed to memory" (10). The theory of programmatic and spectatorial intertextuality that I advance here runs counter to this assertion (10).
13. B. Davis, *Repertory Movie Theaters*, 8.
14. Historians mark François Truffaut's 1954 article in *Cahiers du Cinéma*, "Les Politiques des Auteurs," as the beginnings of this discourse. Andrew Sarris's 1962 essay "Notes on the Auteur Theory" then imported the concept into the United States. See Staples, "The Auteur Theory Reexamined."
15. Wasson, *Museum Movies*, 108.
16. B. Davis, *Repertory Movie Theaters*, 42.
17. B. Davis, *Repertory Movie Theaters*, 42.
18. It would be useful to have a more detailed study of programmers' attitudes toward film studies, especially as the field takes up semiotics, Marxism, feminism, and other structuralist approaches post-1968.
19. I see a connection here to what Gerwin van der Pol calls the "cinephile game," which is when the cinephile looks for a past film's influence or citation in a later film, wonders if the connections are intentional, and thereby explores the creative genealogies of auteurs. But whereas the ci-

nephile game tests intertextual expertise and memory, the double bill is a more immediate game (if you will) of comparison in which the viewer is challenged to understand a film's meaning as it is dependent on its relation to its co-feature. Inevitably the double bill's intertextuality will extend beyond its dyadic borders into other discourses, genres, and traditions, but it is not requisite for the comparative exercise I am interested in here. See van der Pol, "The Secret Passion of the Cinephile."

20. See Gorfinkel, *Lewd Looks*, 62.
21. L. Williams, *Screening Sex*, 114.
22. *Village Voice*, August 3, 1974 45.
23. Spivak, "Translator's Preface," xxvii.
24. "Carnegie Hall Cinema," Pacific Film Archive (BAMPFA), Berkeley, CA.
25. L. Williams, *Screening Sex*, 119.
26. Williams explains that Bertolucci was inspired by the writings of Georges Bataille, who wrote that eroticism is an attempt for bodies to find continuity and unity only for it to vanish and give way to discontinuity, that is, the reality that humans will always return to their singular states upon the break with erotic time and space. For Bataille, erotic impulses attempt to overcome this discontinuity. If *Last Tango in Paris* is about the sex drive driven to its logical limits (that is, death) in the Bataillian sense, it is also effectively about the unsustainability of erotic fantasy to translate to practicable life. The last tango between Brando and Schneider at the end of the film, full of maudlin frenzy and awkwardness, exemplifies this discontinuity, a prelude to the film's representation of the most extreme discontinuity of all: murder. See Bataille, *Erotism*.
27. The modern culture industry of romance and sentimentality has long invested in the idea of lovers becoming vulnerable and therefore coming undone as the ultimate sacrifice to love's sustainability. As Lauren Berlant aptly notes in *The Female Complaint*, "when people enter into love's contract with the promise of recognition and reciprocity, they hope memory will be reshaped by it, minimizing the evidence of failure, violence, ambivalence, and social hierarchy that would otherwise make love a most anxious desire for an end to anxiety" (179).
28. For more on "reading against the grain," see Aspasia Kotsopoulos, "Reading Against the Grain Revisited," *Jump Cut* 44 (2001).
29. Elsewhere I've explored the blurred boundaries and uneven temporal developments of feminist and queer theories in what I consider a crisis of attribution. See Marc Francis, "Splitting the Difference: On the Queer-Feminist Divide in Scarlett Johansson's Recent Body Politics," *Jump Cut: A Review of Contemporary Media* 57 (2016).
30. Marks, "The Ethical Presenter," 43.

31. Bem, "Cinema | Diptych," 3.
32. Bem, "Cinema | Diptych," 3.
33. Marks, "The Ethical Presenter," 43.
34. Caroline Bem compares these dynamic contact points to the diptych's hinge; the interstice between the two films offers a space within which spectators ask what is the relation between the two frames, toggle back and forth between the films' comparable scenes, climactic moments, endings, notable style attributes, performance techniques, intertextual allusions (that course between and outside of the diptych), to set in motion a tennis match of compare and contrast. This movement between the two parts establishes an ethical dialogic scene for the viewer. See Bem, "Cinema | Diptych," 5–7.
35. Eco, *A Theory of Semiotics*, 122.
36. Fawaz, *Queer Forms*, 13.
37. "Strand Theatre," Pacific Film Archive (BAMPFA), Berkeley, CA.
38. Wood, *Hollywood from Vietnam to Reagan*, 53. It is unclear if the two were playing a double bill in this exact instance.
39. "filmcalendar," Pacific Film Archive (BAMPFA), Berkeley, CA.
40. Harris, "*Klute*: Trying to See Her."
41. The closeted gay man can be interpreted as a symbol of denied liberation and therefore violent repression writ large. Some have found it to be homophobic.
42. For more discussion of *Looking for Mr. Goodbar*, see Molly Haskell, "Exposing a Nerve," review of *Looking for Mr. Goodbar*, *New York*, October 31, 1977; Fran Moira, Margie Crow, and Terri Poppe, review of *Looking for Mr. Goodbar*, *Off Our Backs* 7, no. 10 (December 1977); Benson-Allott, "Looking for *Looking for Mr. Goodbar*," 127; Wood, *Hollywood from Vietnam to Reagan*; and Bruce LaBruce, "Bruce LaBruce's Academy of the Underrated: *Looking for Mr. Goodbar*," *Talkhouse*, July 19, 2016.
43. I am invoking Michael Warner and Lauren Berlant's challenge to the privacy of sexuality in their excellent piece "Sex in Public." See the essay in Warner, *Publics and Counterpublics*, 187–208.
44. One can also track this via Fonda's meta- and paratextual indicators. For instance, the mugshot in *Klute* mirrors her iconic real-life one, and from that same year, 1970. *Klute* and *They Shoot Horses, Don't They?* arguably mark a dark departure from *Barbarella*-era Fonda. Likewise, *Looking for Mr. Goodbar* marked a departure for Keaton from *Annie Hall* and other lighter Woody Allen collaborations.
45. I have not aimed to exhaust the potential intertextual readings of these films that were shown together. There are many cogent ways to make

sense of their juxtaposition that move beyond restrictive binary logic. Eco reminds us of this by way of his allusion to the "infinite peripheries" cultivated by semiotic processes (*Theory of Semiotics*, 122). I would argue that intertextuality—left undiscussed by Eco in relation to unlimited semiosis—amplifies these opportunities. "Unlimited" here does not simply mean that a person can derive whatever meaning they want from the text. On the contrary, a text's meaning is moored by context and discourse; these cannot be jettisoned willy-nilly.

46. Stewart, *Ordinary Affects*, 128. This is not the same thing as saying affect works beyond or somehow outside of signification, which I do not believe.

47. Sontag, *Against Interpretation*, 284.

48. In their psychoanalytic comparative study, Betty Robbins and Roger Myrick write, "The fetish is . . . represented politically in *Priscilla* in a way that is missing in *Rocky Horror*, a move which further acts to throw the construction of gender into relief" ("The Function of the Fetish in *The Rocky Horror Picture Show* and *Priscilla, Queen of the Desert*," 275).

49. Sobchack, *Carnal Thoughts*, 4–8.

50. They showed together in double bills also in more mainstream theaters. See *Village Voice*, October 15, 1970, 60.

51. For Eco, cult films live on in their "glorious incoherence." Eco, "'Casablanca,'" 4.

52. Stam, *Subversive Pleasures*, 86.

53. See also Foucault, "Of Other Spaces." Foucault's concept of the *heterotopia*—a "counter-site" of living that marks an "absolute break with . . . traditional time"—allows another theoretical direction that might arrive at some of the same conclusions (26). I am avoiding it because Foucault's formulation is notoriously slippery, if not inconsistent. (It is worth noting that the article was a lecture that was published shortly before Foucault's death.) The *carnivalesque* (which Foucault includes in his examples of heterotopic space) has much more affective and definitional specificity to it. Nevertheless, I want to mention that Foucault's subcategory of "heterotopias of deviation" might resonate with my thinking here; he defines these as spaces designated for "individuals whose behavior is deviant in relation to the required mean or norm" (25). His examples are retirement homes, nursing homes, prisons, and psychiatric hospitals. Elsewhere in the lecture, Foucault mentions the cinema, but more as a space of simultaneous heterogeneity, not necessarily one of "deviant" suspension from normative time and place. Lauren Berlant eloquently describes the heterotopia as "a transitional space where the social reaches a limit and opens a window to an outside, to new dictionaries and the counternormative"

(*On the Inconvenience*, 14). This gets much closer to the carnivalesque imaginings I am describing in this section.

54. Stam, *Subversive Pleasures*, 87.

55. This double feature's sensibility can be applied to numerous other arrangements. Just consider these perverse worlds produced through repertory time: Paul Morrissey's *Heat* and *Trash* at the Bleecker Street Cinema in the summer of 1977; *The Bitter Tears of Petra von Kant* (dir. Rainer Fassbinder, 1973) and *Les Biches* at Carnegie Hall in the fall of 1976; and *Liquid Sky* (dir. Slava Tsukerman, 1982) and *The Hunger* at the Vista Theatre in Hollywood in the fall of 1984. "Bleecker Street Cinema" and "Carnegie Hall Cinema," Pacific Film Archive (BAMPFA), Berkeley, CA; Nuart Theatre's program archive, Los Angeles. These double bills represent the extended lengths of time in which richly textured and transgressive worlds are animated to the possible disbelief and curiosity of the spectator.

56. In "Portrait of a Cult Film Audience," Bruce A. Austin locates 1977 as the year *Rocky Horror*'s midnight screenings became a national phenomenon.

57. For more on *The Rocky Horror Picture Show*, see Weinstock, *Reading Rocky Horror*.

58. See Freeman, *Time Binds*, 3; and Halberstam, *The Queer Art of Failure*, 72–82.

59. Stam, *Subversive Pleasures*, 89.

60. Umberto Eco maintains that cult films are always already composites or "intertextual collages" that elude a logic of totality, seamlessness, and polish ("'Casablanca,'" 3). Using *Casablanca* (dir. Michael Curtiz, 1942) as his example of a cult film, Eco claims that fans of the film "unhinge it [and] break it up or take it apart so that one then may remember only parts of it, regardless of their original relationship to the whole" (4). *Casablanca* is for Eco a "hodgepodge of sensational scenes strung together implausibly, which makes it ideal as a cult text" (3). Despite the criticism that Eco's claim can be applied to any number of films that are nowhere near "cult," his point that cult films live on in their "glorious incoherence" accurately captures the extent to which cult films are loved precisely because they are disjointed narratively, logically, philosophically, and aesthetically (4). For the critique of Eco, see Grant, "Science Fiction Double Feature."

61. Nuart Theatre's program archive, Los Angeles.

62. L. Williams, "Skin Flicks on the Racial Border," 290.

63. I say this because a substantial amount of repertory programming today, which tends to be associated with museums and major institutions such as the Film Society of Lincoln Center, BAMPFA, and MoMA is indeed syntagmatic in that programs tend to be *thematized* and unified by a particular auteur, actor, movement, era, or nation, and so on.

64. "Agglutination" is a phenomenon found both in biology and linguistics that occurs when simple parts form masses, clumps, and compounds with other simple parts, without resulting in full assimilation. In language, agglutination means rearranging and reassigning prefixes and suffixes to help generate new connective tissues among words and concepts never before considered. (For instance, the prefix "bio-," meaning "life," continues to find new suffixes, as does the suffix "-poiesis," which comes from ancient Greek understandings of making, producing, and forming.)

65. "Strand Theatre," Pacific Film Archive (BAMPFA), Berkeley, CA. Mike Thomas purchased the Strand in 1977. According to Jack Stevenson, "Thomas personally booked and oversaw daily operations at The Strand" until it closed in 1989 (*Land of a Thousand Balconies*, 84). Stevenson gives the impression that Thomas had to negotiate the theater's programmatic identity. It had to be "hip" and eccentric, but not go so far as to become a grindhouse. Thomas is quoted as saying, "If you play nothing but nasty, violent movies you get nothing but nasty, violent people" (82). He added, "If you think your customers are animals and give them nothing but exploitation pictures, they'll treat your theatre accordingly" (82). With Thomas at the helm, Stevenson notes, the Strand established itself "on a diet of subtitled foreign films, widescreen epics, vintage Hollywood pictures and cult 'specials' like house-filling bargain-priced marathons on Sundays, and a 'Scary Movie Festival' every Tuesday. Thomas sought to maintain a classic grind house [*sic*] style of exhibition in the manner of his beloved old Market St movie houses. This meant continuous programming, daily multiple-bills stacked with cartoons, shorts and trailers. No intermissions . . . non-stop movies. The lights never went up" (83). Fittingly, Thomas drew "a new audience composed of students, senior citizens from the neighbourhood and film buffs from all over town who appreciated extras like the restored décor and displays of original one-sheet lobby posters" (83).

66. See Bataille, *Erotism*.

67. See chapter 2 for discussions of Rubin's "outer limits" and a Butleresque notion of "queer kinship."

68. For more information, see Bonnie Malkin, "*Last Tango in Paris* Director Suggests Maria Schneider 'Butter Rape' Scene Not Consensual," *Guardian*, December 3, 2016, https://www.theguardian.com/film/2016/dec/04/last-tango-in-paris-director-says-maria-schneider-butter-scene-not-consensual; and Lina Das, "I Felt Raped by Brando," *Daily Mail*, July 19, 2007, http://www.dailymail.co.uk/tvshowbiz/article-469646/I-felt-raped-Brando.html.

69. That is, not including the many in sexploitation and pornographic films far too abundant to list.

70. Russo, *The Celluloid Closet*, 190. I insert a "[sic]" in the quote because *Something for Everyone* is clearly a bisexual film, not a gay one.
71. San Filippo, *The B Word*, 22.
72. Russo is quite correct to point out the two films' topical bonds. They are unified by the gay appeal, of which urban art house programmers would have been well aware. In addition, they were both released in 1970. But beyond the superficial markers of "queer interest," their copresence may be difficult to ascertain. *The Boys in the Band*, based on Mart Crowley's play of the same name, takes place one evening as seven friends gather for a birthday party. As the night wears on, their internalized homophobia becomes all the more apparent as the culprit of their fraying lives and relations. Russo's mention of these two films in the same breath suggests that while they might not appear to participate in the same exact representational politics, the homoerotic draw of *Something for Everyone* conceals the disparaging and self-loathing subtext of both films. See chapter 5 for a critique of Russo's paranoid reading practice.
73. "filmcalendar," Pacific Film Archive (BAMPFA), Berkeley, CA.
74. San Filippo, *The B Word*, 41.
75. San Filippo uses the blurring of reality and dreams in films such as *Persona* and *Mulholland Drive* as art house examples of bi-textuality. I find such a method also vexes the separation of "good" and "bad" objects. For instance, *Teorema* (a critical darling) and *Something for Everyone* (a seemingly tawdry forgotten relic) both use the family as the locus to illustrate how bisexuality can undo a number of social orders such as class and gender, or at least expose them for their tenuousness.
76. *Something for Everyone* is set in Bavaria and based on a German book, but it was adapted for the screen by a British screenwriter and features an all-British cast speaking English. The argument can easily be made that the film comments on the British class system, but I say "European" here to include the film's German literary roots. It's not surprising that *Something for Everyone* was also shown with Hal Prince's other class farce, *A Little Night Music* (about the secret tristes and affairs among Victorian bourgeoisie) (at the UC Theater, July 1978), and also Buñuel's *Discreet Charm of the Bourgeoisie* (about the unconscious desires and anxieties of the contemporaneous middle class) (at the Times Theatre, June 1974).
77. "filmcalendar," Pacific Film Archive (BAMPFA), Berkeley, CA.
78. The film has clear resemblances to *Midnight Cowboy*, released eight months later. The premise for *Flesh* was cribbed from *Midnight Cowboy*, then in production, as a preemptive response to the later commercial release. Maurice Yacowar discusses Warhol's interest in featuring friends from his Factory who had been relegated to the background in *Midnight Cowboy*. See Yacowar, *The Films of Paul Morrisey*, 23.

79. For more on these changes, see Mulvey, *Death 24x a Second*. VHS and home viewing of film and media find their own collective forms of queerness (such as bootlegging), but the experience of sitting next to strangers in a dark room, without control of the moving images or the setting as well as, at times, without knowledge of a co-feature, becomes an increasingly marginalized experience. For more on bootlegging subcultures, see Hilderbrand, *Inherent Vice*.

80. The *Oxford English Dictionary* says the term "binge-watching" originates in the 1990s. The earliest scholarly text I could find using it is Thorne, "*The Seven Up!* Films." For more on streaming and binge-watching, see McDonald and Smith-Rowsey, *The Netflix Effect*.

81. On streaming platforms, algorithms extrapolate from users' past selections, browsing history, and even scrolling patterns (among a plethora of other factors). The interface even entices the viewer/user to keep watching after one film or TV show has finished by inserting suggestions; its curation stems from an automated predictor of taste.

82. Benson-Allott, "The Ennui of the Scroll."

83. Alexander, "Rage Against the Machine."

84. Some more prestige streaming platforms have a complicated relationship not only to repertory exhibition but with the practice of curating itself. Criterion Collection, known for canonizing DVDs and Blu-rays it sees as "classics" in their own right, has its own streaming platform in which series are imaginatively assembled by human curators working invisibly behind the scenes, and met with great fanfare among online cinephile communities. See Joshua Hunt, "Sure, It Won an Oscar. But Is It Criterion?," *New York Times*, February 29, 2024, https://www.nytimes.com/2024/02/29/magazine/criterion-collection.html.

85. It is suspicious that these film festivals grow in popularity at the same time that VHS starts to dominate the market and repertory houses plummet in numbers. B. Ruby Rich in conversation suggested to me that this could be due to an emphasis on liveness and newness as the new qualifications of cinephilic experience. Unfortunately, I have not had a chance to pursue this question further here, but this correspondence without a doubt warrants deeper investigation.

86. See Ma, "Days of Heaven."

87. At both festivals and in double features, there is an impossible amount of focus demanded of the spectator. But there is always the possibility of distraction or redirected attention, contemplation, and other behavioral and perceptual markers of spectatorial distance from a text. There is also the possibility of interruption in the theater, due to audience reaction or more banal sources, from candy wrappers to talking to ringing cell

phones. (Virtual Reality [VR]—the new *immersive* videographic technology—in some ways aims to eliminate these conditions by putting viewers directly in the diegetic world.) Although these factors fall outside of the scope of this study, I emphasize that repertory time, as immersive, is frequently not a time of escape or continuity, which might call for or induce narrative and stylistic absorption. It is full of disjunction and ambiguity. The immersive quality of repertory time does not therefore foreclose or prohibit the practices of spectatorial distance but rather encourages them and gives them intertextual basis and justification. Even when double bills appear to fully lure spectators into queer diegeses of anti-normative play, the logics and norms of these worlds can be incoherent and off-putting, and therefore are not continuous in their ostensibly immersive aim.

In regards to contemporary repertory houses, Netflix has purchased several at-risk repertory houses, notably the Paris Theater in New York and the Egyptian Theater in Los Angeles. There they exhibit Netflix's new releases as well as repertory titles and series, which may or may not tie in with Netflix's latest theatrical releases. In the wake of COVID-19 lockdowns and quarantines, repertory cinemas have made a strong comeback—stronger than struggling new-release art houses—and movie pop-ups and "microcinemas" continue to make their mark in cities across the United States. In "The Heroic Age of New York Movie Theaters," Phillip Lopate writes about contemporary art house programming: "I do not think we need to lament so lachrymosely the decline of the repertory houses, since new ones such as the Metrograph and the renovated Quad keep appearing, the venerable Film Forum keeps chugging along, and the nonprofit institutions, such as MoMA, the Film Society of Lincoln Center, the Museum of the Moving Image, Japan Society, BAM, and the Asia Society, do a bang-up job of presenting new and old global cinema." The Metrograph's playful anti-institutional personality shines through in its programming; in its first summer, it did one weeklong program on disco and the movies and another on films starring the pop star Madonna. In Los Angeles, the New Beverly, Quentin Tarantino's cinema, devotes itself to double features at a low price; the Egyptian had the same practice until shutting down and being bought by Netflix. In this sense, repertory time and repertory programming have largely bifurcated, preserved only in those rare spaces that dare to serve a small cinephile market.

5. For Shame!

A previous version of this chapter with the same title was published in *The Oxford Handbook of Queer Cinema* (Ronald Gregg and Amy Villarejo, eds, Oxford University Press, 2021).

1. That year at Frameline, now-canonical queer classics were showcased as well: *Paris Is Burning* won the audience award for best documentary feature and *Tongues Untied* won for best video.
2. "Frameline," MoMA Archive, New York City.
3. For references to critiques from that era, see Rich, "What's New, Pussycat?"; Mayne, *Framed*; and Cook, "Film Culture."
4. William Friedkin's *Cruising* (1980) is perhaps the most popular example of the last ten years. I take up a variety of the film's readings that accumulated throughout the years in my video essay "Cruising *Différance* in 3 Scenes."
5. This is a nod to the "descriptive turn" that Heather Love describes in "Close but Not Deep." While I worry that this methodology runs the risk of depoliticizing cultural studies, it has use value at times, especially in instances when objects require a double take.
6. My use of "with" here takes after Lauren Berlant's. Berlant writes, "I do not read things; I read with things. When I read with theorists, with art, with a colleague or a friend, *to read with* is to cultivate a quality of attention to the disturbance of their alien epistemology, an experience of nonsovereignty that shakes my confidence in a way from which I have learned to derive pleasure, induce attachment, and maintain curiosity about the enigmas and insecurities that I can also barely stand or comprehend. This is what it means to say that excitement is disturbing, not devastating; ambivalent, not shattering in the extreme. Structural consistency is a fantasy; the noise of relation's impact, inducing incompletion where it emerges, is the overwhelming condition that enables the change that, within collaborative action, can shift lived worlds" (Berlant and Edelman, *Sex, or the Unbearable*, 125).
7. I am invoking Heather Love's use of "trauma" to refer to queer spectatorship, but I'm thinking also of the countless histories that presume as their starting points the misrepresentation of queer life as it is rendered on-screen. These historians' energies are focused on the harm that these representations induce. Vito Russo's account in *The Celluloid Closet* is perhaps the most prominent and enduring example.
8. Feng, "Recuperating Suzie Wong," 47.
9. See Benson-Allott, "Looking for *Looking for Mr. Goodbar*"; Crozier, "Making it After All," 7; Paasonen, "Strange Bedfellows"; Pawan Singh, "Queer Bollywood: The Homo-textuality of Celebrity Talk Show Gossip," *Spectator* 34, no. 1 (Spring 2014).
10. White, *Uninvited*, xxiv.
11. Sedgwick, *Touching Feeling*, 126.

12. In my research, I found only one article on how queer spectators recuperate "bad objects" that have in the past been associated with epistemic or representational harm: Crémieux, "Exploitation Cinema." Crémieux's convincing reading attributes the shift to time: temporal distance strengthens current forms of detachment and disavowal, which then lay the foundation for historical amnesia. In other words, given that queers were considerably more oppressed and repressed—especially before queer went "in vogue" and became mainstream in 1990s North America and Europe—previously injurious representations could now be read as quaint or campy, a relic of social panic or phobia that has since diminished. Compelling as this kind of reading may seem at first glance, it ignores the fact that homophobia and sexism might still be of concern (not just disavowed) in contemporary reparative reading practices. Moreover, it locates reclamation primarily along generational lines, which, in effect, elides reparative readings of films at the time of their releases prior to the 1990s. Assessing the programming of these "bad objects" adds complexity to these narratives because they become part of a contact zone in which other texts and histories collide, where desires struggle to find articulation even as their presence is felt within a curated network. (I am invoking Donna Haraway's and Kathleen Stewart's notion of the *contact zone*. See Haraway, *When Species Meet*; and Stewart, *Ordinary Affects*.)

13. I am adopting Lauren Berlant's usage of the "historical present" in *Cruel Optimism*.

14. See Barthes, "Death of the Author," in *Image, Music, Text*.

15. Berlant and Edelman, *Sex, or the Unbearable*, 61. The second part of the sentence reads, "as when a comic orientation toward aggression and pleasure produces new capacities for bearing, and not repairing, ambivalence." My sense is that there can be more relationships to ambivalence than are suggested by the dyad of bearing/repairing. In *The Female Complaint*, Berlant notes, "The usual solution to the conundrum of ambivalence" is "to understand it as a crisis that can first be fixed by attachment to a new form from which one can then be liberated until the next crisis, and so on" (261). Ambivalence here provides a kind of railway switch to guide temporary attachments. But couldn't it also be a kind of "holding station" like the one Berlant refers to in relation to impasses? For more on impasses, see *Cruel Optimism*, 199.

16. Here is how the story tends to go: in pre-Code Hollywood and European films, there were quite overt representations of homosexuals and gender deviants. When the Production Code was instated, Hollywood had to encode representations of queer people, exacerbating already rampant homophobia and transphobia. The course was set and—with only a few unanimously embraced films—it would not be until the 1990s that

queers would really get to make their own films that would supposedly authentically and realistically speak to their struggles.

17. It would be disingenuous to suggest Russo's views were only one-note. A critic with a rhetorical strategy but a critic nonetheless, Russo's tastes and philosophies would—as parenthetically noted above—vacillate at times. Russo's pleasures make brief appearances in the pages of *The Celluloid Closet*, especially in his expressed love for *The Rocky Horror Picture Show* and *Mädchen in Uniform* (52–57). Still, these moments are few and far between in his polemical text.

18. For examples, see the introduction to San Filippo, *The B Word*; and Benshoff and Griffin, *Queer Images*. Tyler's *Screening the Sexes*, which is somewhere between a precursor and counterpart to *The Celluloid Closet*, is largely ignored by scholars because it has not been seen as academic or historical enough. Roger N. Lancaster writes, "Which method has prevailed and not just in writing about film is not difficult to discern. Even in the heyday of queer theory (which was supposedly presided over by a carnivalesque and transgressive ethos not unlike the unruly deity Tyler dubbed 'Homeros'), the real money was in scholarship that ruthlessly demonstrated, one more time and with ever more exacting theoretical firepower, the heteronormative character of this text or that discourse" ("Text, Subtext, and Context").

19. Representative of the arguments made on social media is Garrett Schlichte's op-ed, "*Call Me by Your Name* Is a Gay Love Story. The Film Should Have Included Gay Sex," *Washington Post*, December 18, 2017.

20. Love, *Feeling Backward*, 15.

21. Love, *Feeling Backward*, 15.

22. Love's point is in service to her thesis that shame and melancholia continue to live on in the postmemory and affective lives of the very queers who disavow it, her adversary appearing to be queer liberal ideology rather than anything steeped in intellectual work in academe and beyond.

23. There are some exceptions to this. In the queer film criticism canon, B. Ruby Rich, Alexander Doty, Judith Mayne, and Patricia White have numerous generous readings of "bad objects." Richard Dyer's brilliant essay "Judy Garland and Gay Men," in *Heavenly Bodies*, poignantly demonstrates the affective ties between gay fans and their diva.

24. Besides Russo, see also Benshoff and Griffin, *Queer Images*.

25. Sedgwick, *Touching Feeling*, 146. By "the past," does Sedgwick mean historicity itself, its retelling (i.e., the construction of history), or could she be speaking to the presence of multiple histories and temporalities? Even the endnote following the sentence in her essay does not provide ample clarification.

26. Doty writes, "'Mainstream' films and other popular culture texts and performers, for all their potential to alienate, have been, and continue to be, positive formative influences for many lesbians, gays, bisexuals, and other queers" (*Flaming Classics*, 15).
27. I have written elsewhere about how Doty tends to read queer texts through an LGBT lens, forgoing different kinds of deviance in the name of identity politics. See Newman, "Deviant Programming."
28. "Roxie Cinema," Pacific Film Archive (BAMPFA), Berkeley, CA. Russo did several lectures on the subject throughout the United States in the 1970s and 1980s. See Schiavi, *Celluloid Activist*.
29. Haraway, *When Species Meet*, 4.
30. See Freeman, *Time Binds*, 12.
31. hooks, *Black Looks*, 126.
32. Dyer, *Pastiche*, 130.
33. R. Williams, "Structures of Feeling," 130.
34. Fawaz, *Queer Forms*, 344. See also Baron, "The Ethical Cringe."
35. Likierman, *Melanie Klein*, 127.
36. Sontag, *Against Interpretation*, 285.
37. See especially Miller's cheeky exegesis in "*Cruising*."
38. Ditzler, "Curation and Cinema," 124.
39. Shimizu, *The Hypersexuality of Race*.
40. See Gould, *Moving Politics*, 33–34.
41. The clashing that Russo describes is ironic for several reasons. Most conspicuously, his sentiment is shocking in that it seems to wholly contradict what *The Celluloid Closet* enterprise set out to do: to advocate for more authentic representations of LGBT life in the face of hackneyed and harmful typologies. Russo, "Losing It at the Movies," 56.
42. "Frameline," MoMA Archive, New York City.
43. "Frameline," MoMA Archive, New York City.
44. Weiss, *Vampires and Violets*, 101.
45. "Castro Theatre," Pacific Film Archive (BAMPFA).
46. Several other factors play a part as well, such as a theater's ongoing curation, or the curation at nearby theaters that the spectator might also frequent. Take, for example, the 1980 program at the Castro Theatre that was devoted to screen divas. Surely both Greta Garbo and Marlene Dietrich provided cross-appeal for queers of all genders and straights of different persuasions. And in New York City, the Carnegie Hall Cinema encouraged its own intertextual and affective spectatorial practices. In 1976, it

exhibited *The Bitter Tears of Petra von Kant* and *Les Biches* in a double bill. Two years later, it presented *Mädchen in Uniform* in contrast to *The Children's Hour*.

47. White, *Uninvited*, xviii.
48. Butler, "What Is Critique?," 320.
49. Butler, "What Is Critique?"
50. "Frameline," MoMA Archive, New York City.
51. Mayne, *Framed*, 114.
52. For a reparative reading of Pam Grier's star persona, see Holmlund, "Wham! Bam! Pam!"
53. Mayne, *Framed*, 133.
54. This was written before "Don't Say Gay" and other trans- and homophobic legislation advanced by extreme right-wing conservatives such as Ron DeSantis. The question of humorously responding to the idea of "contagion" can be geographically and temporally contingent.
55. Mayne, *Framed*, 136.
56. Babuscio, "The Cinema of Camp," 128.
57. Amy Villarejo has also expressed this sentiment. In *Ethereal Queer*, she writes, "[Television] is deserving of deeper analyses of its specific function as a technology of sexual becoming and erotic life beyond the terms of *recognition* and *identification* most often used to describe relationships between spectators and particular programs" (7).
58. Gates, "Activating the Negative Image," 623. Unsurprisingly, Gates speaks of excess in depictions of Black women "acting out" on unscripted TV shows. If, for Gates, "acting right" is effectively "acting white," shows such as *Love and Hip Hop* flout white notions of respectability. Camp as a kind of excess can also allow for readings that push against the liberal imperative for respectability politics, especially in the intersection of race, gender, and sexuality, as the Pam Grier example demonstrates.
59. Sedgwick, *Touching Feeling*, 146.
60. Sedgwick, *Touching Feeling*, 150.
61. The art house reverence of Meyer's work is representative of what I've deemed in chapter 1 *promiscuous programming*, which was characteristic of the 1970s and 1980s art house scenes. During this period, programmers exercised infidelity to the auteurist bias of their forefathers and foremothers. They instead leaned into eclecticism, mixing filmic traditions and genres, low-, medium-, and highbrow tastes, and effectively ditching thematic or tonal coherence.
62. "Cineprobe," MoMA Film Library.

63. Hatch, "The Sweeter the Kitten the Sharper the Claws," 146.
64. Rich, "What's New, Pussycat?"
65. Barthes comments that the cult auteur "nourishes" the text "in the same relation of antecedence to his work as a father to his child" (*Image, Music, Text*, 145).
66. Rich, "What's New, Pussycat?"
67. It is worth noting here the place of programming within feminist film criticism. In art house series or at festivals, it was common to see low-, middle-, and highbrow fare coexisting. For example, it was frequent to find the films of Dorothy Arzner programmed alongside *Mädchen in Uniform* and experimental work by Carolee Schneeman and Constance Beeson. This heterogeneous mixture was, in part, because of the few examples available of work done by women directors. One could argue that this animated the imagination of lesbian film critics by opening them up to serious scholarly or critical considerations of work deemed unsophisticated. Additionally, the practice of reading "against the grain" became a feminist strategy. One can see some continuity between this practice and reparativity.
68. Lippit, "Plus Surplus Love," 88.
69. Avgi Saketopoulou's book *Sexuality Beyond Consent: Risk, Race, Traumatophilia* presents a wonderfully generative alterative to trauma's treatment that feels in the same spirit as New Queer Cinema's. Saketopoulou writes, "Trauma, I argue, needs to circulate; it needs to be revisited ... Traumatophilia does not overlook or diminish the impact of trauma but offers, instead, a way of working with the recognition that we cannot turn away from our traumata, that we are strangely drawn to them" (2).
70. Realizing this temporal separation invites the question of generational division, which I raised in the beginning. However, because I am also dealing with the baby boomer generation, I am putting aside for a moment how subsequent generations might encounter them. Surely this is a worthy topic of investigation, to be saved for another time.

Afterword

1. See Brody, "The Returns of *Cleopatra Jones*."
2. B. Ruby Rich, who coined the term New Queer Cinema in 1992, identifies several films and makers as precursors to NQC in her 2013 book, *New Queer Cinema: The Director's Cut*: Kenneth Anger's *Fireworks*, Jean Genet's *Un Chant D'Amour*, Luchino Visconti's *The Leopard* and *Death in Venice*, Pier Paolo Pasolini's *Teorema*, Claude Chabrol's *Les Biches*, Bernardo Bertolucci's *The Conformist*, Milton Miron's *Tricia's Wedding* (1971), Jim Bidgood's *Pink Narcissus*, Jan Oxenberg's *A Comedy in Six Unnatural*

Acts (1975), and Barbara Hammer's *Thunkercrack!* (1975) and *Dyketactics* (1974), among several others. She gives special attention to John Waters: "He's an indelible part of NQC prehistory, a patron saint presiding over its doings, chuckling at its follies, applauding its successes" (4–6).

3. For a list of theater closures in New York City, see B. Davis, *Repertory Movie Theaters*, 207. Filmmaker and co-programmer of the Carnegie Hall Cinema and Bleecker Street Cinema Jackie Raynal remarked in 1990 that cinephiles now collected tapes like avid readers collect books (Laermer, "Revival Houses in the Era of Videocassettes"). According to Ben Davis, emergent cable television (such as HBO) around the same time too began to offer classics and cult fare, "once exclusive domain of the repertory houses" (*Repertory Movie Theaters*, 91). Davis also cites that in New York City, rent prices had already begun to increase, pushing out repertory houses whose profit was not enough to keep up with the mushrooming real estate market. This would seem to anticipate New York's "clean up" during the Mayor Giuliani years and subsequent muscular forms of gentrification that follow.

4. See Hilderbrand, *Inherent Vice*. See also *Videoheaven* (dir. Alex Ross Perry, 2025).

5. B. Davis, *Repertory Movie Theaters*, 91.

6. See Rich, "Collision, Catastrophe, Celebration," 79–84.

7. Rich, "Collision, Catastrophe, Celebration."

8. One could also see classics and B movies on television during the years that this book covers, for instance, but with heavily compromised picture and sound quality.

9. There are now undergraduate courses and master's degrees devoted to curatorial studies. Several books on the topic have been published in recent years: Balzer's *Curationism*; and Marstine and Ho's *Curating Art*.

10. Lou Stoppard suggests the word's overuse "speaks of a generation anxious for authority and authorship, and also for meaning." No doubt this coincides with the rise of social media. Google Books Ngram Viewer shows a steady increase in the word *curation* from 1960, but it takes a sharp, exponential increase around 2005, with no sign of its growing usage letting up. Stoppard, "These Days, Everyone's a Curator."

11. See Hornaday, "The Movie Business May Be Struggling."

12. Welk, "How to Get Young Audiences in Theaters? Show Old Movies." At the same time, the outlook for new theatrical releases, including art house films, is not nearly as optimistic. Theaters themselves are in danger, as well. See Brueggemann, "As Cinemas Close, America Watches Its Moviegoing Deserts Grow."

13. I went to several of these screenings and they were well attended and the crowd was often quite audible in their amusement. Also imaginative, BAMcinématek (as part of the Brooklyn Academy of Music or BAM) programmed in 2014 a series entitled "Vengeance Is Hers," which focused on films about women seeking retribution for violence or harm done to them and/or the ones they love. Films as far ranging as *Coffy* (dir. Jack Hill, 1973), *Ms. 45* (dir. Abel Ferrara, 1981), *Medea* (dir. Pier Paolo Pasolini, 1969), and *Jeanne Dielman, 23 Quai du Commerce, 1080 Bruxelles* (dir. Chantal Akerman, 1975) filled this feminist program. What made it radically deviant perhaps—besides the fact that it forcibly excised men from the diegetic space of the screen—is that many of the films, in their membership to genres such as horror and exploitation, revel in bizarre characterizations, taboo desires, and worlds thrown off kilter.

Bibliography

Aaron, Michele, ed. *New Queer Cinema: A Critical Reader*. Rutgers University Press, 2004.

Abel, Richard. *French Cinema: The First Wave, 1915–1929*. Princeton University Press, 1984.

Adams, Rachel. *Sideshow U.S.A: Freaks and the American Cultural Imagination*. University of Chicago Press, 2001.

Ahmed, Sara. *Queer Phenomenology: Orientations, Objects, Others*. Duke University Press, 2006.

Alexander, Neta. "Rage Against the Machine: Buffering, Noise, and Perpetual Anxiety in the Age of Connected Viewing." *Cinema Journal* 56, no. 2 (2017): 1–24.

Allen, Graham. *Intertextuality*. 2nd ed. New Critical Idiom. Routledge, 2011.

Amazonas, Lee. "Guerilla Cinematheque Comes of Age: The Pacific Film Archive." *Chronicle of the University of California: A Journal of University History*, no. 6 (Spring 2004): 147–59.

Anderson, Melissa. "The Quad Relaunches (and Pleasingly Confounds) with an Unanticipated Pick." *The Village Voice*, April 11, 2017, 28.

Austin, Bruce A. "Portrait of a Cult Film Audience: The Rocky Horror Picture Show." *Journal of Communication* 31, no. 2 (June 1, 1981): 43–54.

Babuscio, Jack. "The Cinema of Camp (aka Camp and the Gay Sensibility)." In *Camp: Queer Aesthetics and the Performing Subject: A Reader*, edited by Fabio Cleto. Edinburgh University Press, 1999.

Bad Object-Choices. *How Do I Look? Queer Film and Video*. Bay Press, 1991.

Balon, Richard. *Practical Guide to Paraphilia and Paraphilic Disorders*. Springer International Publishing, 2016.

Balzer, David. *Curationism: How Curating Took Over the Art World and Everything Else*. Coach House, 2014.

Barol, Bill, et al. "The Last Picture Shows." *Newsweek*, June 8, 1987.

Baron, Jaimie. "The Ethical Cringe, or the Dated Film as Revelatory Genre." *Television and New Media* 24, no. 5 (2023): 584–94.

Barthes, Roland. *Image, Music, Text*. Hill and Wang, 1977.

Barthes, Roland. "Leaving the Movie Theater." In *The Rustle of Language*. Hill and Wang, 1986.

Bataille, Georges. *Erotism: Death and Sensuality*. City Lights, 1986.

Becker, Edith, Michelle Citron, Julia Lesage, and B. Ruby Rich. "Lesbians and Film." *Jump Cut* no. 24–25 (March 1981): 17–21.

Bem, Caroline. "Cinema | Diptych: Grindhouse | Death Proof." *JCMS* 58, no. 2 (2019): 1–22.

Benshoff, Harry M. *Monsters in the Closet: Homosexuality and the Horror Film*. Manchester University Press, 1997.

Benshoff, Harry M., and Sean Griffin. *Queer Images: A History of Gay and Lesbian Film in America*. Rowman and Littlefield, 2006.

Benson-Allott, Caetlin. "The Ennui of the Scroll." *Film Quarterly* 75, no. 2 (2021): 84–88.

Benson-Allott, Caetlin. 'Looking for *Looking for Mr. Goodbar*." *Feminist Media Histories* 1, no. 3 (July 1, 2015).

Berlant, Lauren. *Cruel Optimism*. Duke University Press, 2011.

Berlant, Lauren. *The Female Complaint: The Unfinished Business of Sentimentality in American Culture*. Duke University Press, 2008.

Berlant, Lauren. *On the Inconvenience of Other People*. Duke University Press, 2022.

Berlant, Lauren, and Lee Edelman. *Sex, or the Unbearable*. Duke University Press, 2014.

Bersani, Leo. "Is the Rectum a Grave?" *October* 43 (1987): 197–222.

Betz, Mark. "High and Low and in Between." *Screen* 54, no. 4 (December 1, 2013): 495–513.

Bornstein, Kate. *Gender Outlaw: On Men, Women, and the Rest of Us*. Routledge, 1994.

Bosma, Peter. *Film Programming: Curating for Cinemas, Festivals, Archives*. Columbia University Press, 2015.

Bourdieu, Pierre. *Distinction: A Social Critique of the Judgement of Taste*. Harvard University Press, 1984.

Bourdieu, Pierre. *The Field of Cultural Production: Essays on Art and Literature.* Polity, 1993.

Breen, Dana, Sara Flanders, and Alain Gibeault. *Reading French Psychoanalysis.* Routledge, 2010.

Brinkema, Eugenie. *The Forms of the Affects.* Duke University Press, 2014.

Brinkema, Eugenie. *Life-Destroying Diagrams.* Duke University Press, 2022.

Brody, Jennifer DeVere. "The Returns of *Cleopatra Jones.*" *Signs: Journal of Women in Culture and Society* 25, no. 1 (1999): 91–121.

Brueggemann, Tom. "As Cinemas Close, America Watches Its Moviegoing Deserts Grow." *IndieWire* (blog), February 12, 2024. https://www.indiewire.com/news/box-office/american-cities-without-movie-theaters-1234912768/.

Butler, Judith. "Doing Justice to Someone: Sex Reassignment and Allegories of Transsexuality." *GLQ: A Journal of Lesbian and Gay Studies* 7, no. 4 (January 1, 2001): 621–36.

Butler, Judith. *Gender Trouble: Feminism and the Subversion of Identity.* Routledge, 2006.

Butler, Judith. "Is Kinship Always Already Heterosexual?" *differences* 13, no. 1 (May 1, 2002): 14–44.

Butler, Judith. "What Is Critique? An Essay on Foucault's Virtue." In *The Judith Butler Reader*, edited by Judith Butler and Sara Salih. Blackwell, 2004.

Caillois, Roger. "Mimicry and Legendary Psychasthenia." Translated by John Shepley. *October* 31 (1984): 28.

Campany, David. *Photography and Cinema.* Exposures. Reaktion, 2008.

Capino, José B. "Seizing Moving Image Pornography." *Cinema Journal* 46, no. 4 (2007).

Carroll, Noël. "The Future of Allusion: Hollywood in the Seventies (and Beyond)," *October* 20 (Spring 1982): 51–81.

Cesare, Tony. "Pasolini's Theorem." *Film Criticism* 14, no. 1 (1989): 22–25.

Champagne, John. "'Stop Reading Films!': Film Studies, Close Analysis, and Gay Pornography." *Cinema Journal* 36, no. 4 (1997): 76–97.

Church, David. "Queer Ethics, Urban Spaces, and the Horrors of Monogamy in *It Follows.*" *Cinema Journal* 57, no. 3 (2018): 3–28.

Chute, David. "Outlaw Cinema." *Film Comment* 19, no. 5 (1983): 9–15.

Cohen, Cathy J. "Punks, Bulldaggers, and Welfare Queens: The Radical Potential of Queer Politics?" *GLQ: A Journal of Lesbian and Gay Studies* 3, no. 4 (May 1, 1997): 437–65.

Cook, Pam. "Film Culture: 'Exploitation' Films and Feminism." *Screen* 17, no. 2 (Summer 1976): 122–27.

Crémieux, Anne. "Exploitation Cinema and the Lesbian Imagination." *Transatlantica: Revue d'études Américaines / American Studies Journal* no. 2 (December 15, 2015).

Crozier, Susan. "Making It After All: A Reparative Reading of *The Mary Tyler Moore Show*." *International Journal of Cultural Studies* 11, no. 1 (2008): 51–67.

Davis, Ben. *Repertory Movie Theaters of New York City: Havens for Revivals, Indies and the Avant-Garde, 1960–1994*. McFarland, 2017.

Davis, Heather, and Paige Sarlin. "'On the Risk of a New Relationality': An Interview with Lauren Berlant and Michael Hardt." *Reviews in Cultural Theory* 2, no. 3 (2012).

Davis, Nick. *The Desiring-Image: Gilles Deleuze and Contemporary Queer Cinema*. Oxford University Press, 2013.

Delany, Samuel R. *Times Square Red, Times Square Blue*. NYU Press, 1999.

de Lauretis, Teresa. "Popular Culture, Public and Private Fantasies: Femininity and Fetishism in David Cronenberg's 'M. Butterfly.'" *Signs: Journal of Women in Culture and Society* 24, no. 2 (1999): 303–34.

Deleuze, Gilles. *Masochism*. Zone Books, 1989.

D'Emilio, John, and Estelle B. Freedman. *Intimate Matters: A History of Sexuality in America*. 2nd ed. University of Chicago Press, 1997.

Dempsey, Michael. "Ken Russell, Again: In Print and Film." *Film Quarterly* 31, no. 2 (1977): 19–24.

Derrida, Jacques. *Of Grammatology*. Translated by Gayatri Chakravorty Spivak. Johns Hopkins University Press, 1976.

Derrida, Jacques. "Phenomenology and Deconstruction." In *The Phenomenology Reader*, edited by Dermot Moran and Timothy Mooney. Routledge, 2002.

Derrida, Jacques. *Writing and Difference*. University of Chicago Press, 1978.

Ditzler, Andy. "Curation and Cinema." PhD. diss., Emory University, 2015.

Doane, Mary Ann. *The Emergence of Cinematic Time: Modernity, Contingency, the Archive*. Harvard University Press, 2002.

Doerfler, J. "Radley Metzger: Let 'Em See Skin . . ." *Boston After Dark*, February 9, 1971.

Doty, Alexander. *Flaming Classics: Queering the Film Canon*. Routledge, 2000.

Doty, Alexander. *Making Things Perfectly Queer: Interpreting Mass Culture*. University of Minnesota Press, 1993.

Doty, Alexander, and Patricia Clare Ingham. "The 'Evil Medieval': Gender, Sexuality, Miscegenation, and Assimilation in *Cat People*." In *Bad: Infamy, Darkness, Evil, and Slime on Screen*, edited by Murray Pomerance. SUNY Press, 2004.

Downing, Lisa. "'Citizen-Paraphiliac': Normophilia and Biophilia in John Money's Sexology." In *Fuckology: Critical Essays on John Money's Diagnostic Concepts*, edited by Lisa Downing, Iain Morland, and Nikki Sullivan. University of Chicago Press, 2019.

Downing, Lisa. "A Disavowed Inheritance: Nineteenth-Century Perversion Theory and John Money's 'Paraphilia.'" In *Fuckology: Critical Essays on John*

Money's Diagnostic Concepts, edited by Lisa Downing, Iain Morland, and Nikki Sullivan. University of Chicago Press, 2019.

Downing, Lisa, Iain Morland, and Nikki Sullivan. "Introduction: On the 'Duke of Dysfunction.'" In *Fuckology: Critical Essays on John Money's Diagnostic Concepts*, edited by Lisa Downing, Iain Morland, and Nikki Sullivan. University of Chicago Press, 2019.

Dyer, Richard. *The Culture of Queers*. Routledge, 2002.

Dyer, Richard. *Gays and Film*. Rev. ed. Zoetrope, 1984.

Dyer, Richard. *Heavenly Bodies: Film Stars and Society*. 2nd ed. Routledge, 2004.

Dyer, Richard. *Pastiche*. Routledge, 2007.

Eagleton, Terry. "Capitalism, Modernism, and Postmodernism." *New Left Review* (July 1, 1985): 60–73.

Eco, Umberto. "'Casablanca': Cult Movies and Intertextual Collage." *SubStance* 14, no. 2 (1985): 3–12.

Eco, Umberto. *A Theory of Semiotics*. Indiana University Press, 1976.

Edelman, Lee. *No Future: Queer Theory and the Death Drive*. Duke University Press, 2004.

Eilers, James McColley. "Sebastian's Nocturnal Dream Shows." *The Gay and Lesbian ReviewWorldwide* 15, no. 3 (May–June 2008).

Elsaesser, Thomas. "Film Festival Networks: The New Topographies of Cinema in Europe (2005)." In *The Film Festival Reader*, edited by Dina Iordanova. St Andrews Film Studies, 2013.

Eng, David L., Judith Halberstam, and José Esteban Muñoz. "Introduction." In "What's Queer about Queer Studies Now?," edited by David L. Eng, Judith Halberstam, and José Esteban Muñoz. *Social Text*, nos. 84–85 (2005): 1–17.

Fawaz, Ramzi. *Queer Forms*. NYU Press, 2022.

Feng, Peter X. "Recuperating Suzie Wong: A Fan's Nancy Kwan-dary." In *Countervisions: Asian American Film Criticism*, edited by Darrell Y. Hamamoto and Sandra Liu. Temple University Press, 2000.

Ferguson, Roderick A. *Aberrations in Black: Toward a Queer of Color Critique*. University of Minnesota Press, 2004.

Ferguson, Roderick A. *One-Dimensional Queer*. Polity Press, 2018.

First, Michael B. "DSM-5 and Paraphilic Disorders." *The Journal of the American Academy of Psychiatry and the Law* 42, no. 2 (2014): 191–201.

Foster, Hal. "The 'Primitive' Unconscious of Modern Art." *October* 34 (Autumn 1985): 45–70.

Foucault, Michel. *The History of Sexuality*. Vintage Books, 1990.

Foucault, Michel. "Of Other Spaces." *Diacritics* 16, no. 1 (1986): 22–27.

Francis, Marc. "Cruising *Différance* in 3 Scenes." *[In]Transition: Journal of Videographic Film and Moving Image Studies* 5, no. 3 (2018).

Francis, Marc. "Tokyo Unmasked." Essay for Blu-ray restoration of *Funeral Parade of Roses*, Cinelicious/Arbelos (November 2017). https://www.cineliciouspics.com/2999-2/.

Francoeur, Robert T. *A Descriptive Dictionary and Atlas of Sexology*. Greenwood Press, 1991.

Freeman, Elizabeth. *Time Binds: Queer Temporalities, Queer Histories*. Duke University Press, 2010.

Freud, Sigmund. *Three Essays on the Theory of Sexuality*. Verso, 2016 (1905).

Frost, Laura. *Sex Drives: Fantasies of Fascism in Literary Modernism*. Cornell University Press, 2018.

Gagliano, Rico. "The Elgin and EL TOPO plunge NYC into 'Midnite Madness.'" *MUBI Podcast*, July 7, 2022. https://mubi.buzzsprout.com/1788738/episodes/10912182-the-elgin-and-el-topo-plunge-nyc-into-midnite-madness.

Gaines, Jane. "Political Mimesis." In *Collecting Visible Evidence*, edited by Jane Gaines and Michael Renov. University of Minnesota Press, 1999.

Galt, Rosalind, and Karl Schoonover. *Global Art Cinema: New Theories and Histories*. Oxford University Press, 2010.

Gates, Racquel. "Activating the Negative Image." *Television and New Media* 16, no. 7 (2015): 616–30.

Gates, Racquel. *Double Negative: The Black Image and Popular Culture*. Duke University Press, 2018.

Geritz, Kathy. "Edith Kramer: A Focus on Cinema, in Her Own Words." *Film Quarterly* 75, no. 1 (September 1, 2021): 70–78.

Geritz, Kathy, Josslyn Luckett, Cornelius Moore, et al.. "Film Culture—the Legacy of the Pacific Film Archive and Non-Profit Exhibition" (webinar). *Film Quarterly*, December 2, 2021. https://www.youtube.com/watch?v=Ev227WiDMJ4.

Giles, Jane. *Scala Cinema 1978–1993*. FAB Press, 2018.

Gillespie, Michael Boyce. *Film Blackness: American Cinema and the Idea of Black Film*. Duke University Press, 2016.

Goffman, Erving. *Stigma: Notes on the Management of Spoiled Identity*. Simon and Schuster, 1986.

Goldin, Nan. "Feeding the Appetites: Nan Goldin's Movie Obsessions," interview with Hilary Weston. September 10, 2020. https://www.criterion.com/current/posts/7094-feeding-the-appetites-nan-goldins-movie-obsessions.

Gomery, Douglas. *Shared Pleasures: A History of Movie Presentation in the United States*. University of Wisconsin Press, 1992.

Gorfinkel, Elena. *Lewd Looks: American Sexploitation Cinema in the 1960s*. University of Minnesota Press, 2017.

Gould, Deborah B. *Moving Politics: Emotion and ACT UP's Fight against AIDS*. University of Chicago Press, 2009.

Grant, Barry K. "Science Fiction Double Feature: Ideology in the Cult Film." In *The Cult Film Experience: Beyond All Reason*, edited by J. P. Telotte. University of Texas Press, 1991.

Gunning, Tom. "An Aesthetic of Astonishment: Early Film and the (In)Credulous Spectator." *Art and Text* 34 (Spring 1989).

Gustafson, Irene. "Putting Things to the Test: Reconsidering *Portrait of Jason*." *Camera Obscura* 26, no. 2 (2011): 1–31.

Halberstam, Jack. "The Anti-Social Turn in Queer Studies." *Graduate Journal of Social Science* 5, no. 2 (January 2008), 140–56.

Halberstam, Jack. *The Queer Art of Failure*. Duke University Press, 2011.

Halberstam, Jack. *Wild Things: The Disorder of Desire*. Duke University Press, 2020.

Hall, Stuart. "Deviance, Politics, and the Media." In *The Lesbian and Gay Studies Reader*, edited by Henry Abelove. Routledge, 1993.

Halperin, David M. *Saint Foucault: Towards a Gay Hagiography*. Oxford University Press, 1995.

Hanson, Ellis. *Decadence and Catholicism*. Harvard University Press, 1997.

Haraway, Donna J. *When Species Meet*. University of Minnesota Press, 2008.

Harris, Mark. "*Klute*: Trying to See Her." The Criterion Collection. July 16, 2019. https://www.criterion.com/current/posts/6492-klute-trying-to-see-her.

Hatch, Kristen. "The Sweeter the Kitten the Sharper the Claws: Russ Meyer's Bad Girls." In *Bad: Infamy, Darkness, Evil, and Slime on Screen*, edited by Murray Pomerance. SUNY Press, 2004.

Hawkins, Joan. *Cutting Edge: Art-Horror and the Horrific Avant-Garde*. University of Minnesota Press, 2000.

Hebdige, Dick. *Subculture: The Meaning of Style*. Routledge, 1979.

Hennefeld, Maggie. "Affect Theory in the Throat of Laughter." *Feminist Media Histories* 7, no. 2 (2021): 110–44.

Hilderbrand, Lucas. *Inherent Vice: Bootleg Histories of Videotape and Copyright*. Duke University Press, 2009.

Hirsch, Foster. *The Hollywood Epic*. Barnes, 1978.

Hoberman, J. "A Tale of a Tokyo Drag Queen, Circa 1969." *The New York Times*, June 8, 2017, sec. Movies. https://www.nytimes.com/2017/06/08/movies/atale-of-a-tokyo-drag-queen-circa-1969.html.

Hoberman, J., and Jonathan Rosenbaum. *Midnight Movies*. Harper and Row, 1983.

Holmlund, Chris. "John Waters: *Multiple Maniacs* Relaunch." *Film Quarterly* 71, no. 1 (September 1, 2017): 97.

Holmlund, Chris. "Wham! Bam! Pam! Pam Grier as Hot Action Babe and Cool Action Mama," *Quarterly Review of Film and Video* 22, no. 2 (March 9, 2005): 97–112.

hooks, bell. *Black Looks: Race and Representation*. South End Press, 1992.

Hornaday, Ann. "The Movie Business May Be Struggling, but You Wouldn't Know It at These Thriving Independent Theaters: Across America, Art Houses Aren't Just Bouncing Back, They're Renovating and Expanding." *The Washington Post*. 2021.

Iampolski, M. B. *The Memory of Tiresias: Intertextuality and Film*. University of California Press, 1998.

Iordanova, Dina, ed. *The Film Festival Reader*. St. Andrews Press, 2013.

Irvine, Janice M. *Disorders of Desire: Sexuality and Gender in Modern American Sexology*. Rev. and expanded ed. Temple University Press, 2005.

Jameson, Fredric. *Postmodernism, or, The Cultural Logic of Late Capitalism*. Duke University Press, 1991.

Jenny, Laurent. "The Strategy of Forms." In *French Literary Theory Today*, edited by Tzvetan Todorov. Cambridge University Press, 1982.

Kael, Pauline. "Circles and Squares." *Film Quarterly* 16, no. 3 (1963): 12–26.

Kael, Pauline. "Trash, Art, and the Movies" (1969). In *American Movie Critics: An Anthology from the Silents Until Now*, edited by Phillip Lopate. Library of America, 2006.

Kaye, Richard A. "Losing His Religion: Saint Sebastian as Contemporary Gay Martyr." In *Outlooks: Lesbian and Gay Sexualities and Visual Cultures*, edited by Peter Horne and Reina Lewis. Taylor and Francis, 2002: 88–99.

Keegan, Cael M. *Lana and Lilly Wachowski*. University of Illinois Press, 2018.

Kellow, Brian. *Pauline Kael: A Life in the Dark*. Viking, 2011.

Kleinhans, Chuck. "Pornography and Documentary: Narrating the Alibi." In *Sleaze Artists: Cinema at the Margins of Taste, Style, and Politics*, edited by Jeffrey Sconce. Duke University Press, 2007.

Krafft-Ebing, Richard von. *Psychopathia Sexualis; a Medico-Forensic Study*. Putnam, 1965.

Krips, Henry. *Fetish: An Erotics of Culture*. Cornell University Press, 2018.

Laermer, Richard. "Revival Houses in the Era of Videocassettes." *New York Times*, April 15, 1990.

Lancaster, Roger. "Text, Subtext, and Context: Strategies for Reading Alliance Theory." *American Ethnologist* 32, no. 1 (2005): 22–27.

Lang, Brent. "Björn Andrésen on His Tortured Relationship with Luchino Visconti's *Death in Venice*: 'That Son of a Bitch Sexualized Me.'" *Variety*, November 30, 2021. https://variety.com/2021/film/news/bjorn-andresen-sexual-exploitation-luciano-visconti-death-in-venice-1235122373/.

Lanza, Joseph. *Phallic Frenzy: Ken Russell and His Films*. Review Press, 2007.

Laplanche, Jean, and J.-B. Pontalis. "Fantasy and the Origins of Sexuality." In *Reading French Psychoanalysis*, edited by Dana Breen, Sara Flanders, and Alain Gibeault. Routledge, 2010.

Lee, Grant. "A Never-Ending Film Festival." *Los Angeles Times*, October 11, 1977.

Lévi-Strauss, Claude. *The Savage Mind*. University of Chicago Press, 1962.

Lewis, Charlton T., and Charles Short. *A Latin Dictionary*. Nigel Gourlay, 2020.

Likierman, Meira. *Melanie Klein: Her Work in Context*. Continuum, 2001.

Lippit, Akira Mizuta. "Plus Surplus Love: Jacques Derrida's Echopoiesis and Narcissism Adrift." *Discourse* 37, no. 1 (October 7, 2015).

Lopate, Phillip. "The Heroic Age of New York Movie Theaters." *The New York Review of Books*. November 6, 2017.

Love, Heather. "Close but Not Deep: Literary Ethics and the Descriptive Turn." *New Literary History* 41, no. 2 (2010): 371–92.

Love, Heather. *Feeling Backward: Loss and the Politics of Queer History*. Harvard University Press, 2007.

Love, Heather. *Underdogs: Social Deviance and Queer Theory*. University of Chicago Press, 2021.

Luckett, Josslyn. "The Black Film Ambassador: The Ecstatic World of Albert Johnson." *Film Quarterly* 75, no. 1 (September 1, 2021): 62–69.

Ma, Jean. "Days of Heaven: Il Cinema Ritrovato on Its Thirtieth Anniversary," *Film Quarterly* 70, no. 2 (December 1, 2016): 68–73.

Ma, Jean. *Melancholy Drift: Marking Time in Chinese Cinema*. Hong Kong University Press, 2010.

MacDonald, Scott. *Cinema 16: Documents Toward a History of the Film Society*. Temple University Press, 2002.

MacDonald, Scott, Frank Stauffacher, and Art in Cinema Society. *Art in Cinema: Documents Toward a History of the Film Society*. Temple University Press, 2006.

Magilow, Daniel. "Introduction: Nazisploitation! The Nazi Image in Low-Brow Cinema and Culture." In *Nazisploitation*, edited by Daniel Magilow, Elizabeth Bridges, and Kristin T. Vander Lugt. Continuum International Publishing Group, 2012.

Marks, Laura U. "Coeditor's Foreword," *The Moving Image* 4, no. 1 (2004): ix–xi.

Marks, Laura U. "The Ethical Presenter: Or How to Have Good Arguments over Dinner." *The Moving Image* 4, no. 1 (2004): 34–47.

Marks, Laura U. *The Skin of the Film: Intercultural Cinema, Embodiment, and the Senses*. Duke University Press, 2000.

Marriott, David. *On Black Men*. Columbia University Press, 2000.

Marrone, Gaetana. "*The Night Porter*: Power, Spectacle, and Desire." The Criterion Collection. December 9, 2014. https://www.criterion.com/current/posts/3393-the-night-porter-power-spectacle-and-desire.

Marstine, Janet, and Oscar Ho Hing Kay. *Curating Art*. Routledge, 2021.

Martin, Nina K. "Never Laugh at a Man with His Pants Down: The Affective Dynamics of Comedy and Porn." In *Pornography: Film and Culture*, edited by Peter Lehman. Rutgers University Press, 2006.

Mayne, Judith. *Framed: Lesbians, Feminists, and Media Culture*. University of Minnesota Press, 2000.

McDonald, Kevin, and Daniel Smith-Rowsey, eds. *The Netflix Effect: Technology and Entertainment in the 21st Century*. Bloomsbury Academic, 2016.

McRuer, Robert. *Crip Theory: Cultural Signs of Queerness and Disability*. NYU Press, 2006.

Michalak, Joseph. "Thalia, West Side Muse of Reruns, is Revived," *New York Times*, August 12, 1977.

Miller, D. A. "Cruising." *Film Quarterly* 61, no. 2 (December 1, 2007): 70–73.

Milner, J. S., C. A. Dopke, and J. L. Crouch. "Paraphilia Not Otherwise Specified: Psychopathology and Theory." In *Sexual Deviance: Theory, Assessment, and Treatment*, edited by William T O'Donohue, and D. Richard Laws. Guilford Press, 2008.

Money, John. *The Destroying Angel: Sex, Fitness, and Food in the Legacy of Degeneracy Theory, Graham Crackers, Kellogg's Corn Flakes, and American Health History*. Prometheus Books, 1985.

Mulvey, Laura. *Death 24x a Second: Stillness and the Moving Image*. Reaktion Books, 2006.

Mulvey, Laura. "Notes on Sirk and Melodrama." In *Visual and Other Pleasures*, edited by Laura Mulvey. Palgrave Macmillan, 1989.

Mulvey, Laura. *Visual and Other Pleasures*. Macmillan, 1989.

Muñoz, José Esteban. *Cruising Utopia: The Then and There of Queer Futurity*. NYU Press, 2009.

Muñoz, José Esteban. *Disidentifications: Queers of Color and the Performance of Politics*. University of Minnesota Press, 1999.

Newman, Marc Francis. "Deviant Programming: Curating Queer Spectatorial Possibilities in U.S. Art House Cinemas, 1968–1989." PhD diss., University of California, Santa Cruz, 2018. ProQuest (10829410).

Noriega, Chon. "On Curating." *Wide Angle* 1, no. 4 (1995): 292–304.

North, Anna. "The Disturbing Story Behind the Rape Scene in Bernardo Bertolucci's *Last Tango in Paris*, Explained." Vox, November 26, 2018. https://www.vox.com/2018/11/26/18112531/bernardo-bertolucci-maria-schneider-last-tango-in-paris.

Nyong'o, Tavia. *Afro-Fabulations: The Queer Drama of Black Life*. NYU Press, 2018.

Obrist, Hans Ulrich. *Ways of Curating*. Allen Lane, 2014.

O'Donohue, William T., and D. Richard Laws. *Sexual Deviance: Theory, Assessment, and Treatment*. Guilford Press, 2008.

Ohmer, Susan. "Speaking for the Audience: Double Features, Public Opinion, and the Struggle for Control in 1930s Hollywood." *Quarterly Review of Film and Video* 24, no. 2 (February 1, 2007): 143–69.

Orpen, Valerie. *Film Editing: The Art of the Expressive*. Wallflower, 2003.

Osterweil, Ara. *Flesh Cinema: The Corporeal Turn in American Avant-Garde Film*. Manchester University Press, 2014.

Paasonen Susanna. "Strange Bedfellows: Pornography, Affect and Feminist Reading." *Feminist Theory* 8, no. 1 (2007): 43–57.

Parvulescu, Anca. *Laughter: Notes on a Passion*. Short Circuits. MIT Press, 2010.

Patton, Cindy. *L.A. Plays Itself/Boys in the Sand: A Queer Film Classic*. Arsenal Pulp Press, 2014.

Peirce, Charles S. *Collected Papers*. Belknap Press of Harvard University Press, 1958.

Peterson, Thomas E. "The Allegory of Repression from Teorema to Salò." *Italica* 73, no. 2 (1996): 215–32.

Potolsky, Matthew. *Mimesis*. Routledge, 2006.

Powell, Adam. "Nicolas Winding Refn and the Ken Russell Style." In *The Films of Ken Russell*, edited by Matthew Melia. Edinburgh University Press, 2023.

Rapfogel, Jason. "Repertory Film Programming: A Critical Symposium Featuring Commentary by John Ewing, John Gianvito, Bruce Goldstein, Haden Guest, Jim Healy, Kent Jones, Laurence Kardish, Marie Losier, Richard Peña, James Quandt, David Schwartz, Adam Sekuler, Dylan Skolnick and Tom Vick." *Cinéaste* 35, no. 2 (2010): 38–53.

Ravetto, Kriss. *The Unmaking of Fascist Aesthetics*. University of Minnesota Press, 2001.

Rhodes, Gary D. "'The Double Feature Evil': Efforts to Eliminate the American Dual Bill." *Film History: An International Journal* 23, no. 1 (2011): 57–74.

Rich, B. Ruby. *Chick Flicks: Theories and Memories of the Feminist Film Movement*. Duke University Press, 1998.

Rich, B. Ruby. "Collision, Catastrophe, Celebration: The Relationship between Gay and Lesbian Film Festivals and Their Publics." In "Queer Publicity: A Dossier on Lesbian and Gay Film Festivals Essays by B Ruby Rich, Eric O. Clarke, and Richard Fung, with an Introduction by Patricia White." *GLQ: A Journal of Lesbian and Gay Studies* 5, no. 1 (January 1, 1999): 73–93.

Rich, B. Ruby. *New Queer Cinema: The Director's Cut*. Duke University Press, 2013.

Rich, B. Ruby. "What's New, Pussycat?" *The Village Voice*. January 17, 1995.

Robbins, Betty, and Roger Myrick. "The Function of the Fetish in *The Rocky Horror Picture Show* and *Priscilla, Queen of the Desert*." *Journal of Gender Studies* 9, no. 3 (November 1, 2000): 269–80.

Rubin, Gayle. *Deviations: A Gayle Rubin Reader*. Duke University Press, 2011.

Rubin, Gayle. "Thinking Sex: Notes for a Radical Theory of the Politics of Sexuality." In *Culture, Society and Sexuality: A Reader*, edited by Peter Aggleton and Richard Parker. Routledge, 2007.

Russo, Vito. *The Celluloid Closet: Homosexuality in the Movies*. Rev. ed. Perennial Library, 1987.

Russo, Vito. "Losing it at the Movies." *Advocate* 504, July 2, 1988.

Saketopoulou, Avgi. *Sexuality Beyond Consent: Risk, Race, Traumatophilia*. NYU Press, 2023.

San Filippo, Maria. *The B Word: Bisexuality in Contemporary Film and Television*. Indiana University Press, 2013.

Schaefer, Eric. *"Bold! Daring! Shocking! True!": A History of Exploitation Films, 1919–1959*. Duke University Press, 1999.

Schaefer, Eric. "Introduction: Sex Seen: 1968 and Rise of 'Public' Sex." In *Sex Scene: Media and the Sexual Revolution*, edited by Eric Schaefer. Duke University Press, 2014.

Schiavi, Michael R. *Celluloid Activist: The Life and Times of Vito Russo*. University of Wisconsin Press, 2011.

Schlib, John. "Future Historiographies of Rhetoric and the Present Age of Anxiety." In *Writing Histories of Rhetoric*, edited by Victor J. Vitanza. Southern Illinois University Press, 2013.

Schlüpmann, Heide. "Queen Kelly." *Frauen und Film* no. 39 (1985): 40–48.

Schrader, Paul. *Transcendental Style in Film: Ozu, Bresson, Dreyer*. University of California Press, 2018.

Sconce, Jeffrey. "Introduction." In *Sleaze Artists: Cinema at the Margins of Taste, Style, and Politics*, edited by Jeffrey Sconce. Duke University Press, 2007.

Sconce, Jeffrey. "Movies: A Century of Failure." In *Sleaze Artists: Cinema at the Margins of Taste, Style, and Politics*, edited by Jeffrey Sconce. Duke University Press, 2007.

Sconce, Jeffrey. "'Trashing' the Academy: Taste, Excess, and an Emerging Politics of Cinematic Style." *Screen* 36, no. 4 (1995): 371–93.

Scott, Joan Wallach. "Gender: A Useful Category of Historical Analysis," *The American Historical Review* 91, no. 5 (December 1, 1986): 1053–75.

Sedgwick, Eve Kosofsky. *Touching Feeling: Affect, Pedagogy, Performativity*. Duke University Press, 2003.

Seitler, Dana. "Queer Physiognomies; Or, How Many Ways Can We Do the History of Sexuality?" *Criticism* 46, No. 1 (Winter 2004): 71–102.

Sekula, Allan. "The Body and the Archive." *October* 39 (1986): 3–64.

Shaviro, Steven. *The Cinematic Body*. University of Minnesota Press, 1993.

Shimizu, Celine Parreñas. *The Hypersexuality of Race: Performing Asian/American Women on Screen and Scene*. Duke University Press, 2007.

Simon, William. "Deviance as History: The Future of Perversion." *Archives of Sexual Behavior* 23, no. 1 (1994): 1–20.

Singh, Pawan. "Queer Bollywood: The Homo-textuality of Celebrity Talk Show Gossip." *Spectator* 34, no. 1 (Spring 2014): 18–24.

Sobchack, Vivian. *The Address of the Eye: A Phenomenology of Film Experience*. Princeton University Press, 1992.

Sobchack, Vivian. *Carnal Thoughts: Embodiment and Moving Image Culture*. University of California Press, 2004.

Sontag, Susan. *Against Interpretation, and Other Essays*. Farrar, Straus and Giroux, 1966.

Spade, Dean. *Normal Life: Administrative Violence, Critical Trans Politics, and the Limits of Law*. Duke University Press, 2015.

Spivak, Gayatri Chakravorty, "Translator's Preface." Derrida, Jacques. *Of Grammatology*. Translated by Gayatri Chakravorty Spivak, 1967.

Stacey, Jackie. *Star-Gazing: Hollywood Cinema and Female Spectatorship*. Routledge, 1993.

Staiger, Janet. *Perverse Spectators: The Practices of Film Reception*. NYU Press, 2000.

Stam, Robert. *Subversive Pleasures: Bakhtin, Cultural Criticism, and Film*. Johns Hopkins University Press, 1989.

Staples, Donald E. "The Auteur Theory Reexamined." *Cinema Journal* 6 (1966): 1–7.

Stein, Elliott. "*Maîtresse*." The Criterion Collection, February 2, 2004. https://www.criterion.com/current/posts/309-matresse.

Stevenson, Jack. *Land of a Thousand Balconies: Discoveries and Confessions of a B- Movie Archeologist*. Headpress, 2003.

Stewart, Kathleen. *Ordinary Affects*. Duke University Press, 2007.

Stiglegger, Marcus. *Sadiconazista: Faschismus und Sexualität im Film*. Gardez! Verlag, 2000.

Stone, Sandy. "The Empire Strikes Back: A Posttranssexual Manifesto." *Camera Obscura* 10, no. 2 (1992): 150–76.

Stoppard, Lou. "These Days, Everyone's a Curator: Style Desk." *The New York Times*, March 3, 2020.

Straayer, Chris. *Deviant Eyes, Deviant Bodies: Sexual Re-Orientations in Film and Video*. Columbia University Press, 1996.

Studlar, Gaylyn. *In the Realm of Pleasure: Von Sternberg, Dietrich, and the Masochistic Aesthetic*. Columbia University Press, 1992.

Sullivan, Nikki, Lisa Downing, and Iain Morland. "On the 'Duke of Dysfunction.'" In *Fuckology*. University of Chicago Press, 2014.

Talbot, Daniel. *In Love with Movies: From New Yorker Films to Lincoln Plaza Cinemas*, edited by Tony Talbot. Columbia University Press, 2022.

Tashiro, C. S. *Pretty Pictures: Production Design and the History Film*. University of Texas Press, 1998.

Taylor, Diana. *The Archive and the Repertoire: Performing Cultural Memory in the Americas*. Duke University Press, 2003.

Tent, Pam. *Midnight at the Palace: My Life as a Fabulous Cockette*. Alyson Books, 2004.

Thorne, Barrie. "*The Seven Up!* Films: Connecting the Personal and the Sociological." *Ethnography* 10, no. 3 (September 1, 2009): 327–40.

Time Magazine. "The New Sociology." January 5, 1970. https://time.com/vault/issue/1970-01-05/page/46/.

Twomey, John E. "Some Considerations on the Rise of the Art-Film Theater (1956)." In *Moviegoing in America: A Sourcebook in the History of Film Exhibition*, edited by Gregor A. Waller. Blackwell Publishers, 2002.

Tyler, Parker. *A Pictorial History of Sex in Films*. 1st ed. Citadel Press, 1974.

Tyler, Parker. *Screening the Sexes: Homosexuality in the Movies*. Anchor Press, 1972.

van der Pol, Gerwin. "The Secret Passion of the Cinephile: Peter Greenaway's *A Zed and Two Noughts* Meets Adriaan Ditvoorst's *De Witte Waan*." In *Cinephilia: Movies, Love and Memory*, edited by Marijke de Valck and Malte Hagener. Amsterdam University Press, 2005.

Villarejo, Amy. *Ethereal Queer: Television, Historicity, Desire*. Duke University Press, 2014.

Vogel, Amos. *Film as a Subversive Art*. D. A. P. /Distributed Art Publishers, 2005.

Vogel, Amos. "Independents: Structures." *Film Comment*, February 1975. https://www.filmcomment.com/article/independents-structures/.

Warner, Michael. *Publics and Counterpublics*. Zone Books, 2002.

Warner, Michael. *The Trouble with Normal: Sex, Politics and the Ethics of Queer Life*. Free Press, 1999.

Warner, Michael, and Lauren Berlant. "Sex in Public." In Michael Warner, *Publics and Counterpublics*: Zone Books, 2002.

Wasson, Haidee. *Museum Movies: The Museum of Modern Art and the Birth of Art Cinema*. University of California Press, 2005.

Waugh, Thomas. *Hard to Imagine: Gay Male Eroticism in Photography and Film from their Beginnings to Stonewall*. Columbia University Press, 1996.

Weinstock, Andrew, ed. *Reading Rocky Horror:* The Rocky Horror Picture Show and Popular Culture. Palgrave Macmillan, 2008.

Weiss, Andrea. *Vampires and Violets: Lesbians in Film*. Penguin Books, 1993.

Welk, Brian. "How to Get Young Audiences in Theaters? Show Old Movies." *IndieWire* (blog), April 25, 2024. https://www.indiewire.com/news/business/how-film-revivals-luring-young-crowds-saving-specialty-cinema-1234975333/.

White, Patricia. *Uninvited: Classical Hollywood Cinema and Lesbian Representability*. Indiana University Press, 1999.

Wilinsky, Barbara. *Sure Seaters: The Emergence of Art House Cinema*. University of Minnesota Press, 2001.

Williams, Linda. "Bad Sex and Obscene Undertakings: Ken Russell's *Women in Love*." *Journal of Adaptation in Film and Performance*. Intellect, 2013.

Williams, Linda. "Film Bodies: Gender, Genre, and Excess." *Film Quarterly* 44, no. 4 (1991): 2–13.

Williams, Linda. *Hard Core: Power, Pleasure, and the 'Frenzy of the Visible.'* University of California Press, 1999.

Williams, Linda. *Screening Sex.* Duke University Press, 2008.

Williams, Linda. "Skin Flicks on the Racial Border: Pornography, Exploitation, and Interracial Lust." In *Porn Studies*, edited by Linda Williams. Duke University Press, 2004.

Williams, Raymond. *Marxism and Literature.* Marxist Introductions. Oxford University Press, 1977.

Williams, Raymond, "Structures of Feeling." In *Marxism and Literature.* Oxford University Press, 1977.

Wolcott, James. "The Decline (and Rise) of the Cinema Revival House," *Vanity Fair*, January 27, 2018.

Wollen, Peter. "Godard and Counter-Cinema: *Vent D'Est.*" In *Movies and Methods: An Anthology*, edited by Bill Nichols. University of California Press, 1976.

Wollen, Peter. *Paris Hollywood: Writings on Film.* Verso, 2002.

Wood, Robin. *Hollywood from Vietnam to Reagan.* Columbia University Press, 1986.

Yacavone, Daniel. "Towards a Theory of Film Worlds." *Film-Philosophy* 12, no. 2 (2008): 83–108.

Yacowar, Maurice. *The Films of Paul Morrissey.* Cambridge University Press, 1993.

Young, Damon R. *Making Sex Public, and Other Cinematic Fantasies.* Duke University Press, 2018.

Zaeske, Susan. "The 'Promiscuous Audience' Controversy and the Emergence of the Early Woman's Rights Movement." *Quarterly Journal of Speech* 81, no. 2 (May 1, 1995): 191–207.

Index

Abrahams, Gary, 241n29
aesthetic sadomasochism, 133, 137, 246n63
affect, 107–9
agglutination, 170, 172, 254n64
Aldrich, Robert. *See Killing of Sister George, The* (1968)
Allen, Tom, 230n88
alternative, 24
American Cinematheque, 213
American Gigolo (1980), 157, 158–59
American International Pictures, 34
amputation, 72
Anderson, Melissa, 217n10
Andrésen, Björn, 18
Anger, Kenneth, 30, 238n73
Anthology Film Archive, 224n48
Antonioni, Michelangelo, 136
apotemnophilia, 72
Arnold, Steven, 46, 227n76
art cinema: accessibility of, pre-1969, 27; audiences' shifting relationships to, 33; as class marker, 31; corporeal turn of, 9–10; defining, 221n6; as following high art and literary traditions, 26–27; Wilinsky on, 221n7
art dealer, 25–26, 222n22

art house cinema(s): closing of, 54–55; deviant practices at, 2; as merging intellectualism and vice, 41–42; promiscuous programming becomes standard among, 38–41; reinvention of, 23
art house film programming: academic questions regarding, 3; modes of deviant, 65–66; scholarship on, 1–4
Art in Cinema film society, 28
Arzner, Dorothy, 264n67

Babuscio, Jack, 199, 234n25
baby boomers, 39
Bacchanal (Medović), 128, 129*f*
background, and bi-textuality of *Cabaret* and *Something for Everyone*, 176–77
Bad (1977), 66, 241n27
"bad objects," 181–85, 204–6; *Cruising* and *Looking for Mr. Goodbar* regarded as, 157; and reclaiming of troublesome texts, 197–204; and temporal removal, 192–97; and trauma of queer spectatorship, 185–92
Baker, Josephine, 242n32
Bakhtin, Mikhail, 166, 167
Balzer, David, 6, 7, 224n41

BAMcinématek, 266n13
Barenholtz, Ben, 104, 239n11
Barry, Iris, 25, 27–28, 43, 149
Barthes, Roland, 264n65
Bataille, Georges, 103, 249n26
bathhouses, 225n57, 226n60
BDSM, 110, 132–39, 247n77. *See also* sadomasochism
Beeson, Constance, 264n67
Bem, Caroline, 155, 248n12, 250n34
Benner, Richard. *See Outrageous!* (1977)
Benshoff, Harry, 80
Benson-Allot, Caetlin, 179
Berger, Helmut, 244n52
Berlant, Lauren, 62, 80, 184, 220n35, 250n27, 252n53, 258n6, 260n15
Bersani, Leon, 121
Bertolucci, Bernardo, 249n26. *See also Last Tango in Paris* (1972)
Betz, Mark, 233n18, 244n52
Beyond the Valley of the Dolls (1970), 42, 118, 119–20, 121, 122, 165–66, 168–69, 243nn41–42
Biches, Les (1967), 68, 69–70, 71f
Big Doll House, The (1971), 198–99
binge-watching, 179, 256n80
Birds, The (1963), 122
bisexuality, 173–78, 255n75
bi-textuality, 176–77, 255n75
Bitter Tears of Petra von Kant, The (1972), 195–96
black deviance, 85
Bleecker Street Cinema, 45, 65, 149–50, 220n1; calendar, 6f
Blonde Venus (1932), 50–51
Blood of a Poet (1932), 190
Blue Angel, The (1930), 75
B movies, 146
body genre, 102, 109
Borden, Lizzie. *See Born in Flames* (1983)
Born in Flames (1983), 18
Bornstein, Kate, 91
Bosma, Peter, 8, 11, 232n4
Bourdieu, Pierre, 25, 31, 32, 193–94, 222n20, 222n22
Boys in the Band, The (1970), 174, 255n72
Boys in the Sand (1971), 43–44
Bradsell, Michael, 122
Brazilian films, 229n85
bricolage / bricoleur, 25–26, 49, 52, 228n81, 230n92

Bright, Susie, 186
Brinkema, Eugenie, 98–99, 108–9, 140, 240n20, 247n74
Brooks, Louise, 50
Brooks, Richard. *See Looking for Mr. Goodbar* (1977)
Butler, Judith, 62, 63, 196, 197, 215n2

Cabaret (1972), 125, 174–76, 177
Cabiria (1914), 123
Caged (1950), 181, 197–98, 200
Call Me by Your Name (2017), 186
Camille 2000 (1969), 42
Cammell, Donald. *See Performance* (1970)
camp, 70–72, 165, 191, 198–99, 263n58
Campany, David, 136
camping out, 188, 191
camp readings, 184–85, 193, 200, 205
Canby, Vincent, 223n36
Canosa, Fabiano, 8, 35–36, 37–38, 223n37
Carnegie Hall Cinema, 15, 63, 154, 225n58, 262n46
carnivalesque, 166–67, 252n53
Casablanca (1942), 253n60
Castle, William, 238n74
Castro Theatre, 174, 194–96, 262n46
Catholicism, 247n76
Cat People (1942), 78, 80, 84
Celluloid Closet, The (1995), 186
Celluloid Closet, The (Russo), 185–86, 188, 260n18, 262n41
Chabrol, Claude. *See Biches, Les* (1967)
Chant D'Amour, Un (1950), 67
"charmed circle," 83, 95
Cherry, Harry & Raquel! (1969), 123, 201
Chicago Art Institute, 70–72, 78–82
Church, David, 215n4
Chute, David, 90–91
Cinema 16, 28–30, 52–53. *See also* Vogel, Amos
cinema attendance, 14–15
Cinema Guild, 33–34
cinematic spaces of debauchery, 123–32
cinematic time, 247n3
cinephile game, 249n19
cinephilia, 145, 235n38, 247n3
Cineprobe series, 201
Cixous, Hélène, 102–3, 104, 106, 239n8
Clarke, Shirley. *See Portrait of Jason* (1967)

classicism, 127–29
classification: of deviance, 62–63, 82–87; as mutable and mobile, 73; programming and, 7, 59, 60–61, 64; in repertory houses, 230n90
Cleopatra Jones (1973), 207, 208, 209
Cleopatra Jones and the Gold Casino (1975), 208
Club 57, 45–46
Cockettes, 46, 48, 227n76, 228n80
Cohen, Cathy, 215n3
collisional form of programming, 52–53
Come Back Little Sheba (1952), 51
Conformist, The (1970), 124, 130–31
"congruency model" of programming deviant films, 65
consumption, excessive scenes of, 123–32
contact zones, 190–92, 193–94
contingence / contingency, 14
conubium, 53
costuming, and material fetish, 77
counter-cinema, 30
Crémieux, Anne, 259n12
Criterion Channel, 212, 213
Criterion Collection, 256n84
critique, 196–97
Cruising (1980), 157–58, 159, 160f, 193, 241n24, 258n4
Cukor, George, 70, 71
cult films, 164–73, 253n60
curating / curation, 212, 216n6, 265n10. *See also* art house film programming; film programming / curation; promiscuous programming
curators. *See* programmers
Curtis, Robin, 216n7

Dallesandro, Joe, 63, 178
Damned, The (1969), 15, 244n52
Dass, Vishnu, 227n76
Daughters of Darkness (1971), 194–96, 205
Davis, Ben, 24, 44–45, 50, 55, 147–48, 151, 154, 211, 220n5, 265n3
Davis, Nick, 139–40
Death in Venice (1971), 15, 18, 67
debauchery, cinematic spaces of, 123–32
Decameron, The (1971), 15, 17f, 125, 188
decay, 130–31
Deep Throat (1972), 44
degenerate index, 99, 239n5
Delany, Samuel R., 44, 226n6

Deleuze, Gilles, 134, 140, 246n65
D'Emilio, John, 39, 225n57
DeMille, Cecil B., 123. *See also Manslaughter* (1930)
Derrida, Jacques, 14, 154, 204, 228n81
desiring-image, 140
Desperate Living (1977), 188
Deuce, The (2017–2019), 44
deviance, 10–13, 57–61; classification of, 62–63, 82–87; defining, 61–64; and fetishism, 73–78; modes of deviant programming, 65–66; and Outlaw Cinema, 87–96; versus queer, 10–11, 61–62, 218n19; and "Sexuality in Cinema" series, 78–82; and Vogel's *Film as a Subversive Art*, 67–68
deviance studies, 62, 64, 95, 233n12
deviance theory, 64, 87
Devils, The (1971), 9–10, 100–107, 117
Diary of a Shinjuku Thief (1968), 223n37
Dietrich, Marlene, 60, 75–77
diptych, 155, 248n12, 250n34
Ditzler, Andy, 193
Divine, 88, 91, 92, 93, 106, 228n80
Doane, Mary Ann, 235n38, 247n3
Doty, Alexander, 80, 187–88, 261nn26–27
double bills, 143–45; Bem on, 248n12, 250n34; as educational time, 149–51; at Elgin Theater, 100–107; enshrined in *The Rocky Horror Picture Show*, 143; featuring bisexual characters, 173–78; feminist-queer crossings in, 156–64; history of, 146–49; oriented around LGBT identity, 65; queer immersion in cult, 164–73; on Roxie Cinema's 1978 winter calendar, 188–90; symbiosis and tension in, 151–56. *See also* "Outlaw Cinema Thursdays" series; repertory time
"Double Feature" (Hayden), 147
Downing, Lisa, 74, 84–85, 237n62
Dracula's Daughter (1936), 194
Dunye, Cheryl, 207–9
Dyer, Richard, 191, 261n23

Eco, Umberto, 14, 156, 166, 168, 251n45, 253n60
ecstasy, 134
edit, eroticized, 117–23
editing, literature on, 243n40
Edwards, Douglas, 241n29

Elgin Theater, 45, 100–107, 152–54
Elsaesser, Thomas, 223n32
emotional habitus, 193–94
Encore, 112
Epstein, Rob. *See Celluloid Closet, The* (1995)
erotic forms, 109–11, 139–41
erotic intertextuality, 97–100; and cinematic spaces of debauchery, 123–32; and erotic forms, 109–11; and eroticized edit, 117–23; laughter in Elgin Theater's programming of *Performance* and *The Devils*, 100–107; and mimesis and affect, 107–9; Nuart Theatre as case study in, 111–17; and stasis in BDSM, 132–39
eroticized edit, 117–23
Essert, Gary, 241n29
exploitation films, 245n55

fantasy, 241n26
"Fascinating Fetishism" series, 50–51, 60, 75–77, 81
fascism, 124–27, 129, 130–31, 243n41, 244n48, 244n52
Fassbinder, Rainer Werner. *See In a Year of 13 Moons* (1978)
Faster, Pussycat! Kill! Kill! (1965), 201, 202–4
Fawaz, Ramzi, 157, 192
Fellini, Federico. *See Roma* (1972); *Satyricon* (1969)
Female Trouble (1974), 18, 66, 91–92, 188, 215n2
feminist film criticism, 264n67
feminist-queer crossings, 156–64
Feng, Richard X., 182
Ferguson, Roderick, 85
fetishism, 3, 73–78
fetish paraphilias, 75
Fierstein, Harvey, 186
"Fifties Melodrama: Post-War Auteurs and the Cinema of Hysteria" (Thalia), 230n88
Film as a Subversive Art (Vogel), 30, 66–68, 233n18
film festivals, 179–80
"Film Noir" series (Thalia), 230n88
film programming / curation, 5–9; as bolstering deviance, 59; as classification apparatus, 60–61; as creating patterns, 97–98; economics of, 32–33; as facilitation camp reading, 193; in feminist film criticism, 264n67; in film studies, 216n7; impact of waning, 210–11; modes of deviant, 65–66; need for more, 213–14; as possibly perverting text's meaning, 126; as praxis strengthening intertextuality, 201; and shift toward queers loving queer "bad objects," 182
film studies, 216n7
First Avenue Screening Room, 35, 36, 38
Fleischer, Richard. *See Mandingo* (1975)
Flesh (1968), 40, 95, 177–78, 255n78
"Flesh Cinema," 231n99
Fonda, Jane, 160, 251n44. *See also Klute* (1971)
foreground, and bi-textuality of *Cabaret* and *Something for Everyone*, 176–77
Foreign Films Movie Club, 41
forms, 240n20. *See also* erotic forms
Fosse, Bob. *See Cabaret* (1972)
Foster, Hal, 49
Foucault, Michel, 62, 85–86, 196, 236n55, 236n57, 252n53
"Four-handkerchief Classics: 35 Years of Tearjerkers" series, 50
Fox Venice, 45, 112–16
frame composition, 127–29
Frameline Film Festival, 181, 194–200
Frank, Adam, 233n14
Freedman, Estelle B., 39
Freeman, Elizabeth, 45, 167, 191, 225n57
frenzy, and eroticized edit, 117–23
Friedkin, William. *See Boys in the Band, The* (1970); *Cruising* (1980)
Friedman, Jeffrey. *See Celluloid Closet, The* (1995)
Frost, Laura, 124–25
Funeral Parade of Roses (1969), 35–37, 223n36
Funny Games (1997), 247n74
Furth, Gregg, 72

Galt, Rosalind, 49, 221n6, 226n67
Gates, Racquel, 199, 216n5, 263n58
"Gay Perspectives" series, 65
Geffen, Sid, 218n12
"generous narcissism," 204
Genet, Jean. *See Chant D'Amour, Un* (1950)

Genette, Gerard, 196
Geritz, Kathy, 15
Ghost Dance (1983), 204
Gillespie, Michael, 216n5
Gilula, Steve, 111–12
Goelman, Jack, 28
Goffman, Erving, 12, 63, 82, 96, 232n6, 234n25, 235n47
Goldin, Nan, 144, 217n10
Goodbye, Dragon Inn (2003), 137, 226n69
Gorfinkel, Elena, 9, 42, 43, 93–94, 126
Gorris, Marlene. *See Question of Silence, A* (1982)
Gottlieb, David, 94
Gould, Deborah, 193–94
Grey Gardens (1975), 188, 191, 200
Griffith, D. W., 123
grindhouse, 144, 226n64

Halberstam, Jack, 167, 236n48, 236n55, 237n65
Hall, Stuart, 65
Halperin, David, 236n55
Hammer, Barbara, 18
Haneke, Michael, 247n74, 247n77
Hanson, Ellis, 239n7, 247n76
Happiness (1965), 152–54, 155, 163–64
Haraway, Donna, 190
Harron, Mary, 227n70
Hatch, Kristen, 201, 202
Haver, Ronald, 241n29
Hayden, Robert, 147, 156
Heat (1972), 40, 95
Hebdige, Dick, 228n84
Hennefeld, Maggie, 102–3
heterotopia, 252n53
Hiroshima, Mon Amour (1959), 98
Hirsch, Foster, 123, 245n58
Hitchcock, Alfred, 122
Hoberman, J., 35–36, 45–46, 90, 223n36, 228n80
Holliday, Jason, 234n24
Hollywood Babylon, 48
"homology model" of programming deviant films, 65–66
homophobia: in *American Gigolo*, 158–59; as perpetuated by mainstream cinema, 185–86
homosexuality: and promiscuity, 225n57; in Vogel's *Film as a Subversive Art*, 67–68. *See also* queerness

hooks, bell, 191
Horak, Jan-Christopher, 216n7
Horowitz, Irving, 94, 95, 238n79
Hu, Marcus, 209–10
Humfress, Paul. *See Sebastiane* (1976)
hustling, 68, 177–78. *See also* sex work
Huyman, Joris-Karl, 239n7

Image of Dorian Gray in the Yellow Press, The (1984), 78, 79
In a Year of 13 Moons (1978), 78, 79, 80, 81f, 91
Indian films, 229n85
interdiegetic, 13–14
International Film Festival (Rotterdam), 212
interracial desire, 169, 170f
intertextuality, 5–6, 8, 13–14, 15–18, 64, 201. *See also* erotic intertextuality; textual promiscuity
In the Realm of the Senses (1976), 39–40, 98, 170–72, 224n45
Intolerance (1916), 123
Irvine, Janice, 84–85, 94

Jacobellis v. Ohio (1964), 151
Jameson, Frederic, 228n84
Jarman, Derek. *See Sebastiane* (1976)
Jenny, Laurent, 98, 126
Johnny Belinda (1948), 51
Johnson, Albert, 7, 36
Johnson, Virginia, 94
Jorgensen, Kim, 112, 115, 241n27
Joseph Papp Public Theater, 35, 37
jump cuts, 105, 118–23, 243n42

Kael, Pauline, 25, 33–35, 154, 222n25, 223n31
Kant Kino, 227n70
Karlyn, Kathleen Rowe, 102–3
Kaye, Richard A., 135, 136
Keegan, Cael, 140
Kellow, Brian, 34
Killing of Sister George, The (1968), 106–7, 193
Kinsey, Alfred, 94
Klein, Melanie, 183
Kleinhans, Chuck, 93, 94, 193
Klute (1971), 158, 159–62, 163–64, 251n44
Krafft-Ebbing, Richard von, 76–77, 85–86

Kramer, Edith, 8, 11, 97
Kuzniar, Alice, 79, 80

Lancaster, Roger N., 260n18
Langlois, Henri, 7
Lanza, Joseph, 118, 242nn35–36
Laplanche, Jean, 241n26
Last Tango in Paris (1972), 18, 98, 133, 137–39, 154–55, 170–72, 249n26
laughter, 101–7, 141, 166, 240n12
lesbian desire, 181, 201–2, 208–9
lesbian vampire film series, 194–96, 200
Les Girls (1957), 70–71, 72
Levine, Caroline, 240n20
Lévi-Strauss, Claude, 228n81, 230n92
Lewis, Marshall, 149–50
LGBT films, 211–12, 213
liberal sexual subject, 218n17, 224n44
Likierman, Meira, 193
Lippit, Akira, 204
Looking for Mr. Goodbar (1977), 157–58, 161–64
Lopate, Phillip, 257n87
Los Angeles Times, 24
Love, Heather, 3, 12; on *The Celluloid Closet*, 186; on classification of sexual and gender deviance, 63; on deviance studies, 233n12; on deviant practices, 2; on queer temporal deviation, 45; on queer theory and sociology, 64; on Sedgwick and Frank's writing on Tomkins, 233n14; on shame and melancholia, 261n22; on stigma, 82
Lovers, The (1958), 151–55, 156, 163–64

Ma, Jean, 137
MacDonald, Scott, 52–53, 216n7
Magilow, Daniel, 245n55
mainstream cinema, depictions of LGBT people in, 185–86
Maîtresse (1975), 132–33, 134–35
Makavejev, Dušan, 219n24
Make Way for Tomorrow (1937), 51
Malle, Louis. See *Lovers, The* (1958)
Mandingo (1975), 169
Manslaughter (1930), 124
Marks, Laura, 61, 155, 216n6, 216n7
Marrone, Gaetana, 129
Martin, Nina K., 102
masochism, 75–76, 134, 246n65; spectatorial, 108

Masters, William, 94
material fetish, 76–77
Matsumoto, Toshio. See *Funeral Parade of Roses* (1969)
Mayne, Judith, 198–99
Medović, Mato Celestin, 128, 129f
Medusa, 103, 104, 107
Medusan laugh, 103–6, 107, 141
Mekas, Jonas, 40
melodrama, 50–52
Member of the Wedding (1952), 63–64, 233n9
Merry Widow, The (1925), 124
Metrograph, 257n87
Metzger, Radley, 42
Meyer, Richard, 91
Meyer, Russ, 42–43, 122, 201–4, 243n42. See also *Beyond the Valley of the Dolls* (1970); *Cherry, Harry & Raquel!* (1969); *Supervixens* (1975); *Vixen* (1968)
middle class, and use of art films, 27
Midnight Cowboy (1969), 255n78
Midnight Movie, 90
Midnight Movies (Hoberman and Rosenbaum), 90
midnight screenings, 104, 143–44, 167
Miller, D. A., 241n24
mimesis, 107–9, 122, 139
Missabu, Rumi, 46–48
Monde Cane (1962), 93
Mondo Freudo (1966), 93
Mondo Trasho (1969), 92, 93, 238n75
Money, John, 12, 72, 75, 86, 92–93, 237n61
montage, 243n42
Moore, Cornelius, 246n67
Morland, Iain, 84–85
Morrissey, Paul, 40, 63, 67, 91, 95, 178
Motion Picture Association of America (MPAA) ratings system, 9, 201
MUBI, 212, 213
Multiple Maniacs (1970), 18, 92–93, 228n80
Muñoz, José Esteban, 17, 18, 220n32
Murrow, Rol, 115
Museum of Modern Art (MoMA), 27–28, 42–43, 201
Music Lovers, The (1970), 9–10, 117, 123
Myra Breckinridge (1970), 166–67, 168, 168f
Myrick, Roger, 252n48

Nazism, 124–25, 126–27
Nazispolitation, 125, 129, 244n48, 244n52
Netflix, 257n87. *See also* streaming platforms
New Beverly, The, 257n87
New German Cinema films, 79, 84
New Queer Cinema (NQC), 206, 209–10, 211, 232n5, 265n2
new sociologists / new sociology, 87, 94–95, 238n79
New Waves, 30, 31
New Yorker Theater, 148
New York Film Festival (1967), 68
Nicholson, Amy, 239n11
Nietzsche, Friedrich, 167
Night Porter, The (1974), 124, 125, 129–32, 133, 137–39, 244n52, 245n55
Ninotchka (1939), 195–96
Nocturnal Dream Show, 46–48, 227n76
Noriega, Chon, 216n7
Nuart Theatre, 66, 87–89, 92–93, 95–96, 111–17, 124, 169, 241n29. *See also* erotic intertextuality
Nyong'o, Tavia, 68, 70

Old Maid, The (1939), 51
Orpen, Valerie, 243n40
Oshima Nagisa, 223n37. *See also In the Realm of the Senses* (1976)
Osterweil, Ara, 9, 231n99
Ottinger, Ulrike. *See Image of Dorian Gray in the Yellow Press, The* (1984)
outlaw, 88, 91, 95–96
Outlaw Cinema, 66, 87–96
"Outlaw Cinema Thursdays" series, 66, 87–89, 92–93, 95–96
outlaw representation, 91
Outrageous! (1977), 4, 5f, 188, 191
outsiders, 63–64, 94
outtakes, compilations of, 52

Pacific Film Archive (PFA), 224n47
Pagoda Palace Theater, 46–48
Pakula, Alan J., 160
Pandora's Box (1929), 195–96
paraphilia, 74–75, 110–11, 234n27, 234n30
Parvulescu, Anca, 102–3, 107
Pasolini, Pier Paolo. *See Decameron, The* (1971); *Salò, or the 120 Days of Sodom* (1975); *Teorema* (1968)
Peirce, Charles Sanders, 99, 156, 239n5

Peña, Richard, 7, 70, 78, 80, 81, 229n85
Performance (1970), 100, 104, 105, 106, 107
Personal Best (1982), 207, 208, 209
perverse spectators, 141
perversion, 74
Piano Teacher, The (2001), 247n77
Pink Flamingos (1972), 18, 91–92, 106, 112
Pontalis, J.-B., 241n26
Poole, Wakefield. *See Boys in the Sand* (1971)
pop art, 30, 31
pornography, 39, 109–11
porn theaters, proliferation of, 44
Porter, Cole, 70, 71
Portrait of Jason (1967), 68–73
postmodernism, 228n84
Powell, Adam, 122
Prince, Harold. *See Something for Everyone* (1970)
Priscilla, Queen of the Desert (1994), 252n48
Prisonnières (1988), 181, 197
Production Code, 124, 201, 260n16
production design, 127–29, 130, 132
programmers, 6–8; as arbiters of taste, 31, 32; as bricoleurs, 49; as diverging from art curators, 224n41; as film classifiers, 59, 60–61; as gatekeepers, 26, 32; as lay sexologists-cum-sociologists for filmgoing public, 58–59, 100
programming: versus curation, 216n6. *See also* art house film programming; film programming / curation; promiscuous programming
program notes, 34, 35
promiscuity, 49
promiscuous, 24–25
promiscuous programming, 23–26, 49–56; becomes standard among art and repertory houses, 38–41; and double bills, 149; genealogy of, pre-1969, 26–31; and postmodernism, 228n84; roadmap of filmic taste and its historical ruptures, 31–33; trashy content as staple of art house programming, 33–38; urban contexts contributing to explosion of, 41–49
Psycho (1960), 122
Public Theater (Joseph Papp), 38

queer, versus deviance, 10–11, 61–62, 218n19
queer cinema, 232n5. *See also* New Queer Cinema (NQC)
queer film studies, 187, 216n5
queer heterosexuality, 215n3
queerness: expansion of criteria for, 3; feminist-queer crossings in double bills, 156–64; of post-1968 programming, 231n99; and promiscuous programming, 35–37, 38–41, 54; queer immersion in cult double bills, 164–73; and repertory house as deviant space, 44–45; and trespassing of sexual identity borders, 43–44. *See also* "bad objects"; homosexuality; lesbian desire
queer studies, 62
queer theory, 3, 12, 62, 64, 91, 215n3, 237n65
Question of Silence, A (1982), 78

Rampling, Charlotte, 244n52
"Rated X: Not for Children (But Not for Porn)," 213
Ravetto, Kriss, 124, 126, 244n48
Raynal, Jackie, 226n60, 265n3
Rebel Without a Cause (1955), 63, 233n9
reclamation, 183
Regency Theater, 55
Reich, Wilhelm, 94
Renan, Sheldon, 224n47
reparative historicizing, 182, 187, 188, 192
reparative reading, 184
reparative relationships, 182
reparative time, 190
reparativity, 182–85, 190, 196, 200–201, 205–6
repertoire, 14
repertory house(s): classification of films in, 230n90; comeback of, 212–13, 257n87; decline of, 54–55, 178–79, 265n3; as deviant space, 45; factors drawing contemporary audiences to screenings, 55; purchased by Netflix, 257n87; queerness of, in *Goodbye, Dragon Inn*, 226n69; as setting for indecent acts, 44–45
repertory time, 143–46, 178–80; and cinematic time, 247n3; defined, 145, 219n28; and double bills featuring bisexual characters, 173–78;

as educational time, 149–51; and feminist-queer crossings in double bills, 156–64; and history of double bills, 146–49; immersive quality of, 257n87; and queer immersion in cult double bills, 164–73; and Roxie Cinema's 1978 winter calendar, 188–90; and symbiosis and tension in double bills, 151–56
repetition, 111, 145, 182
Repulsion (1965), 208, 209
Resnais, Alain. *See Hiroshima, Mon Amour* (1959)
revival, 24
Rich, B. Ruby, 102–3, 202–4, 211, 218n12, 239n8, 256n85, 265n2
Richelieu Cinema, 174
Robbins, Betty, 252n48
Rocky Horror Picture Show, The (1975), 48, 143–44, 165, 167, 168
Roeg, Nicolas. *See Performance* (1970)
Roma (1972), 131
Rosenbaum, Jonathan, 90, 228n80
Ross, Julian, 242n33
Roud, Richard, 68
Roxie Cinema, 188–90, 191, 192
Roxie Theater, 15, 50–51, 60, 75–77
Rubin, Gayle, 3, 12, 65, 82–83, 87, 95, 96, 232n2
Russell, Ken, 117. *See also Devils, The* (1971); *Music Lovers, The* (1970); *Women in Love* (1969)
Russo, Vito, 173, 185–88, 194, 196, 201, 255n72, 259n7, 260n17, 262n41. *See also Celluloid Closet, The* (Russo)

sacrificial paraphilias, 75–76
sadism, 75, 134, 246n65
sadomasochism, 125, 132–39, 246n63, 246n65. *See also* BDSM
Saketopoulou, Avgi, 264n69
Salò, or the 120 Days of Sodom (1975), 124, 125–26, 127–28, 130, 131–32, 137, 245n55
Salon Kitty (1976), 124, 125–28, 130, 131–32
San Filippo, Maria, 173–74, 176, 255n75
San Francisco International Film Festival, 36
Santana, Tura, 202–4
Sarne, Michael. *See Myra Breckinridge* (1970)
Sarris, Andrew, 148

Satyricon (1969), 15, 16f, 131–32, 188, 246n61
Savage Messiah, The (1972), 117
Scala Theater, 227n70
Scarlet Empress, The (1934), 75, 77
Schaefer, Eric, 9, 218n15, 225n49
Scharres, Barbara, 70, 78, 81
Schneeman, Carolee, 264n67
Schneider, Maria, 18
Schoonover, Karl, 49, 221n6, 226n67
Schrader, Paul, 136. See also American Gigolo (1980)
Schroeder, Barbet, 134. See also Maîtresse (1975)
Schwarz, Richard, 8, 49–50, 51–52
Scott, Joan W., 12
Screening the Sexes: Homosexuality in the Movies (Tyler), 57–58, 260n18
Scrubbers (1982), 181, 197
Sebastiane (1976), 132–33, 135–36, 137
Sedgwick, Eve Kosofsky, 166, 182, 183, 187, 199, 200, 233n14, 261n25
Seitler, Dana, 11
Sekula, Allan, 11
semiosis, 111, 150, 151–56
set design, 126–29, 130, 132
sexology, 73–74, 84–85, 94, 95, 238n80
sexploitation, 43, 93–94, 169, 201–2
sexual abuse, 18
sexual identities, trespassing of borders in, 43–44
"Sexuality in Cinema" series, 78–82, 84
sexual revolution, 9, 220n35
sex work, 68, 158–61, 178. See also hustling
Shanghai Express (1932), 75, 77
Sharman, Jim. See Rocky Horror Picture Show, The (1975)
Shaviro, Steven, 108
Shimizu, Celine, 193, 194
Silent Movie Theater, 112
Simon, William, 81, 87
sleazy documentaries, 93–94
Soba, Stephen, 37
Sobchack, Vivian, 77, 108, 119, 140, 165, 243n37
sociology, 64, 73–74, 84–85, 94, 238n80. See also new sociologists / new sociology
Something for Everyone (1970), 173, 174–78, 255n72, 255nn75–76
Sontag, Susan, 68, 124, 165, 193, 217n10

space: in Last Tango in Paris and The Night Porter, 138–39; production of, in Satyricon, 131
spectatorial masochism, 108
Spivak, Gayatri Chakravorty, 154
Staiger, Janet, 40–41, 141
Stam, Robert, 166, 167
stasis, 132–39
Stauffacher, Frank, 28
Stein, Elliott, 133
Steinbock, Eliza, 140
Stevenson, Jack, 254n65
Stewart, Kathleen, 164
Stewart, Potter, 151
Stiglegger, Marcus, 124
stigma, 82, 235n47
Stoppard, Lou, 265n10
Strand Theatre, 158, 163, 170–71, 254n65
streaming platforms, 179, 212, 213, 256n81, 256n84. See also Netflix
Streetcar Named Desire, A (1951), 130, 131–32, 139
Studlar, Gaylyn, 76
Sullivan, Nikki, 84–85
Supervixens (1975), 119, 121
syntagm, 169–70

Talbot, Dan, 7, 148, 150
Talbot, Toby, 7
Tashiro, C. S., 128
taste, 31–33
taxonomania, 86–87
Taylor, Diana, 14
temporal removal, 192–97
Tent, Pam, 48, 227n77
Teorema (1968), 255n75
textual promiscuity, 52–53
Thalia, the, 50–51, 52, 230n88, 230n90
Theatre 80 St. Marks, 226n66
theme bills, 55
Therese and Isabelle (1968), 42
Third World Gay Revolution, 17–18
Thomas, Kevin, 241n27
Thomas, Mike, 254n65
time, in Last Tango in Paris and The Night Porter, 138
Times Theater, 177–78
To Each His Own (1946), 51
Tomkins, Silvan, 233n14
Touch of Evil (1958), 222n25
Tourneur, Jacques. See Cat People (1942)

Toynbee, Philip, 63
Trans-action, 95
transcendence, 136, 137
trans protagonists, in "Sexuality in Cinema" series, 78–82, 84
trans studies, 236n58
Trash (1970), 40, 95
"Trash, Art, and the Movies" (Kael), 34–35
trash films, 143–44
trauma: of queer spectatorship, 185–92, 206, 259n7; Saketopoulou on treatment of, 264n69
triple bills. *See* repertory time
Tsai Ming-Liang, 137, 226n69
Tyler, Parker, 2, 10, 33, 57–58, 87, 123–24, 238n80, 260n18
typage, and bi-textuality of *Cabaret* and *Something for Everyone*, 176–77
typology, 60

UC Theater, 158, 163, 167, 174
underdog, 63, 94, 95
Unknown, The (1927), 72

Valen, Mark, 112, 116, 226n64
van der Pol, Gerwin, 249n19
Varda, Agnès. *See Happiness* (1965)
"Vengeance is Hers" series, 266n13
VHS time, 178–79
Village, The, 41
Village Voice, The, 23, 54
Villarejo, Amy, 263n57
Visconti, Luchino. *See Damned, The* (1969); *Death in Venice* (1971)
Vixen (1968), 23, 201
Vogel, Amos, 28–31, 29f; on Canosa, 37; *Film as a Subversive Art*, 30, 66–68, 233n18; impact of, 7, 40; programming approach of, 25; repeated appearances by, 8; and sexology and sociology in film criticism of 1960s, 238n80; and textual promiscuity, 52–53. *See also* Cinema 16
Vogel, Marcia, 28
von Sternberg, Josef, 60, 75–77
Von Stroheim, Erich, 123. *See* also *Merry Widow, The* (1925)

Warhol, Andy, 30, 40, 201, 255n78
Warner, Michael, 62
Wasson, Haidee, 27, 149
Watermelon Woman, The (1996), 207–9, 211
Waters, John, 18, 86, 88, 91–93, 228n80, 237n61, 238n74, 265n2. *See also Desperate Living* (1977); *Female Trouble* (1974); *Mondo Trasho* (1969); *Multiple Maniacs* (1970); *Pink Flamingos* (1972)
Weiss, Andrea, 194–95, 196
Western (genre), 88
White, Patricia, 63, 183, 196
Whitney Museum, 234n24
Wilinsky, Barbara, 27, 31, 41, 221n7
Willemen, Paul, 235n38
Williams, Linda: on aesthetic sadomasochism, 133, 246n63; on art house cinema and exploration, 39, 108; on Bataille's influence on Bertolucci, 249n26; on gender and sadomasochistic porn, 139; on *The Lovers*, 151–52; on *Mandingo*, 169; on pornography, 109, 119; on *In the Realm of the Senses*, 224n45; on sadism and masochism, 246n65; on sexually explicit content shown in public venues, 9. *See also* body genre
Williams, Raymond, 191–92
Wollen, Peter, 30, 145
Women in Love (1969), 117–19, 121, 122, 242n36
women-in-prison films, 181, 197–99
women's liberation movement, 104. *See also Beyond the Valley of the Dolls* (1970)
Wood, Robin, 158–59
W. R.: Mysteries of the Organism (1971), 219n24

Yacowar, Maurice, 255n78
York, Michael, 174
Young, Damon, 9, 218n17, 224n44

Zimmerman, Patty, 216n7

www.ingramcontent.com/pod-product-compliance
Lightning Source LLC
Chambersburg PA
CBHW050927240426
43670CB00023B/2955